WORLD PRESS PHOTO

2017

Schilt Publishing

Contents

Daily Life

Sports

Nature

Long-Term Projects

Lars Boering

Managing Director, World Press Photo Foundation

Trust? Trust!

'Post-truth' was Oxford Dictionaries Word of the Year for 2016. It was awarded after a tumultuous year in which emotional appeals and personal opinion seemed to trump evidence and facts.

In contrast, the World Press Photo of the Year, and all the other 2017 Photo Contest winners, demonstrate forcefully that accuracy and fairness matter. We know this because the millions who see our exhibitions around the world tell us two important things. The first is that despite the popular view that we are inundated with images, nearly three quarters of the audience are seeing the incredible photographs and stories for the first time. The second, and most important thing, is that they value those photographs and stories because they know they can trust what they see.

Trust is at the heart of what we do and can never be taken lightly. World Press Photo relies on visual journalists to give us the information necessary to verify their photographs and stories. They all do so willingly. We play our part by having a rigorous verification process that ensures our winners are as accurate as possible. Together we produce the best of the best in visual journalism.

When we were founded in 1955, the idea was clear and simple: learn from others and share your work. More than 60 years on that is still at the core of what we do. We help visual journalists present their stories to a global audience that seeks fresh insights and new perspectives, and we celebrate the highest standards of visual journalism, as the great work in this book shows. We train new talent in both the craft of visual storytelling and good journalistic practice, and through research, analysis and debate involving both the profession and the public. We also seek new opportunities and ways forward in meeting the many challenges confronting visual journalism.

Inspiring, educating, supporting. That is our mission for our community. A very strong and vital community. We love and cherish this community, we nurture it and we empower it. We do this to make the world a better place for visual journalism.

Together we need to ensure we live in an era where trust is dominant and 'post-truth' is a myth. Trust is at the core of journalism, it is what the audience wants, and we should all fight to ensure it is secured and valued.

Stuart Franklin

Chairman of the 2017 Jury

Wrapped in blankets we appeared, to me at least, as refugees from a bygone age when photography was omnipotent in the world of visual journalism. Room temperature was lowered purposely to keep us alert as pictures appeared in quick succession on a projection screen. The 2017 World Press Photo General Jury formed a diverse huddle of believers in professional photojournalism negotiating rapid changes to our world.

Outside was a small lawn in a quiet quarter of Amsterdam. There we could pace beside a church dedicated to Jacob Obrecht, a 15th-century composer of very solemn church music, which would have chimed well with the stories of cuts to the industry and some of the harrowing photographs of conflict and ruthless killing that form a staple of this contest.

Jury discussions take place in confidence. We looked at about 80,000 photographs. I saw the vast majority in one week. A second week was used to narrow our choices. The General Jury comprised four women and five men. The US president's unwise executive order stigmatizing citizens from certain Muslim-majority countries, and the ensuing uncertainty, forced one juror (who was replaced) to withdraw.

The net is thrown out at year-end to capture the best of the year's news or documentary pictures. When it's drawn in at the January deadline there's much good work to consider.

Viewing the pictures, and despite a desire for objectivity, differing filters are applied by each juror. These relate to aesthetics, news value, cultural bias, social or environmental significance and so forth. Personally, I looked for an empathetic eye, and am very pleased to have found that in so many of the photographs that made the cut. Photographs need to be of a professional standard and uncontrived, although the People category is open to the established practice of portraiture. Despite efforts to counter stereotypes, they sometimes slip through. The tension between art and journalism, deeply embedded in the medium, is also an unavoidable contingent.

In the end, the important thing is that photographers go to incredible lengths, often putting their lives at risk, to report, to break the silence, and to enlighten us through pictures, because they believe that might, *just might*, inspire change. To sit on the esteemed World Press Photo jury is to help fulfill the other side of the bargain—and World Press Photo is instrumental in this—to respect photographers' efforts, to raise the status of photojournalism, and to display it proudly to the world. Exhibitions produced from the prize-winning photographs are held in 45 countries and seen by four million visitors, and the general public appreciates the trust they can place in the verified work on show.

It's a true honor to celebrate the photographs published here.

Burhan Ozbilici

World Press Photo of the Year 2016 Winner

How did you come to shoot the winning image—were you at the gallery on assignment?
I wasn't assigned to cover the opening officially. A friend phoned to say she would be at a photography exhibition near where I lived, and as I was always so busy and they never saw me, she suggested that we should meet there. I didn't know the Russian ambassador was going to be there. I didn't even know the exhibition was about Russia—so I was there quite by chance.

How did events unfold?
I arrived about 15 minutes late. At first I was standing behind three to four rows of people, listening to Russian and Turkish photographers talk about their work. Then someone announced that the Russian ambassador, Andrey Karlov, would give an address. I always have my cameras and my laptop with me, ready to work at any time. So, I moved closer to the ambassador and started to photograph him, thinking that AP might be able to use the picture for a story on Turkish-Russian relations. He was speaking calmly, very softly, stopping from time to time to allow interpreters to translate. I remember him saying something about 'my homeland'. Then suddenly I heard a gunshot. It was very loud. People were running away in panic, and the ambassador's body was lying on the ground. The gunman raised his left hand, pointing his finger and shouted twice, "*Allahu akbar, Allahu akbar!*" I saw no blood, which was surprising, but later I realized the ambassador had been shot in the back. There was no one between the gunman and myself. He was shouting something I could not understand. I thought it was in Russian, but I learned later it was a slogan of the group he was allegedly part of, al-Nusra Front, one of the main groups fighting in Syria.

Weren't you fearful of your own safety?
When the gunman shouted "*Allahu akbar*", I was really scared because I wasn't sure if there were others with him who would go on to shoot innocent people, as had happened in so many places before. People were screaming, but when I saw the gunman pointing towards them, warning them to leave the hall, I felt a little more secure. He was still shouting, but I didn't pay attention to his words, rather focused on his movements, trying to analyze second by second whether he would shoot us or not. As he moved a little bit away, I got in closer to get in a better position to photograph him. He walked around the ambassador's body and fired one more shot at close range. He seemed very angry, and tore some of the photographs off the wall, throwing them to the ground as an insult. Then he came closer to us and pointed his gun again. I was scared that now he would fire, so I was not moving too fast. I was

extremely calm: running away wasn't a solution, it wasn't safe. I remember thinking: "I might be killed or injured, but the Russian ambassador has been shot. This is very big news, so as a journalist it is my responsibility to stand and do my work." Even if I was killed, there would still be photos.

How quickly did you manage to transmit your images back to AP, and how did your editors respond?
Security guards ordered us all out of the hall, and I called my colleague, Ankara reporter Suzan Fraser, and then the London photo editor, Tony Hicks, to inform him that the Russian ambassador had been shot. He said: "Can you get a picture?" I had not explained myself clearly. I said: "Tony, I was *there*!" His immediate reaction was to ask if I was safe, but I said not to worry, and that I was going straight back to the office to edit and transmit my pictures. On the first two pictures you could see the ambassador speaking and the man standing behind him, in a good suit–like a security guard, or even a friend, but in fact the attacker.

What did you think of the global attention and reaction to the image?
At midnight that day, I saw that the photo had been viewed 18 million times on Facebook. I was shocked! And my own phone was continually busy with newspapers and TV stations wanting to talk to me. In the end, I had to say that I had done my bit, and now I had a responsibility to get on with my work. But I was very aware that I represented a long tradition of good, independent journalism and good news photos. That made me happy and proud–proud of all good journalists, those living and those who have been killed doing their work, at a time when people are trying to manipulate the media, and the quality of journalism is often ignored.

Do you think the image, and winning the award, will change your life?
No, it won't change my life, but I think I will have more responsibility to be a good example for a new generation if I can, and a moral responsibility to good journalism. So, maybe you can say that is a little change in my life. But I will always be the same man.

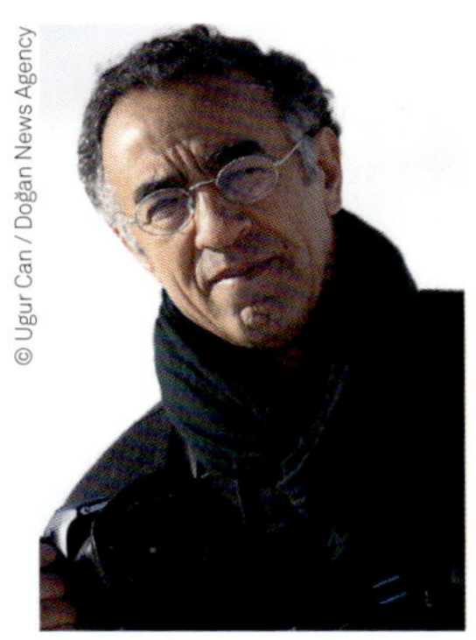

© Ugur Can / Doğan News Agency

Burhan Ozbilici (Turkey, 1955) has been a photographer for The Associated Press (AP) since 1989. Before joining the AP, he worked as an editor and a reporter for several Turkish newspapers. He has covered all the major stories in Turkey and the Middle East.

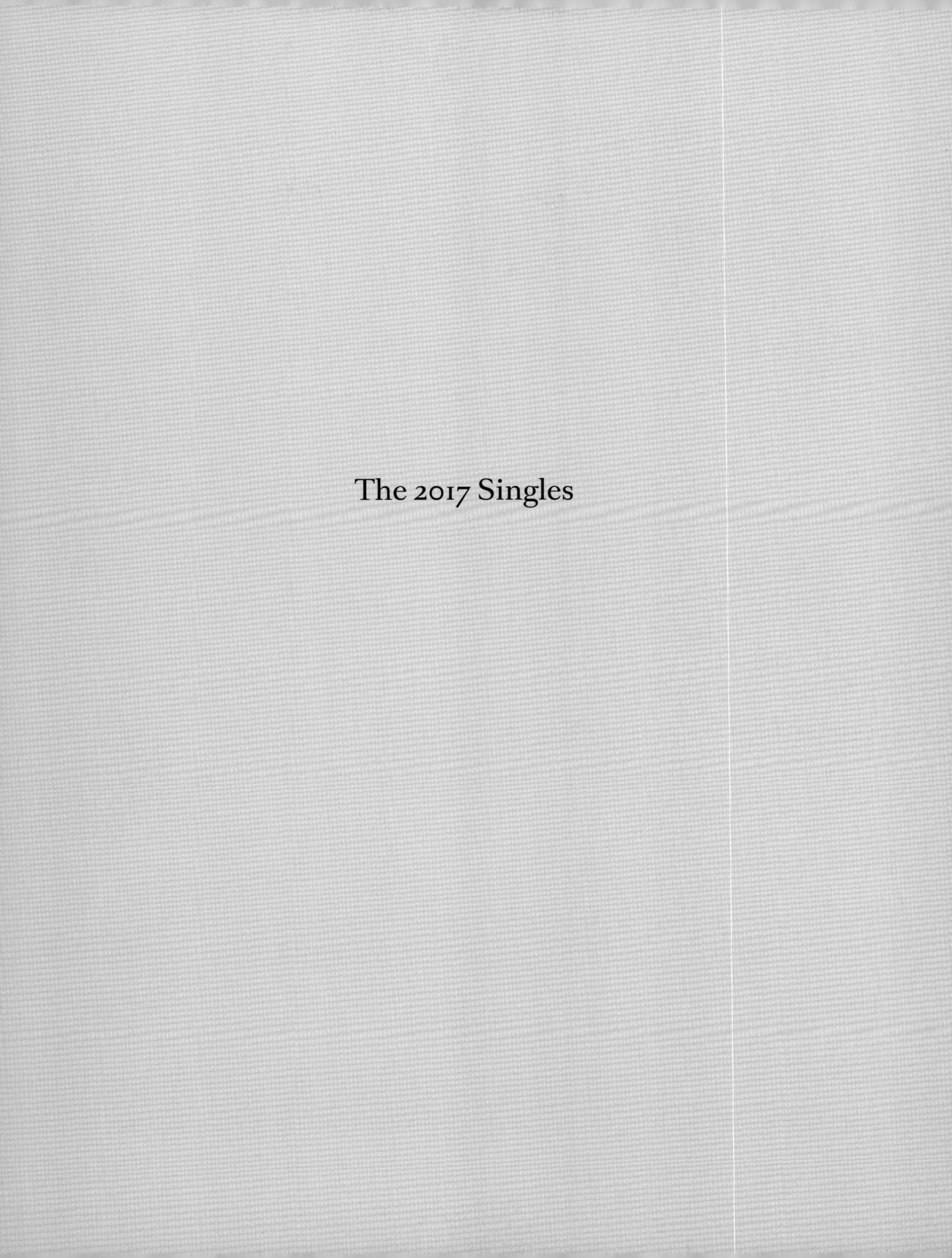

The 2017 Singles

Jonathan Bachman

USA, Reuters /
1st Prize Contemporary Issues

Iesha Evans (27) stands her ground at a rally opposing police violence against black men, outside the Baton Rouge Police Department in Louisiana, USA, on 9 July. Evans had traveled to Baton Rouge to protest the death of Alton Sterling, who was shot at close range while being held to the ground by two white police officers on 5 July. The fatal shooting of Sterling came at a time of heightened tension in the US over the deaths of black men at the hands of the police. Data collected by The Counted, an initiative set up by *The Guardian* to record such fatalities, found that in 2016, black males aged 15-34 were nine times more likely than other Americans to be killed by law enforcement officers. Evans was arrested at the protest, but released later that evening.

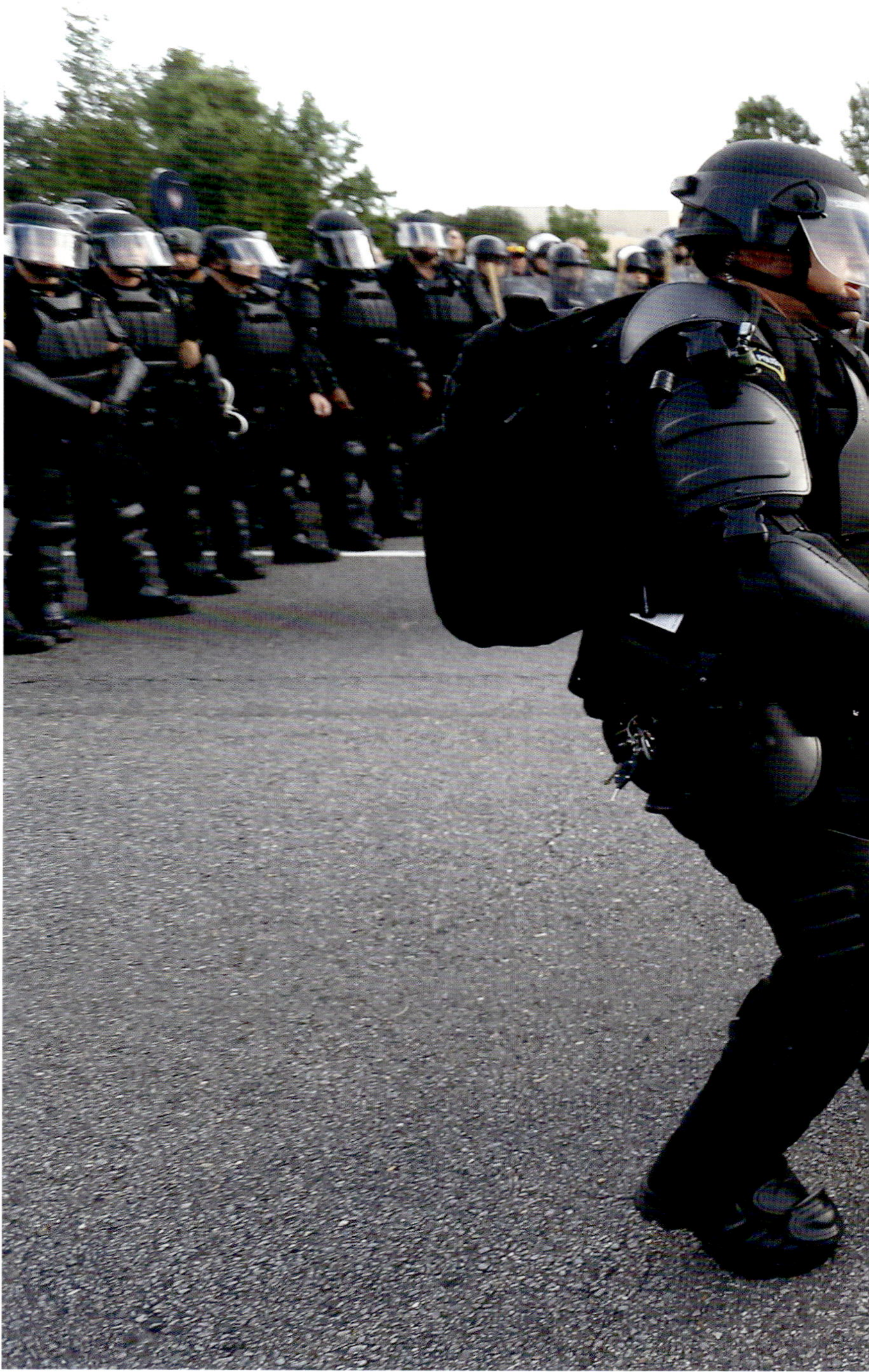

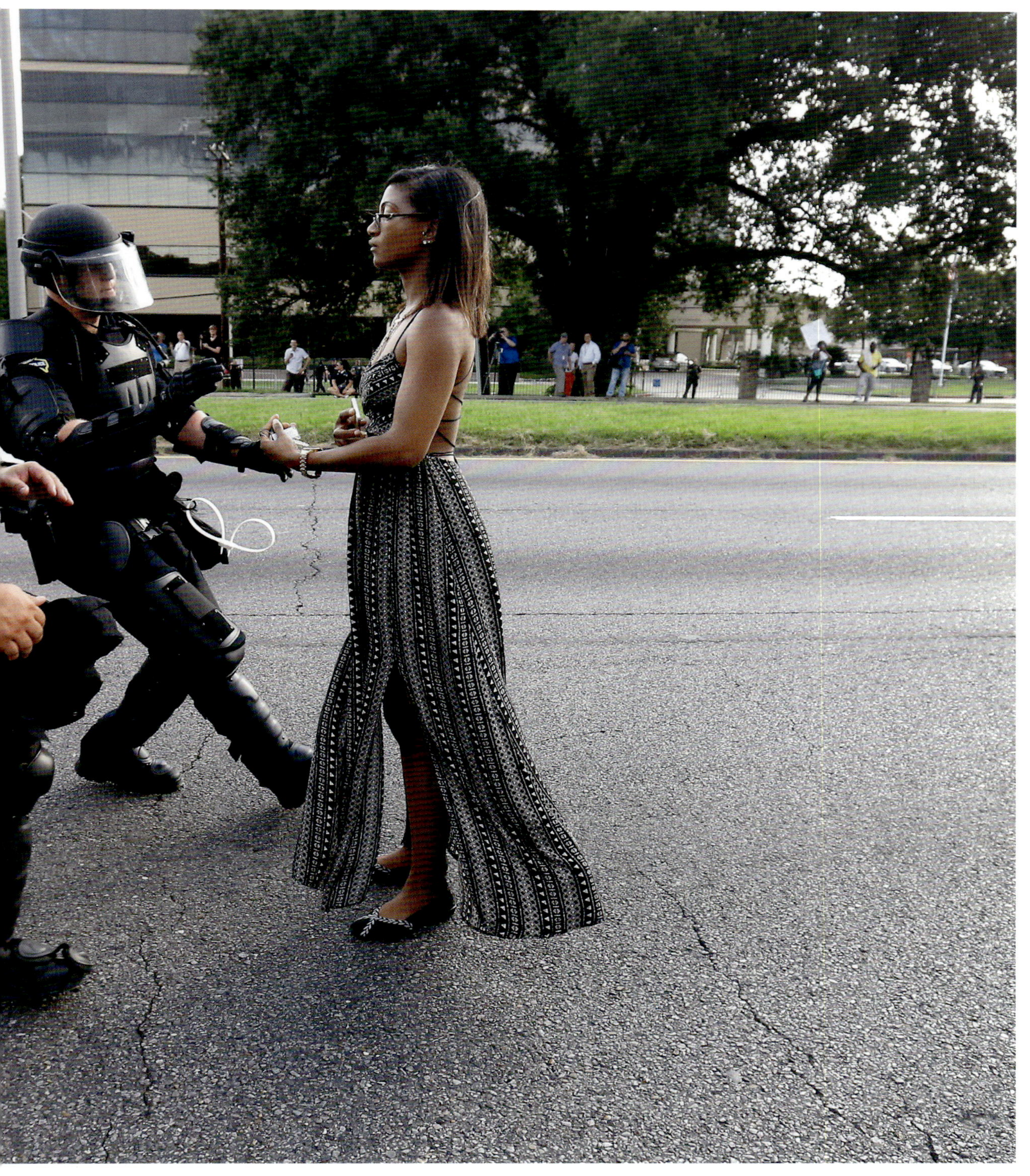

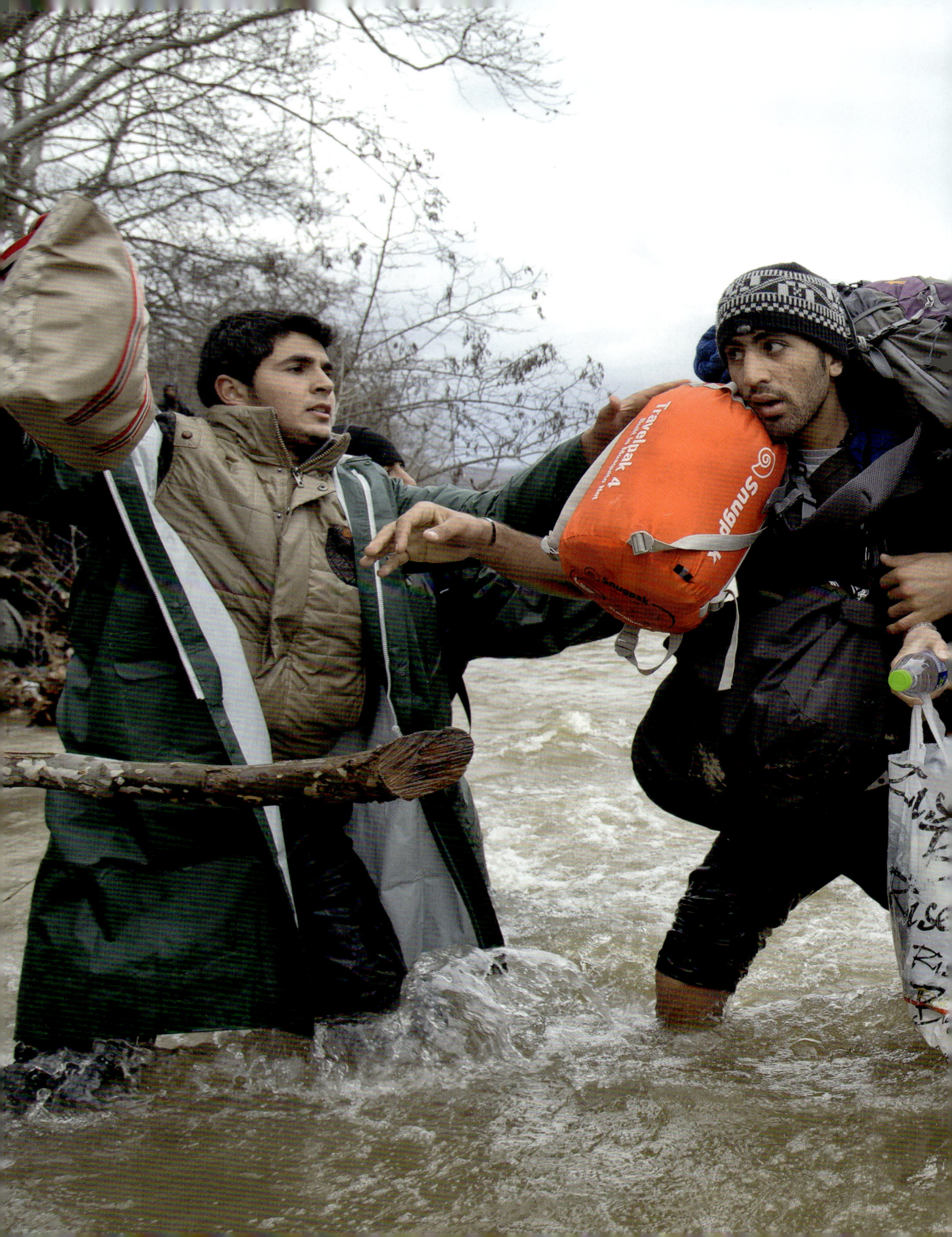
TravelPak 4
Snugpak

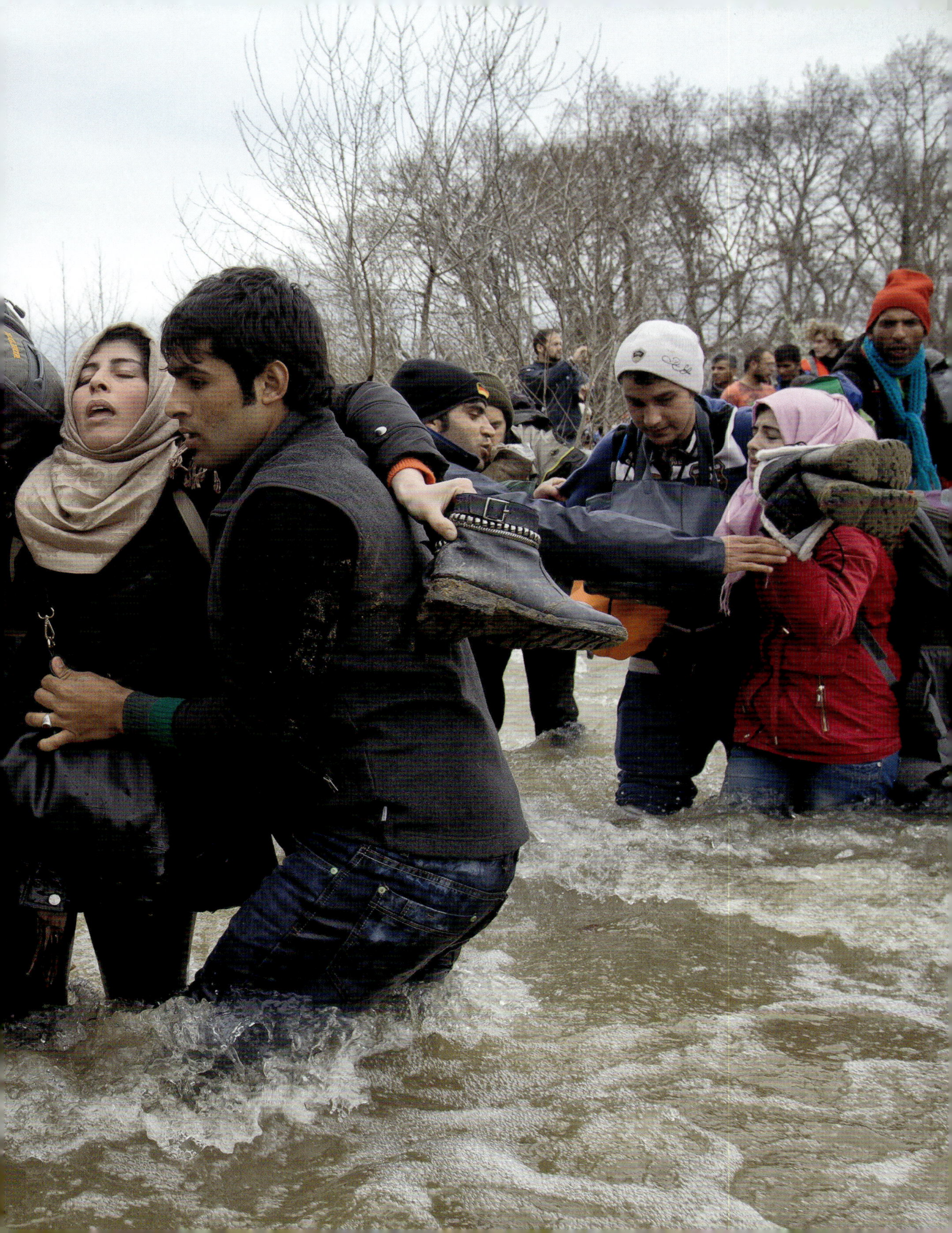

Vadim Ghirda

Romania, The Associated Press / 2nd Prize Contemporary Issues

A woman is supported as refugees cross the Mala Reka river, near the Greek border town of Idomeni, on 14 March. They were attempting a route into Macedonia that would bypass a newly erected border fence. Macedonia, Croatia and Slovenia—countries that lie between Greece and preferred refugee destinations in northern Europe—had all closed their borders five days earlier. Hundreds of thousands of refugees had traveled through Macedonia the previous year, and the UN said that the build-up of people in a holding-camp at Idomeni was turning into a humanitarian disaster.

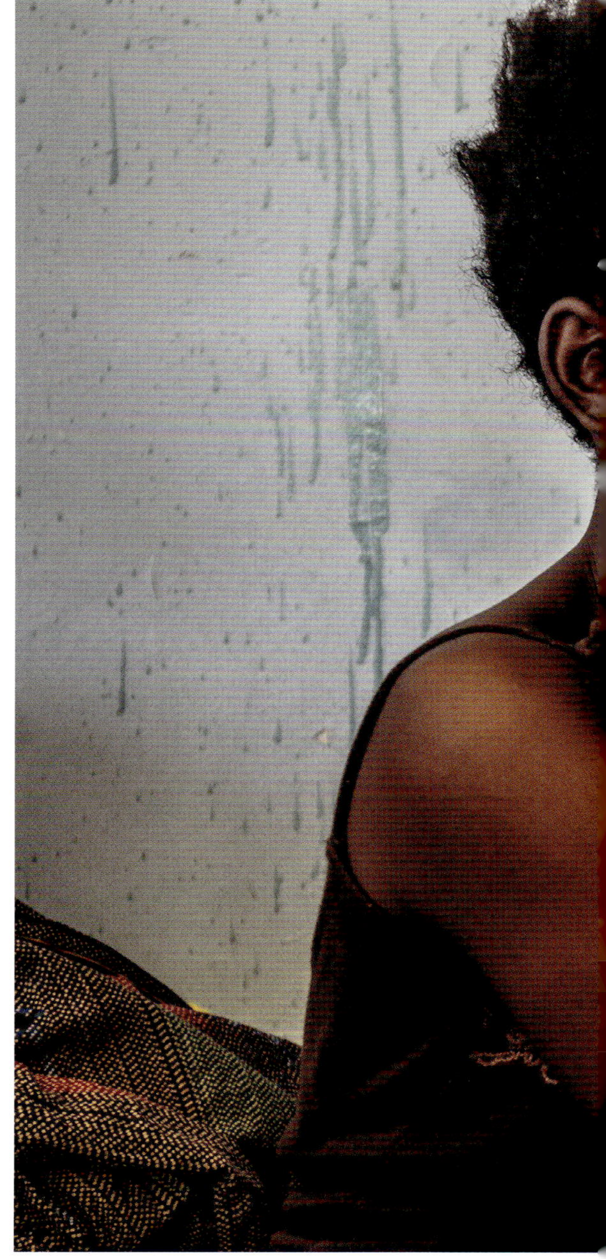

Daniel Etter

Germany, for *Der Spiegel* / 3rd Prize Contemporary Issues

Nigerian refugees cry and embrace in a detention center housing hundreds of women in Surman, Libya. Refugees in such centers face indefinite detention. Many report sexual and physical violence, and insufficient food and water. A large number try to reach Europe by being smuggled over the Mediterranean Sea. According to the International Organization for Migration, the number of Nigerian women travelling by boat from Libya to Italy almost doubled in 2016, to 11,009.

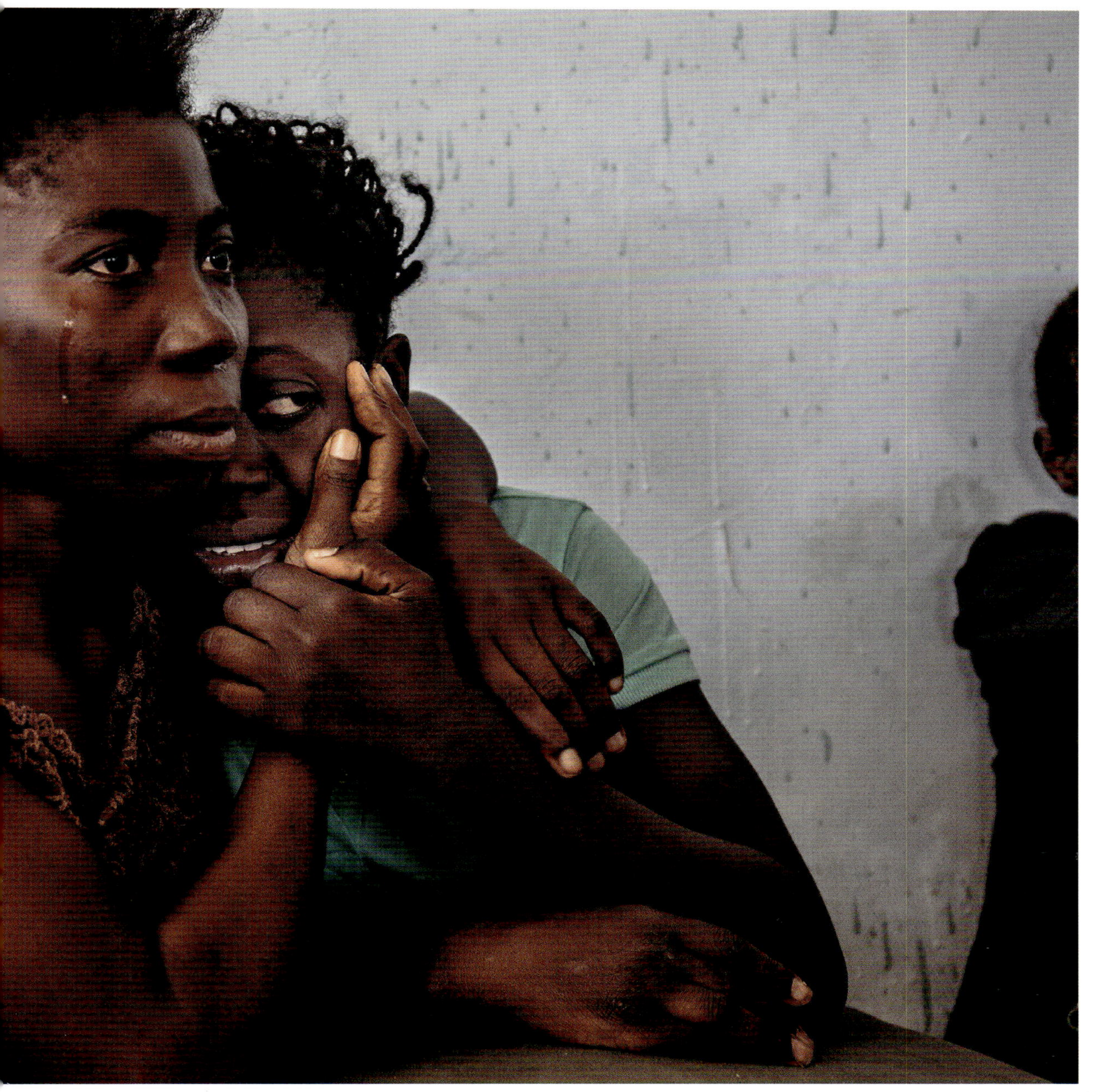

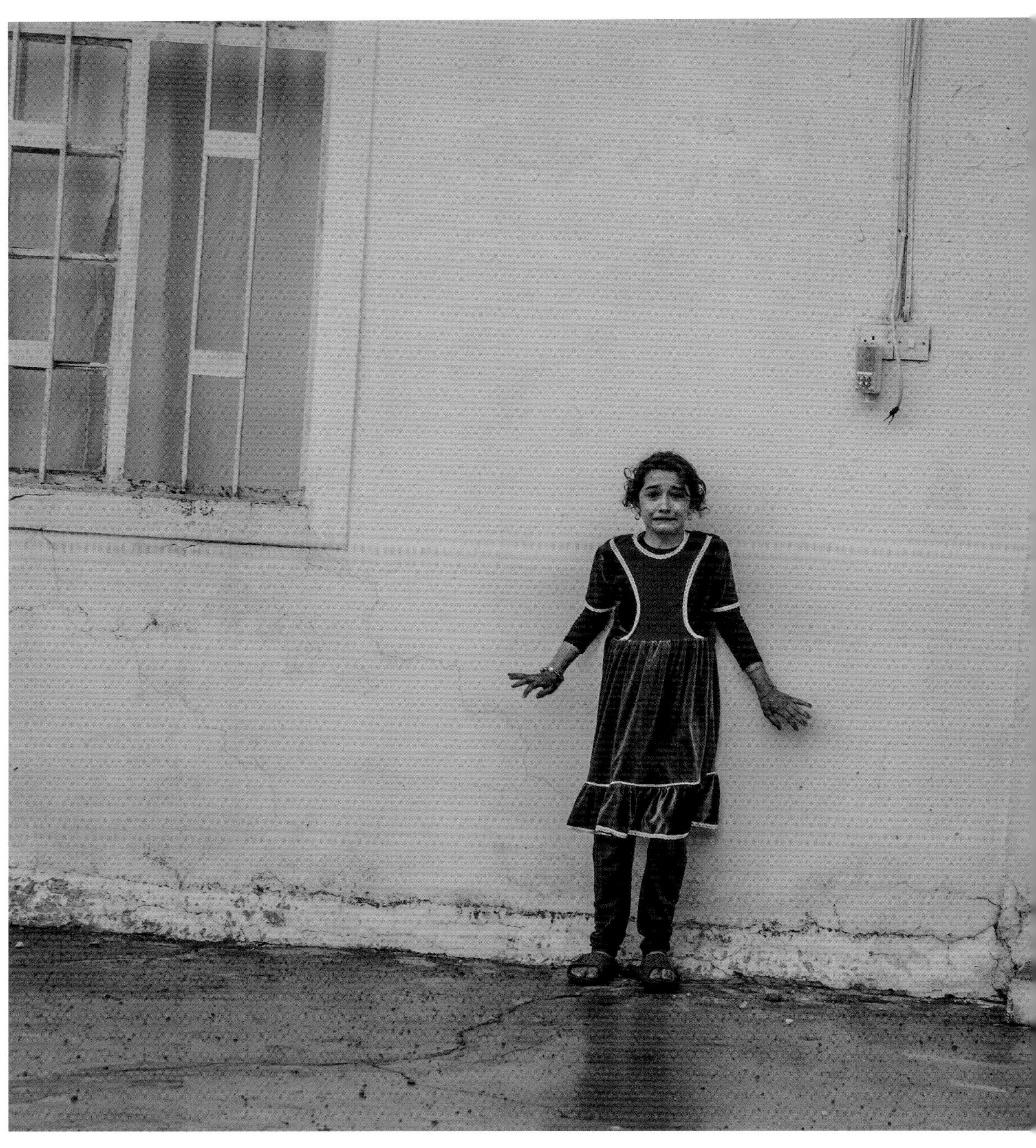

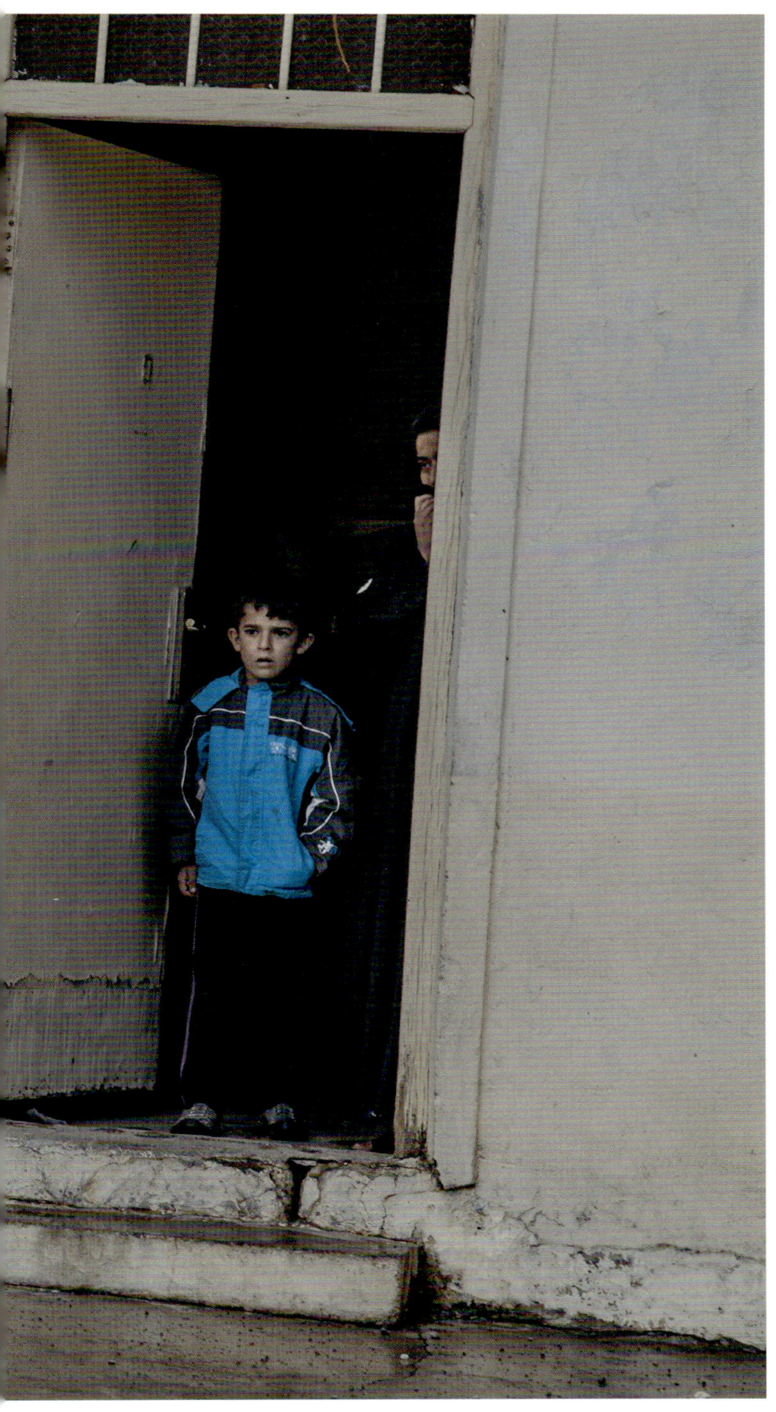

Laurent Van der Stockt

France, Getty Images Reportage for *Le Monde* / 1st Prize General News

A girl stands outside as members of a counter-terrorism battalion of the Iraqi Special Operations Forces (ISOF) search homes in Gogjali, an eastern suburb of Mosul, Iraq, during an offensive to liberate the city. Mosul was the last major stronghold of the Islamic State group (IS) in Iraq. ISOF entered Gogjali in late October, and began looking for IS members, equipment and evidence. Gogjali was retaken in early November, and most of Eastern Mosul by the end of January 2017.

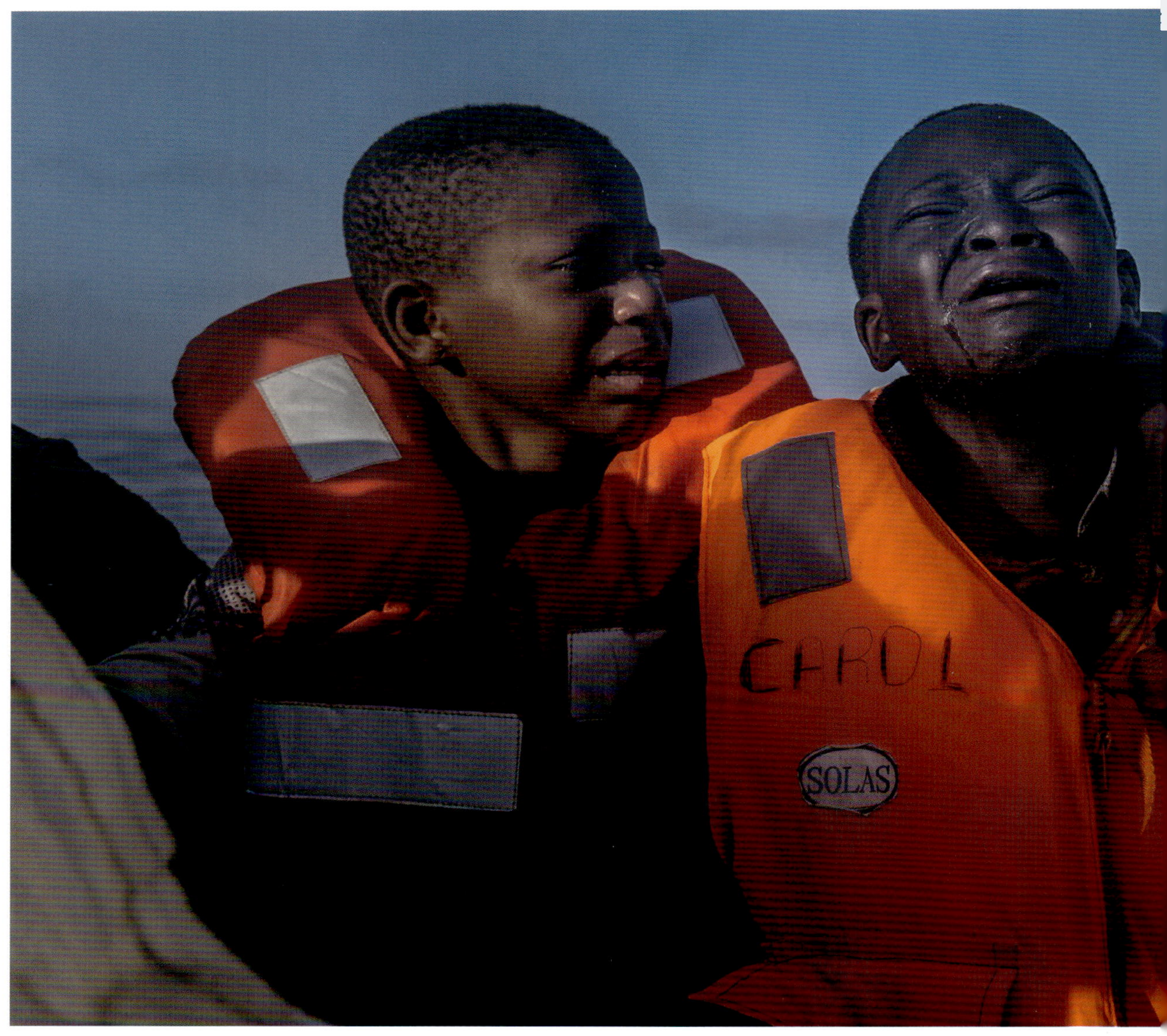

Santi Palacios

Spain, The Associated Press / 2nd Prize General News

An 11-year-old girl (left) from Nigeria, comforts her younger brother aboard a rescue boat after they had been picked up from an overcrowded dinghy in the Mediterranean Sea, en route to Italy, about 23 kilometers north of Sabratha, Libya in July. Their mother had died in Libya, after crossing the Sahara. According to the EU border agency Frontex, arrivals of refugees in Italy from North Africa hit an all-time high of 181,000 in 2016. UNICEF said that some 25,800 of those were unaccompanied children.

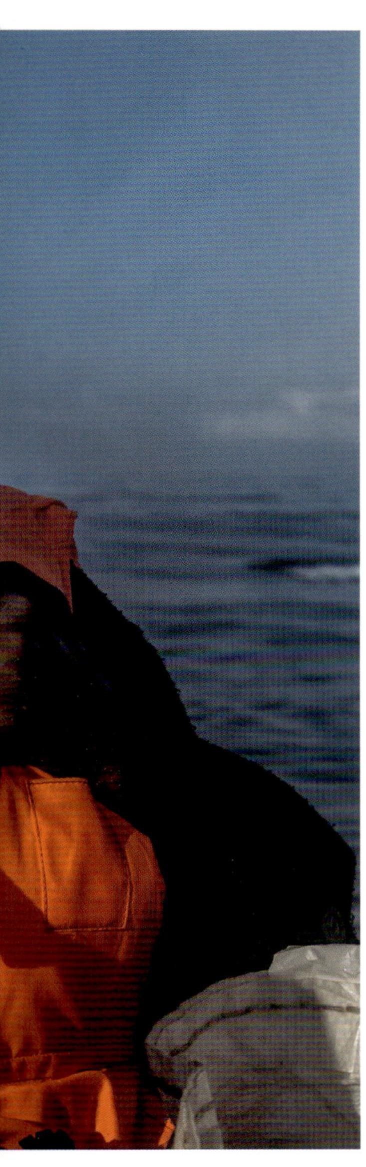

Noel Celis

Philippines, Agence France-Presse / 3rd Prize General News

Prisoners sleep on a staircase inside the Quezon City Jail, at night in Manila, Philippines. The jail was built in 1953 to house 800 people, though the UN says it should accommodate no more than 278. In August, *Time* reported that there were some 3,800 inmates at Quezon. Jail populations in the Philippines rose sharply after newly inaugurated President Rodrigo Duterte announced an all-out war on drugs.

→

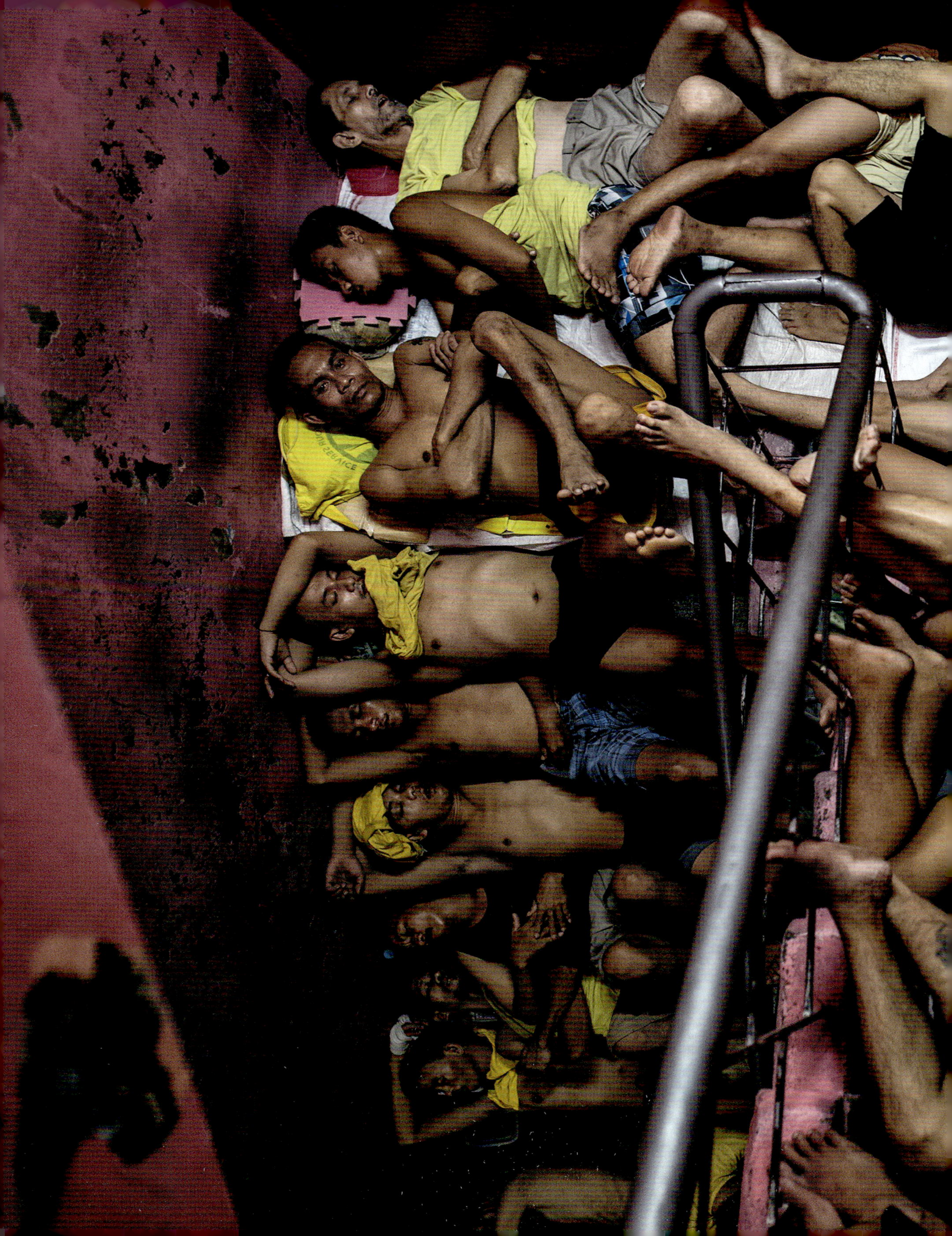

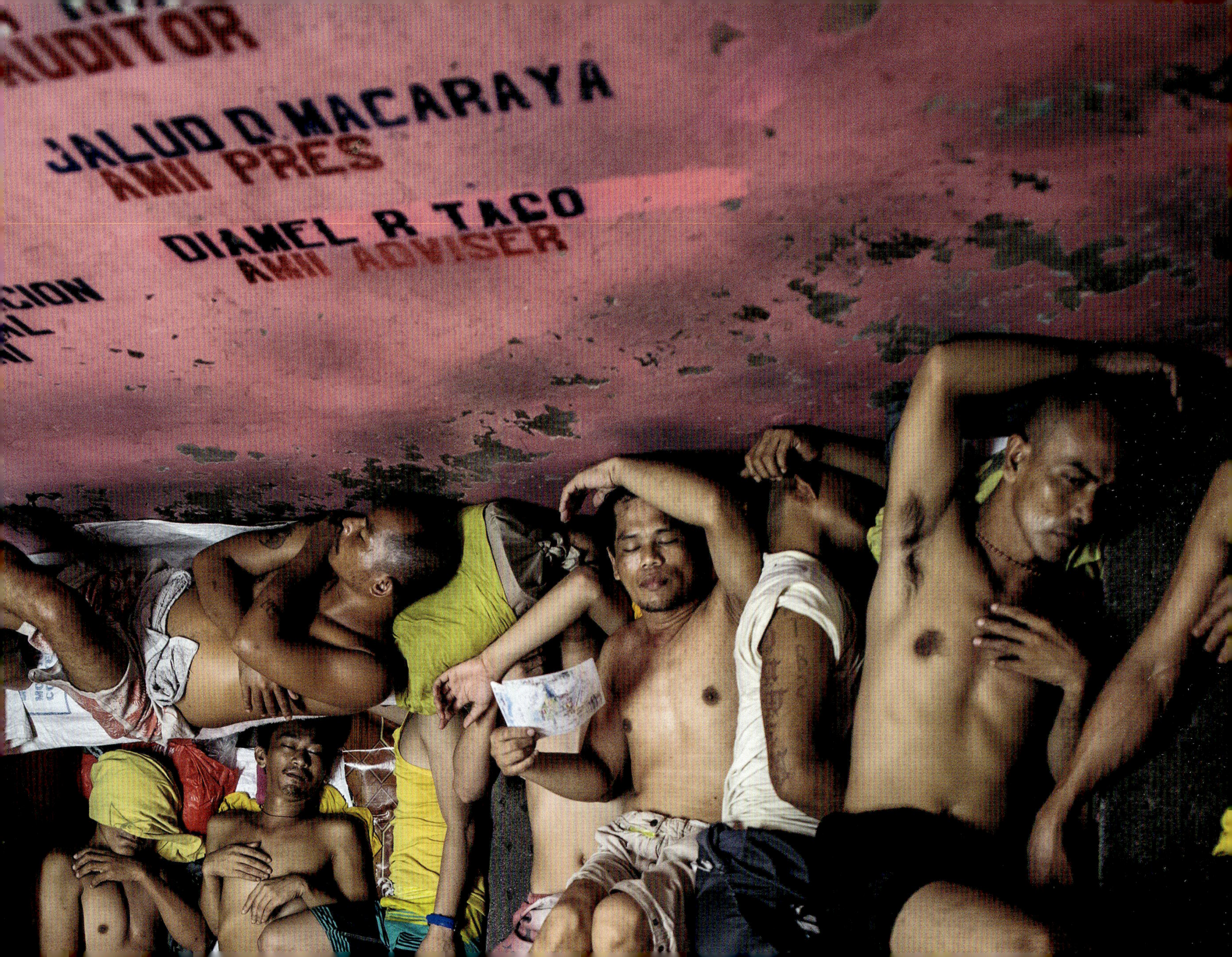
AUDITOR
JALUD D MACARAYA
AMII PRES
DIAMEL R TACO
AMII ADVISER

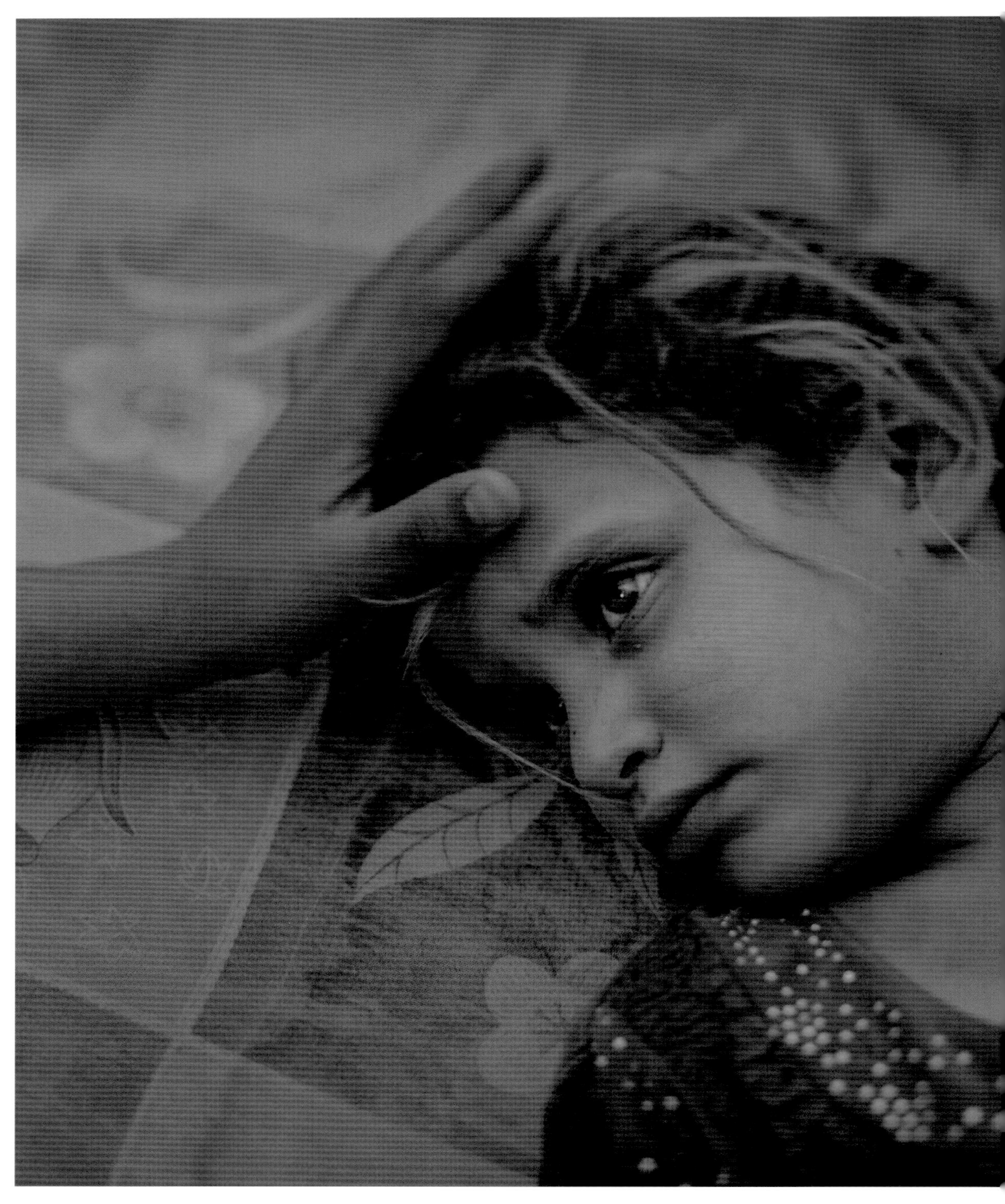

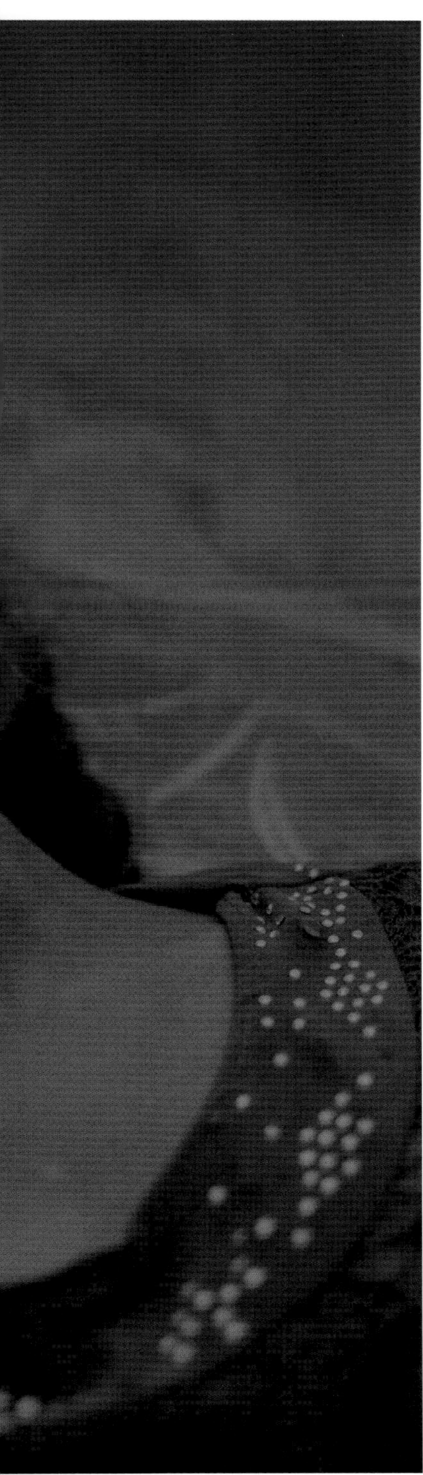

Magnus Wennman

Sweden, *Aftonbladet* / 1st Prize People

Maha (5) is comforted by her mother, in Debaga refugee camp in northeastern Iraq, in September. A week earlier, Maha and her family had fled the town of Hawija, 160 kilometers south of Mosul. Hawija had been under the control of the Islamic State group (IS) since August 2014, and was the last major IS stronghold in oil-rich Kirkuk province, as Iraqi troops recaptured territory on their move towards Mosul. At the time, some 400,000 civilians remained trapped in Hawija and its outlying areas, with little food or medicine, under a blockade from IS that prevented humanitarian aid getting through.

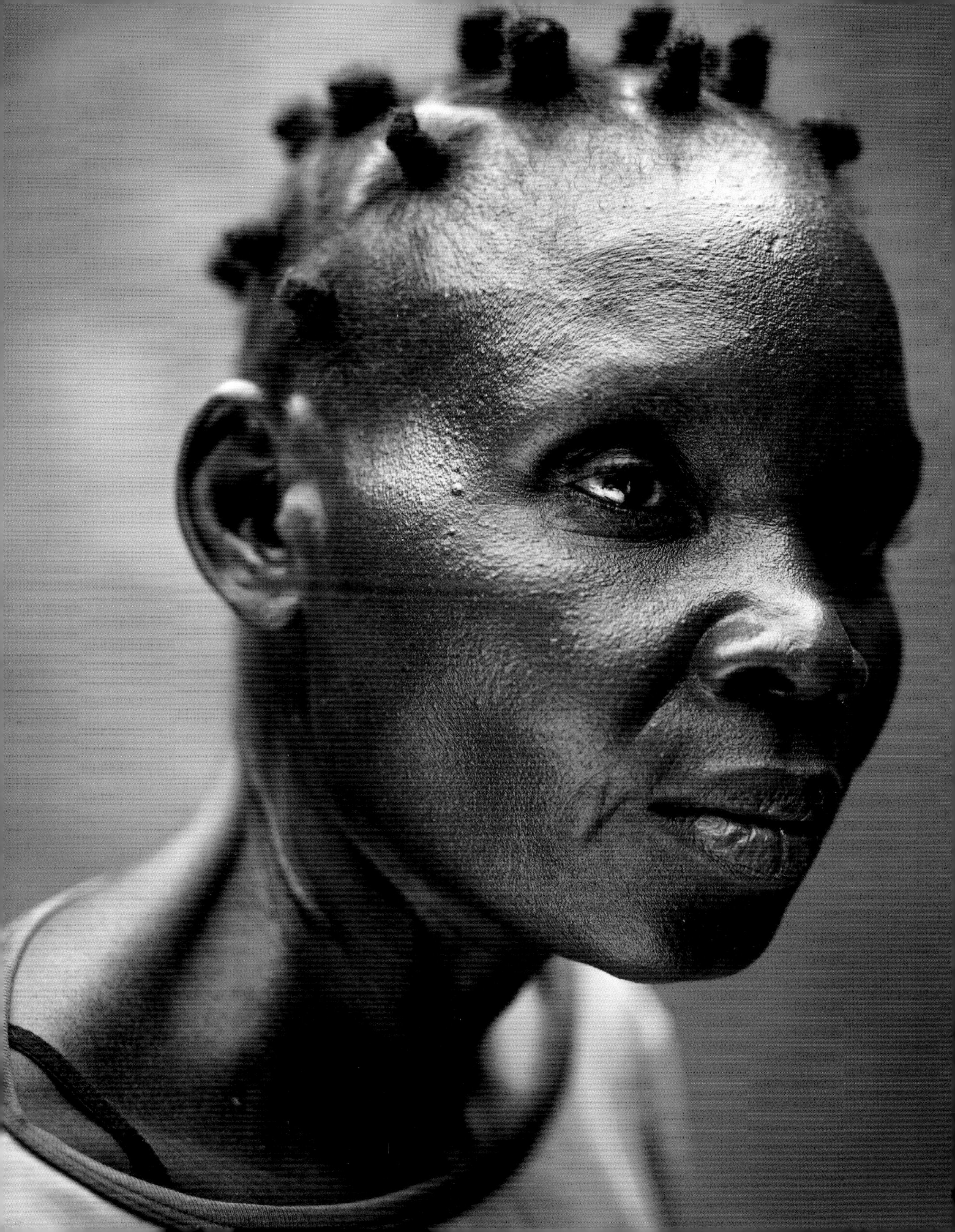

Robin Hammond

New Zealand, NOOR Images for Handicap International / 2nd Prize People

Hellen Alfred (41) lives with a mental health condition, in Juba, South Sudan. She says she fell ill after the birth of her sixth child. Mental illness in South Sudan is often attributed to witchcraft. This means the mentally ill are frequently ostracized, and regarded as a danger to society. Many end up in prison. South Sudan's animist and Christian cultures treat mental illness with traditional cures or prayers, practices that many professionals see as insufficient or as sheer profiteering. Juba has only a handful of qualified psychiatrists and psychologists, but international NGOs are working with the South-Sudanese authorities to improve conditions for the mentally ill.

Kristina Kormilitsyna

Russia, *Kommersant* / 3rd Prize People

A woman and child sit on a sofa at a police station, in Camagüey, central Cuba, a week after the death of Fidel Castro. The former president's funeral procession, which had traveled countrywide, was at the time leaving Camagüey on its way to Santiago, and was being shown on the police station's television set.

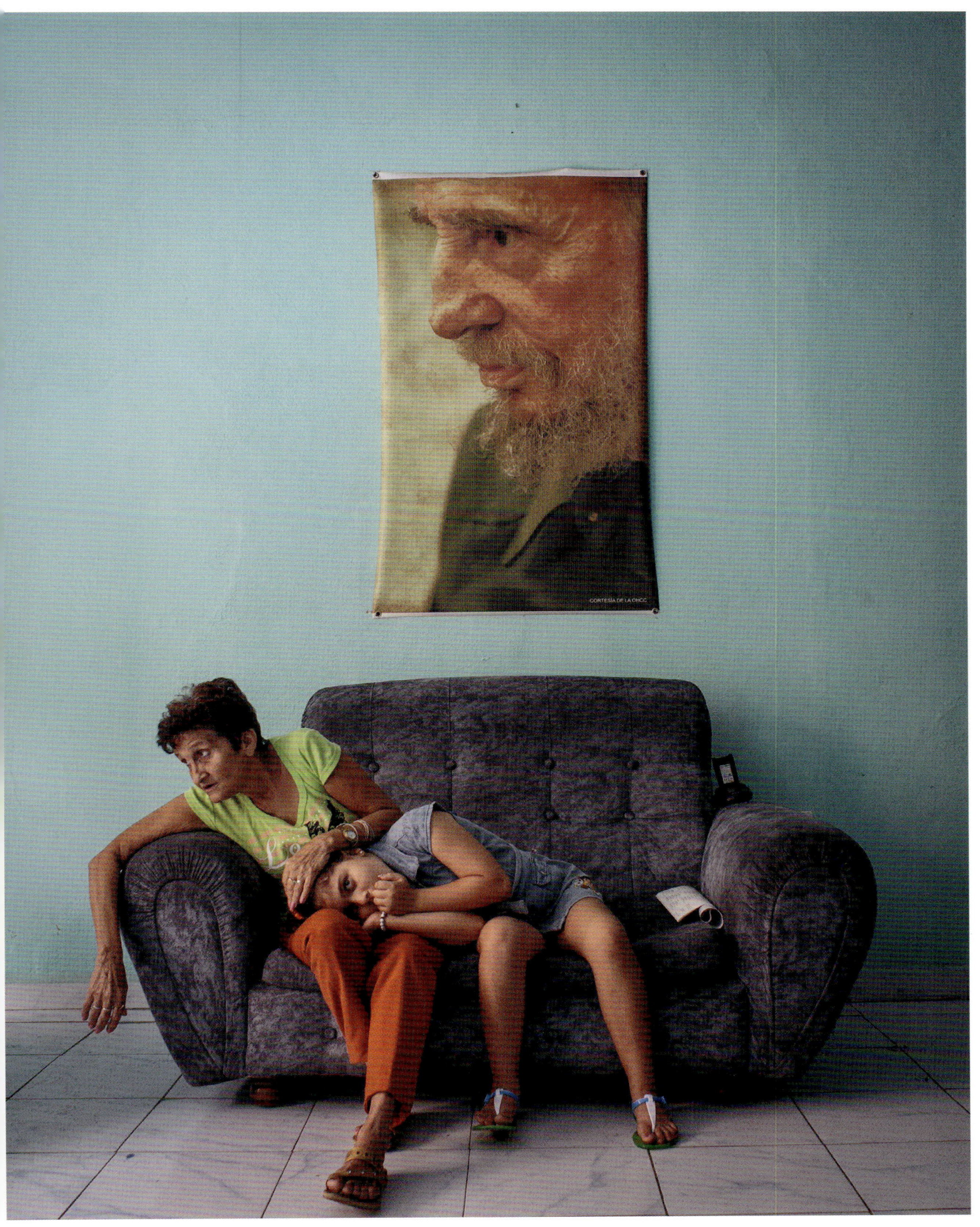
CORTESÍA DE LA OHCC

Jamal Taraqai

Pakistan, European Pressphoto Agency / 1st Prize Spot News

Survivors and onlookers help those injured in a suicide bomb attack at the Civil Hospital in Quetta, Balochistan, Pakistan, on 8 August. Some 200 lawyers, together with journalists, had gathered outside the hospital following the shooting earlier in the day of the president of the Balochistan Bar Council, Bilal Anwar Kasi. Jamaat-ul-Ahrar, a splinter group of the Pakistan Taliban, claimed responsibility for the attack, in which at least 70 people were killed and more than 100 injured. Hospital medical staff said that 60 of those killed were lawyers. Balochistan, which borders on Iran and Afghanistan, is affected by Sunni-Shiite sectarian violence and a separatist Baloch ethnic insurgency. Lawyers form a particular target of attacks, severely impacting the judicial system.

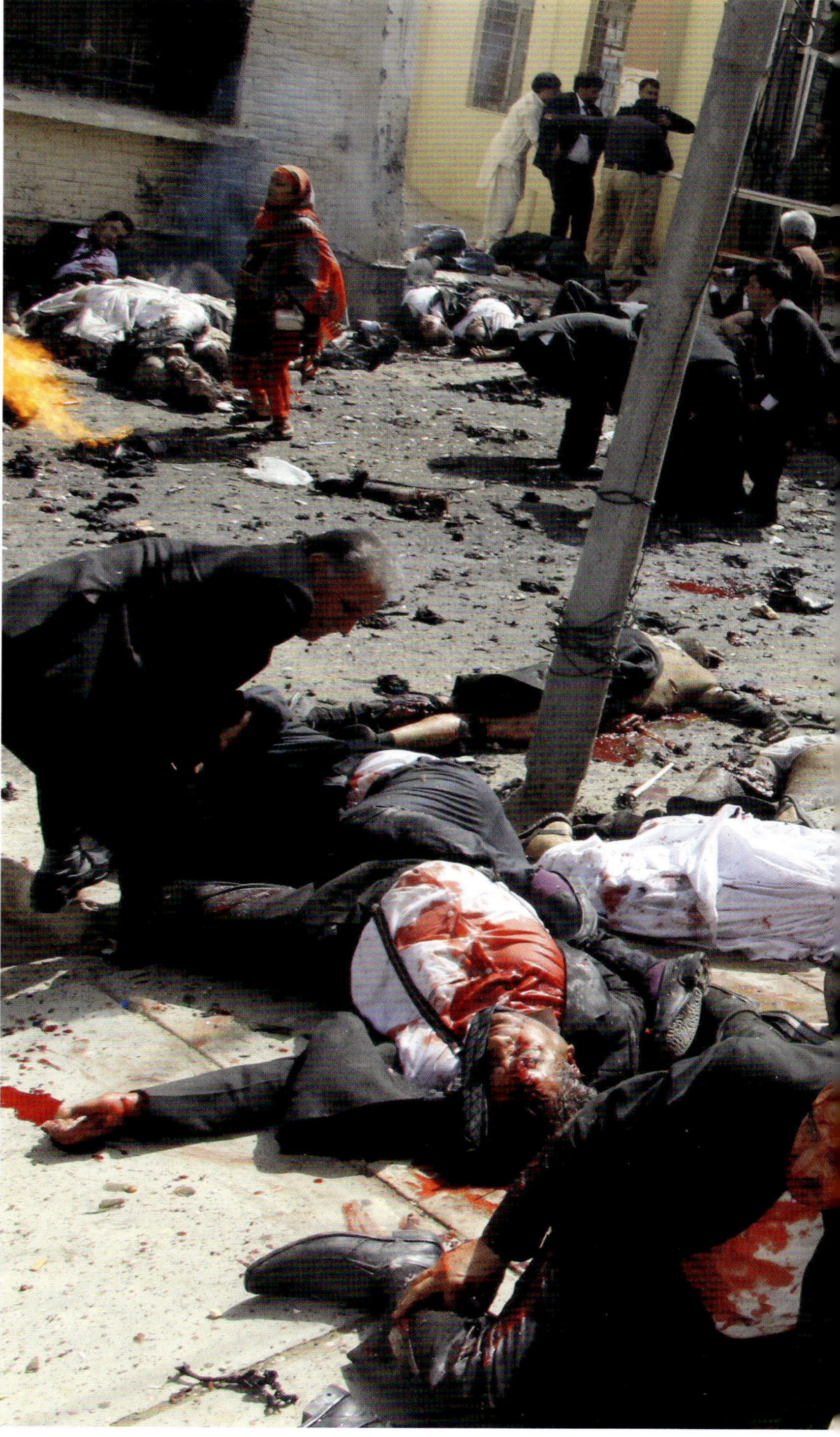

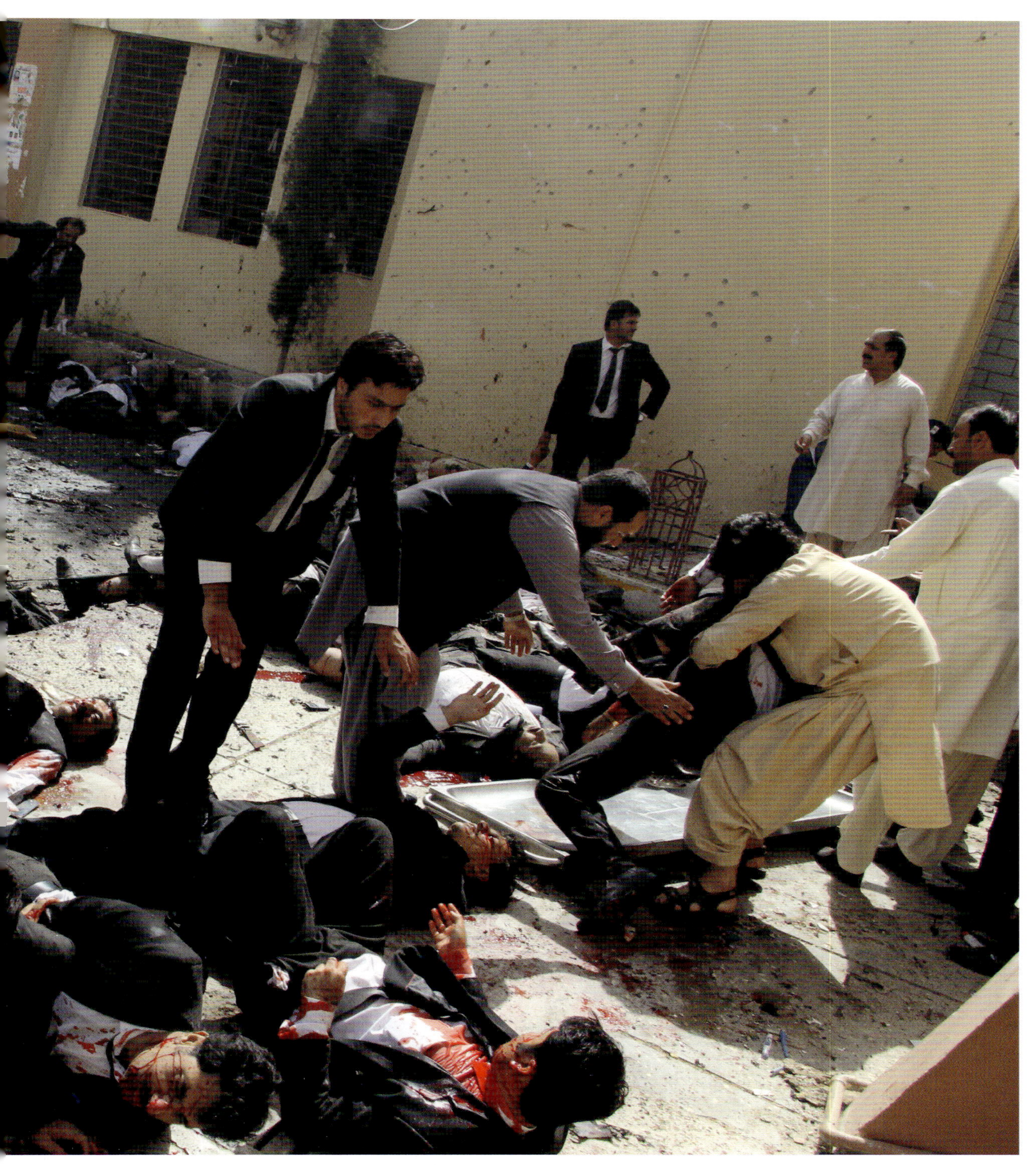

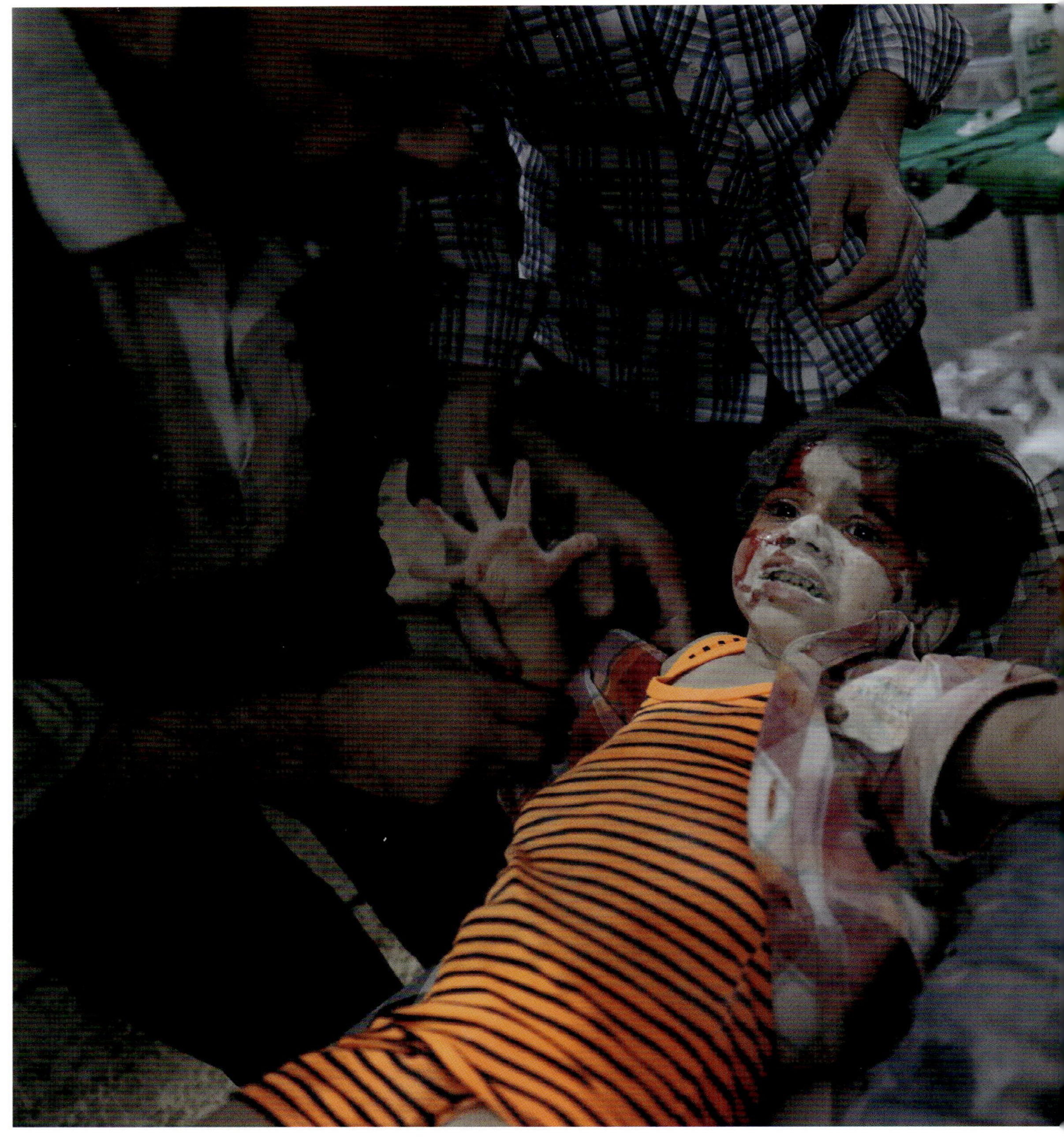

Abd Doumany

Syria, Agence France-Presse / 2nd Prize Spot News

A Syrian child reacts in pain, as another child lies alongside her at a makeshift hospital in the rebel-held town of Douma, following airstrikes and artillery bombardment on 12 September. Douma, on the northeastern outskirts of Damascus, had been under siege by government forces since 2013, and although some aid convoys had managed to reach the town in previous months, supplies of food and medical equipment remained short.

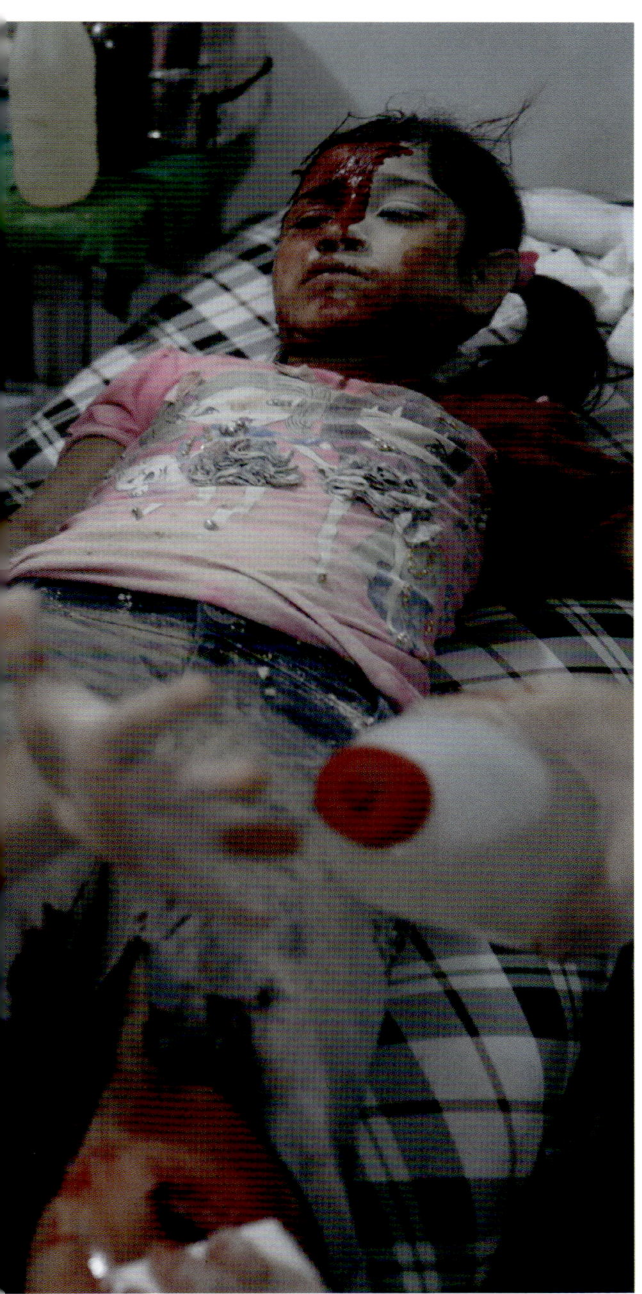

Felipe Dana

Brazil, The Associated Press /
3rd Prize Spot News

A car bomb explodes next to armored vehicles belonging to Iraqi Special Operations Forces (ISOF) as they advance towards territory held by the Islamic State group (IS), in Mosul, Iraq, on 16 November. The convoy's progress was slow, while a bulldozer and tank constructed roadblocks along the route as a buffer against car bombs. The joint offensive by ISOF and allied militias to regain control of Mosul, seized by IS in June 2014, had begun a month earlier and was considered key in the military intervention against IS.

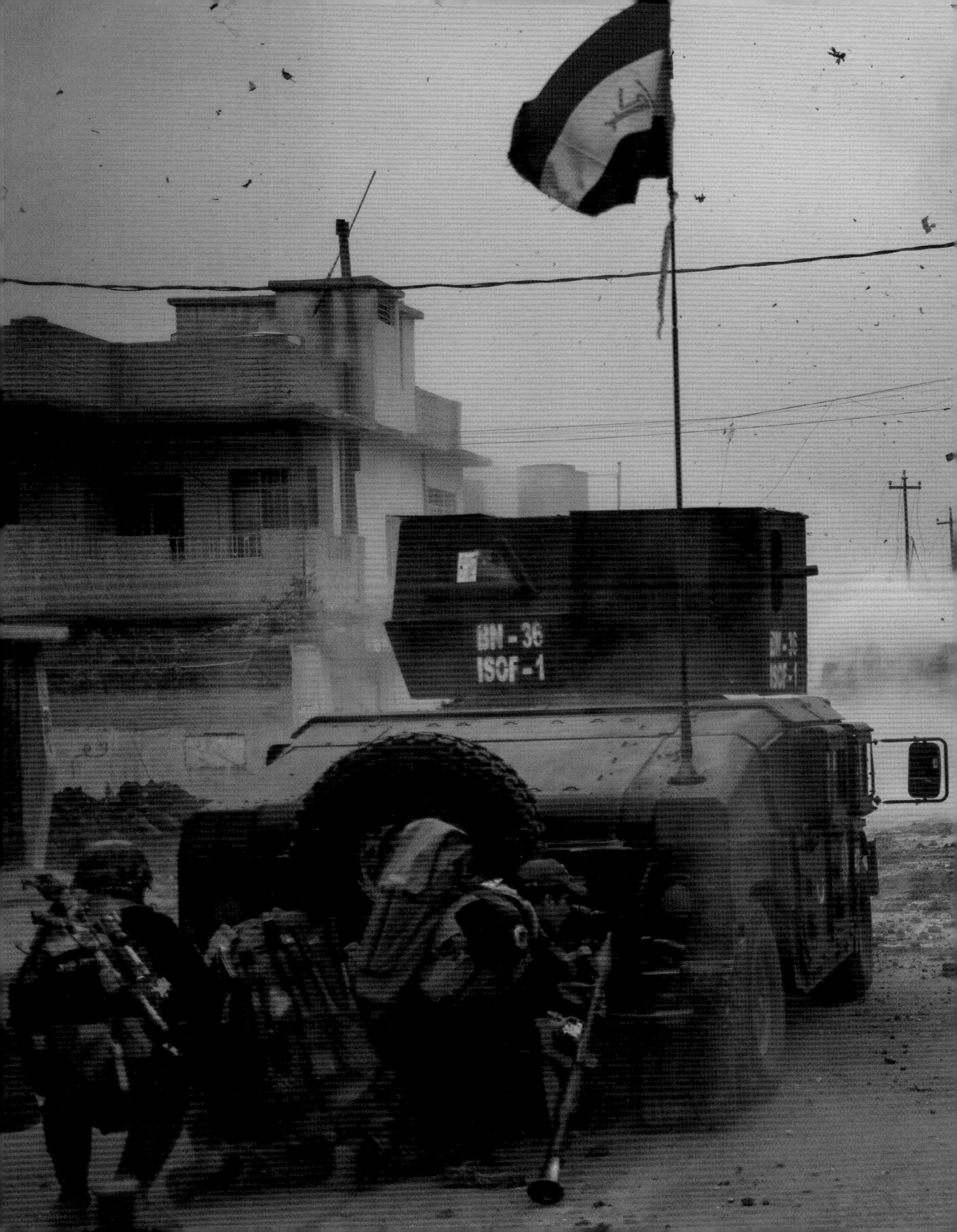
BN - 36
ISOF - 1

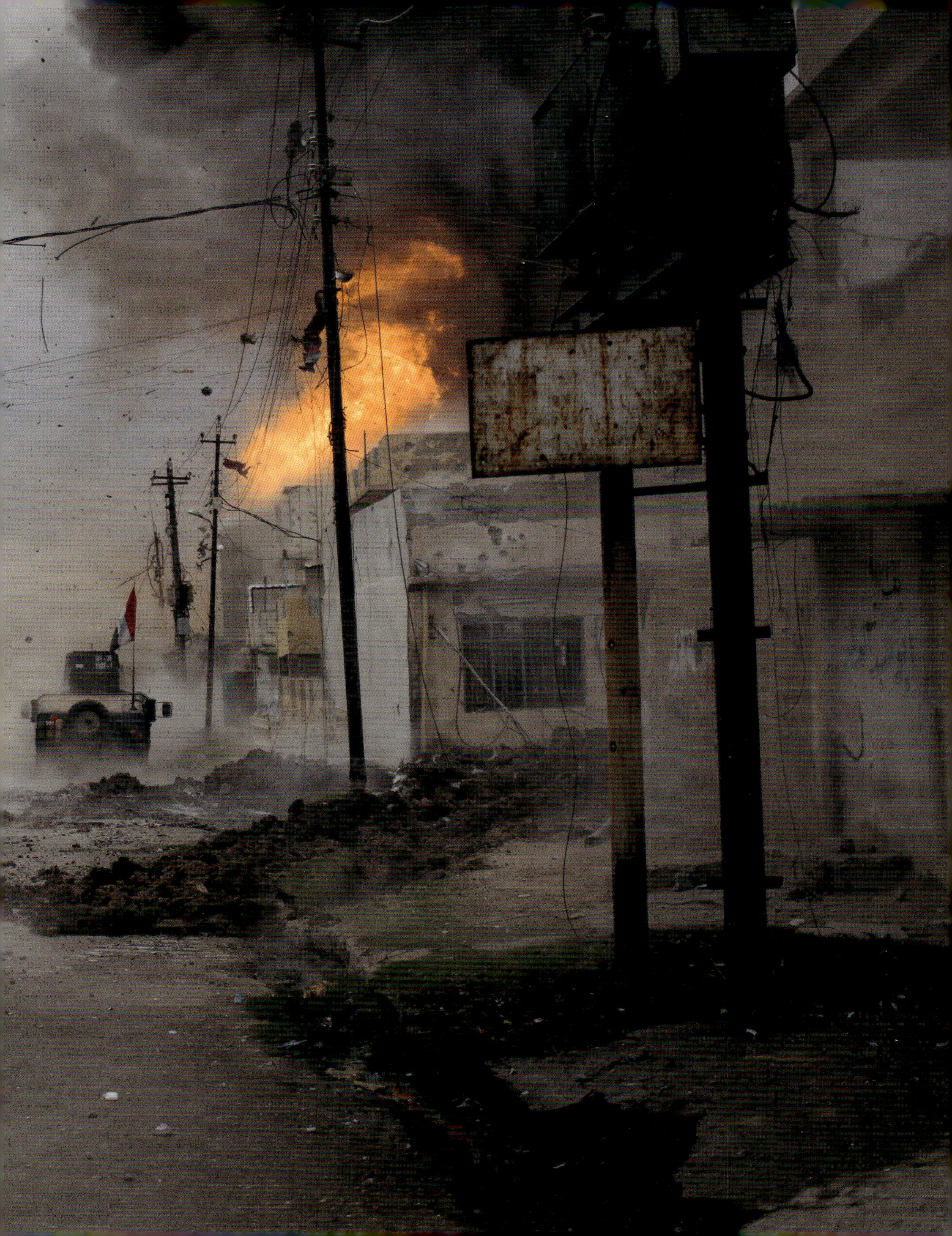

Paula Bronstein

USA, Getty Images Reportage for Pulitzer Center on Crisis Reporting / 1st Prize Daily Life

Najiba holds her nephew Shabir (2), who was injured in a bomb blast that killed his sister, in Kabul, Afghanistan, in March. The bomb exploded in a relatively peaceful part of Kabul while Shabir's mother was walking the children to school. Although the 2001-2014 Afghan War has formally ended, conflict continues in the country, with the Taliban as the chief insurgents and the US and other international forces backing the Afghan military. Fighting moved closer to villages and cities, with an upsurge in suicide bombings and targeted attacks aimed at destabilizing civilian life. According to the UN, child casualties rose by 24 percent in 2016, to 2,589 wounded and 923 killed.

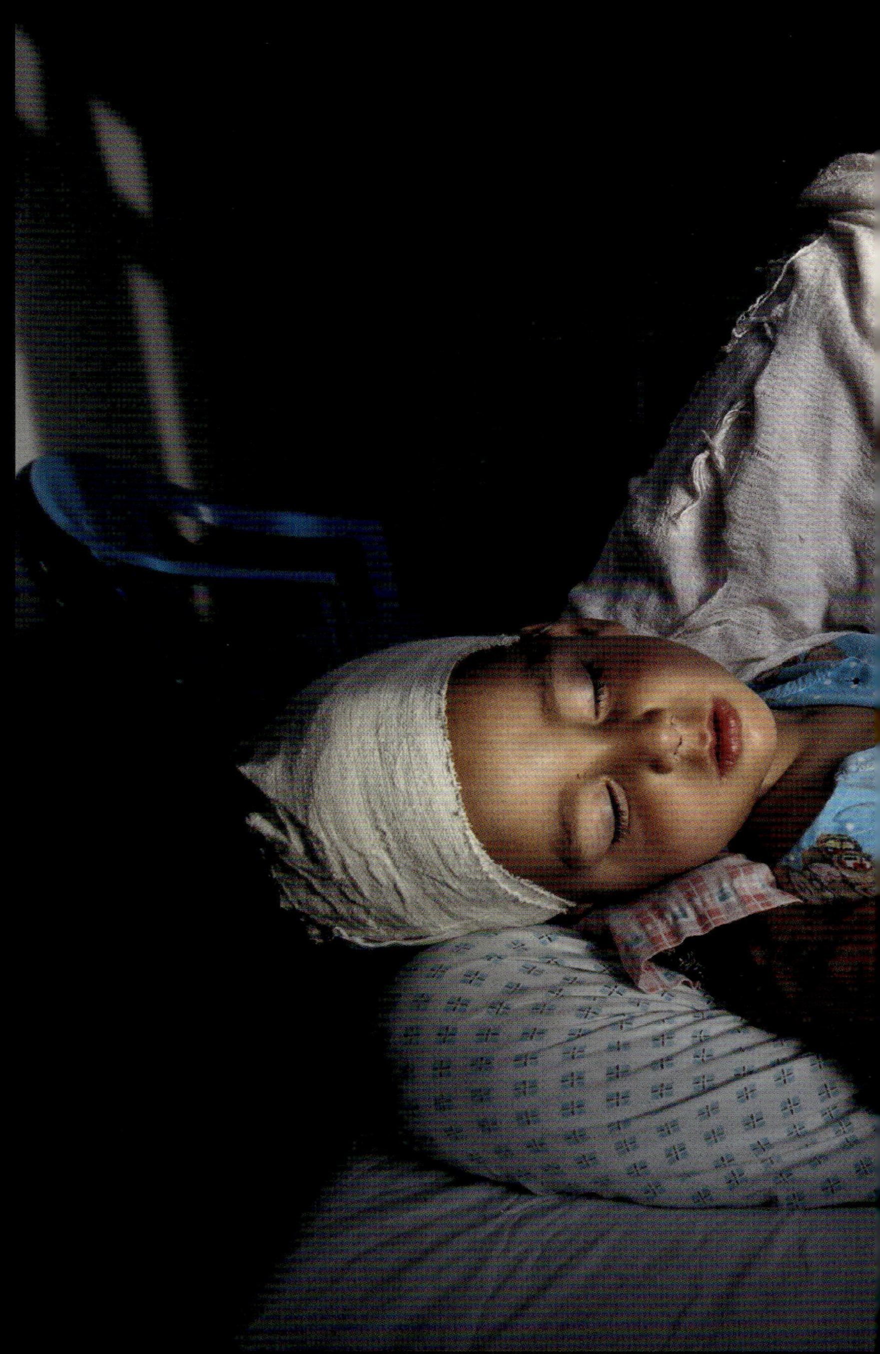

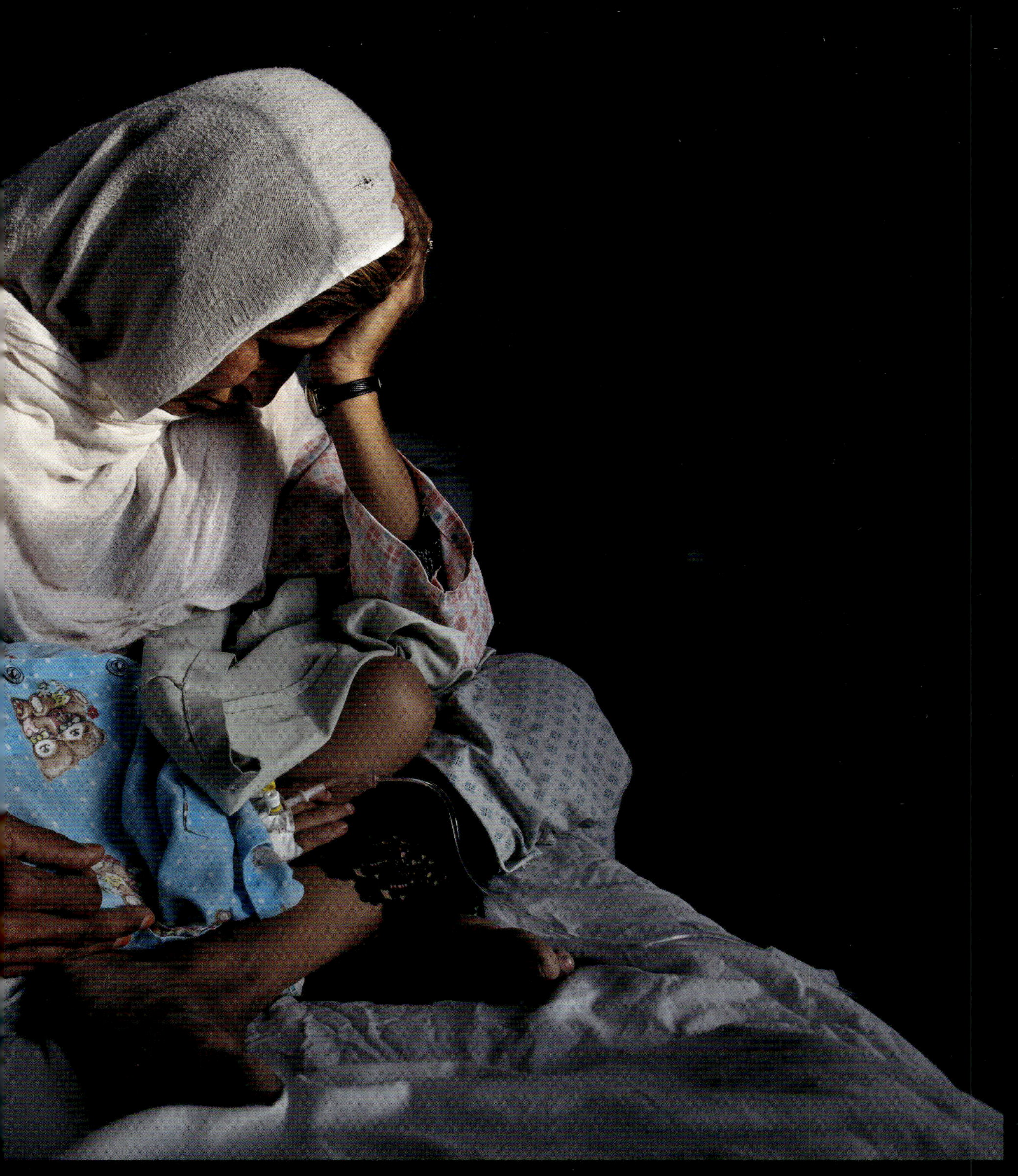

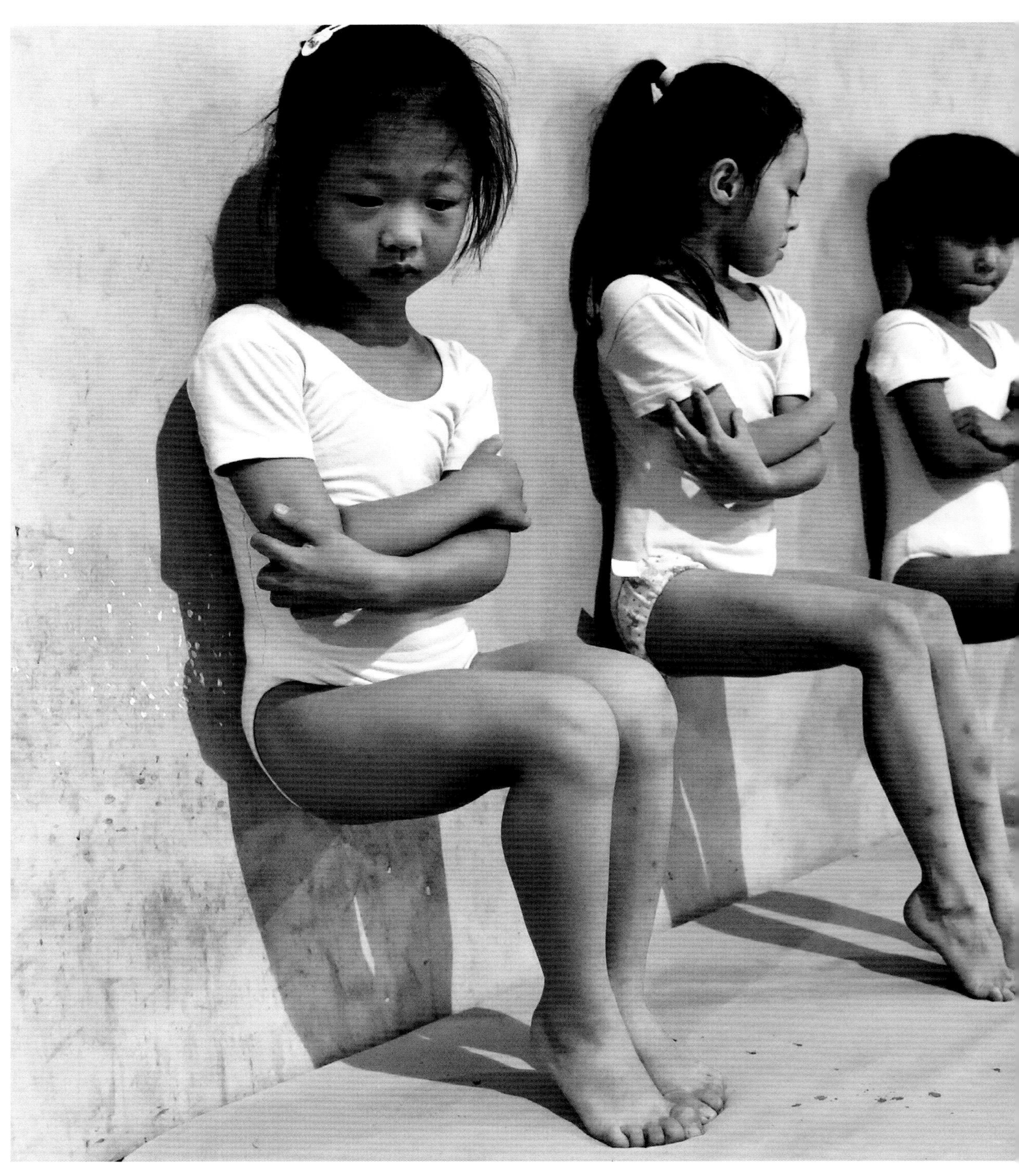

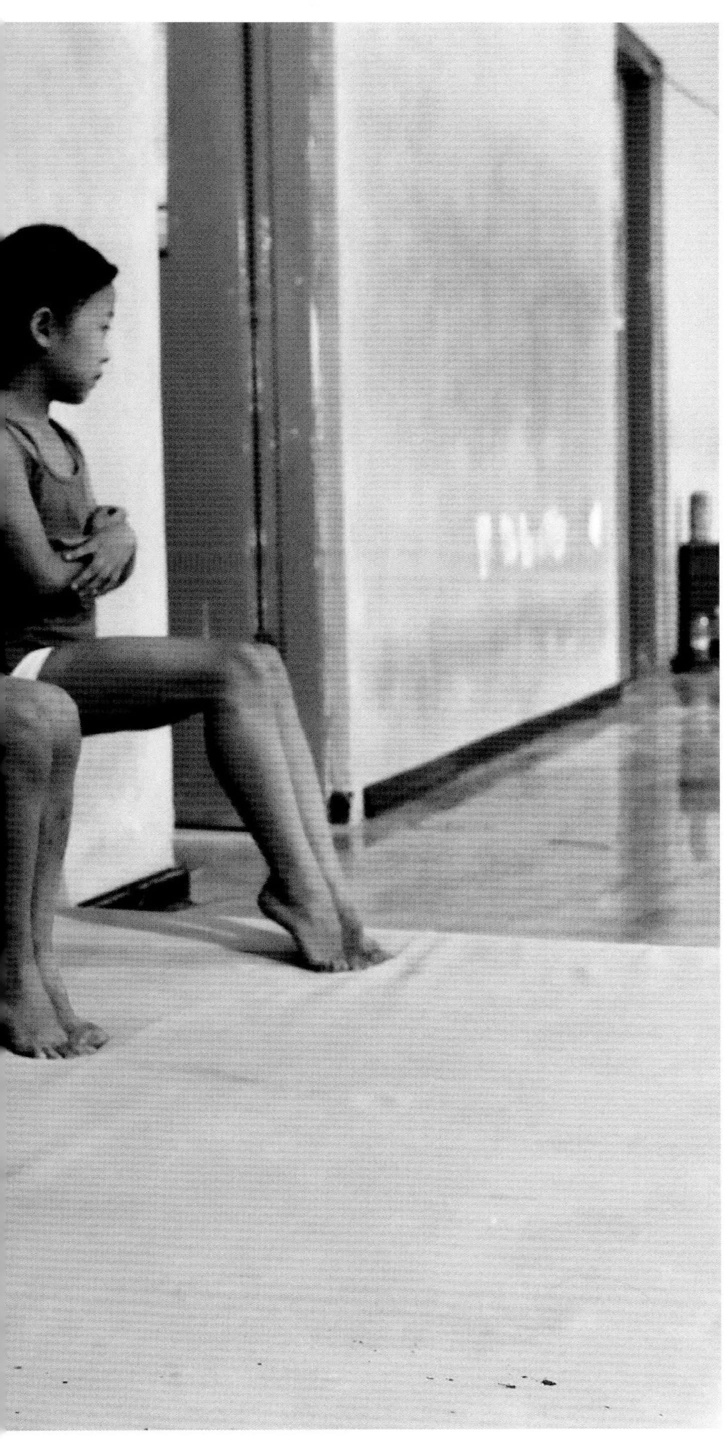

Wang Tiejun

China / 2nd Prize Daily Life

Students of a gymnastics school in Xuzhou, China, do toe-pressure training for 30 minutes in the afternoon. There are over 2,000 sports schools in China, which have produced 95 percent of the country's Olympians. Training is intense, and in today's China fewer parents are willing to let their children endure such grueling routines. Some schools have closed, while others are adjusting the way they work.

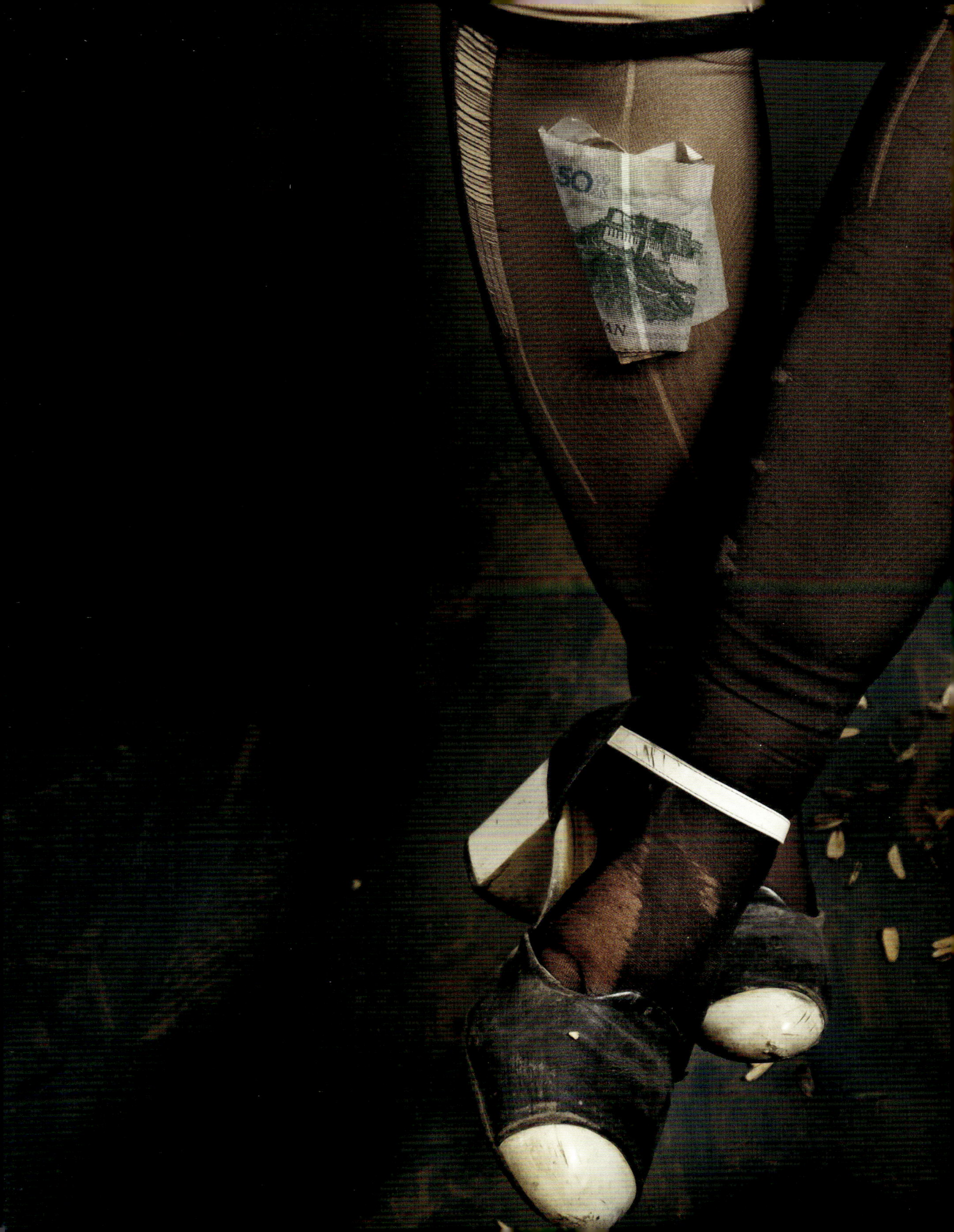
50

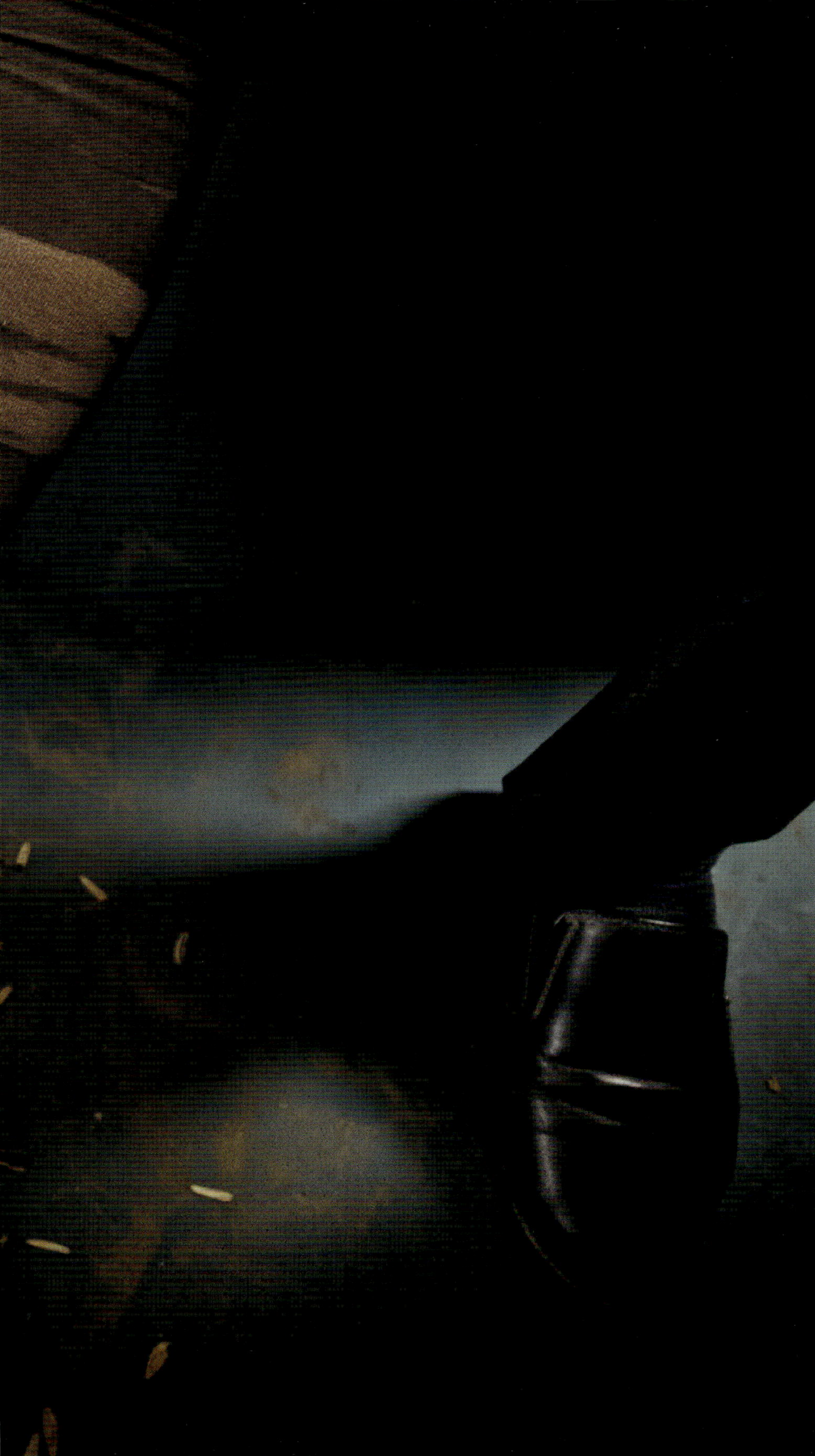

Matthieu Paley

France, for National Geographic / 3rd Prize Daily Life

A Uyghur woman carries money in her stocking, travelling along the old Silk Road by train, between Yarkand and Kashgar, in Xinjiang autonomous region, western China. Uyghur women, while Muslim, do not always adhere to a conservative dress code. The Xinjiang region is home to a diverse ethnic population, with about 46 percent being Uyghur.

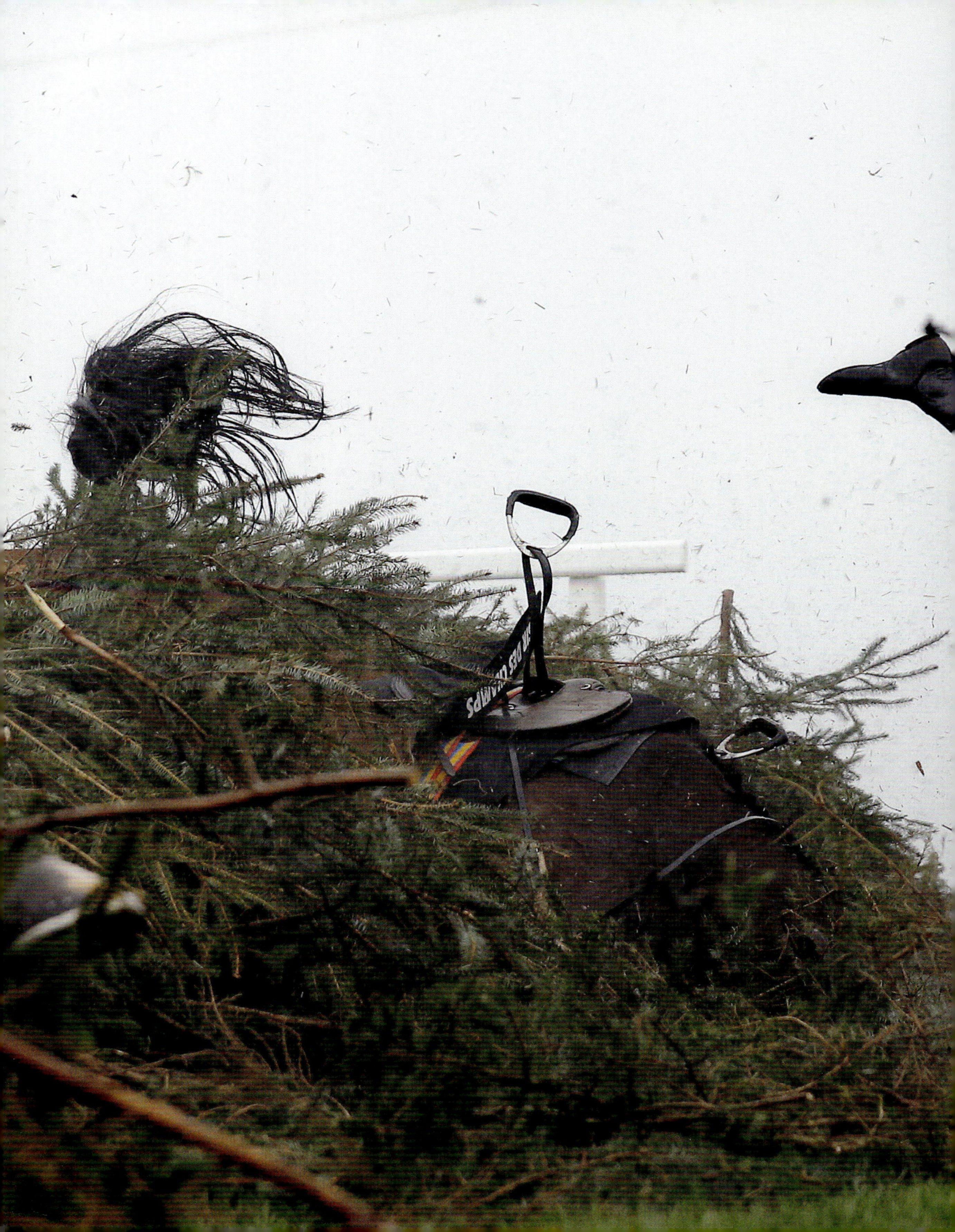

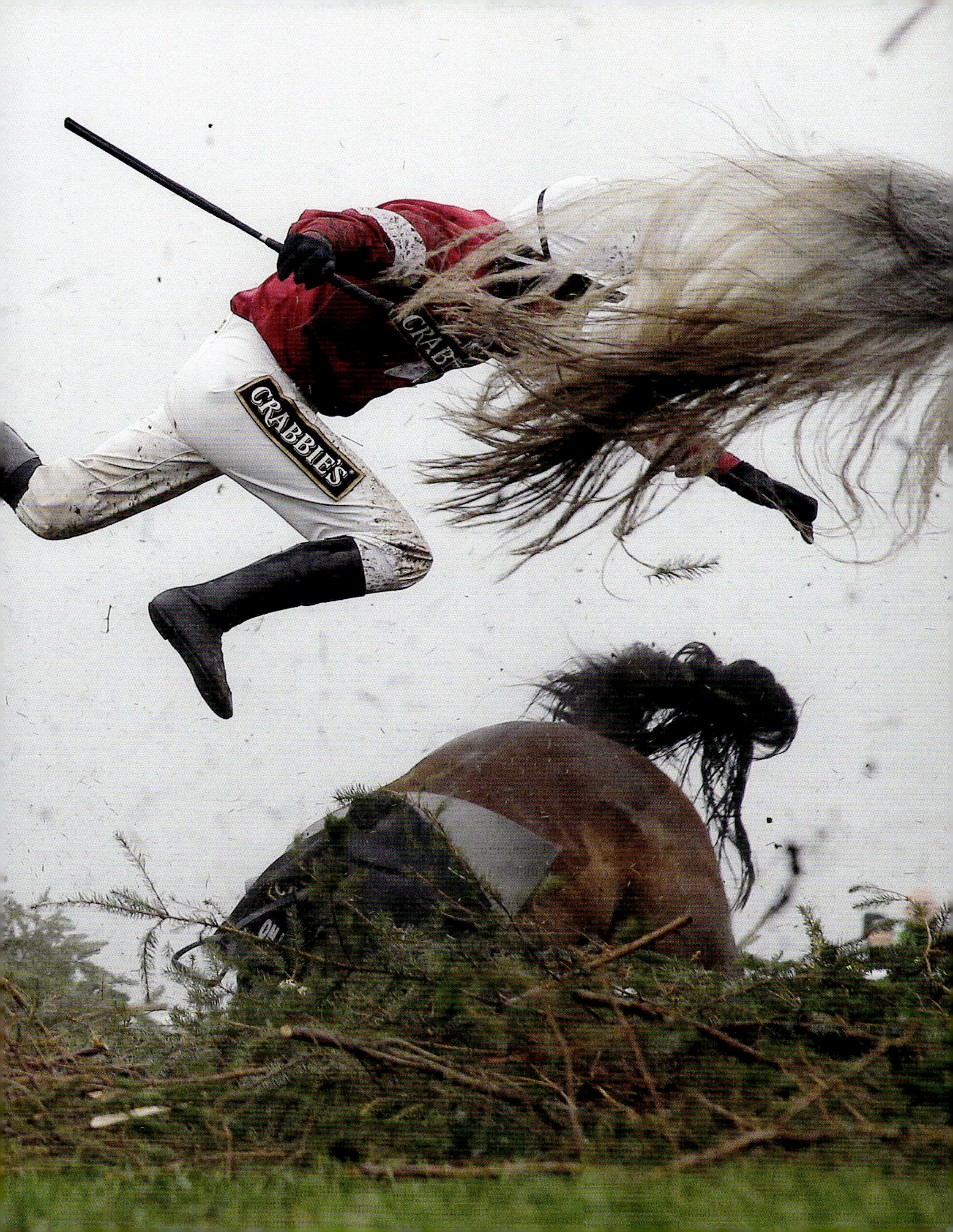
CRABBIE'S

Tom Jenkins

UK, *The Guardian* / 1st Prize Sports

Jockey Nina Carberry flies off her horse Sir Des Champs (left) as they fall at The Chair fence during the Grand National steeplechase, at Aintree Racecourse, Liverpool, UK, on 9 April. A second horse, On His Own (right) also fell at the fence, moments before Sir Des Champs attempted to jump. None of the horses or jockeys involved was injured.

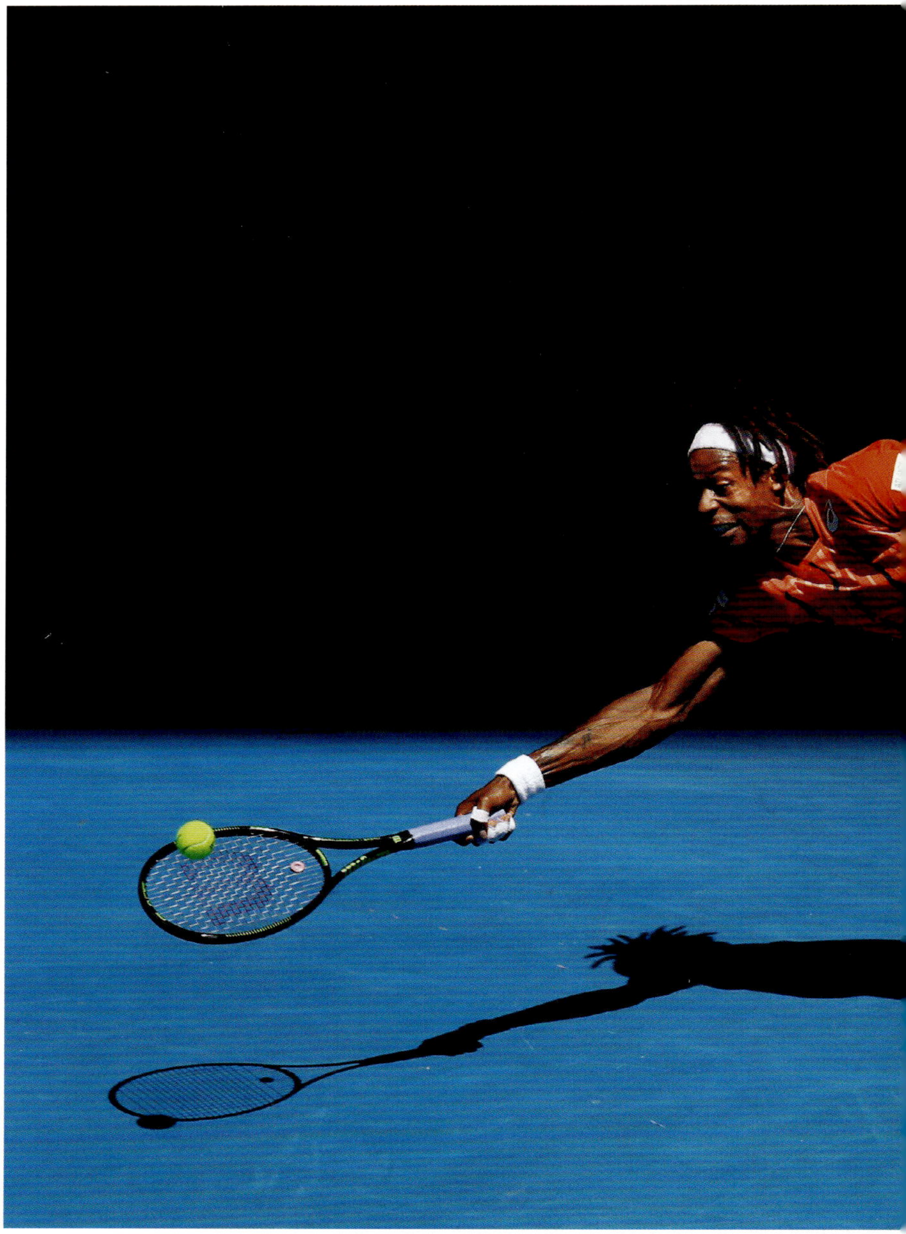

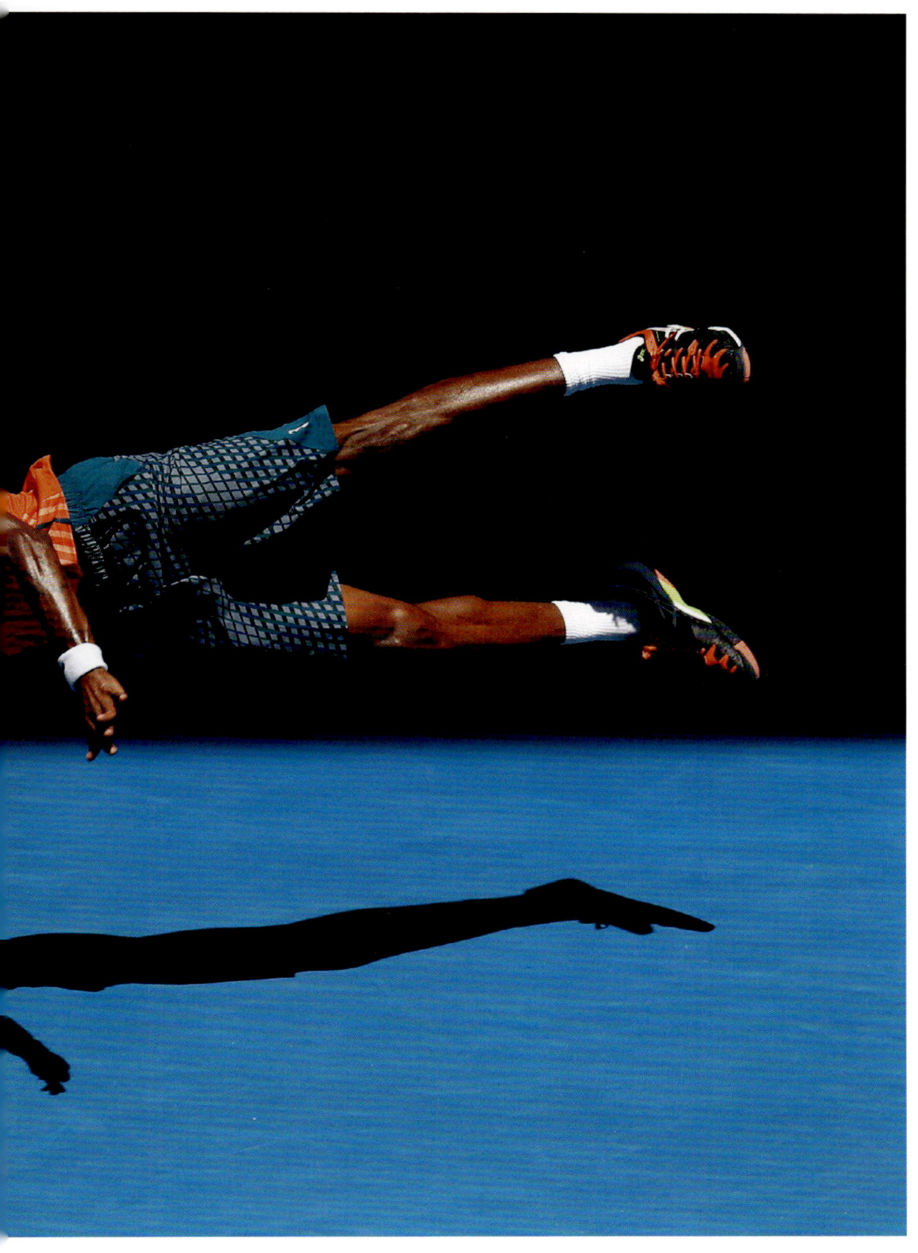

Cameron Spencer

Australia, Getty Images /
2nd Prize Sports

Gaël Monfils of France dives for a forehand, during his fourth-round match against Andrey Kuznetsov of Russia, in the 2016 Australian Open tennis championships at Melbourne Park, Melbourne, Australia, on 25 January. Monfils cut and bruised his hand and required a medical timeout, but went on to win the match.

Kai Oliver Pfaffenbach

Germany, Reuters / 3rd Prize Sports

Jamaican Usain Bolt smiles as he looks back while winning the 100-meter semi-final race at the Summer Olympics in Rio de Janeiro, Brazil, on 14 August. He finished the race in 9.86 seconds. Bolt went on to win a gold medal in the finals, becoming the first athlete to win three Olympic 100-meter titles. He also took gold in the 200-meter race and 4x100-meter relay, thus obtaining the 'triple-triple': three sprinting gold medals in three consecutive Olympics. Bolt later lost this status, after a teammate was found guilty of a doping violation and the 2008 Jamaican relay team was stripped of its gold medal.

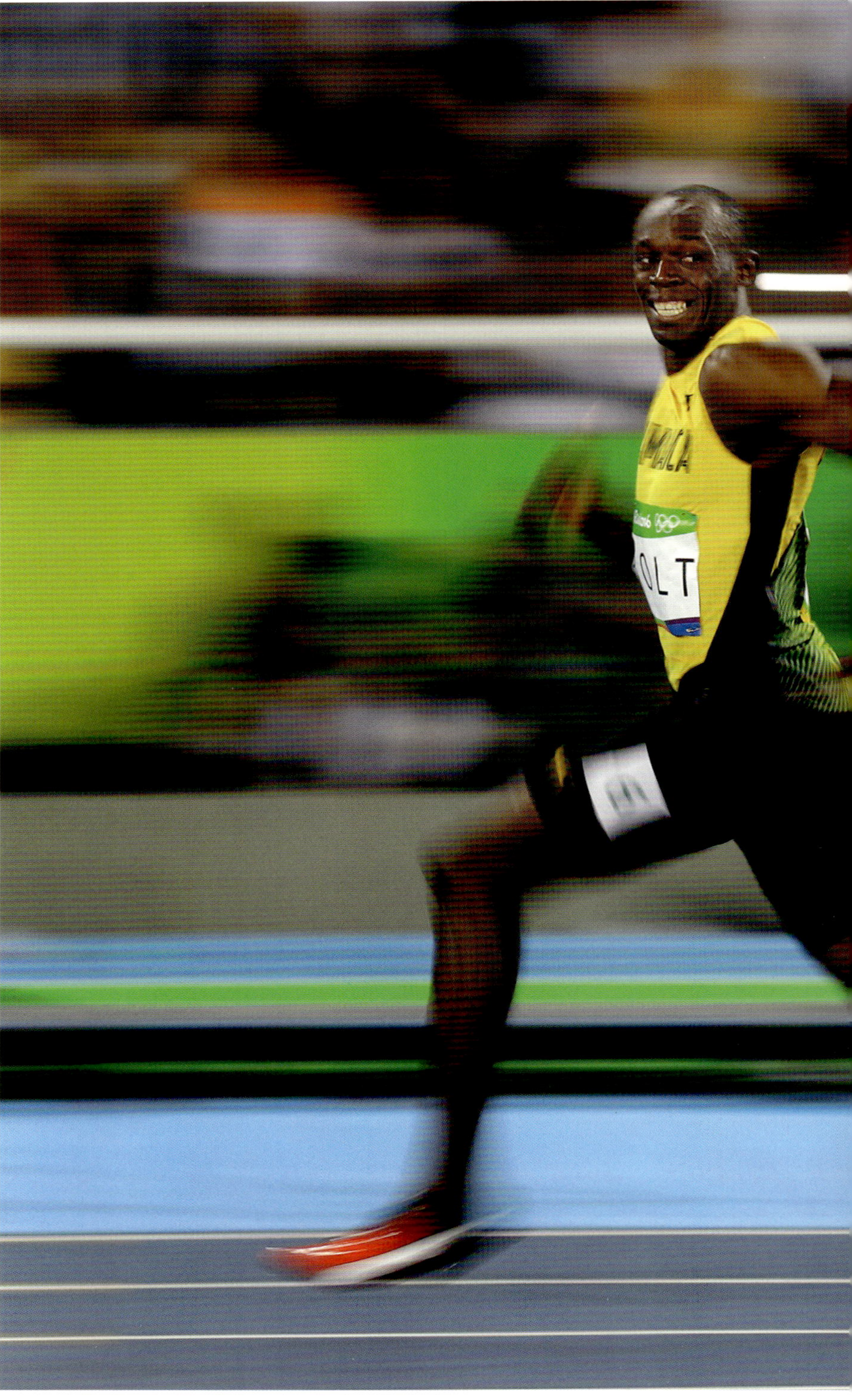

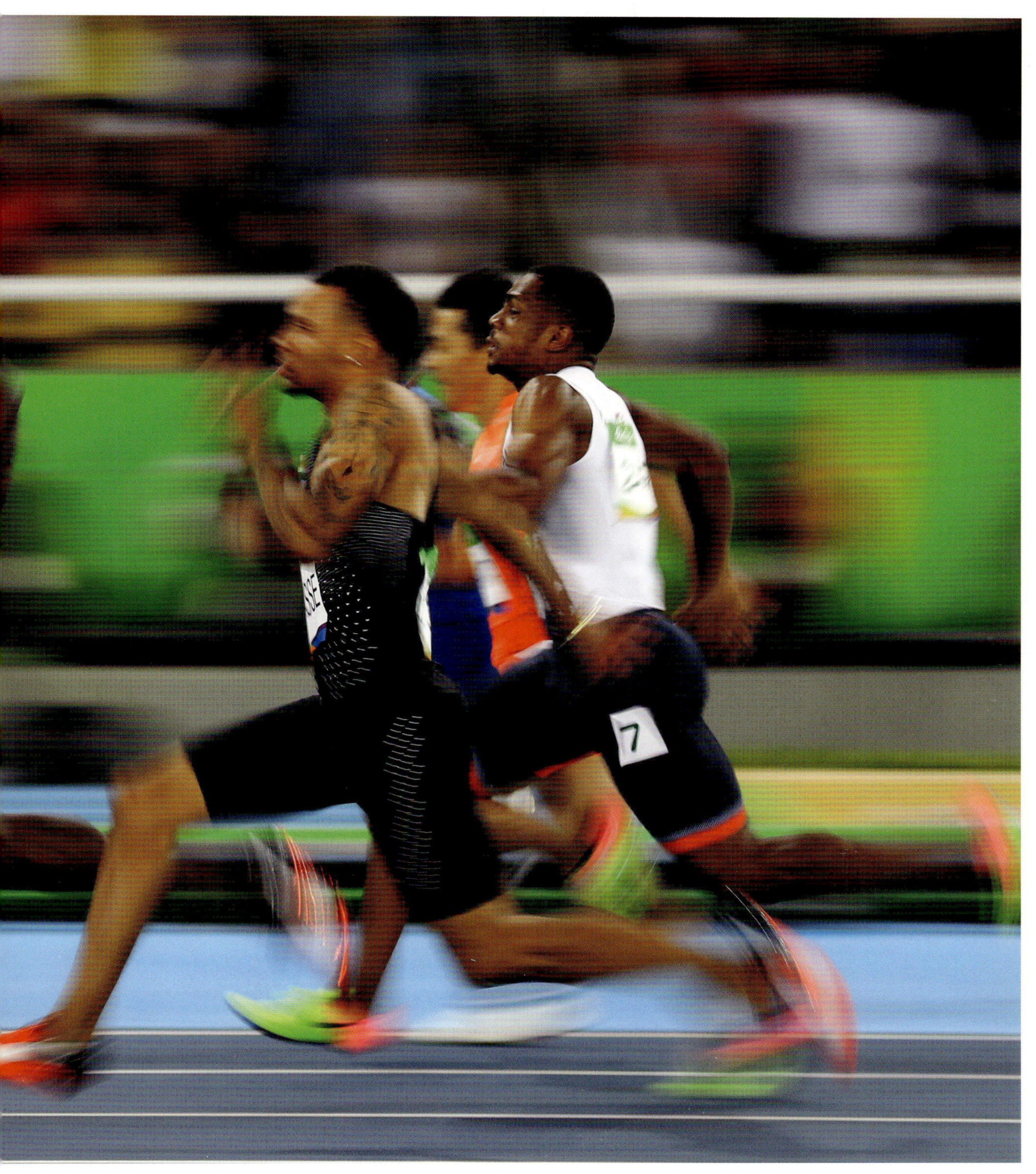
7

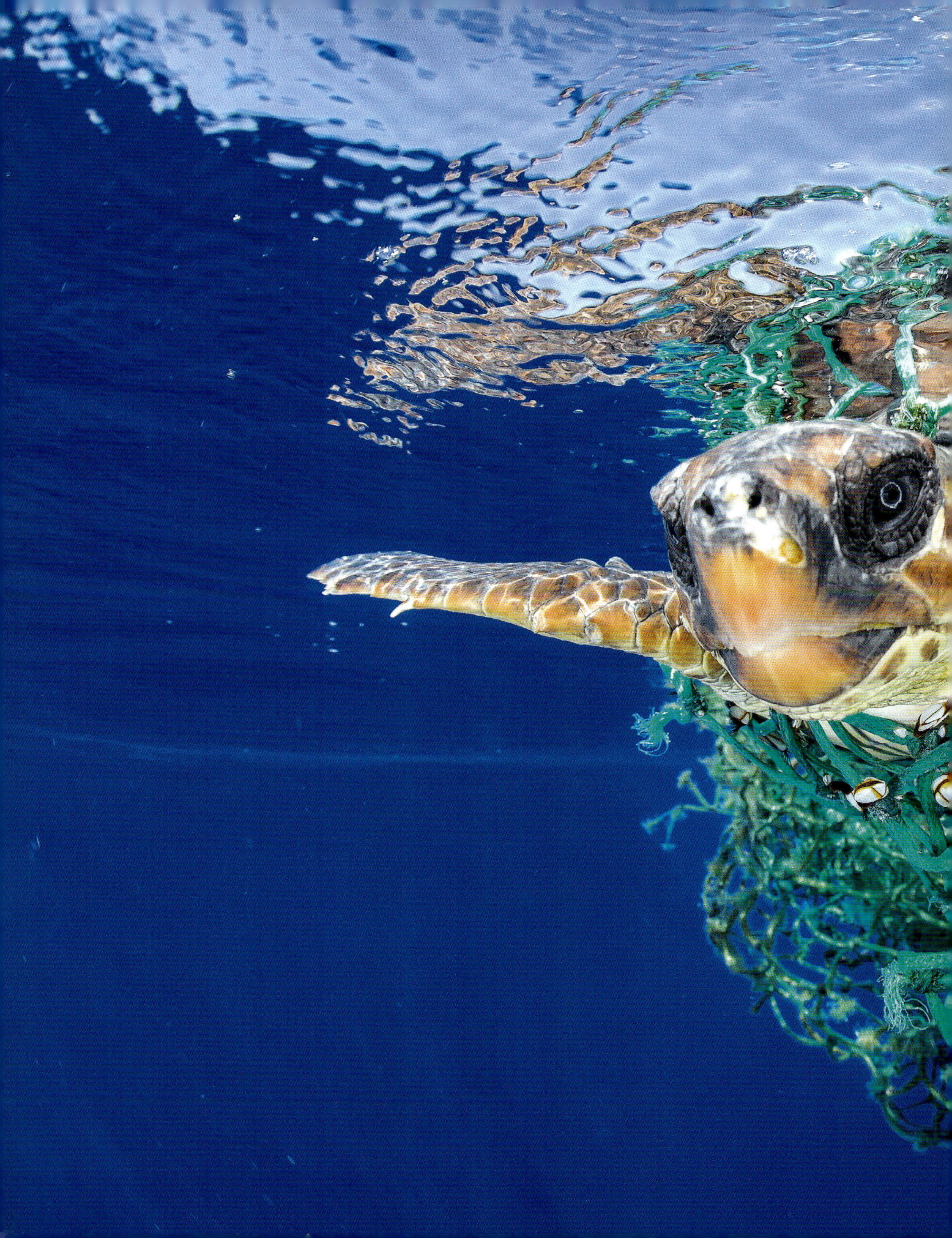

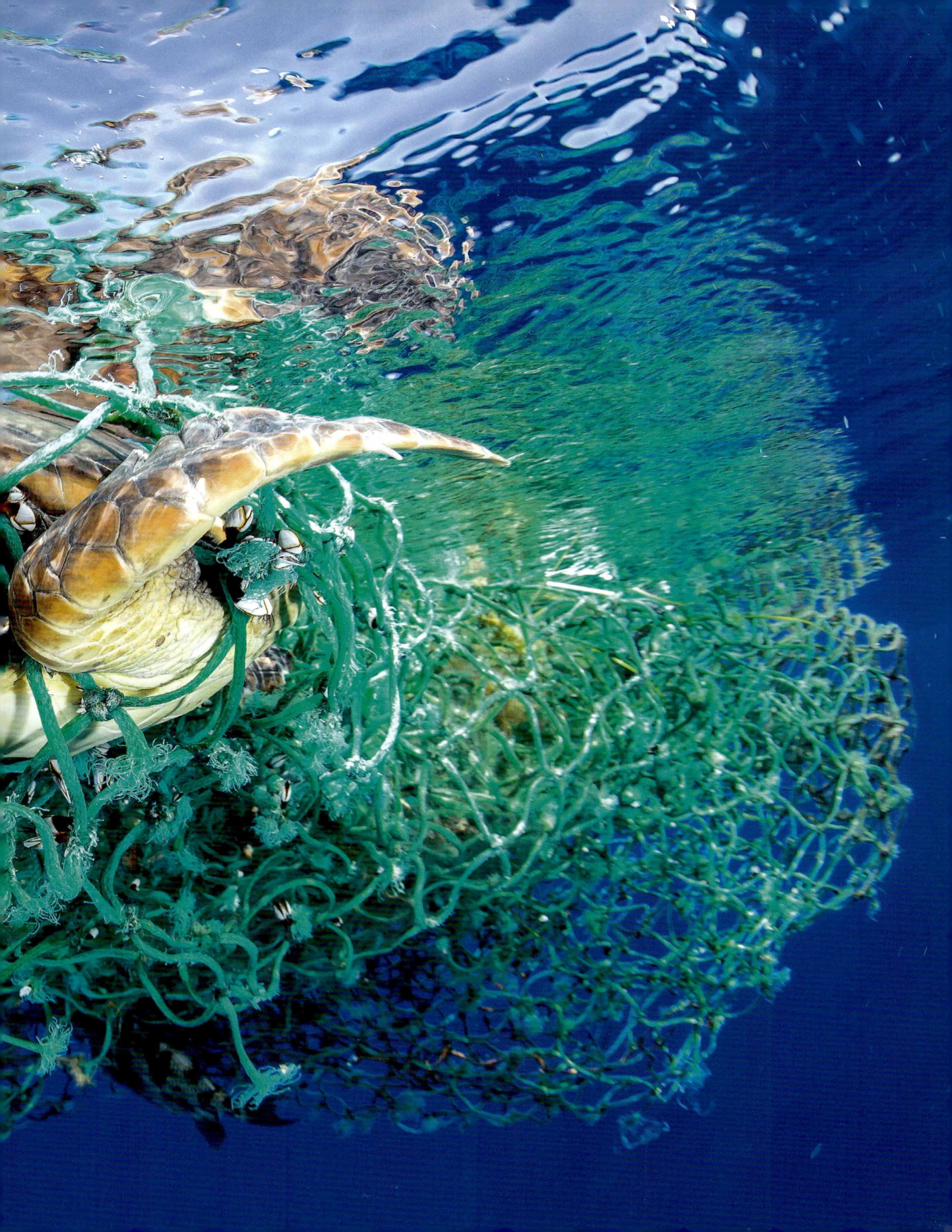

Francis Pérez

Spain / 1st Prize Nature

A loggerhead sea turtle swims entangled in abandoned fishing gear, off the coast of Tenerife, Canary Islands, in the northeast Atlantic Ocean. The loggerhead is classed as a 'vulnerable' species globally by the International Union for Conservation of Nature, but the northeast Atlantic subpopulation is listed as 'endangered'. Entrapment in nets intended for other species, and in gear left abandoned by fishing boats is the prime threat to marine turtles, followed by human consumption of meat and eggs, and coastal development affecting their habitat.

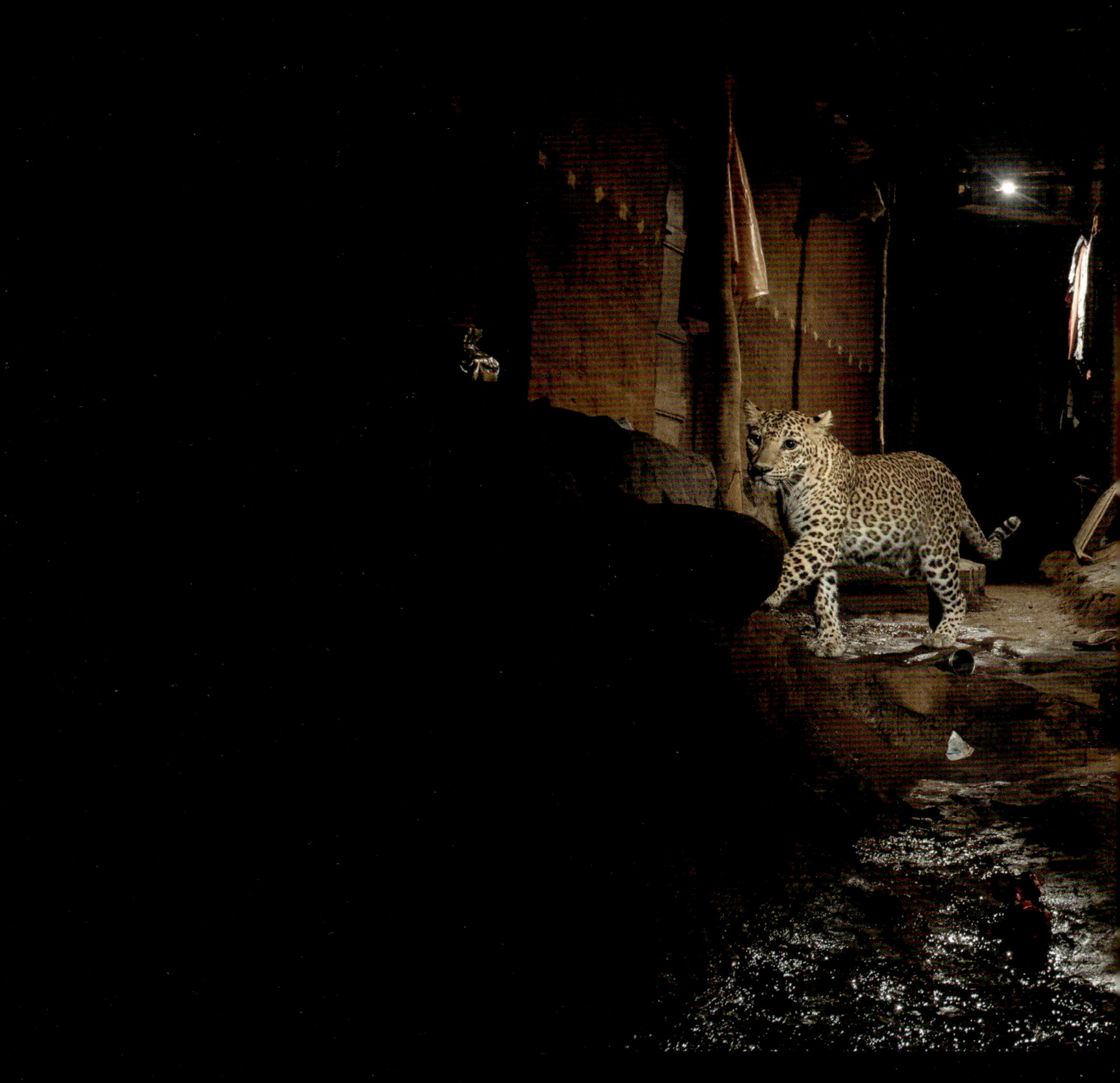

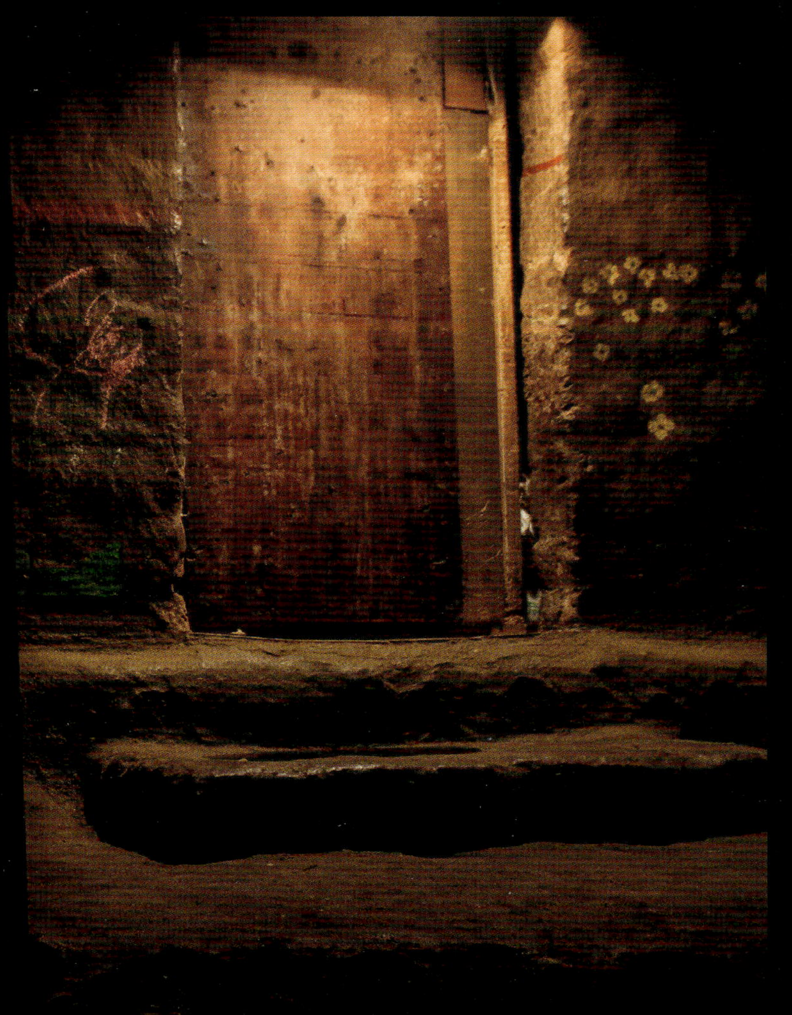

Nayan Khanolkar

India / 2nd Prize Nature

A leopard walks at night through Aarey Milk Colony, a residential, recreational and farming settlement adjacent to the Sanjay Gandhi National Park, in suburban Mumbai. Some 35 leopards live in the park and increasingly venture into surrounding areas in search of prey such as the stray dogs that gather round garbage dumps. This raises the potential for human-leopard conflict, with reports both of attacks on humans, and of leopards caught in poaching traps.

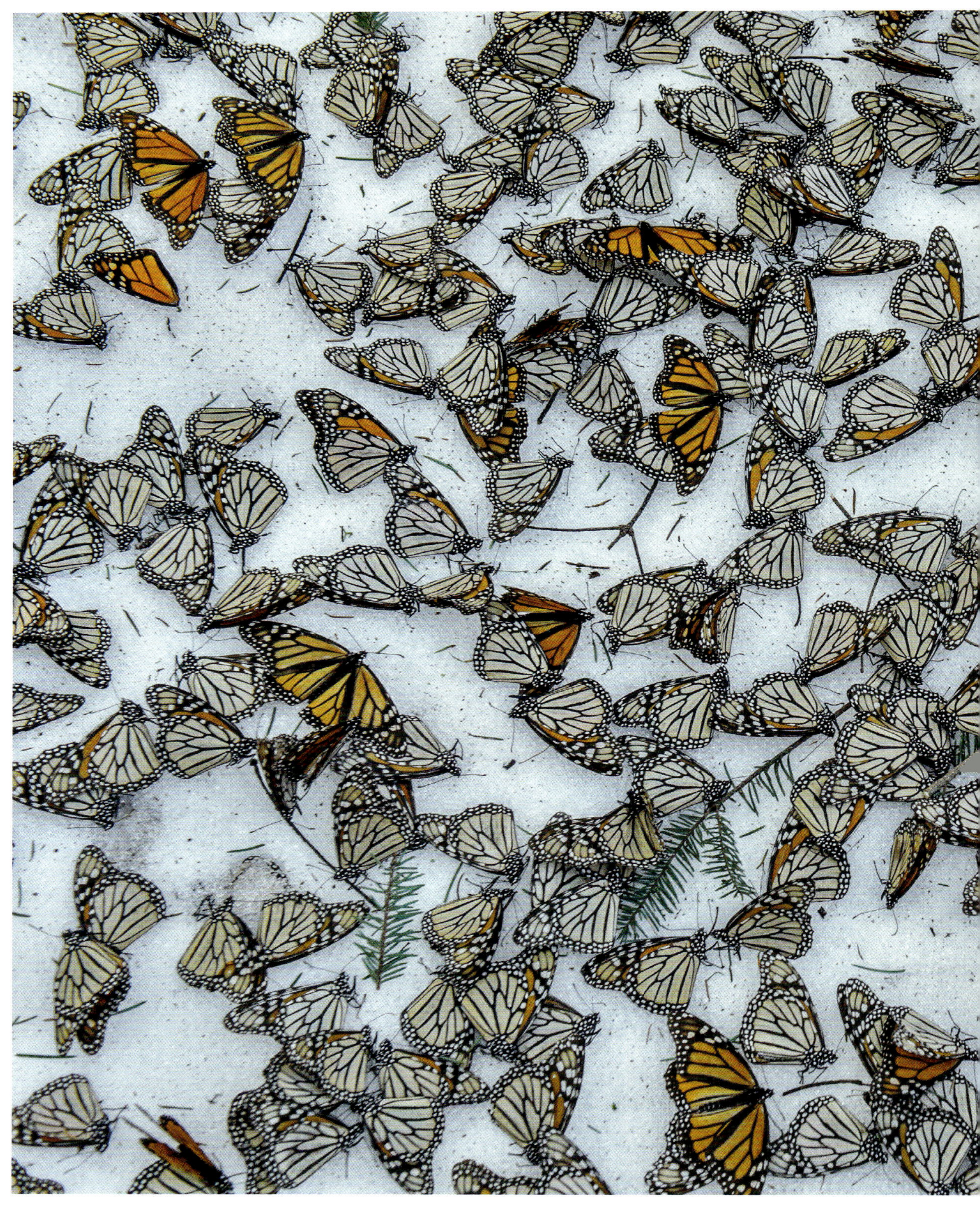

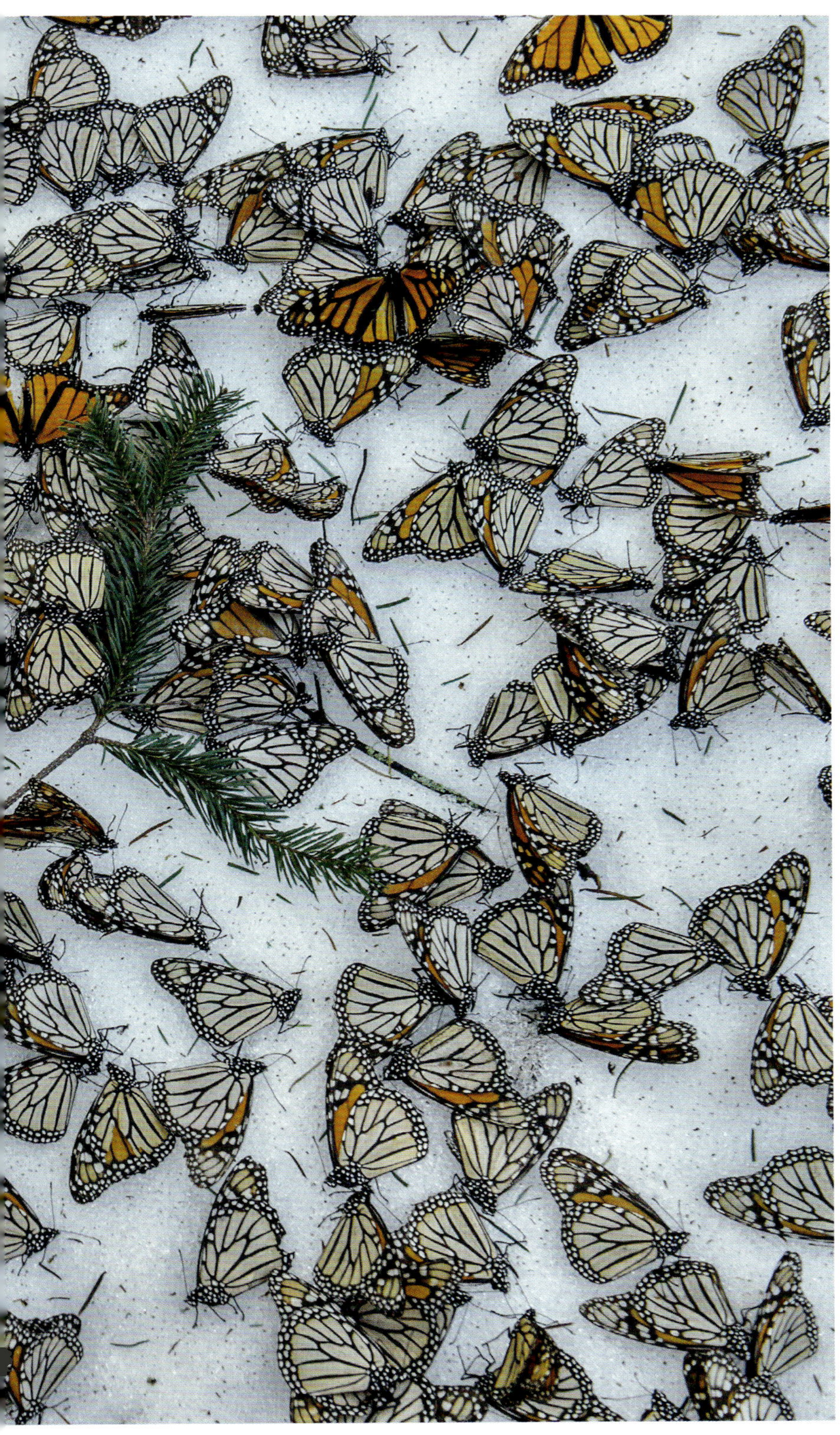

Jaime Rojo

Spain / 3rd Prize Nature

A carpet of monarch butterflies covers the forest floor of El Rosario Butterfly Sanctuary in Michoacán, Mexico, after a snowstorm. The severe storm hit the mountains of Central Mexico on 8 and 9 March, just as wintering colonies of the butterflies were starting their migration back to the USA—a journey of more than 4,500 kilometers. The butterflies are surprisingly resilient and can survive several days in sub-zero temperatures as long as they remain dry, but it was unclear how badly the snowstorm affected the colonies. After a general decline in monarch populations, with numbers dipping by 90 percent since the 1990s, there had been a recent increase, and the winter had been seen as a possible turning point for the species.

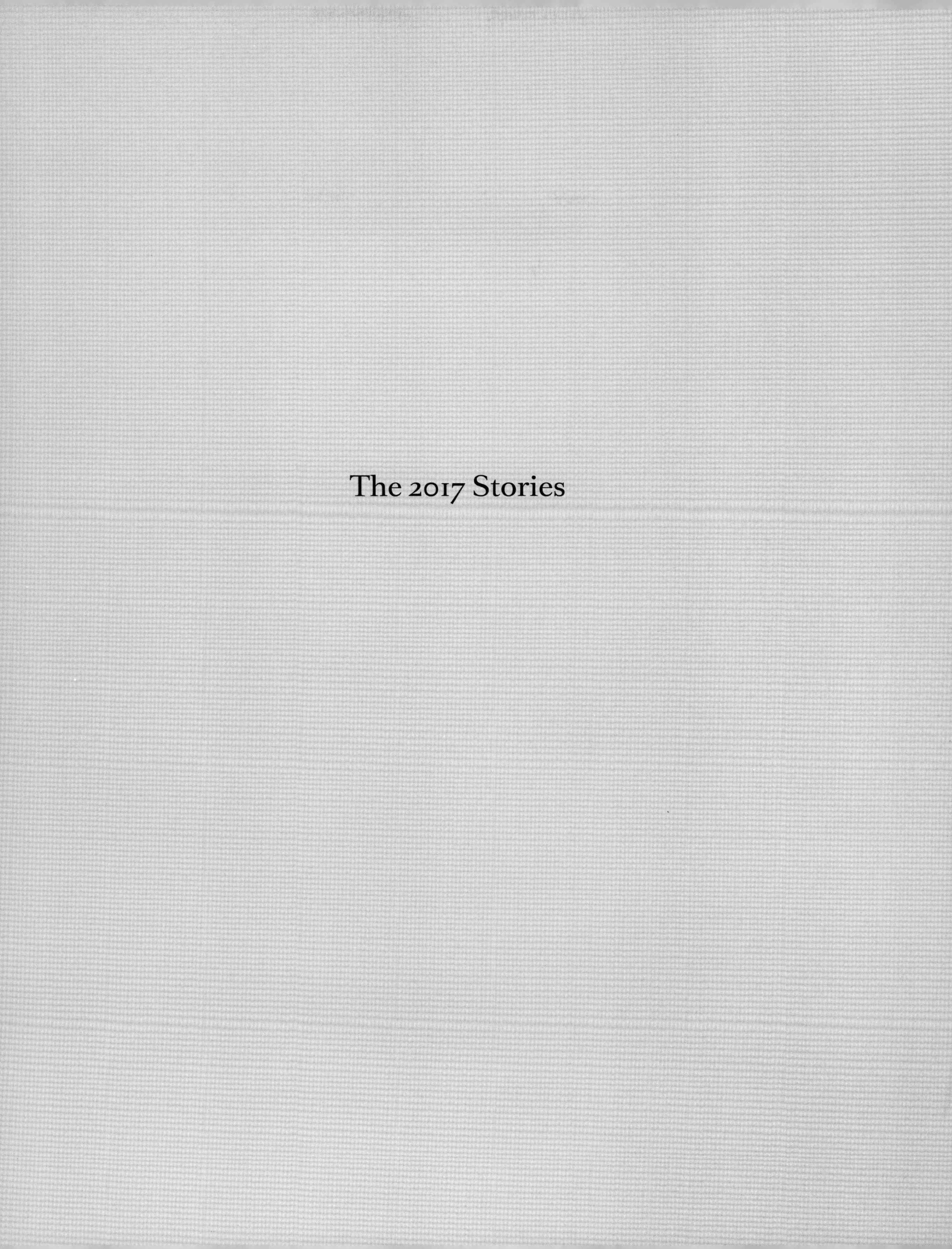

The 2017 Stories

Burhan Ozbilici

Turkey, The Associated Press /
World Press Photo of the Year /
1st Prize Spot News

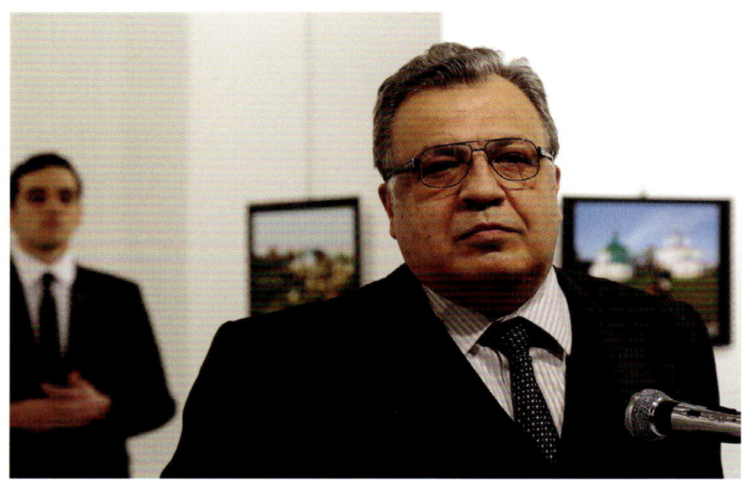

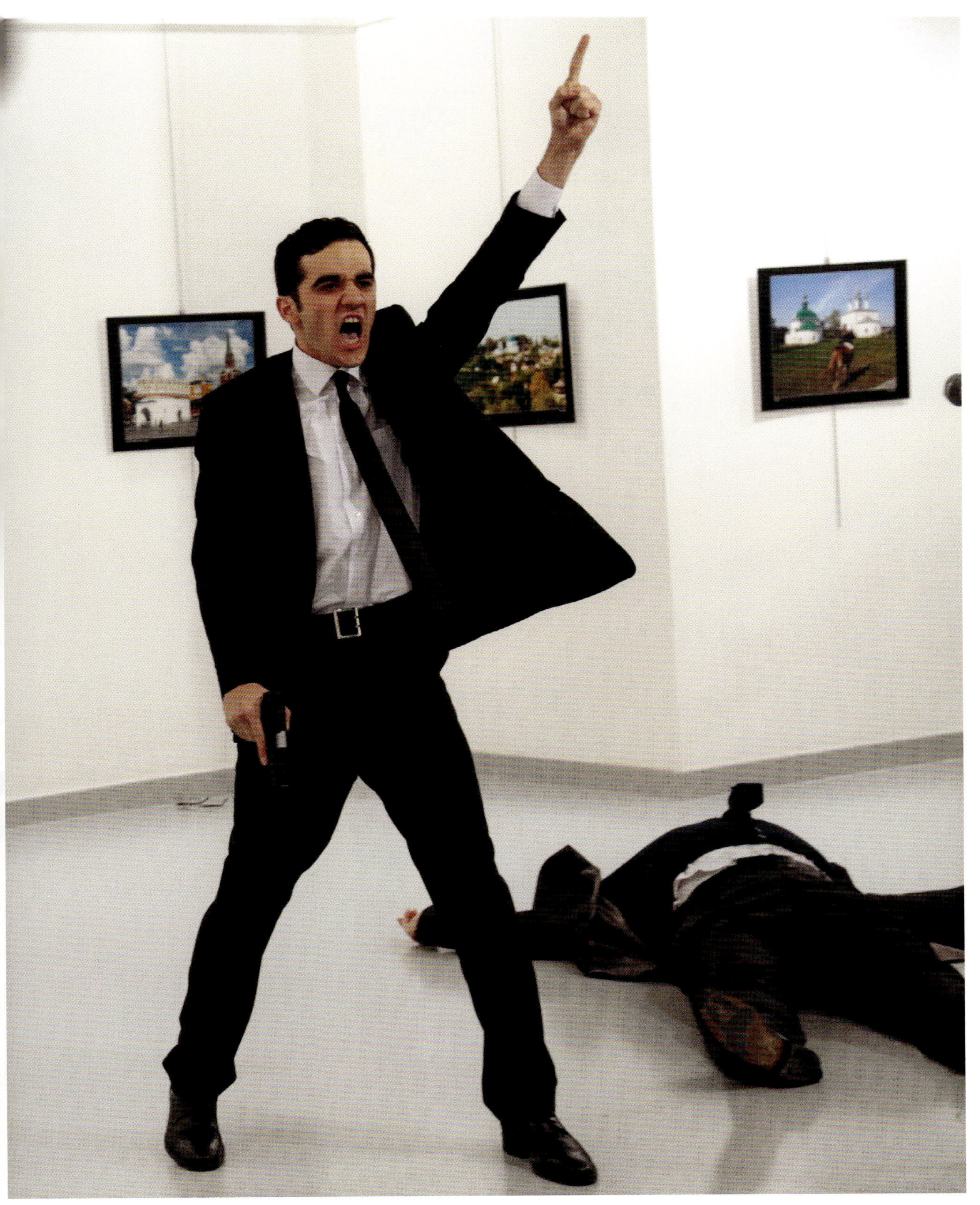

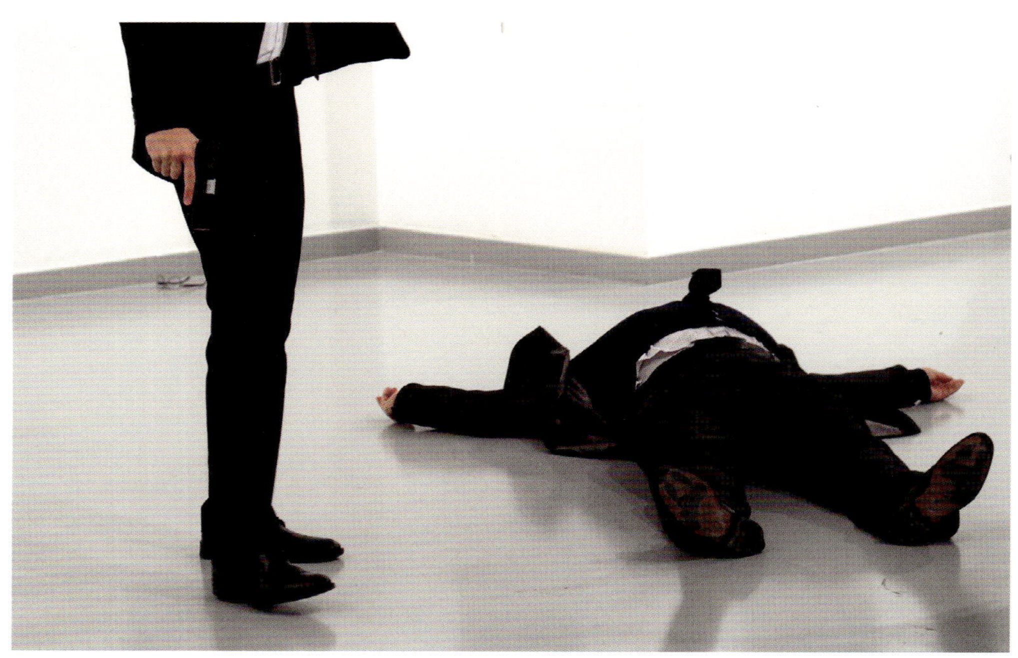

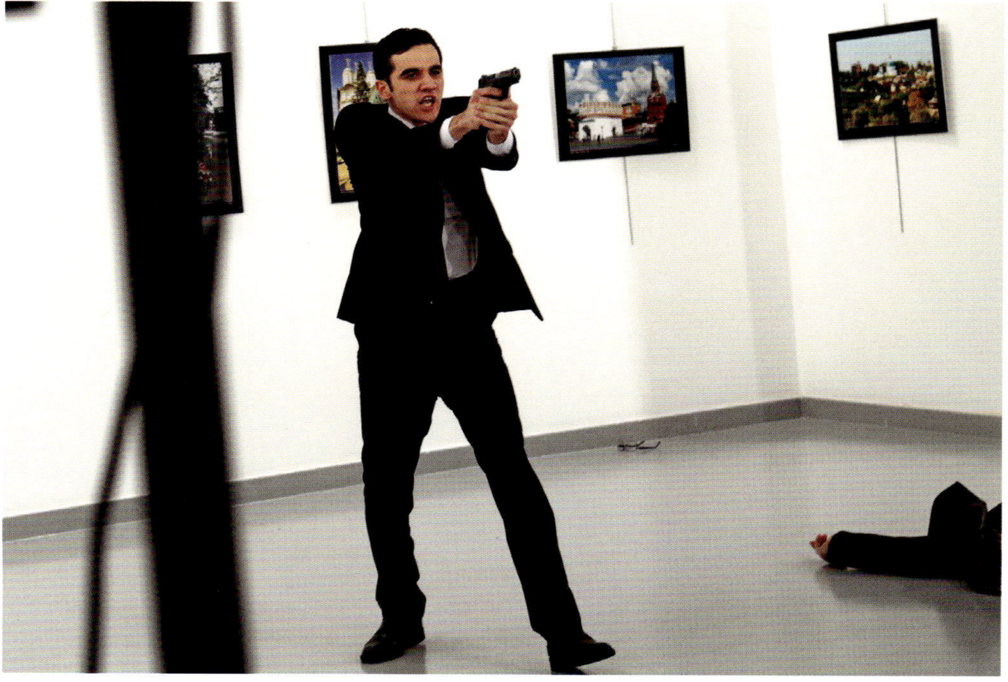

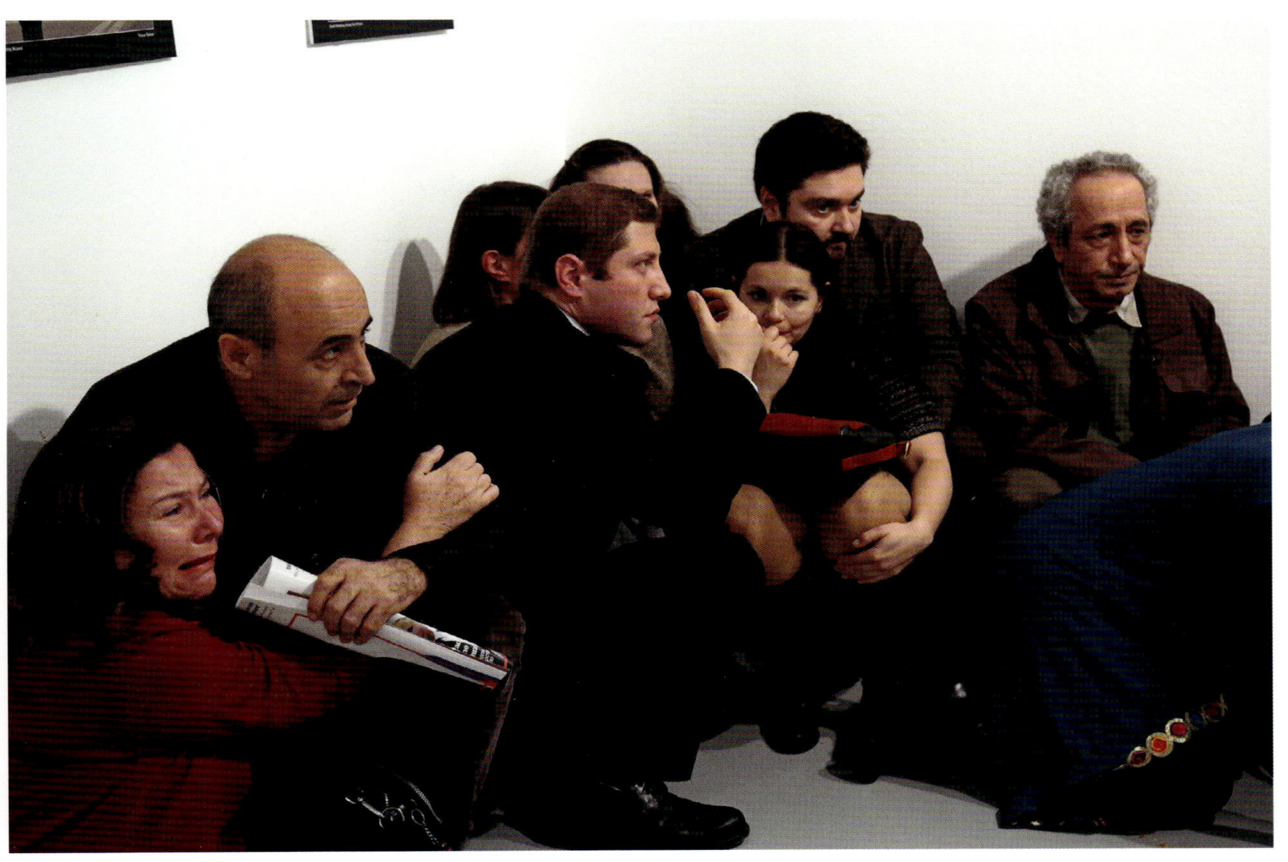

Russian ambassador Andrey Karlov was assassinated by an off-duty Turkish police officer, Mevlut Mert Altintas, while he was speaking at an art gallery in Ankara, Turkey, on 19 December. Altintas shouted "*Allahu akbar*" (God is great) and later said in Turkish: "Don't forget Aleppo. Don't forget Syria." He was killed in a shootout after Turkish Special Forces arrived at the gallery. Russia and Turkey supported opposing sides in the Syrian civil war, with Russia backing forces loyal to the Syrian government and Turkey supporting certain rebel groups. In the months prior to the attack, relations between the two countries had developed into a strategic partnership, with each curbing their support in their own strategic interest. *Previous pages, left*: The Russian ambassador, Andrey Karlov. *Right*: Altintas shouts after shooting the ambassador. *Facing page, top*: Altintas stands over Karlov after shooting him. *Below*: Altintas again holds up a gun after shooting Karlov. *This page*: People crouch in a corner of the gallery after the shooting.

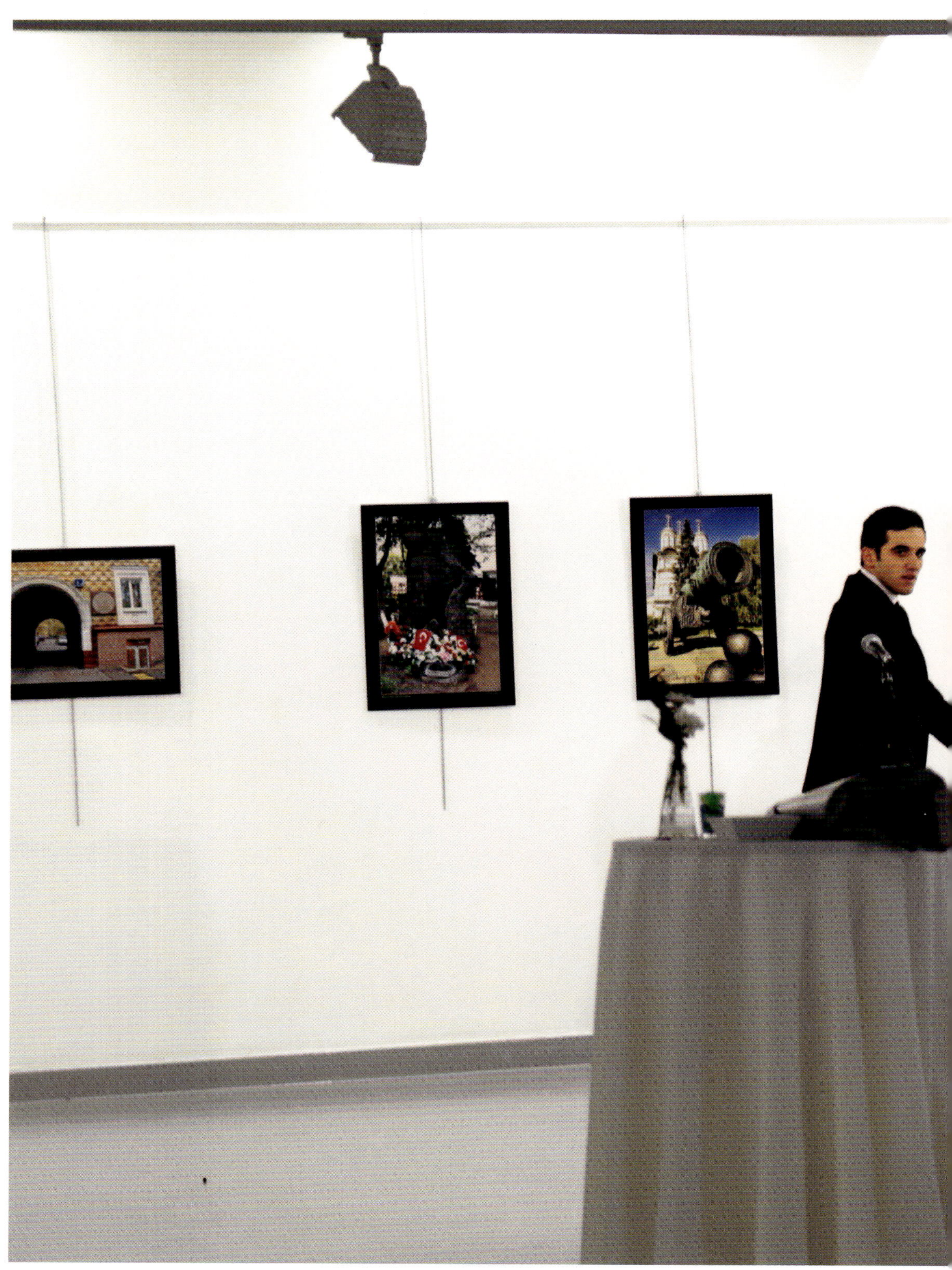

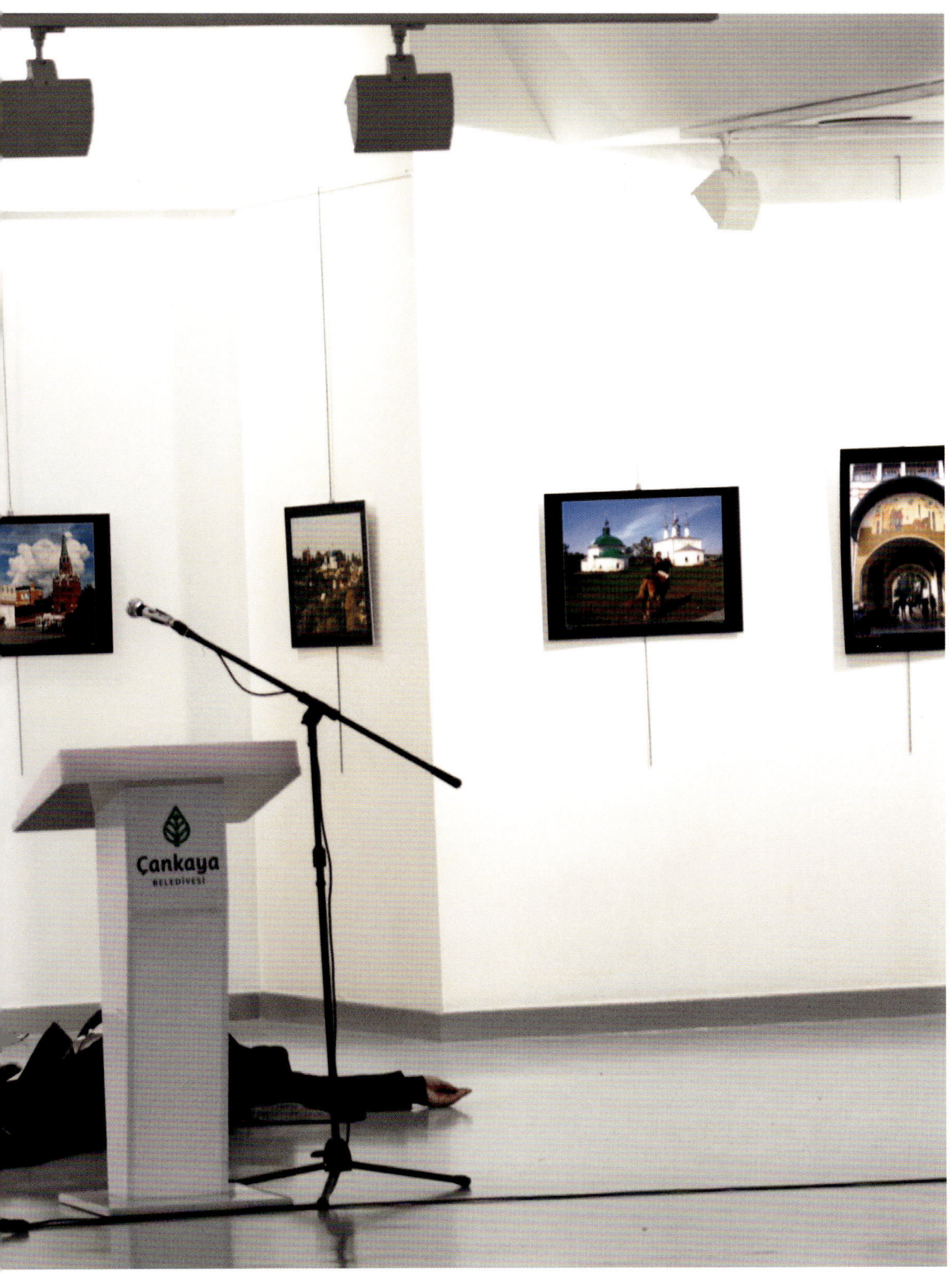
Çankaya
BELEDİYESİ

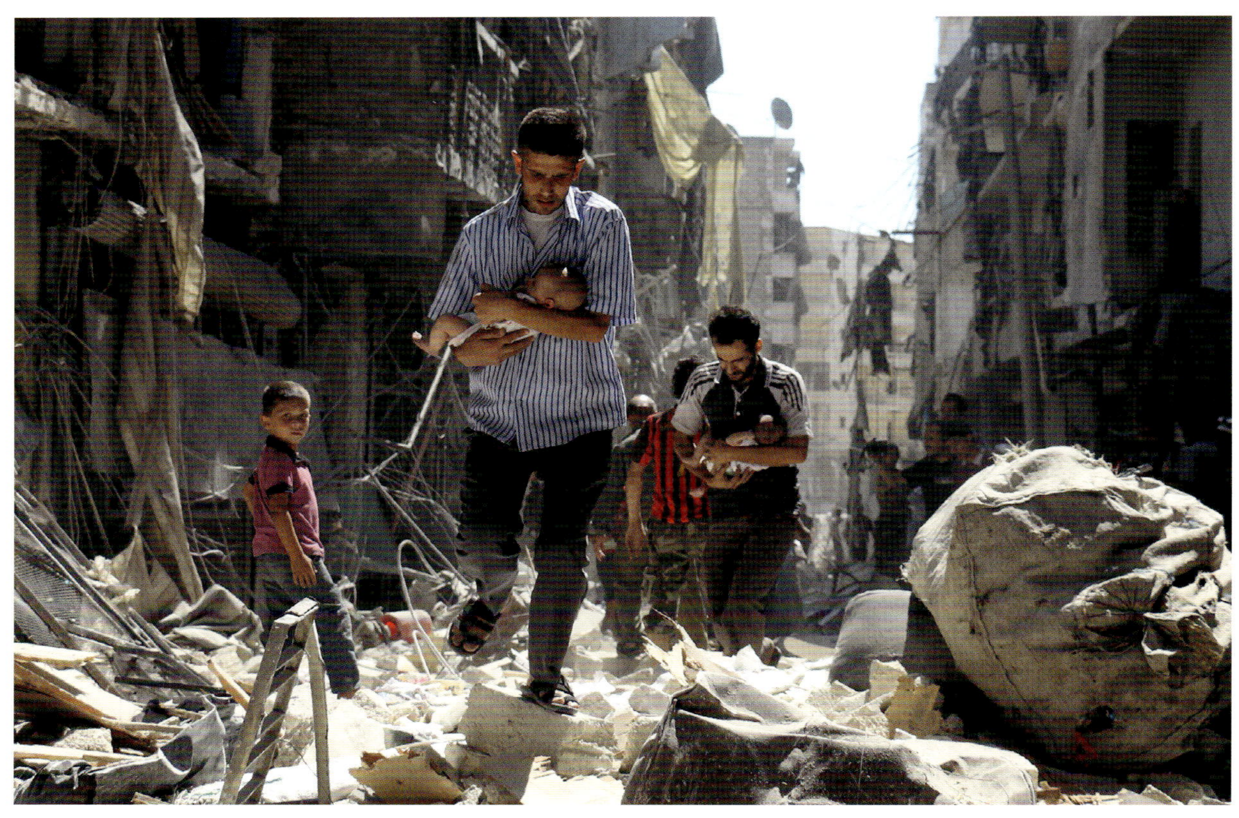

Walid Mashhadi

Syria, Agence France-Presse /
2nd Prize Spot News

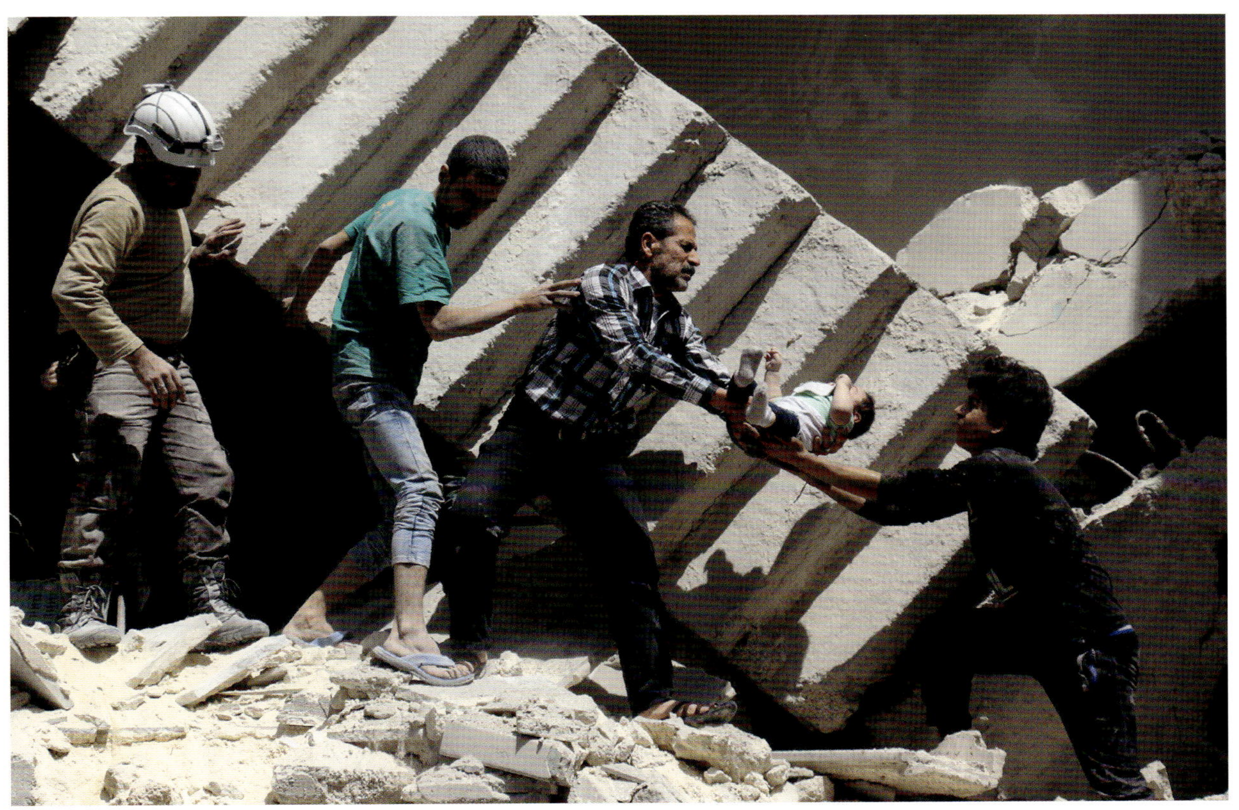

Aleppo, once Syria's largest city and the country's financial and industrial center, was a key battleground in the war between forces loyal to President Bashar al-Assad and rebels who wanted to overthrow him. For four years the city had been roughly divided in half, with the opposition controlling the east and the government the west. As fighting intensified in 2016, the rebels became increasingly besieged. Of the roughly 250,000 people who remained trapped in eastern Aleppo, around 100,00 were children. *Facing page*: Men carrying babies make their way through rubble in the Salihin neighborhood, eastern Aleppo, on 12 September, the day a ceasefire brokered with Russia and the US was due to begin. *This page*: Rescuers remove a baby from the rubble of a destroyed building in the al-Kalasa neighborhood, on 28 April. (*continues*)

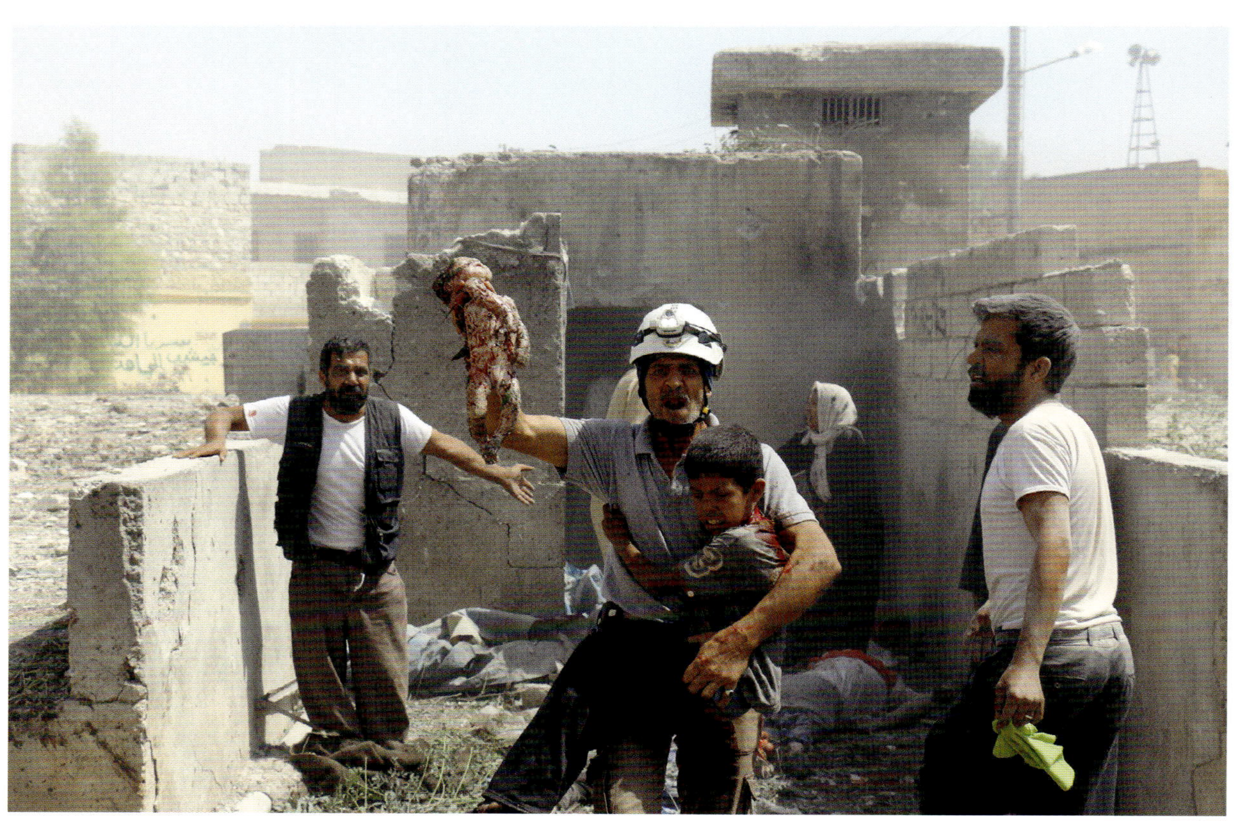

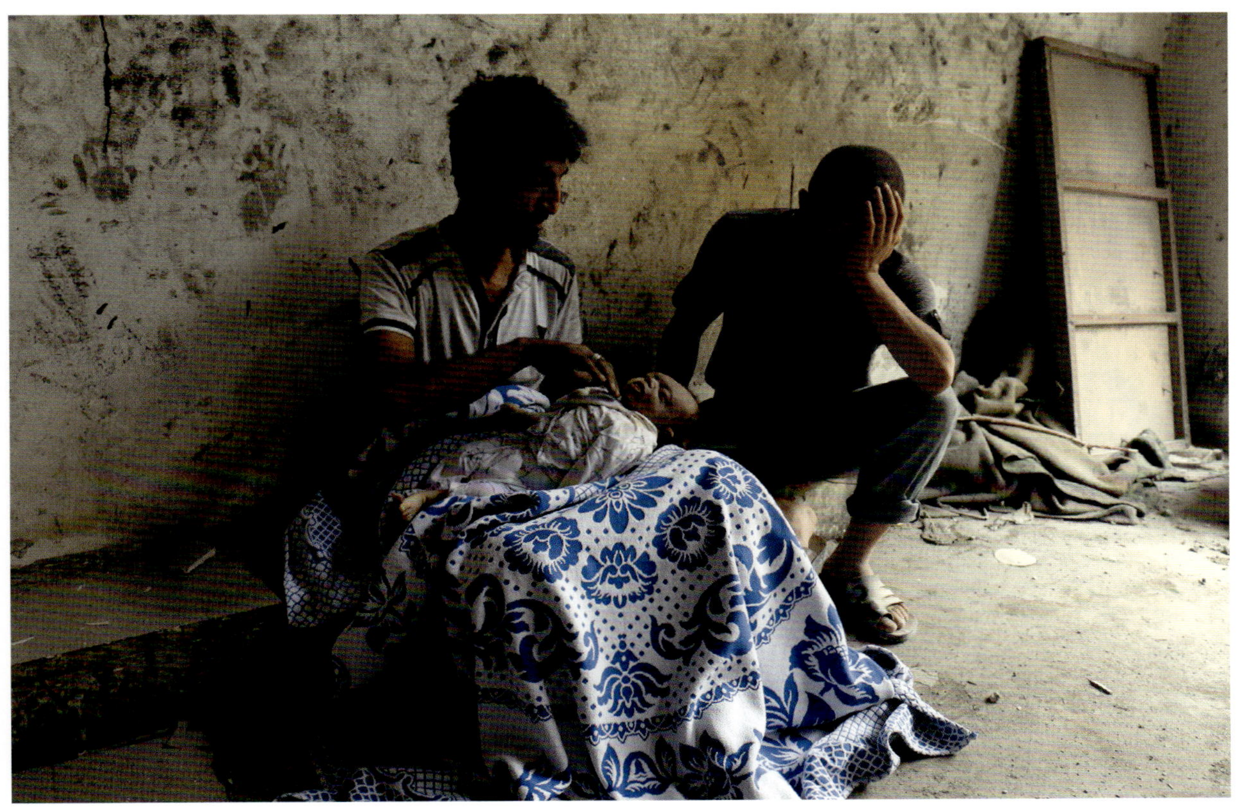

(*continued*) Besieged civilians faced severe food and fuel shortages, and basic infrastructure and healthcare facilities were obliterated. Despite several international attempts at negotiating a ceasefire and allowing civilians passage out of eastern Aleppo, fighting escalated and people remained. Civil defense workers said civilians were mistrustful of government offers of safe passage; the government said rebels were preventing people from leaving. Some were simply reluctant to abandon their homes and property. On 15 December the warring sides reached a ceasefire deal, and on 22 December, following days of evacuations, the Syrian government announced that it had taken control of the city. *Facing page*: A White Helmet civil defense volunteer evacuates a dead baby and a wounded child in the Maadi district of eastern Aleppo, on 27 August. *Above*: Men mourn over the body of a baby, following bombardment of the al-Marja neighborhood, on 23 September.

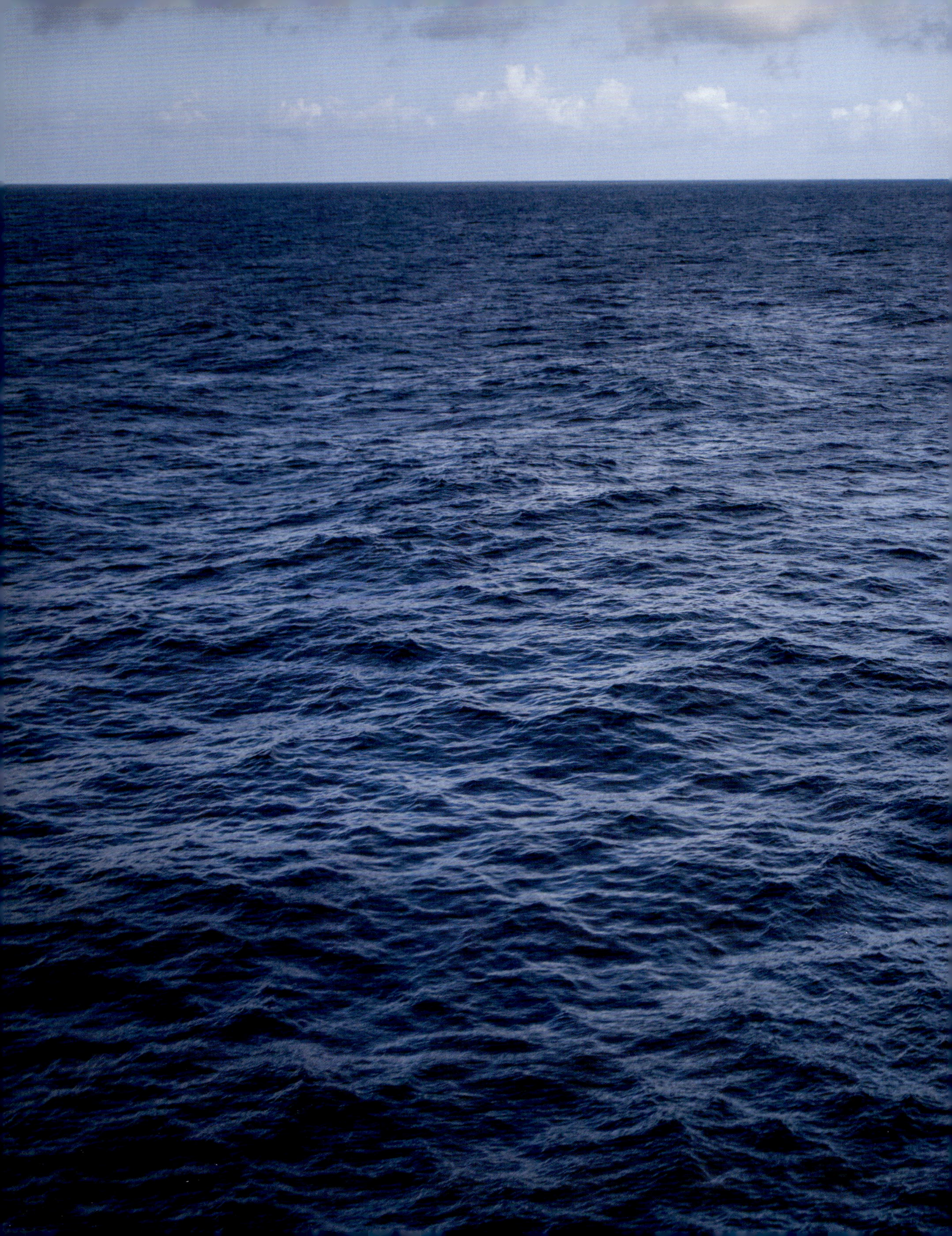

Mathieu Willcocks

UK, MOAS /
3rd Prize Spot News

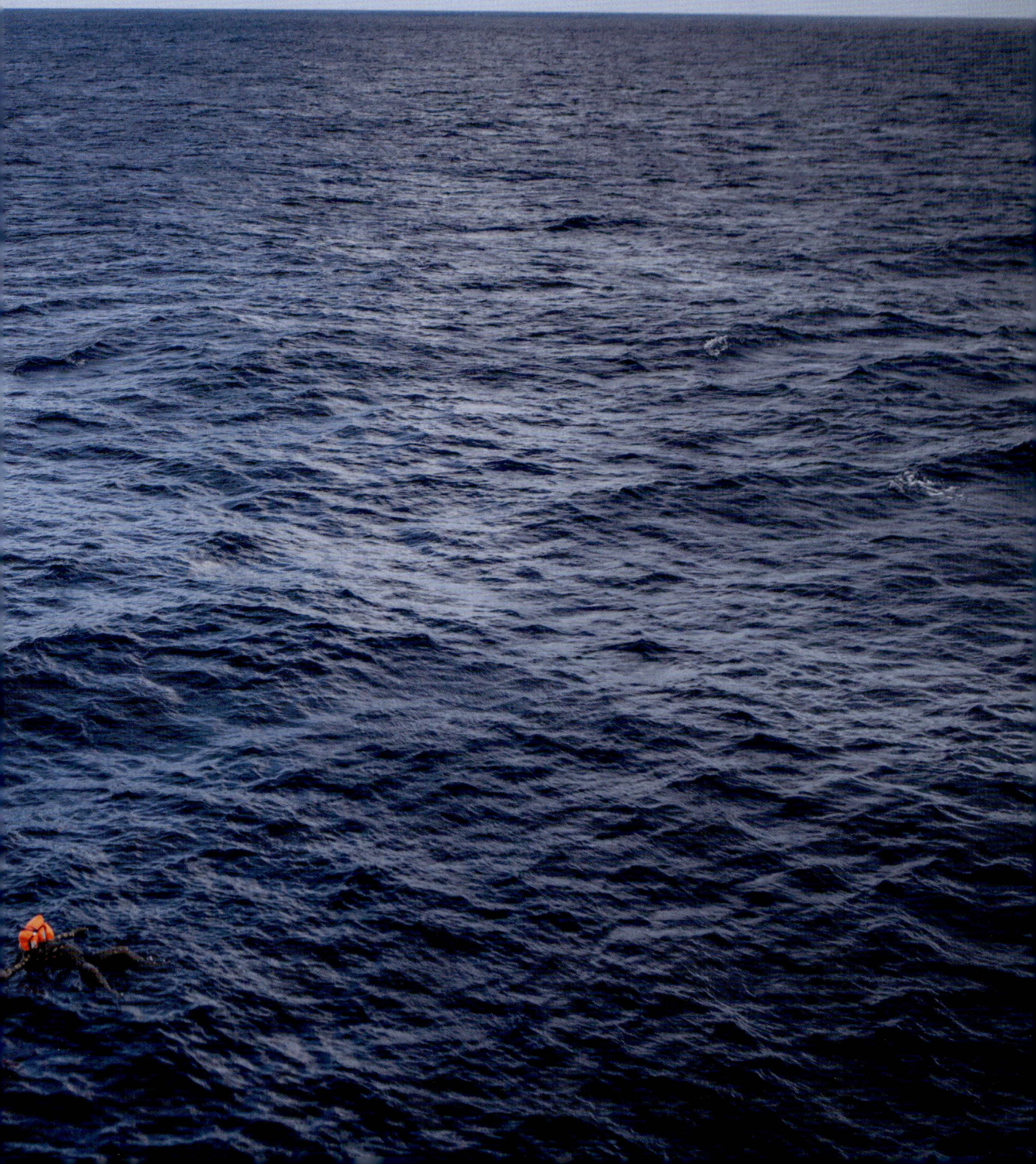

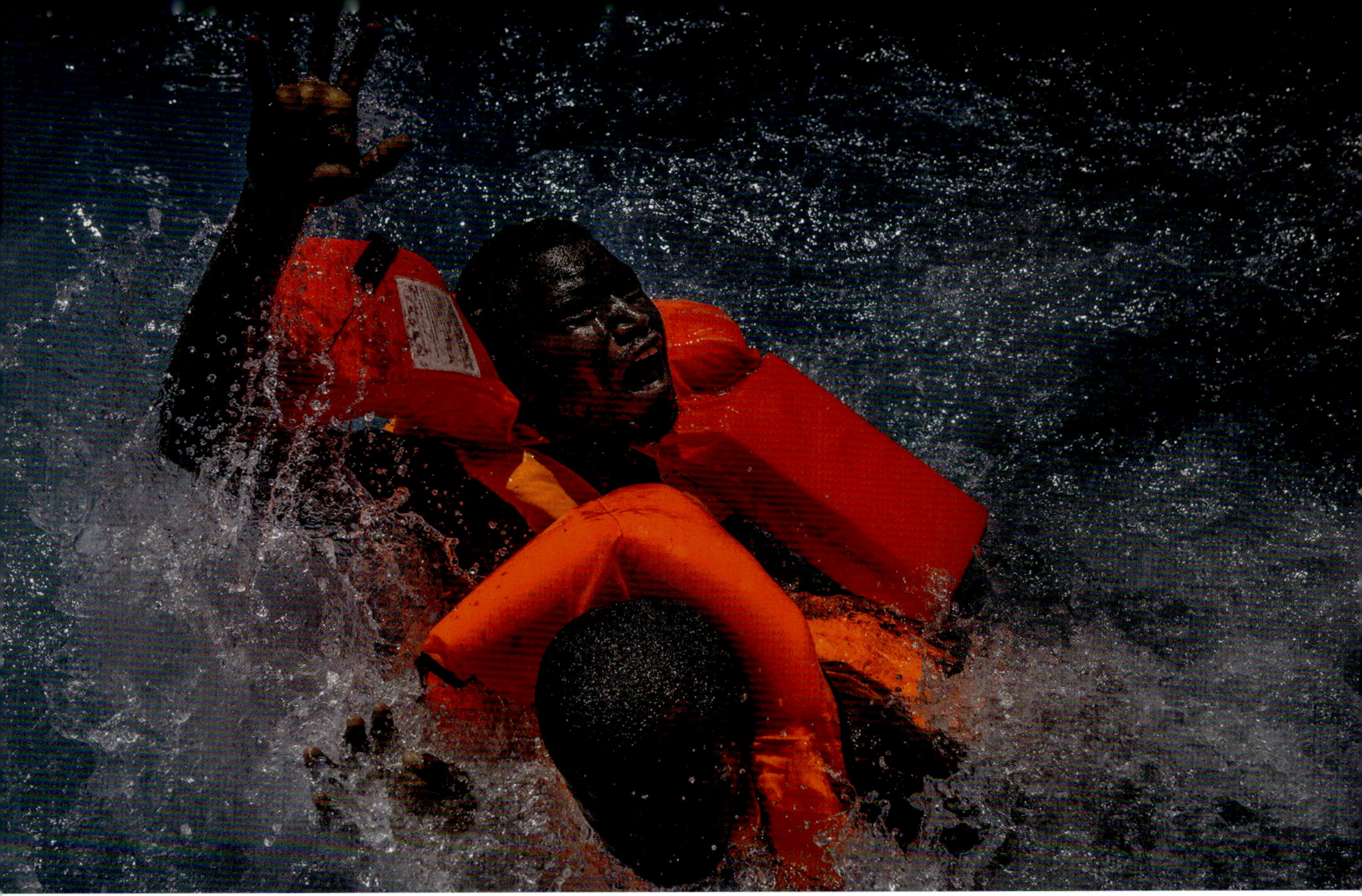

Conflict, persecution, political instability and poverty in parts of Africa and the Middle East continued to compel people to make dangerous sea crossings to seek a better life in Europe. Following a migration deal between the EU and Turkey, the number of refugees crossing the Aegean to Greece dropped, but arrivals in Italy, across the Mediterranean Sea from North Africa, went up sharply. According to the UNHCR, 181,436 people made that crossing in 2016, an 18 percent increase on 2015. Refugees are frequently crammed into unseaworthy craft, often without lifejackets or sufficient food, water or fuel. Many do not survive the three-day journey to Italy. Rescue vessels operated by NGOs and charities patrol international waters off the north Libyan coast to assist people in distress. *Previous spread*: The body of a refugee, still wearing a life jacket, is seen floating in the Mediterranean. *Above*: Two men panic and struggle in the water during a rescue attempt. *Facing page, top*: Refugees cram into the hold of a boat containing more than 500 people. *Below*: Libyan fishermen throw a life jacket to a boat of refugees.

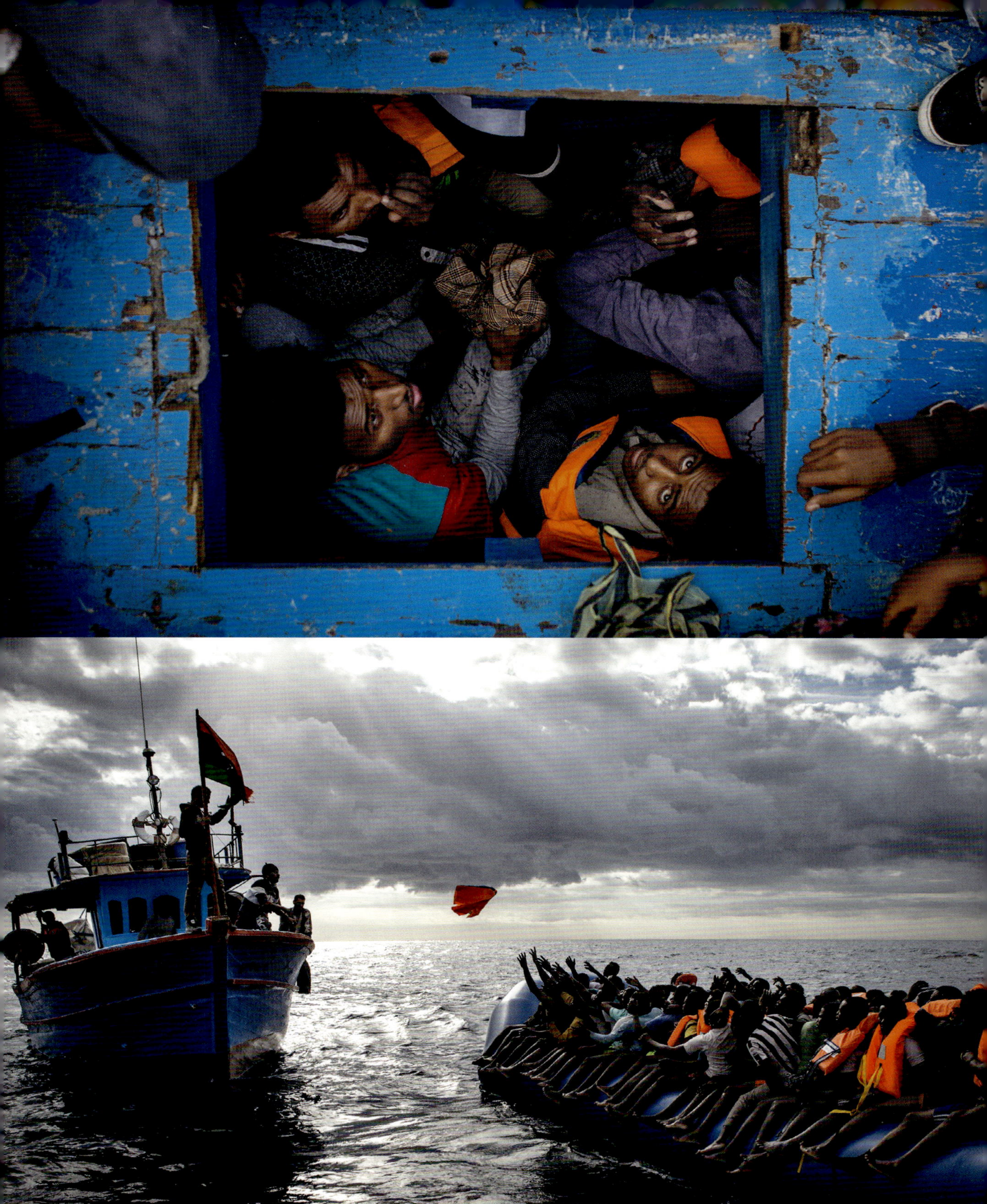

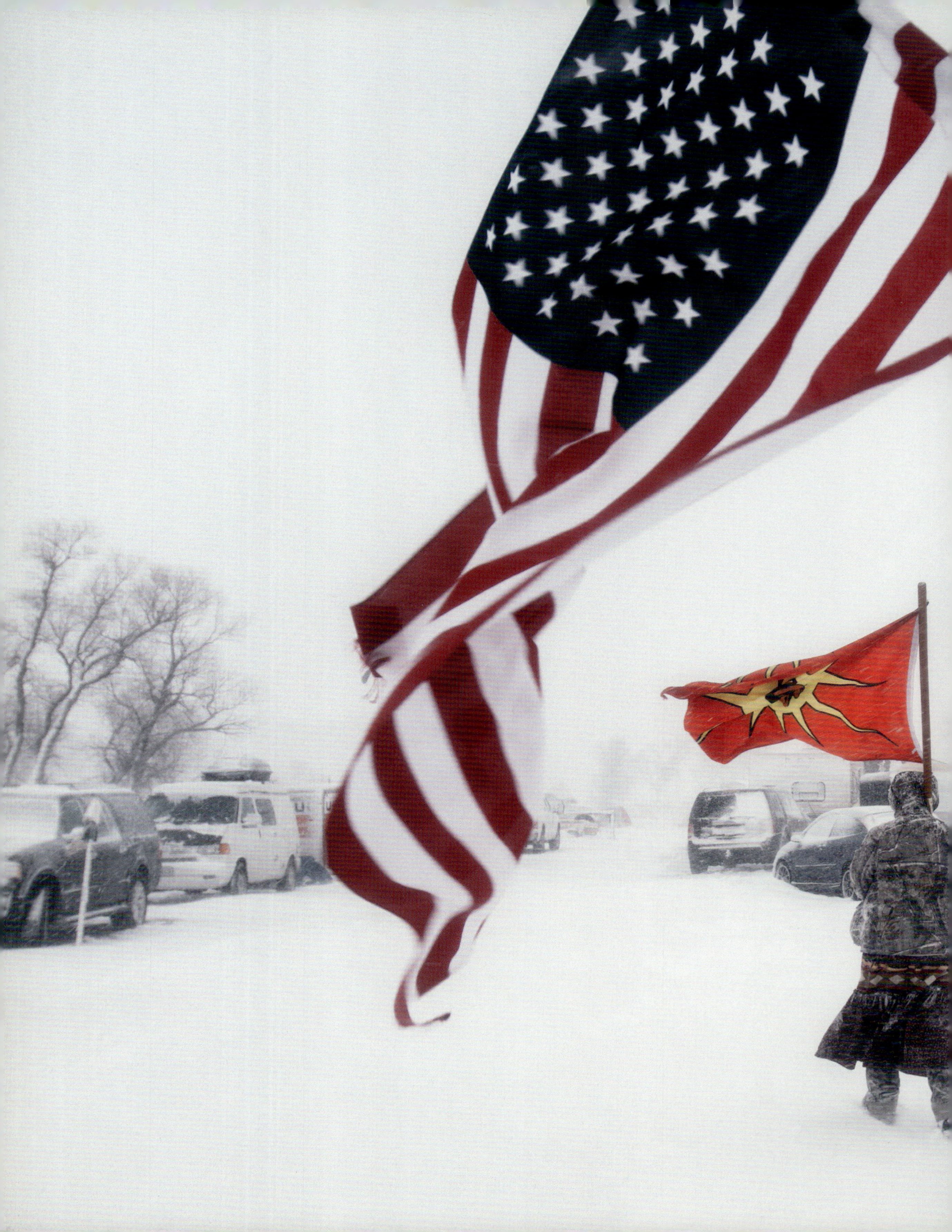

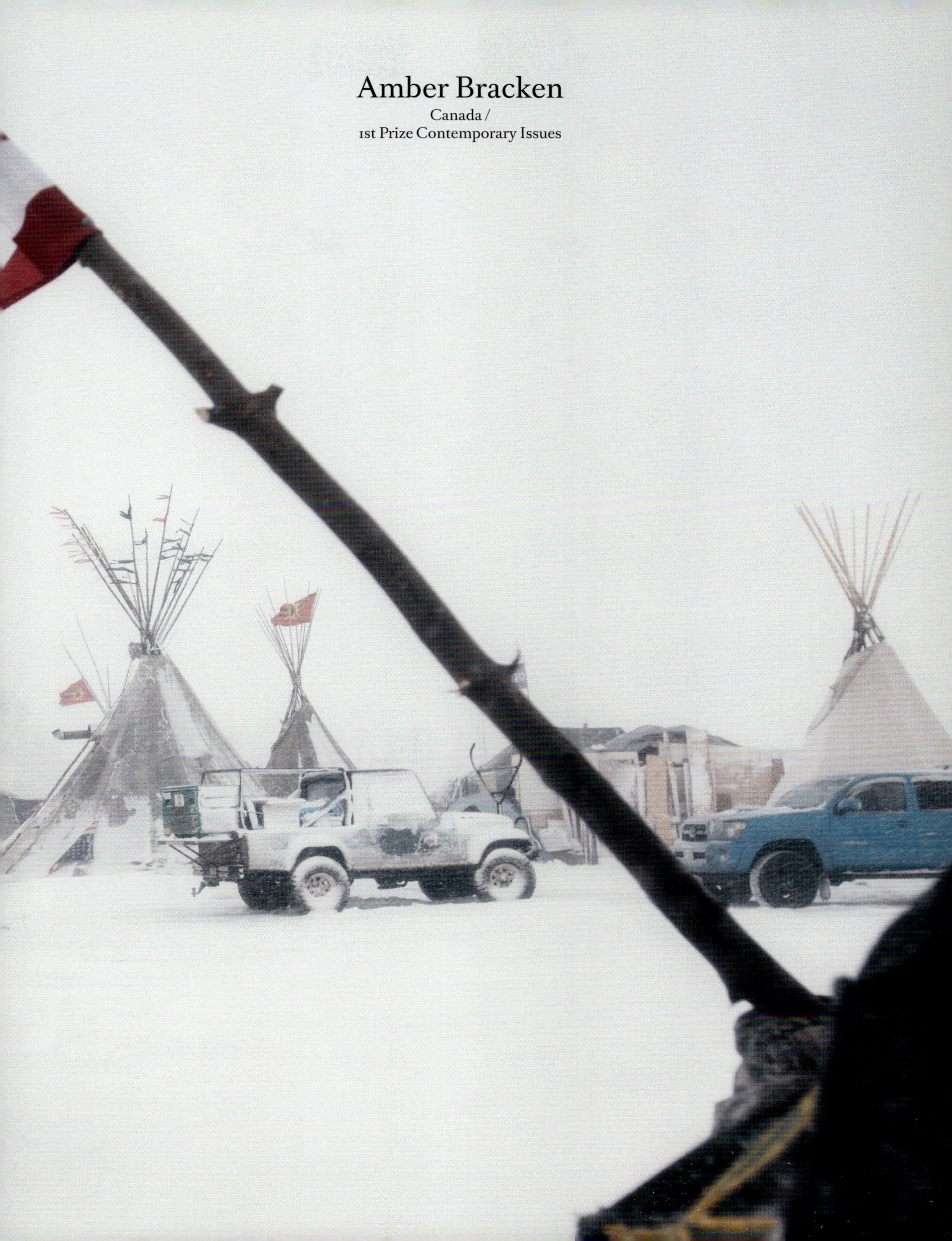

Amber Bracken

Canada /
1st Prize Contemporary Issues

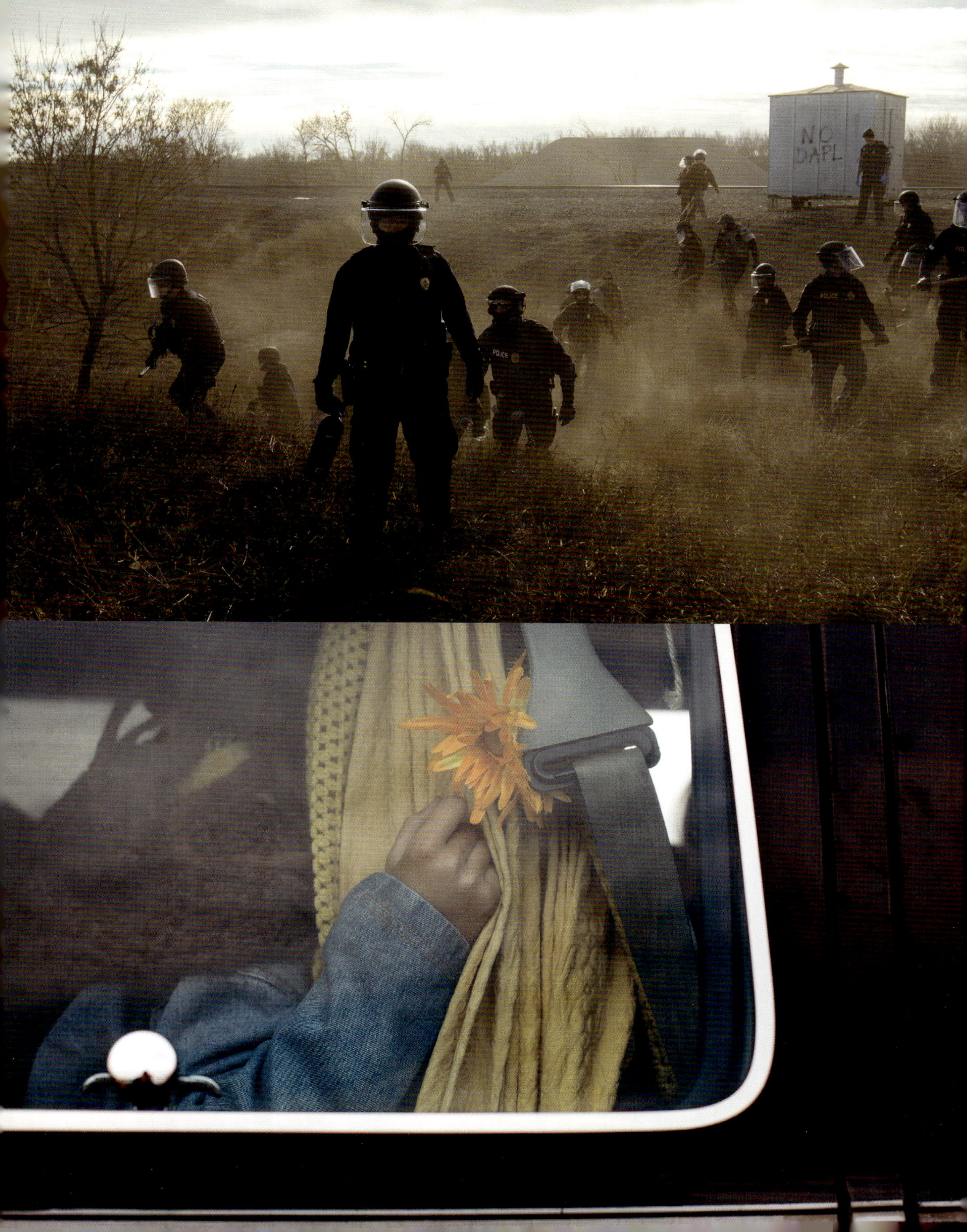
NO DAPL

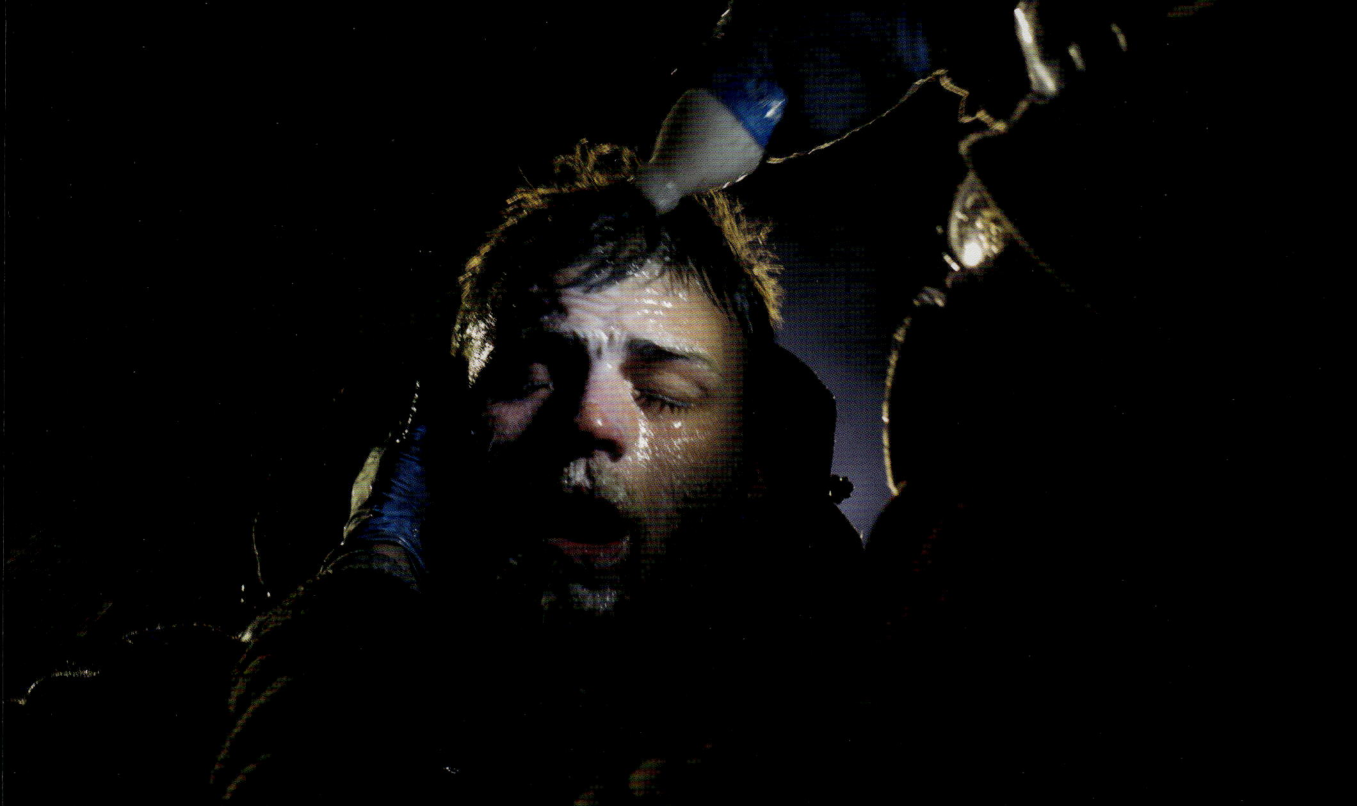

The Dakota Access Pipeline (DAPL) is a 1,886-kilometer-long underground oil pipeline project designed to transport oil from North Dakota to a shipping terminal in Illinois, USA. By 2016, most of the pipeline was complete, but the section closest to the Standing Rock Sioux reservation still awaited federal approval. The Standing Rock Sioux people opposed the DAPL, fearing water contamination and damage to sacred tribal sites. Large protests at Lake Oahe gained national and international attention. *Two spreads back*: People carry an American and a Mohawk Warrior Society flag at a protest camp in Cannon Ball, North Dakota. *Previous spread*: A stretch of the DAPL, already constructed, near Cannon Ball. *Facing page, top*: Riot police clear marchers from outside a DAPL worker camp. *Below*: People prepare to leave camp for a demonstration. *This page*: A protestor is treated after being sprayed with pepper spray. *Next spread*: A man waters his horse, an animal central to Sioux culture.

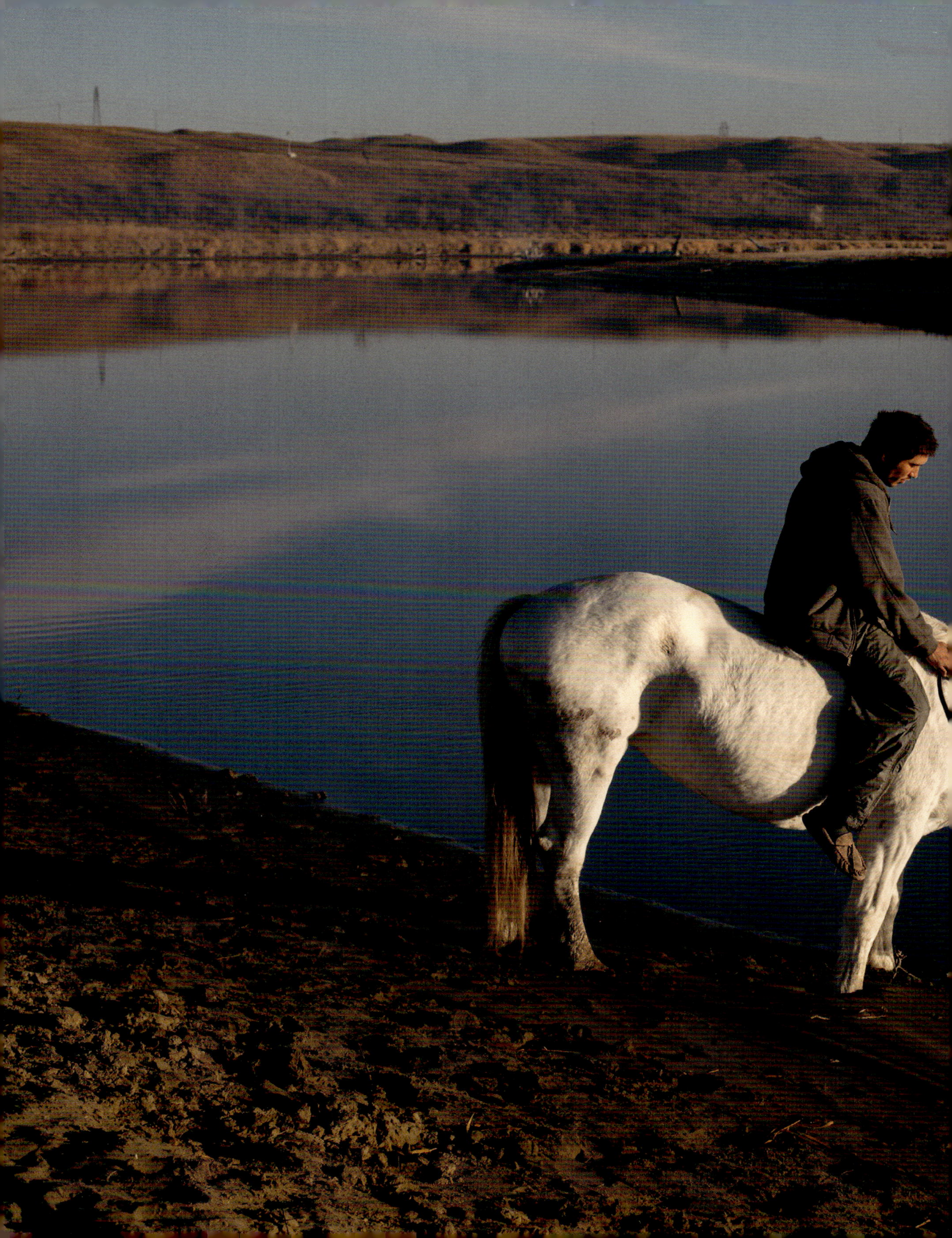

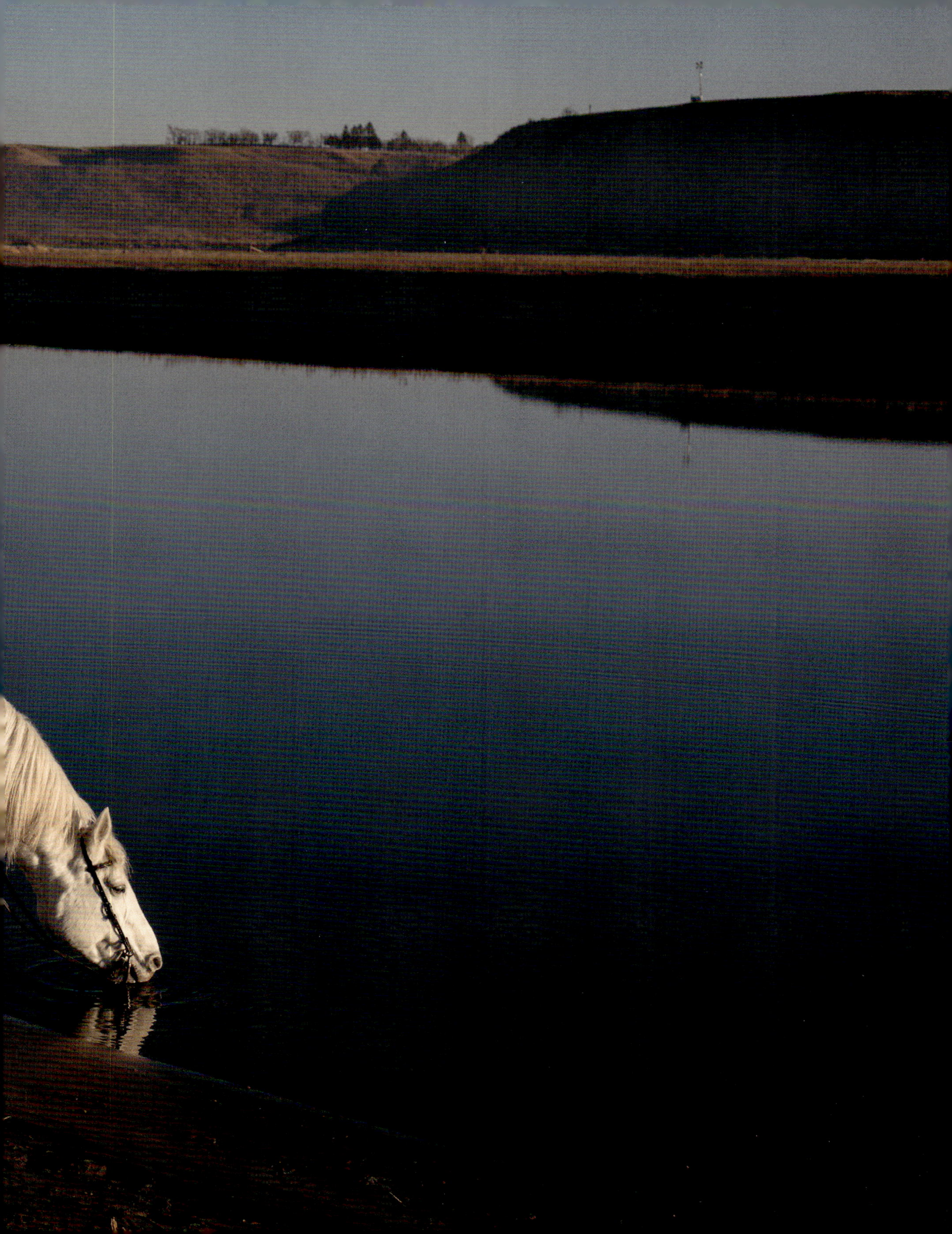

Lalo de Almeida

Brazil, for *Folha de São Paulo* /
2nd Prize Contemporary Issues

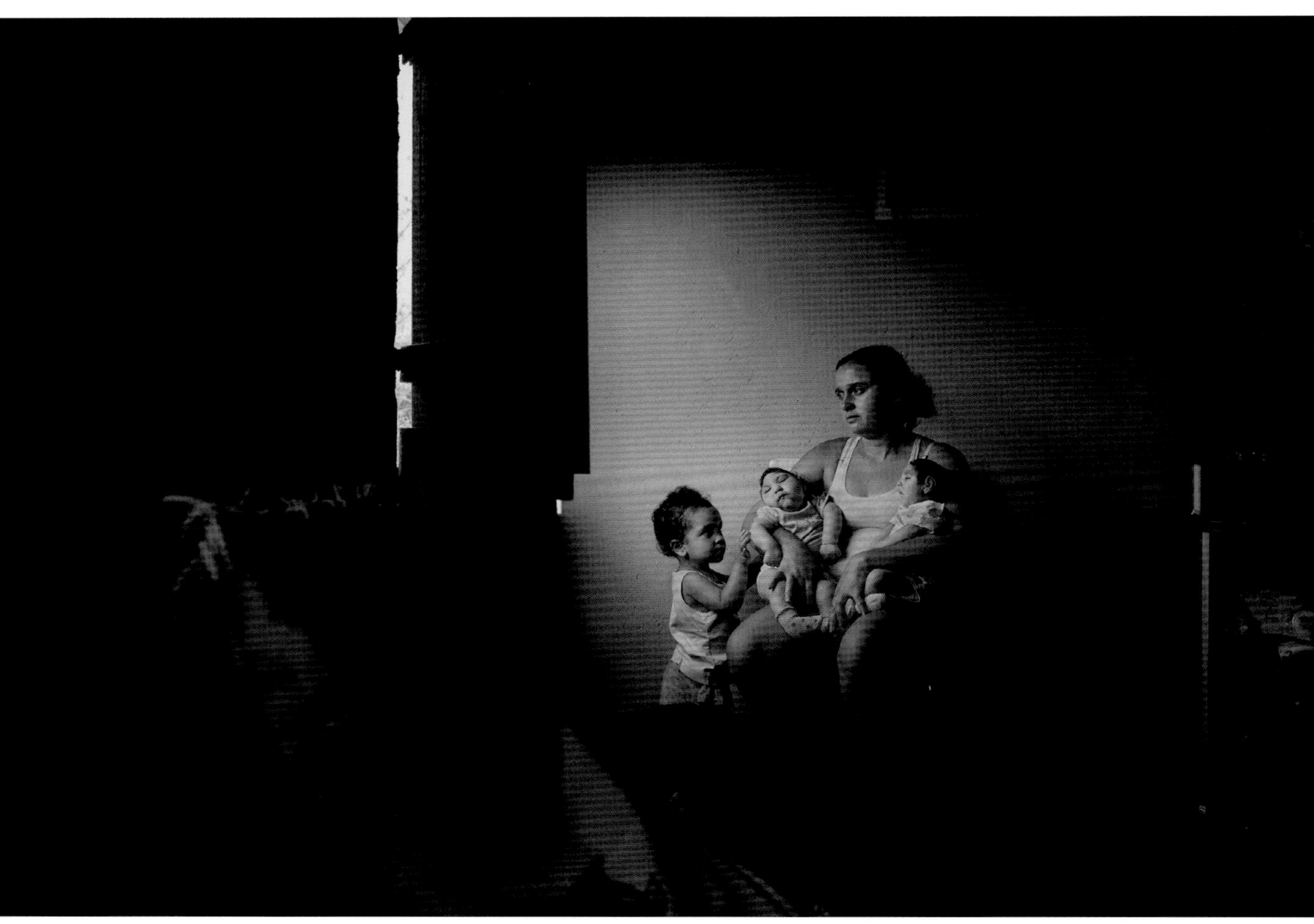

Brazil saw a dramatic increase in numbers of babies born with microcephaly, a condition linked to the Zika virus. Babies with the condition are born with an abnormally small head, or the head stops growing at birth. *Above*: Raquel de Araújo cradles her twins Heloá and Heloisa, both born with microcephaly, as their sister looks on. *Facing page*: Adriana Cordeiro Soares bathes her son João Miguel, who has the condition. (*continues*)

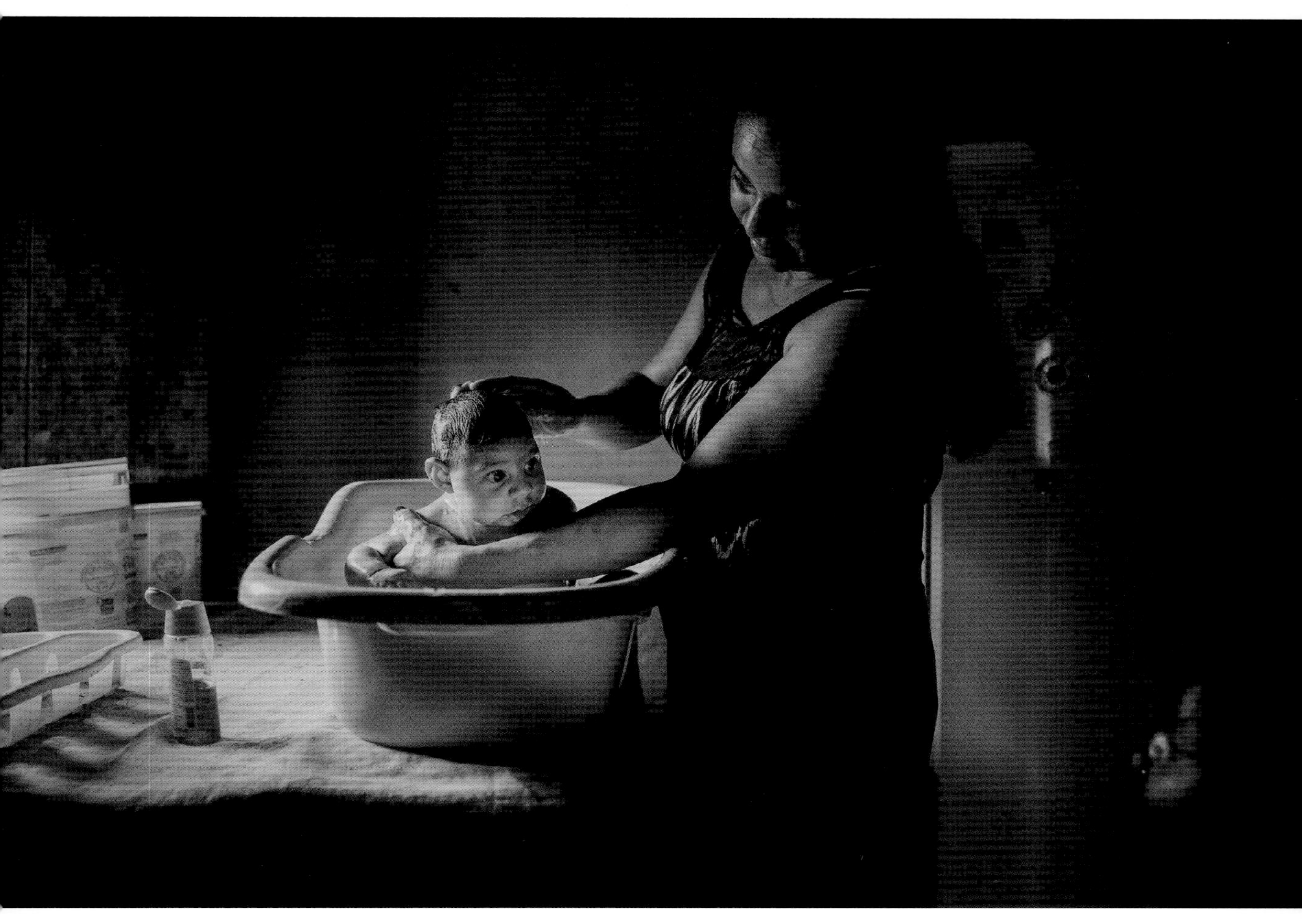

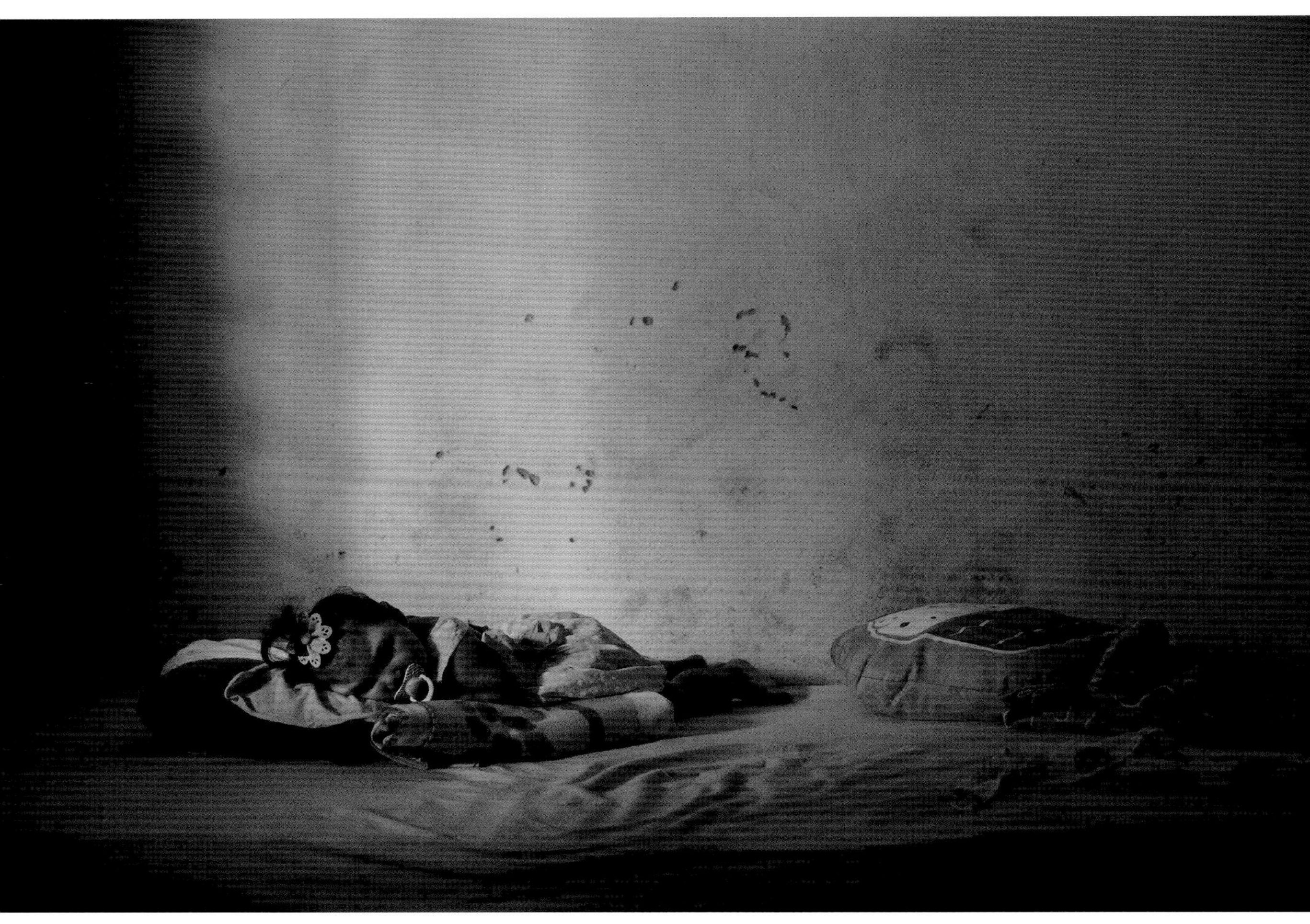

(*continued*) The Zika virus, transmitted by mosquitoes, generally causes mild, flu-like symptoms, and the exact causal link to microcephaly—an otherwise rare condition—is not fully understood. The World Health Organization recorded 2,289 Zika-linked microcephaly cases in Brazil from the beginning of the outbreak in 2015 to the end of 2016, and declared the Zika virus an international public health emergency. *Above*: Pérola da Rocha asleep in Recife, eastern Brazil. *Facing page*: Heloá's grandmother gives her a bottle of milk.

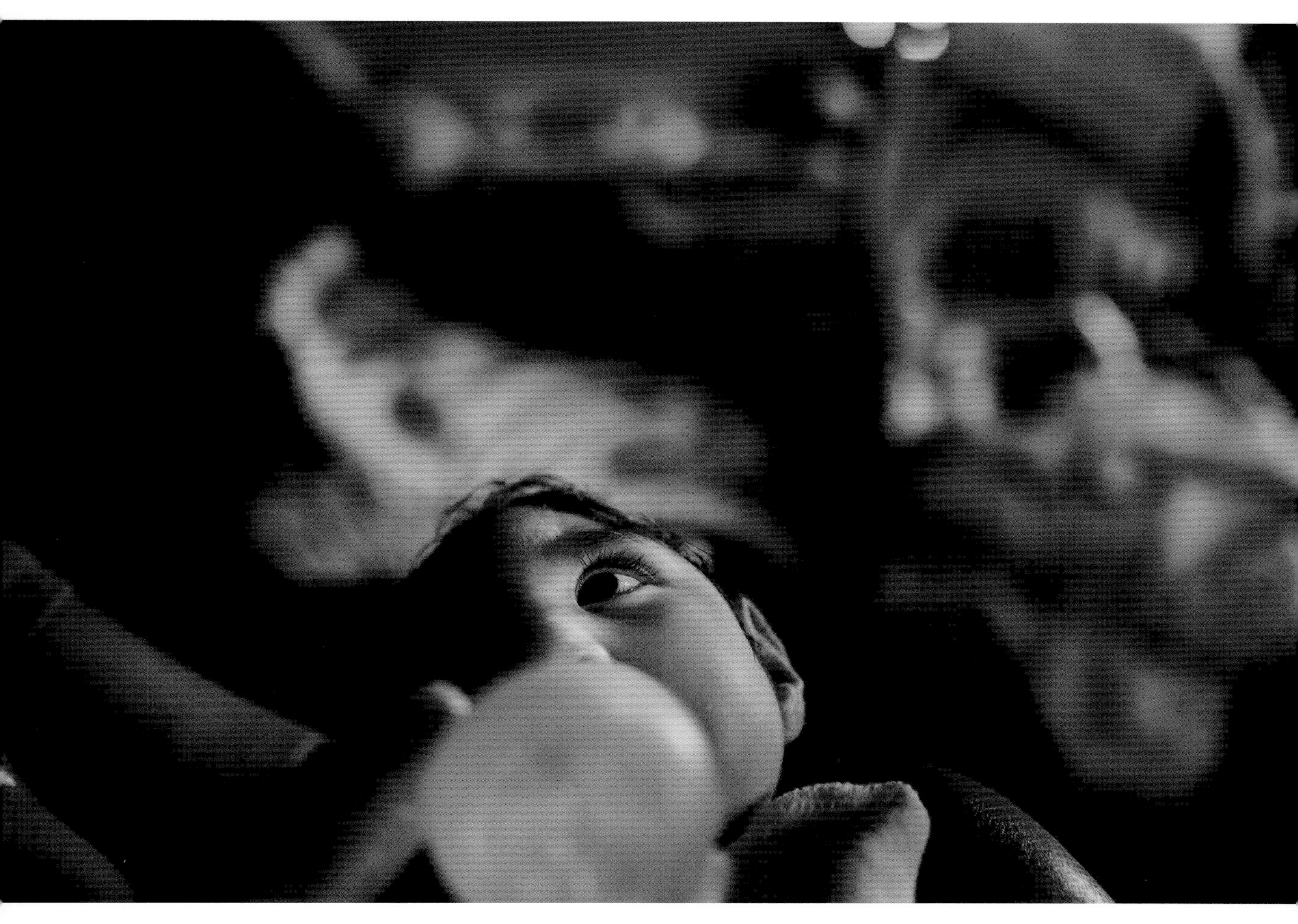

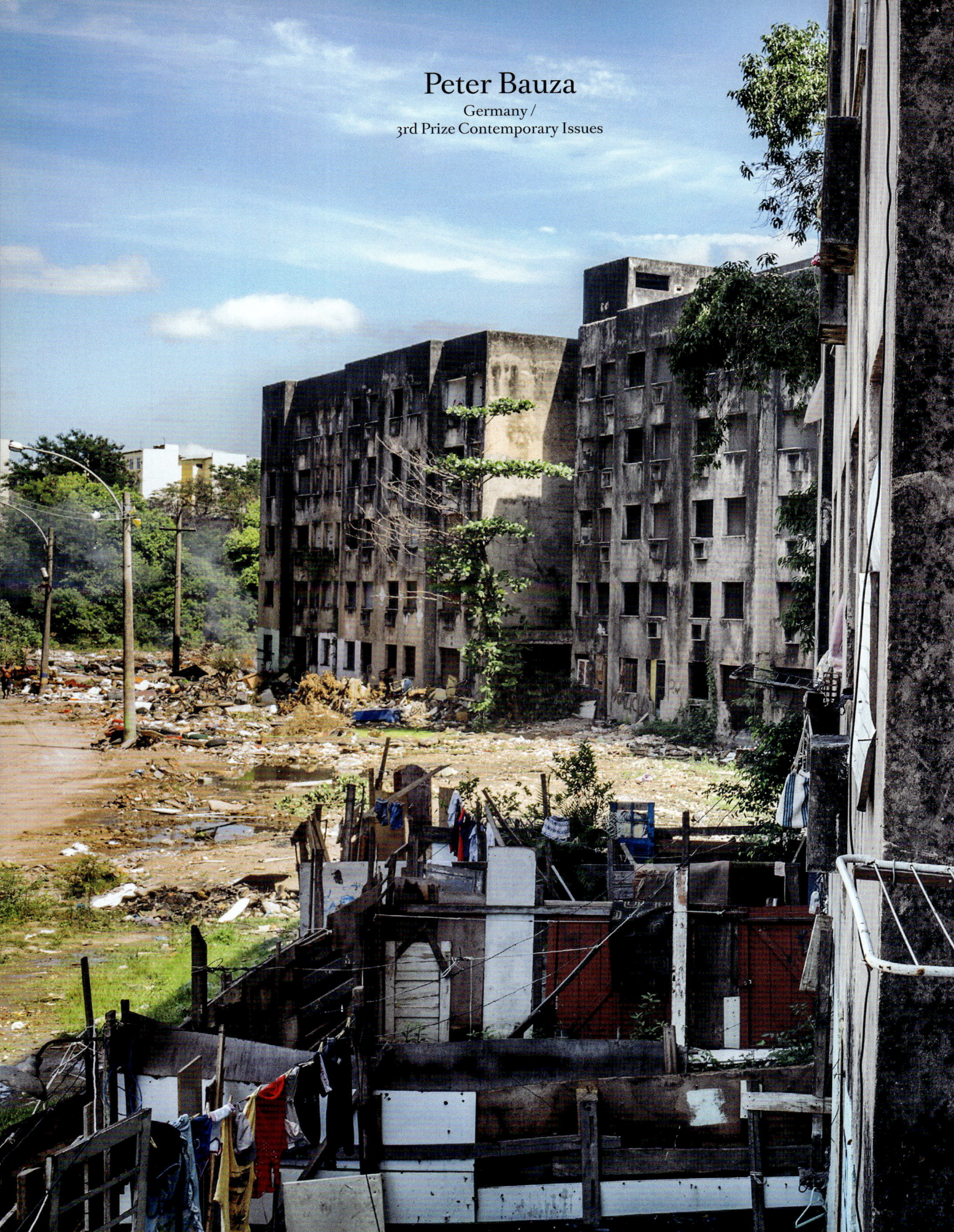

Peter Bauza

Germany /
3rd Prize Contemporary Issues

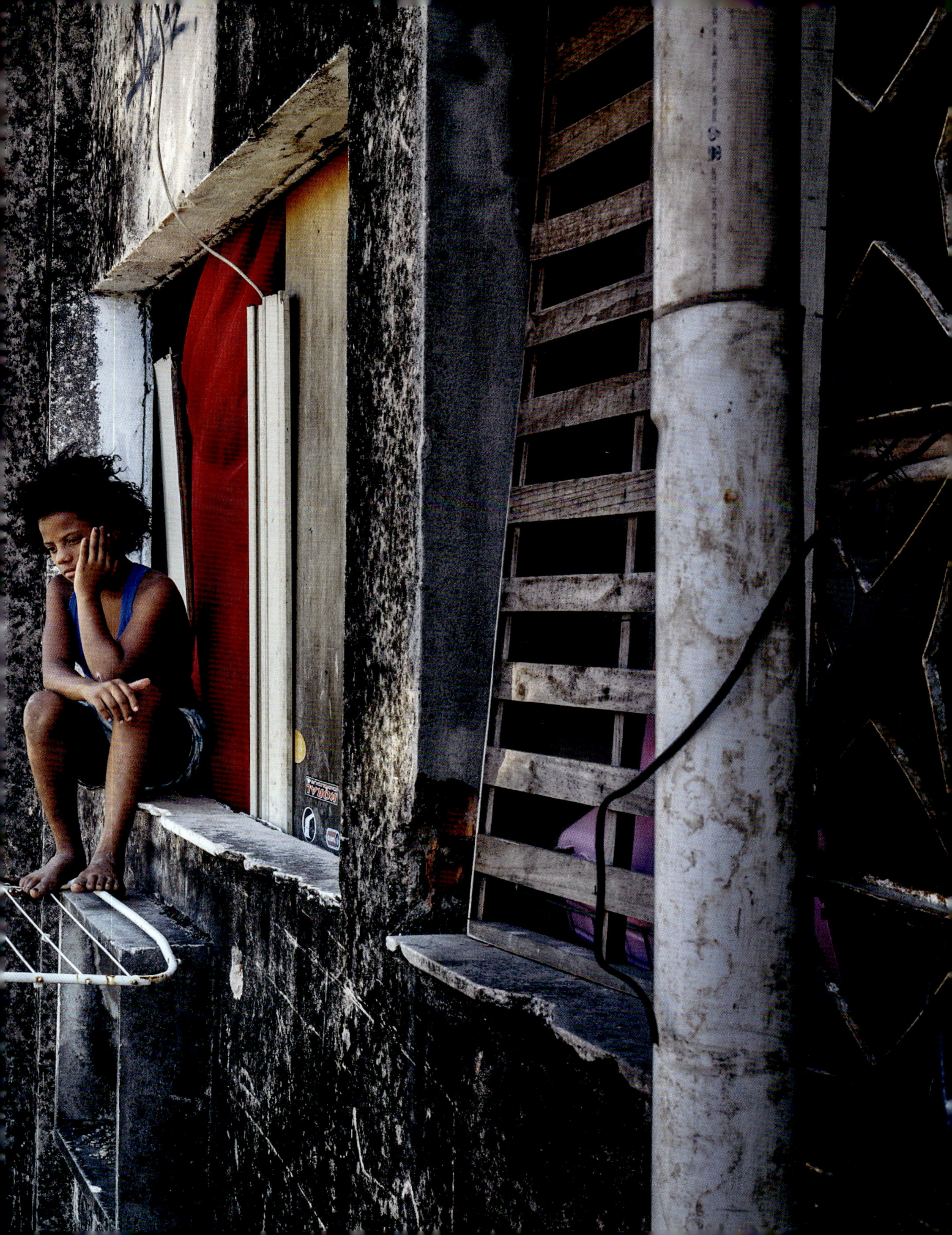
KORAL

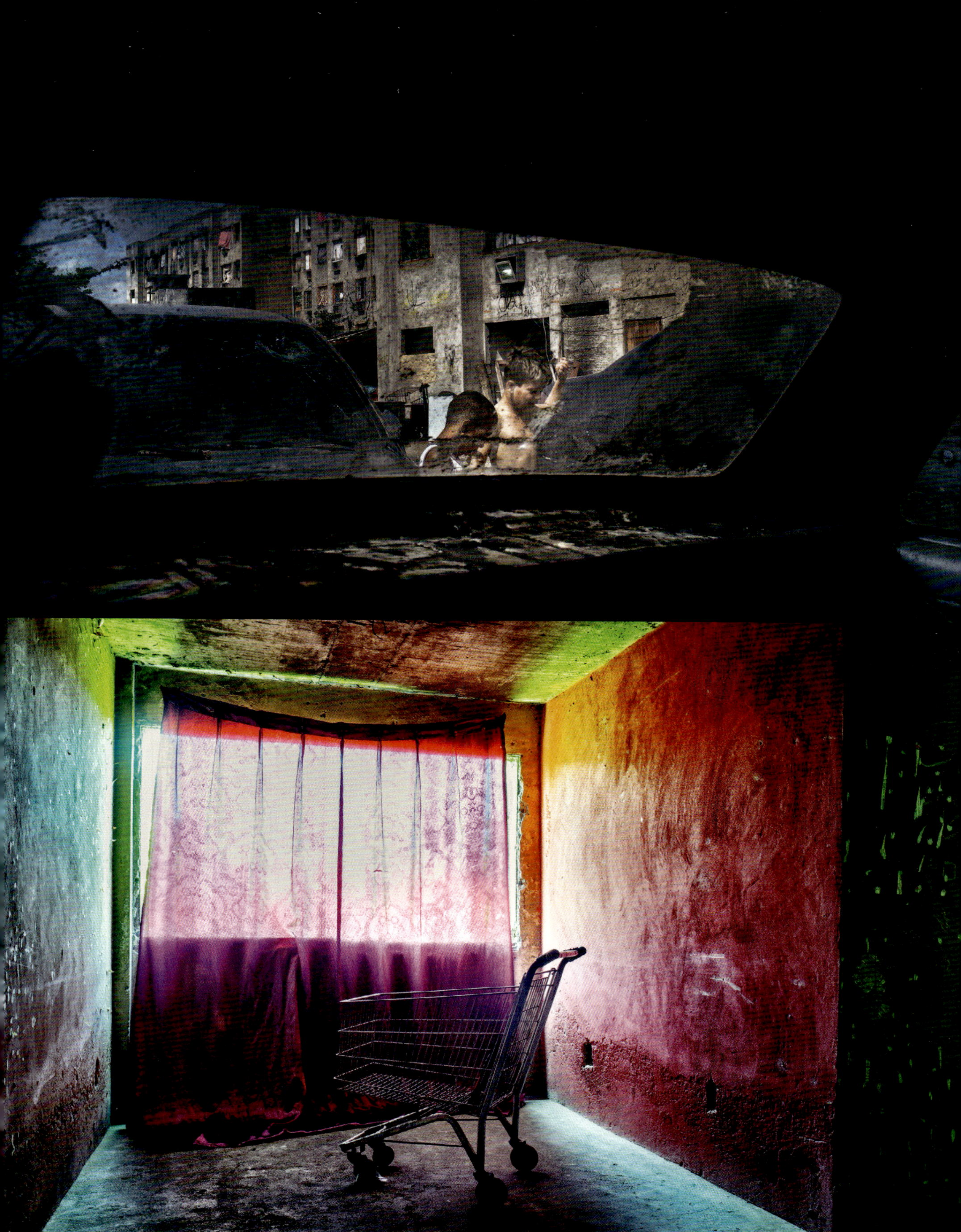

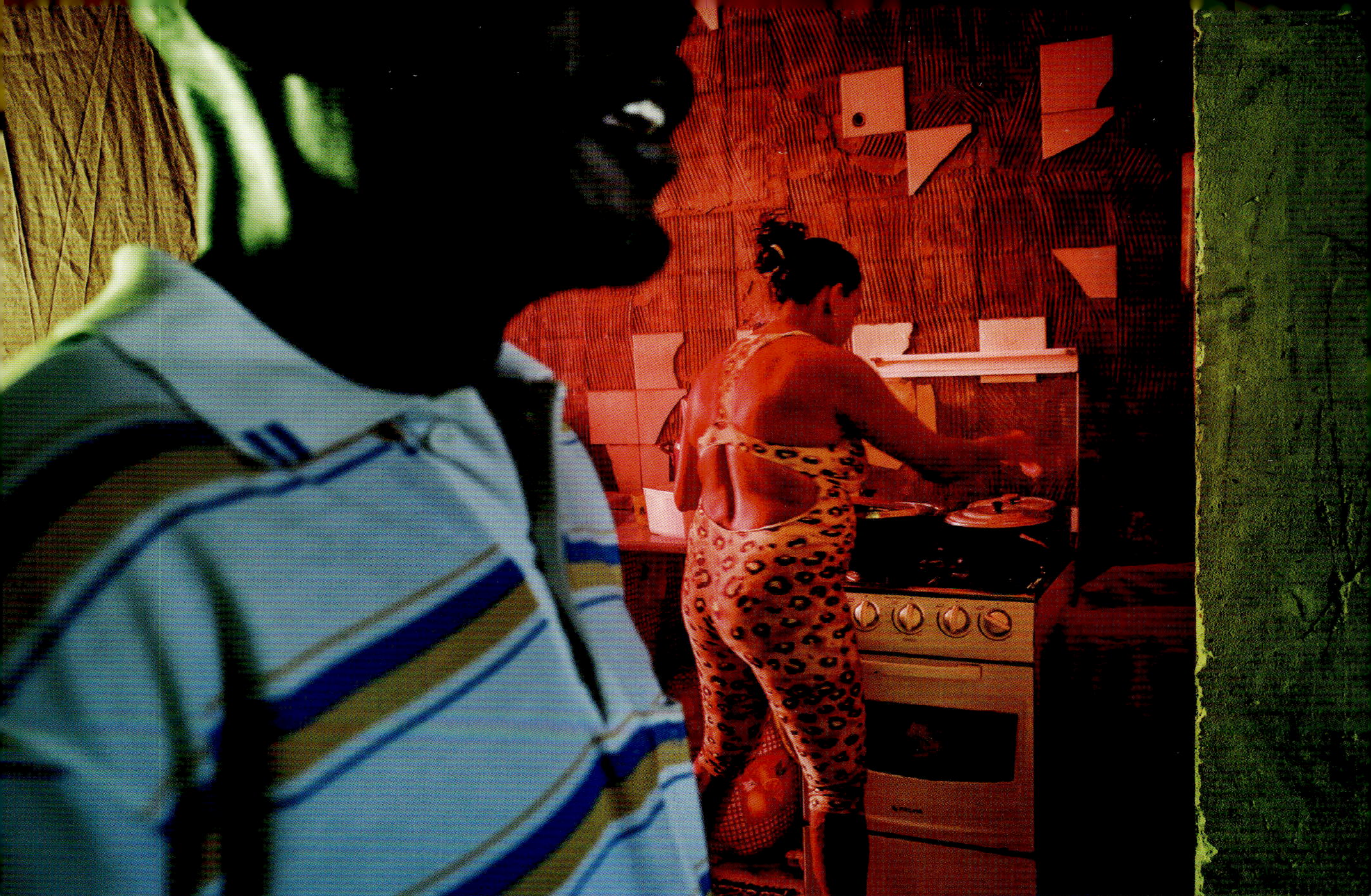

Millions of people in Brazil live without secure housing. Government-backed social housing schemes, aimed at reducing an estimated shortage of 5.24 million homes in Brazil, have had limited impact. Some 300 families live in a neighborhood they call 'Jambalaya', in the western zone of Rio de Janeiro, squatting in derelict apartment blocks: the remnants of a failed middle-class housing development of 30 years ago. The quarter, like many favelas and slums across the country, lacks basic infrastructure and living conditions are poor. *Previous spread*: Eduarda lives with seven siblings in one of the abandoned apartment blocks in Jambalaya. *Facing page, top*: Children play among abandoned cars. *Below*: People try to make the buildings livable. *This page*: Domingo (foreground) came to Brazil from Angola in search of a better life, and lives with Lourdes (cooking) and her five children. *Next spread*: A boy flies a kite from the roof of one of the apartment blocks in Jambalaya.

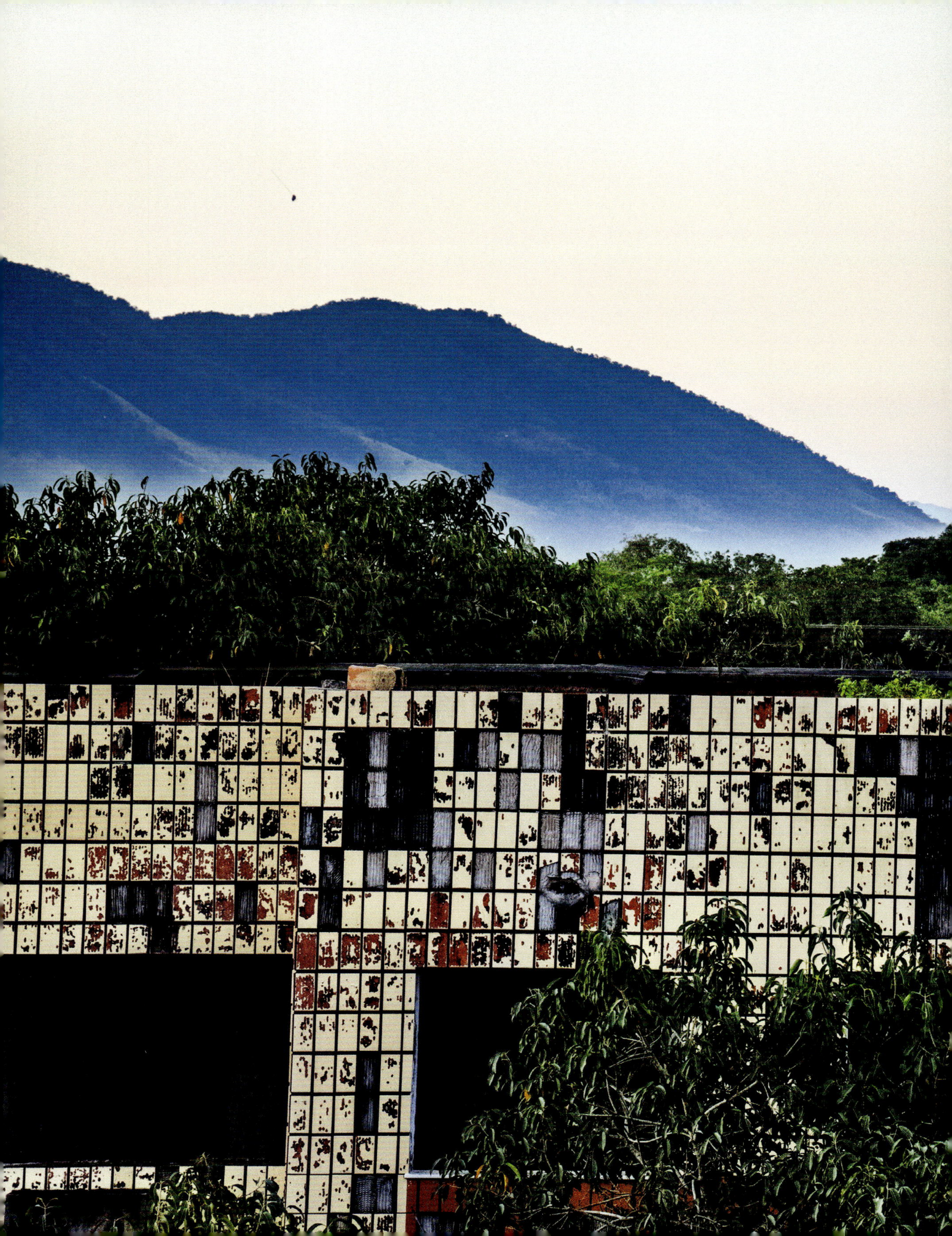

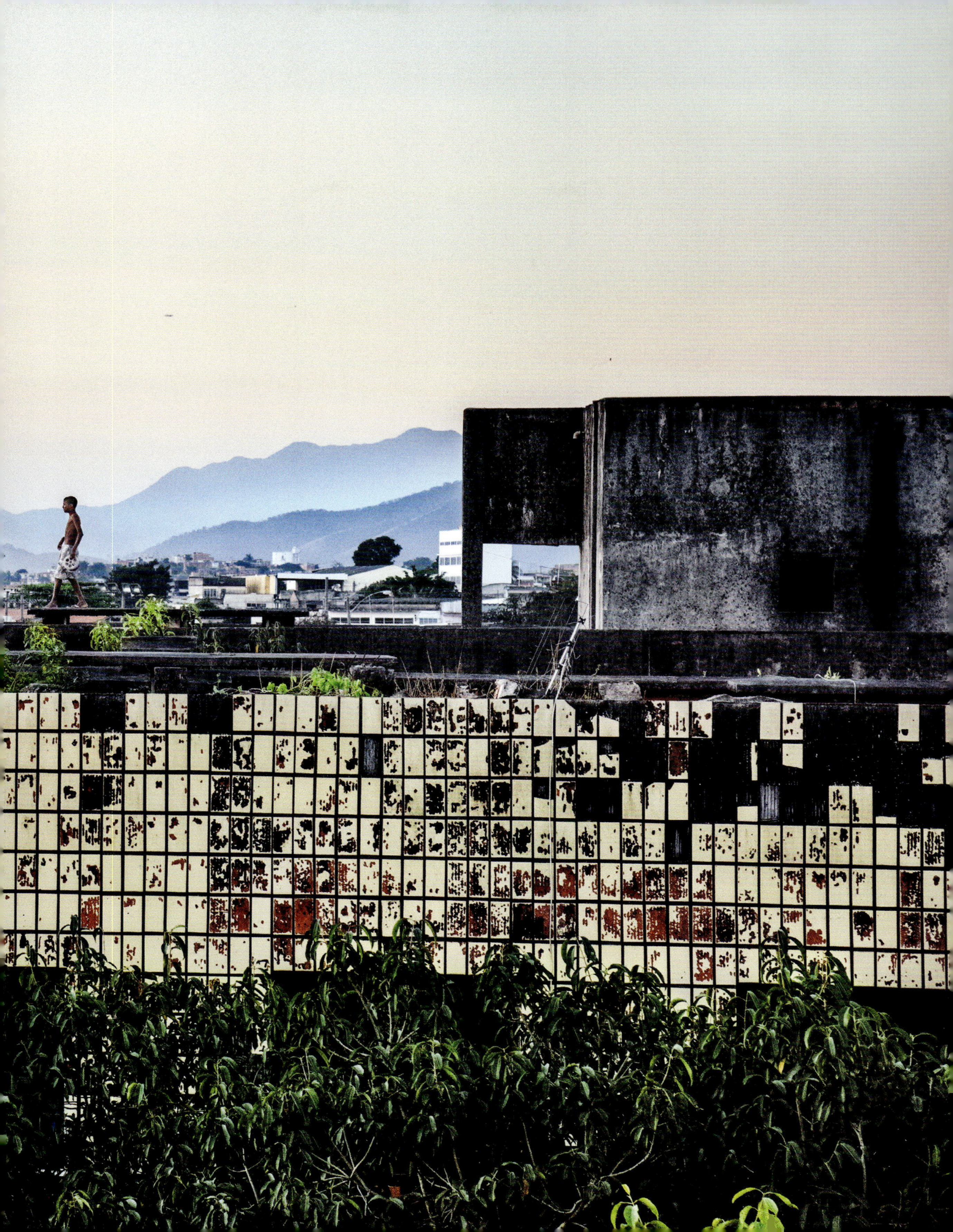

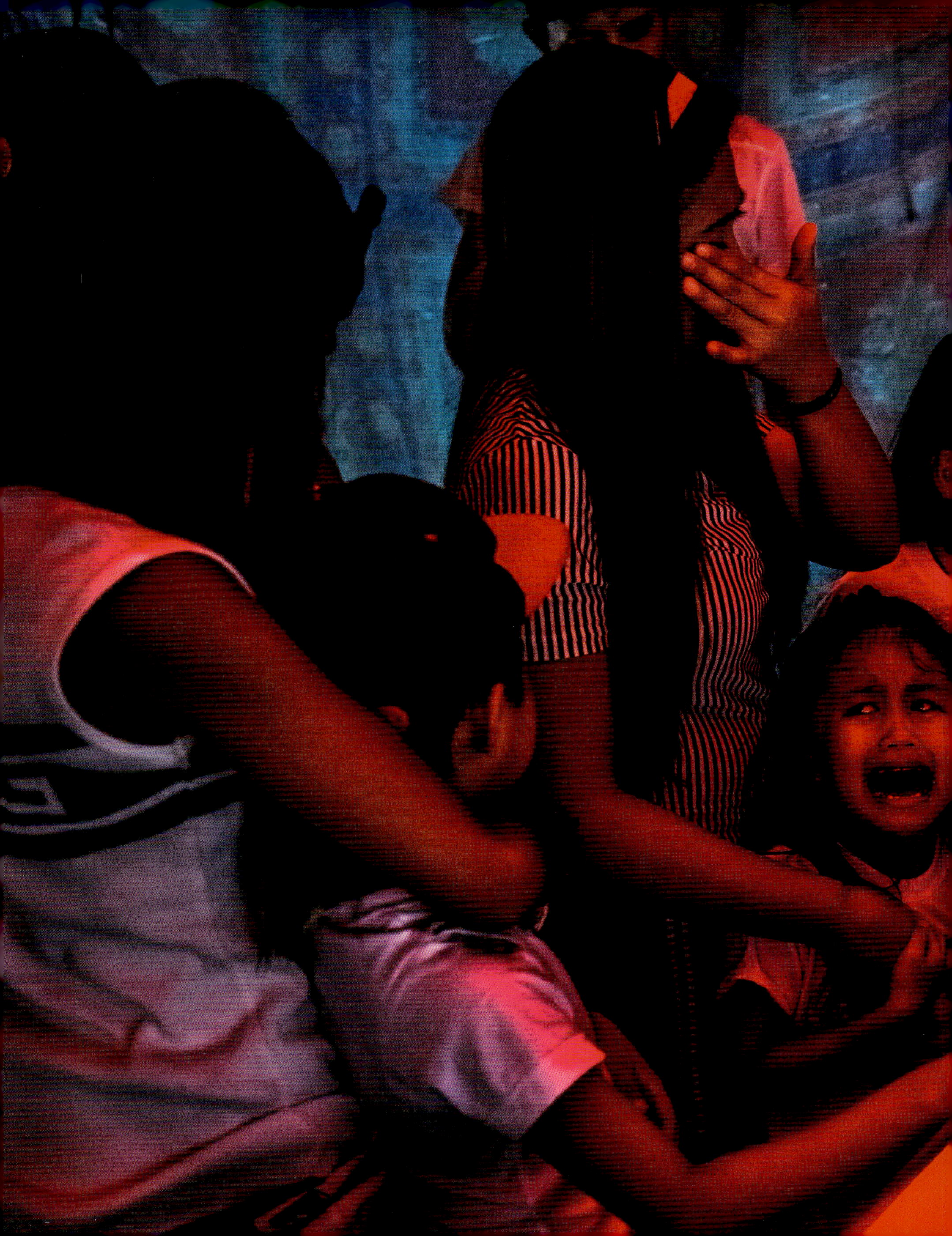

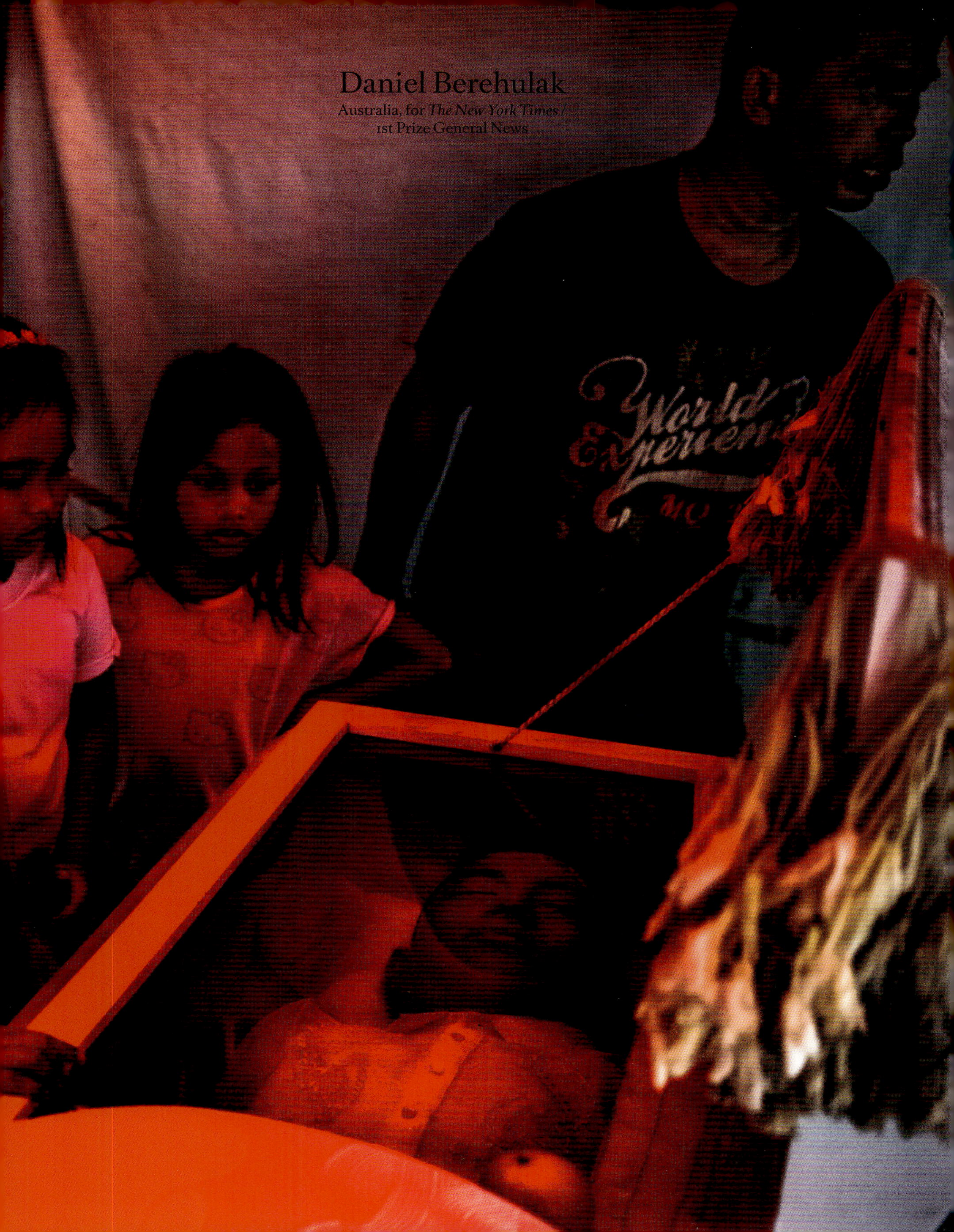

Daniel Berehulak

Australia, for *The New York Times* /
1st Prize General News

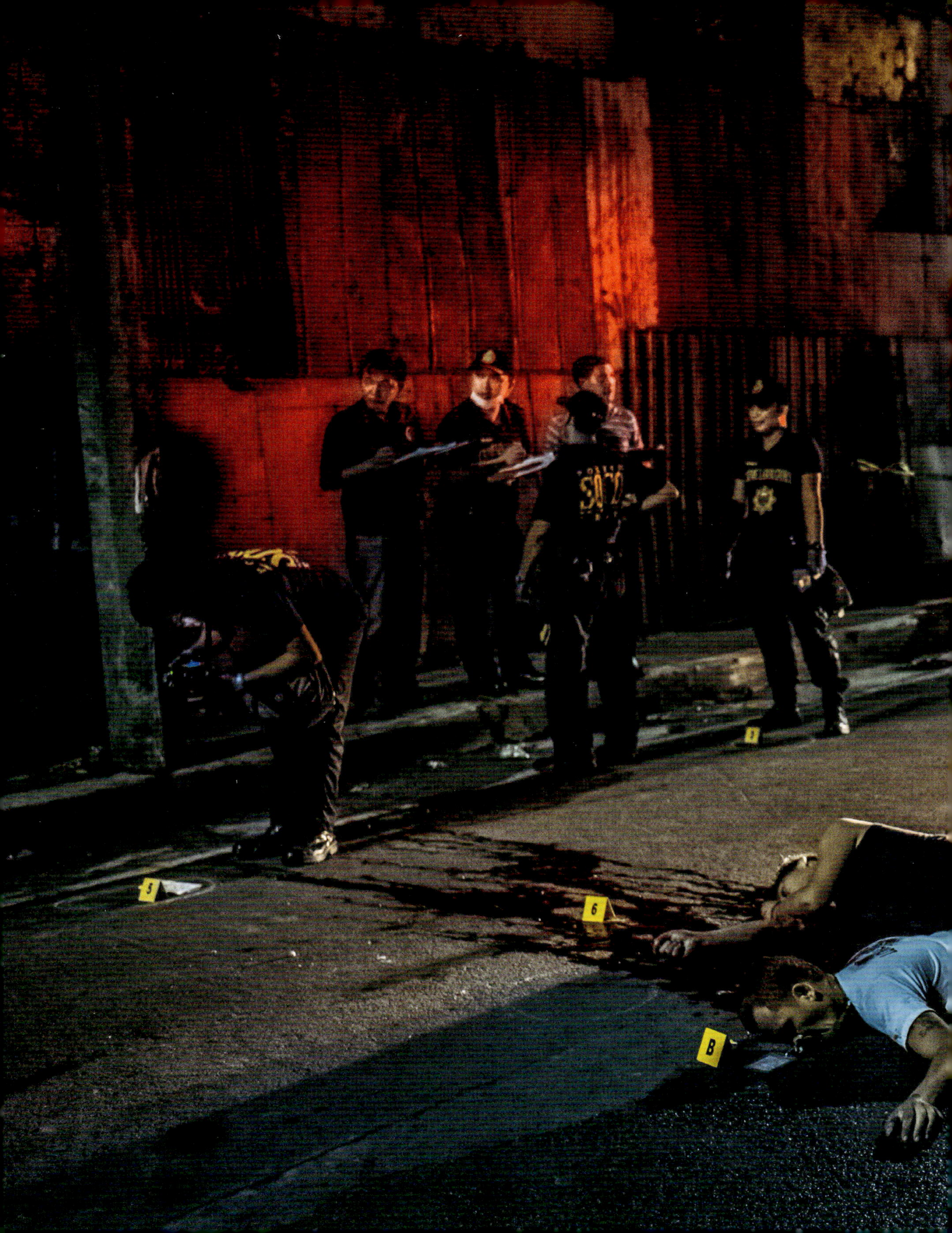

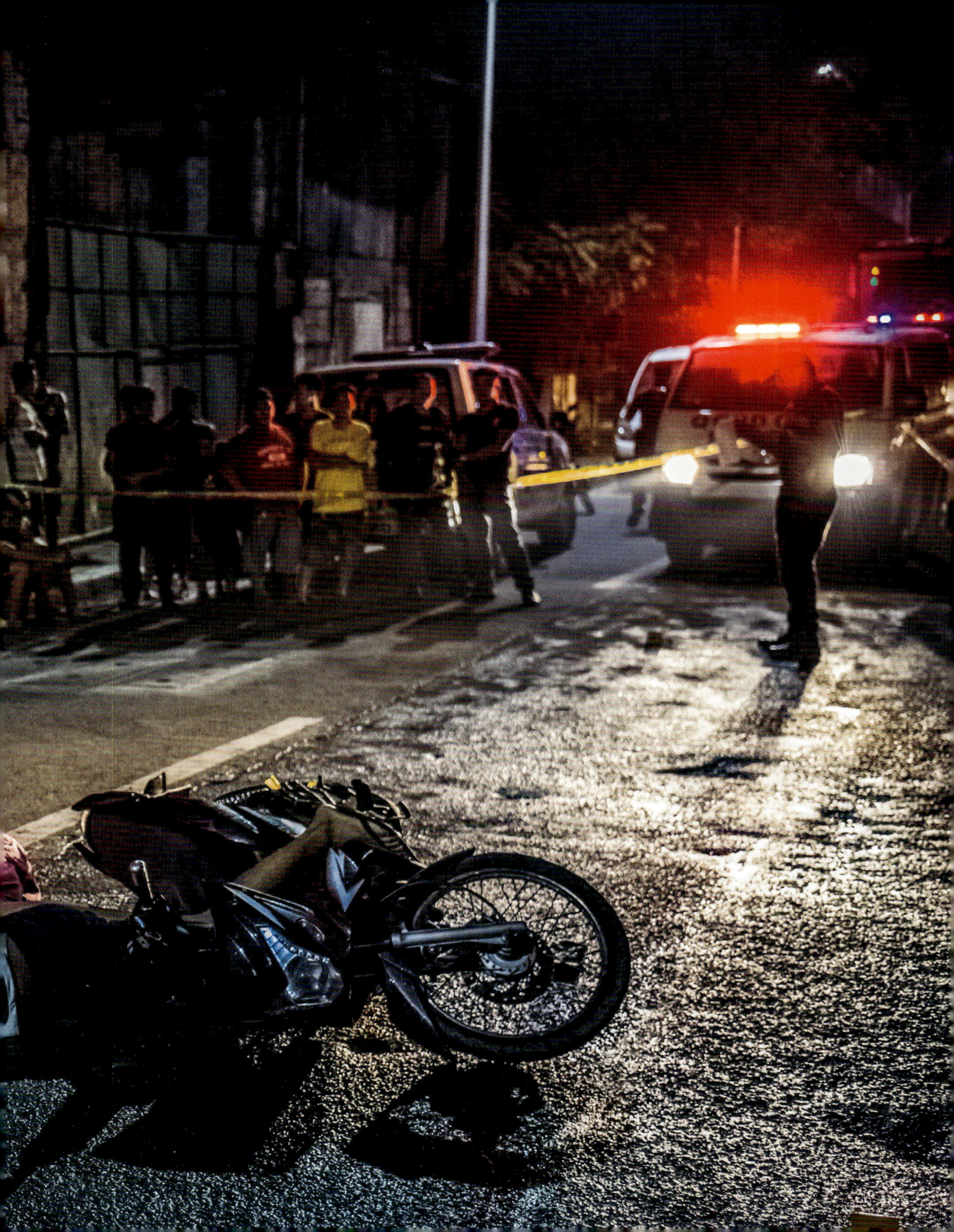

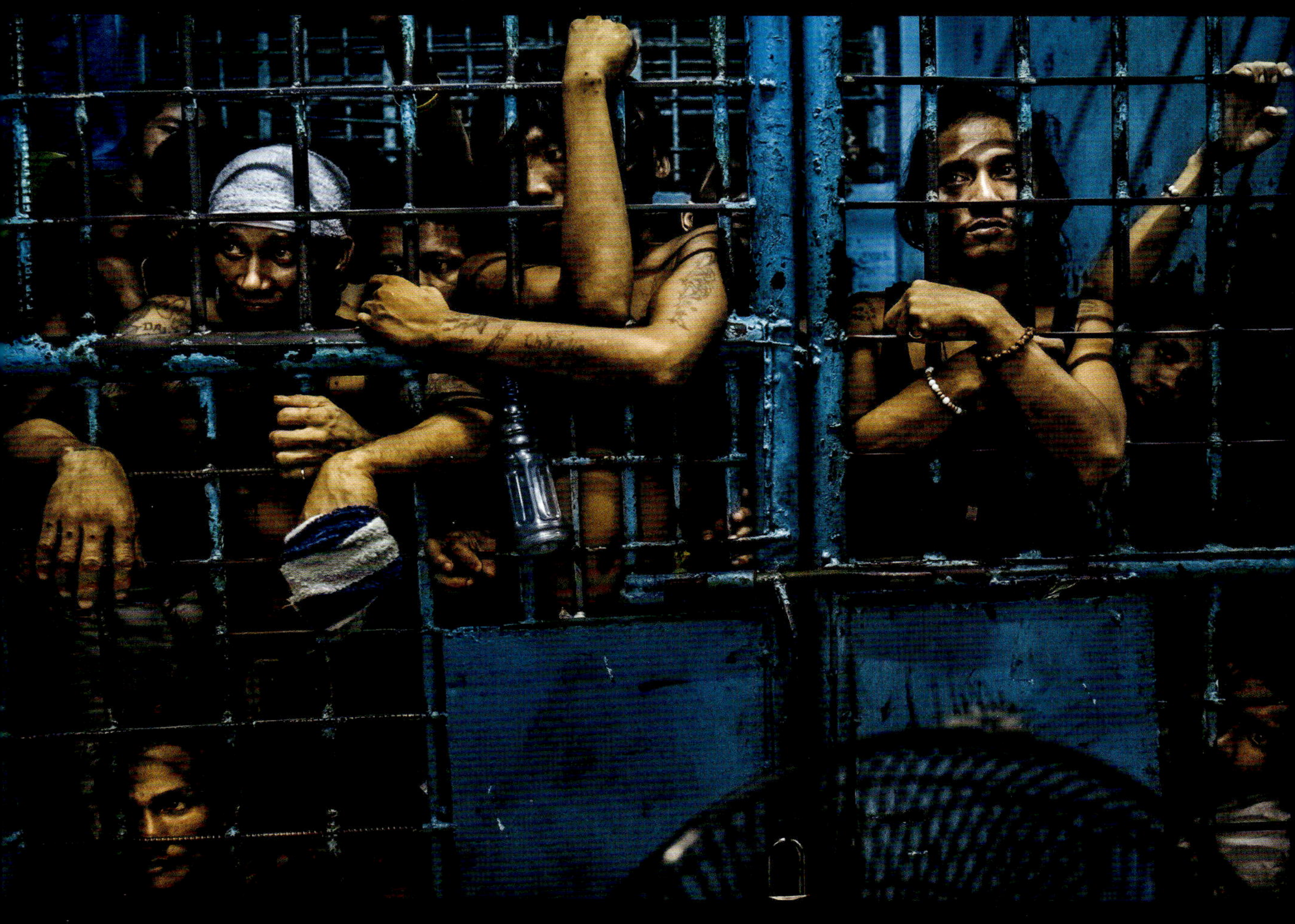

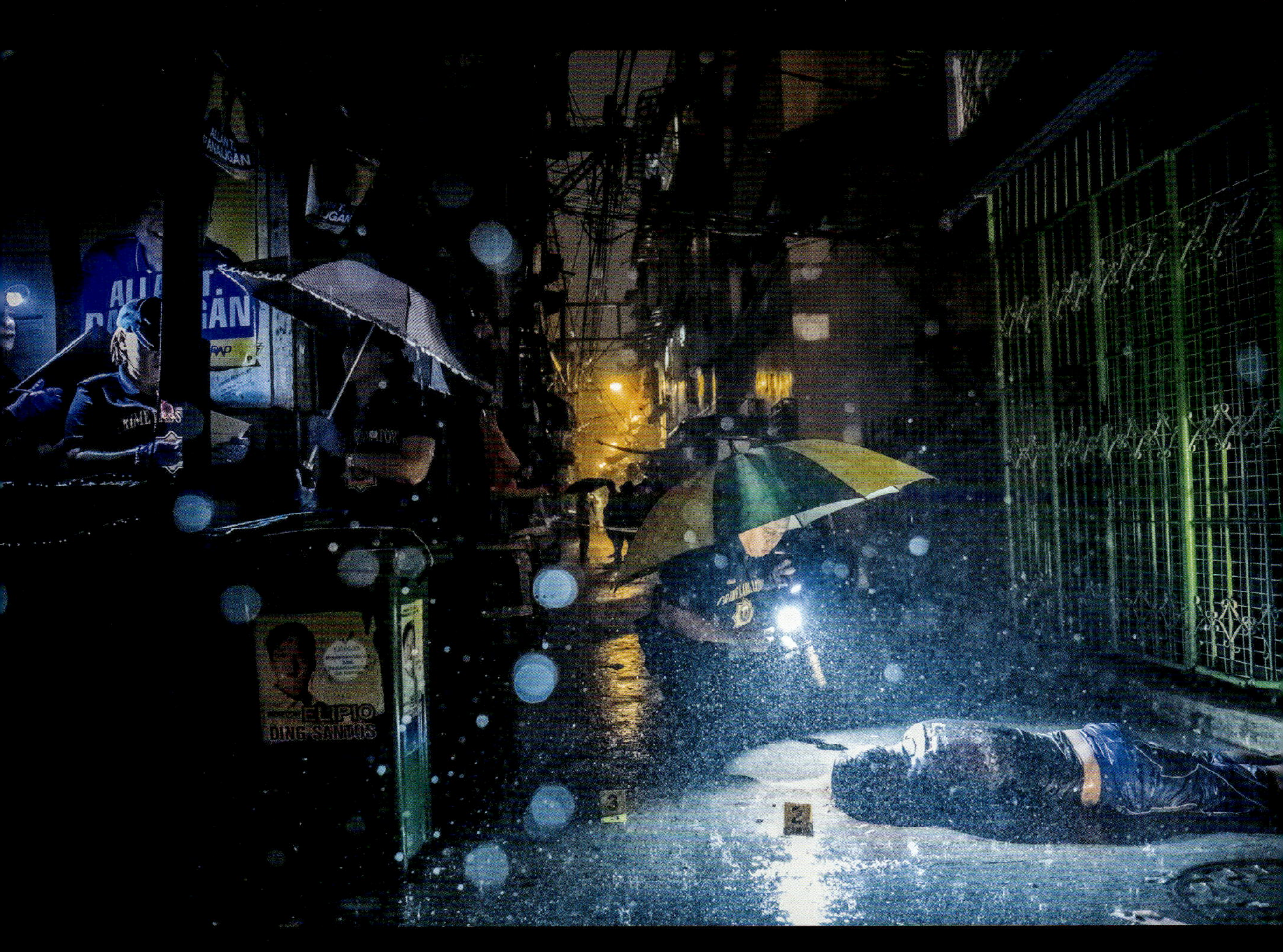

President Rodrigo Duterte of the Philippines began a concerted anti-drug offensive soon after taking office on 30 June. During his presidential campaign, Duterte and senior officials had linked high national crime rates with drugs: an approach popular with voters dissatisfied with the political establishment and its failure to tackle poverty, crime and corruption. The president repeatedly ordered an increase of efforts in the offensive. Amnesty International reports that this led to human rights violations, including extrajudicial killings by both civilians and police. According to the Philippine National Police, officers and unknown armed persons carried out 7,025 drug-related killings between 1 July and 21 January 2017.

Two spreads back: Jimji Bolasa (6) cries before funeral parlor workers remove the body of her father, Jimboy, who was found dead after being abducted by unidentified men. *Previous spread*: Crime-scene investigators gather evidence after Frederick Mafe and Arjay Lumbago were gunned down by unidentified motorcyclists in Manila. *Facing page*: Inmates look on as drug suspects are processed at a Manila police station. *Above*: Investigators examine the scene after Romeo Joel Torres Fontanilla was killed by unknown gunmen riding motorcycles. *Next spread*: The blood of Florjohn Cruz stains the floor in his family home, where he was shot by police while fixing a radio for his mother.

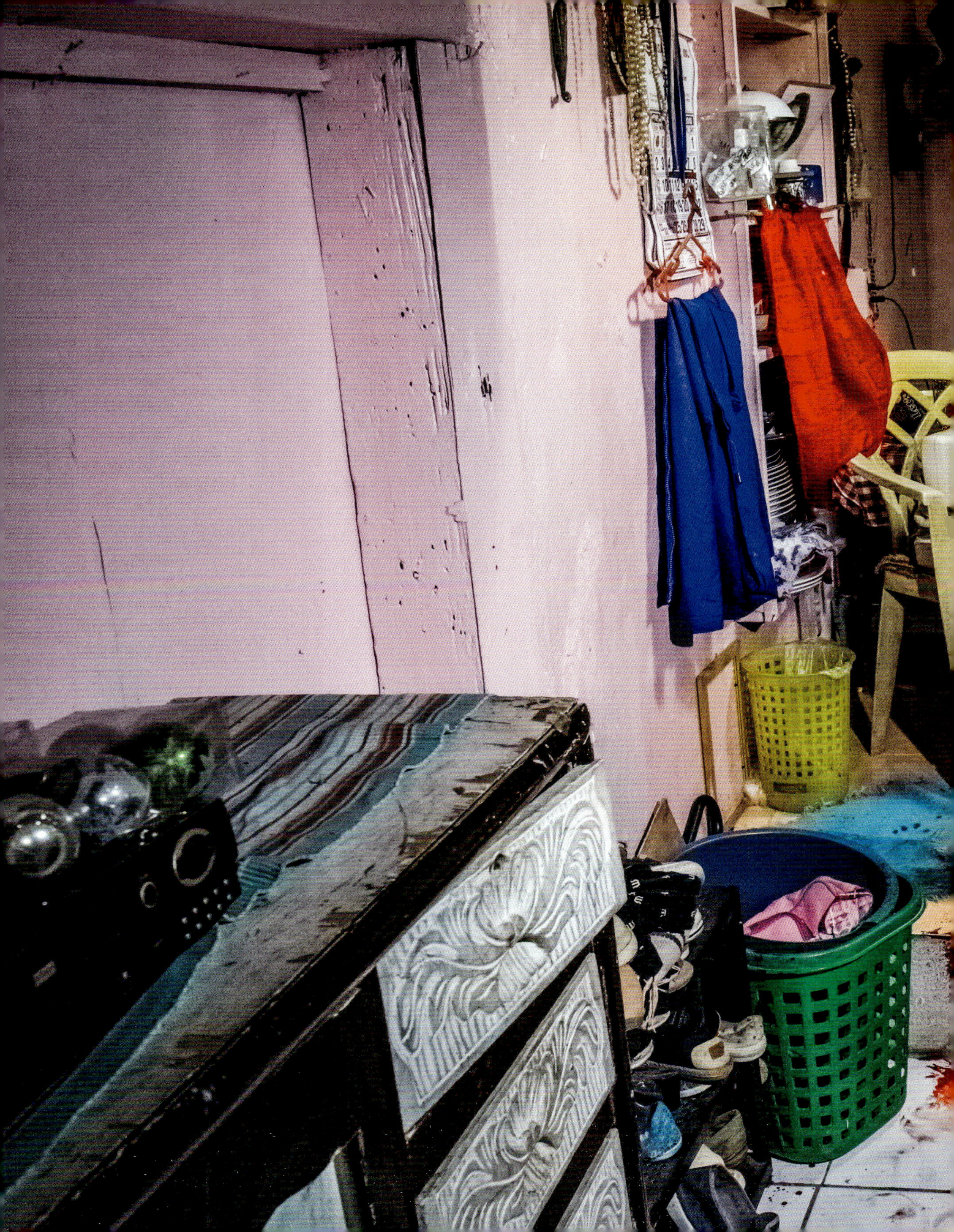

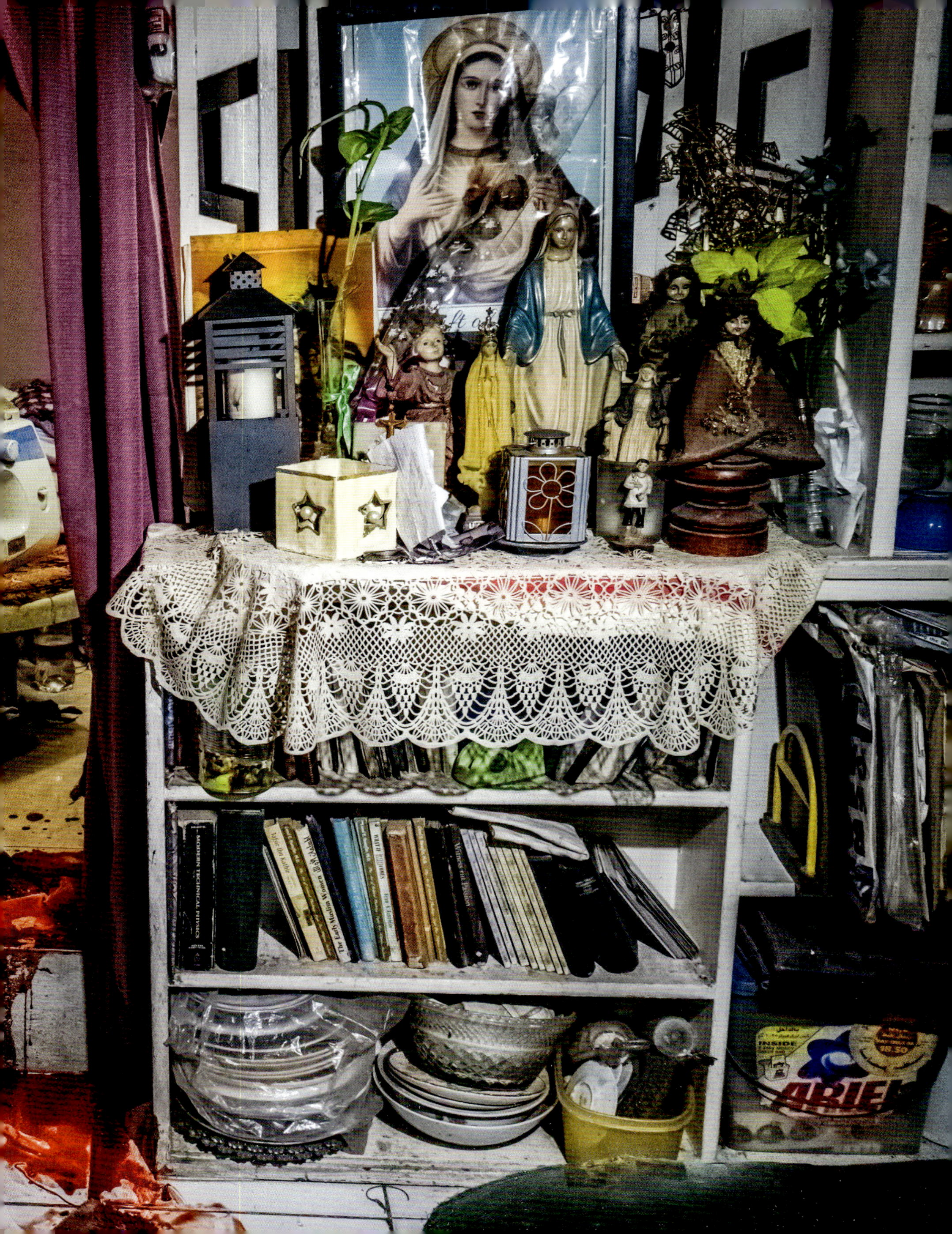
MODERN TECHNICAL PHYSICS
Tafsir Ibn Kathir
The Early Muslim Women
ARIEL

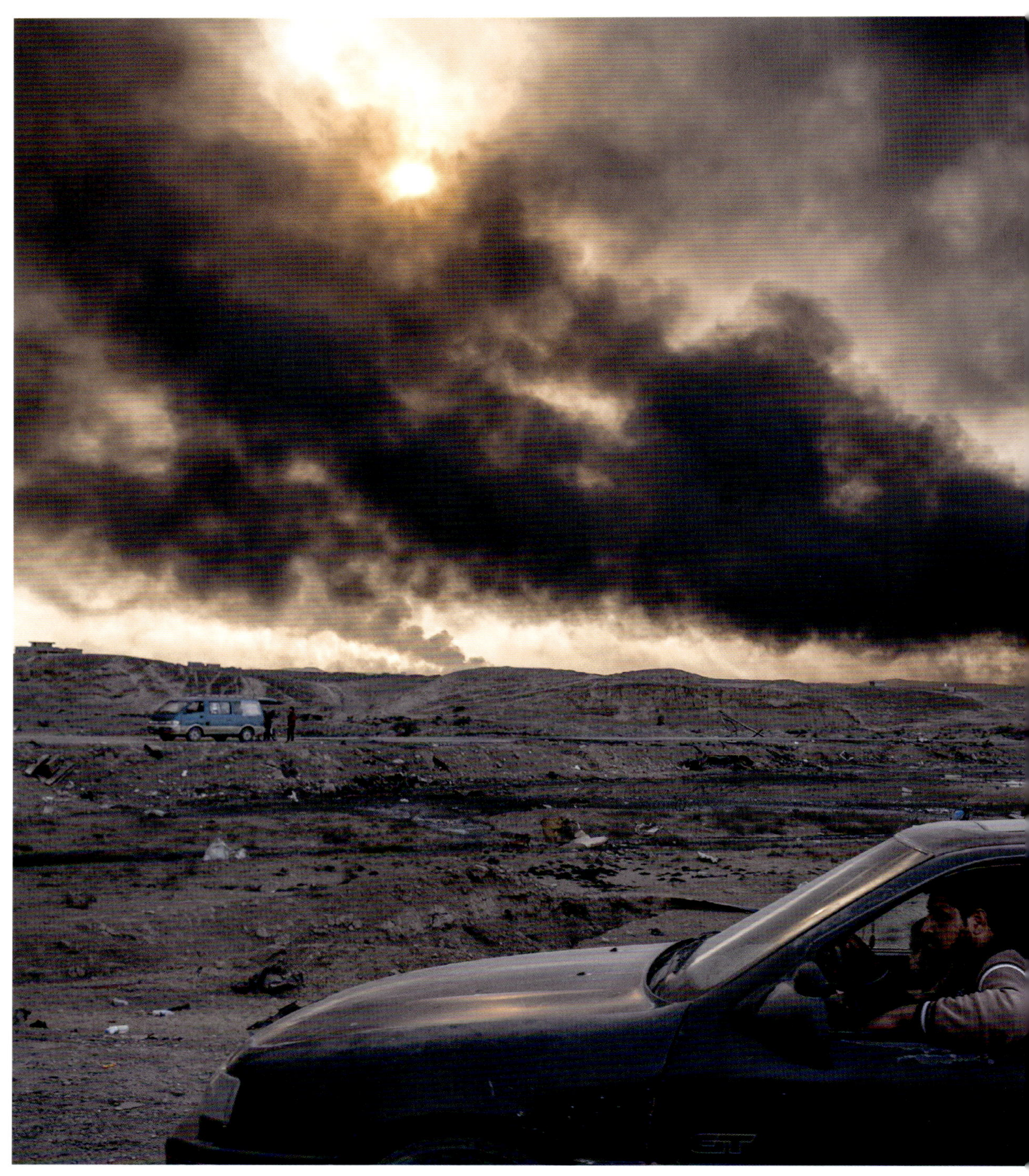

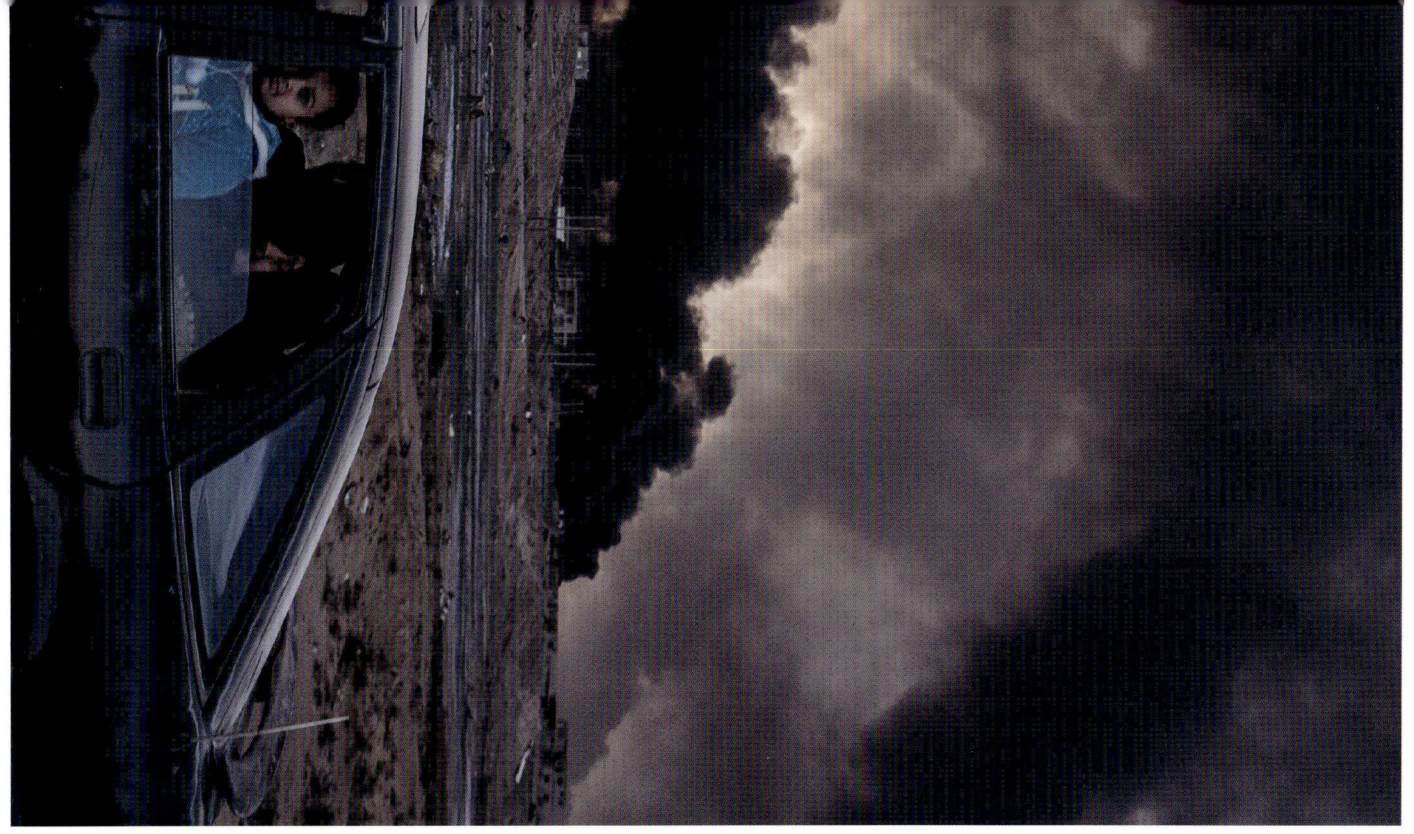

Sergey Ponomarev
Russia, for *The New York Times* /
2nd Prize General News

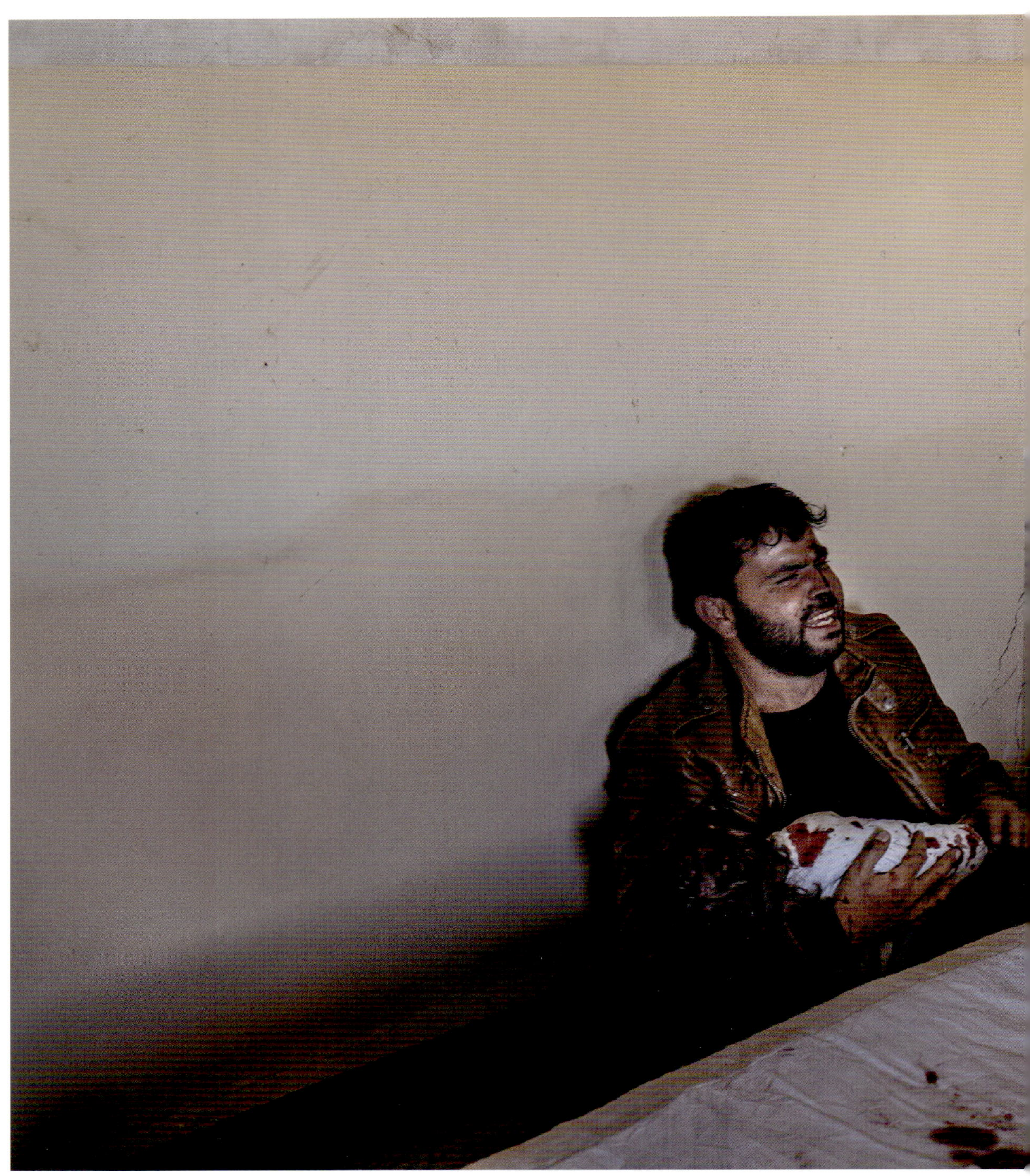

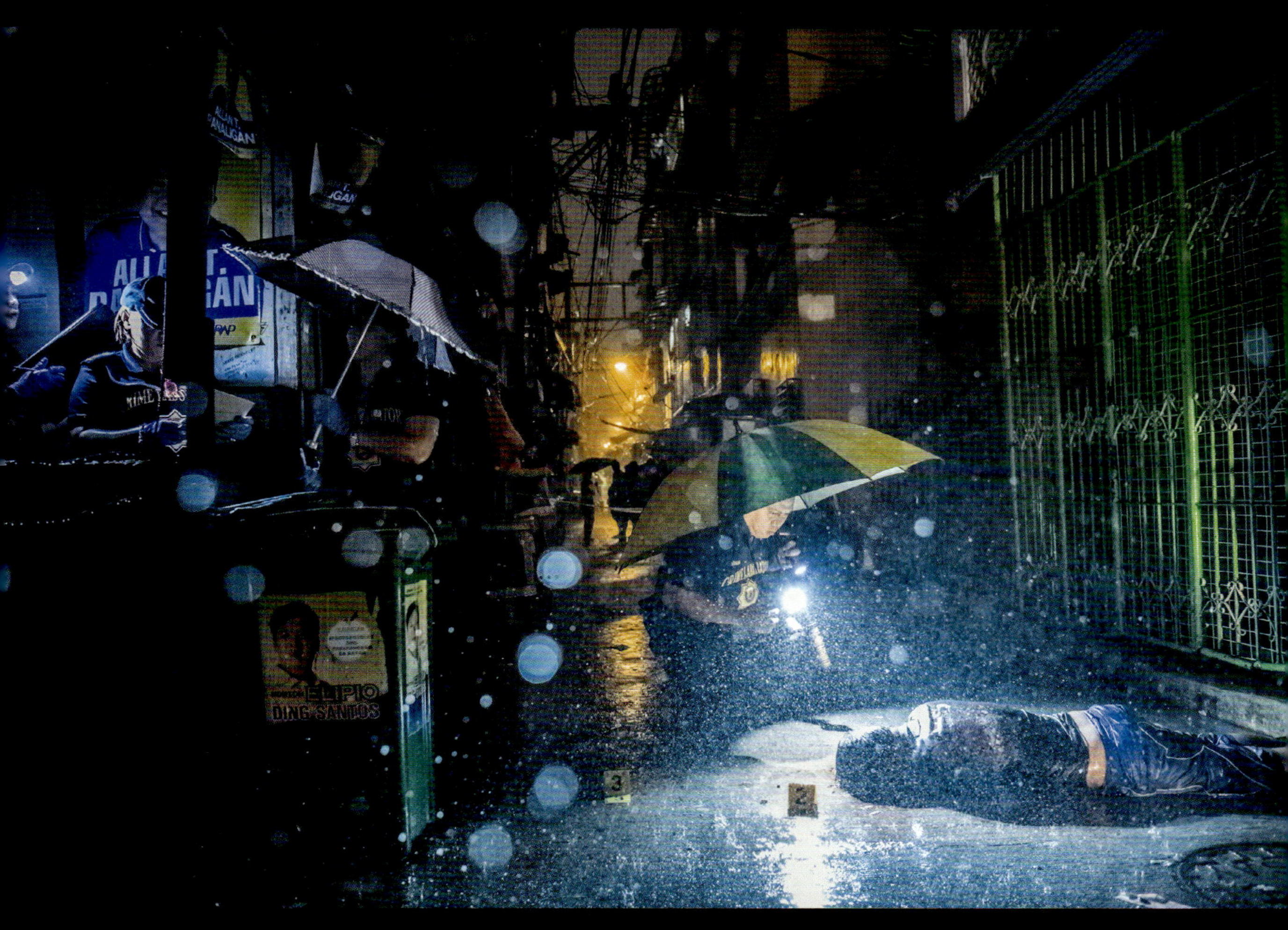

President Rodrigo Duterte of the Philippines began a concerted anti-drug offensive soon after taking office on 30 June. During his presidential campaign, Duterte and senior officials had linked high national crime rates with drugs: an approach popular with voters dissatisfied with the political establishment and its failure to tackle poverty, crime and corruption. The president repeatedly ordered an increase of efforts in the offensive. Amnesty International reports that this led to human rights violations, including extrajudicial killings by both civilians and police. According to the Philippine National Police, officers and unknown armed persons carried out 7,025 drug-related killings between 1 July and 21 January 2017.

Two spreads back: Jimji Bolasa (6) cries before funeral parlor workers remove the body of her father, Jimboy, who was found dead after being abducted by unidentified men. *Previous spread*: Crime-scene investigators gather evidence after Frederick Mafe and Arjay Lumbago were gunned down by unidentified motorcyclists in Manila. *Facing page*: Inmates look on as drug suspects are processed at a Manila police station. *Above*: Investigators examine the scene after Romeo Joel Torres Fontanilla was killed by unknown gunmen riding motorcycles. *Next spread*: The blood of Florjohn Cruz stains the floor in his family home, where he was shot by police while fixing a radio for his mother.

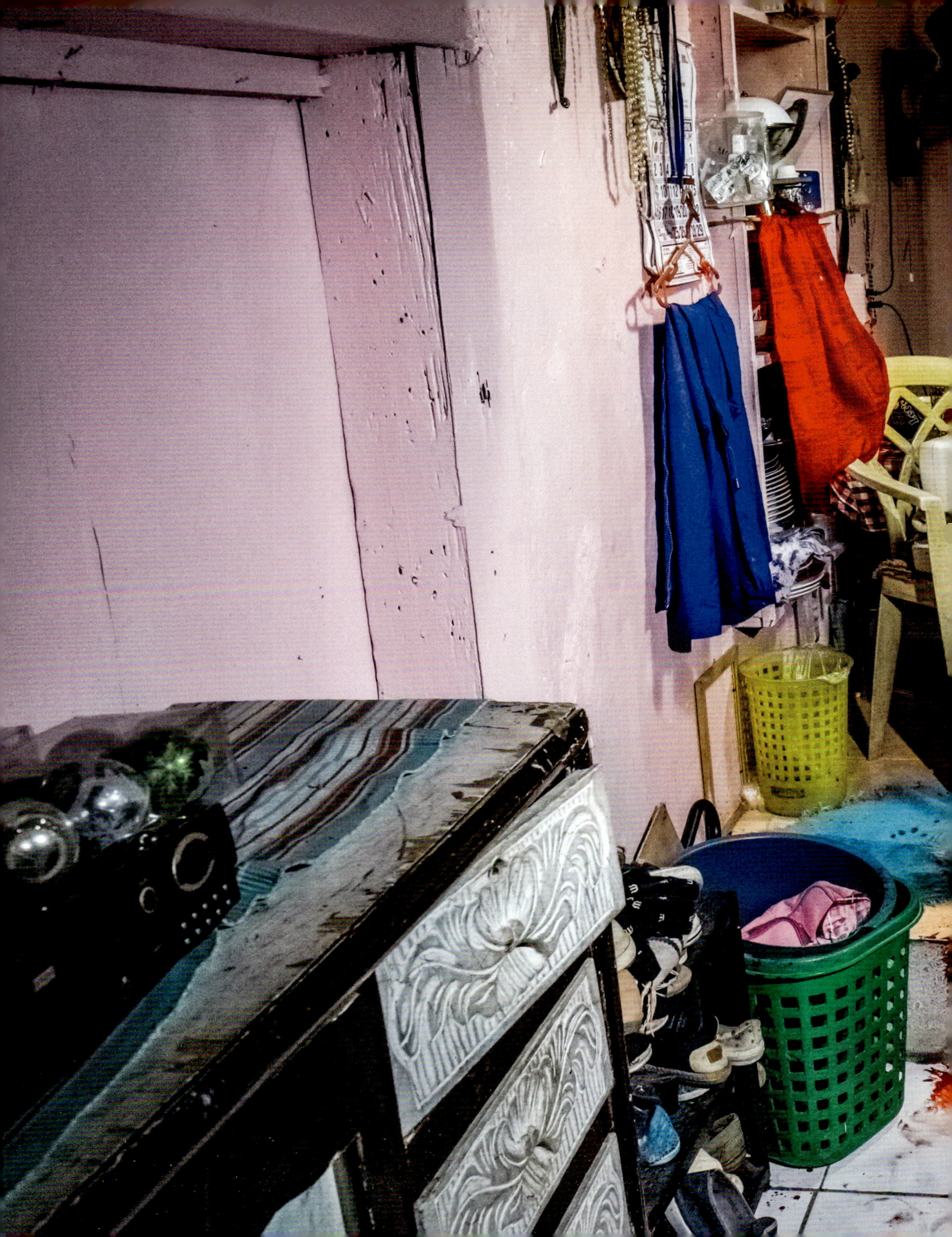

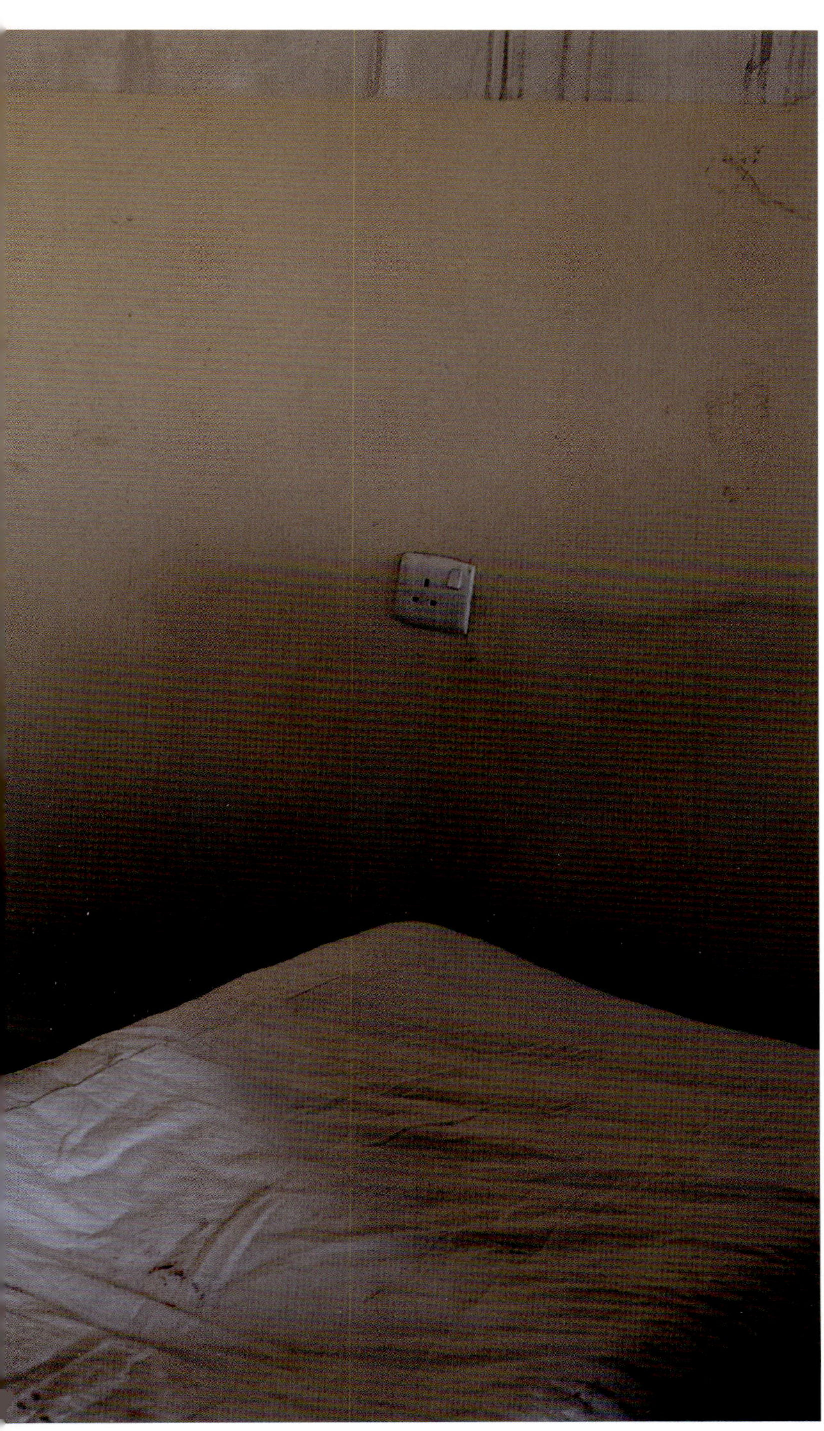

The Iraqi Special Operations Forces (ISOF), backed by US and coalition forces, began an offensive to retake Mosul from the Islamic State group (IS) in October. IS had been entrenched in Mosul for more than two years. The Iraqi government initially dropped leaflets over the city, asking residents to stay in their homes. Many people were caught in the crossfire, but some chose to escape. *Previous spread*: A family flees Mosul, as oil fields burn in Qayyarah, 60 kilometers south of the city, in November. *This spread*: A relative of one-year-old Amira Omar weeps as he holds her body in a field hospital near Mosul. (*continues*)

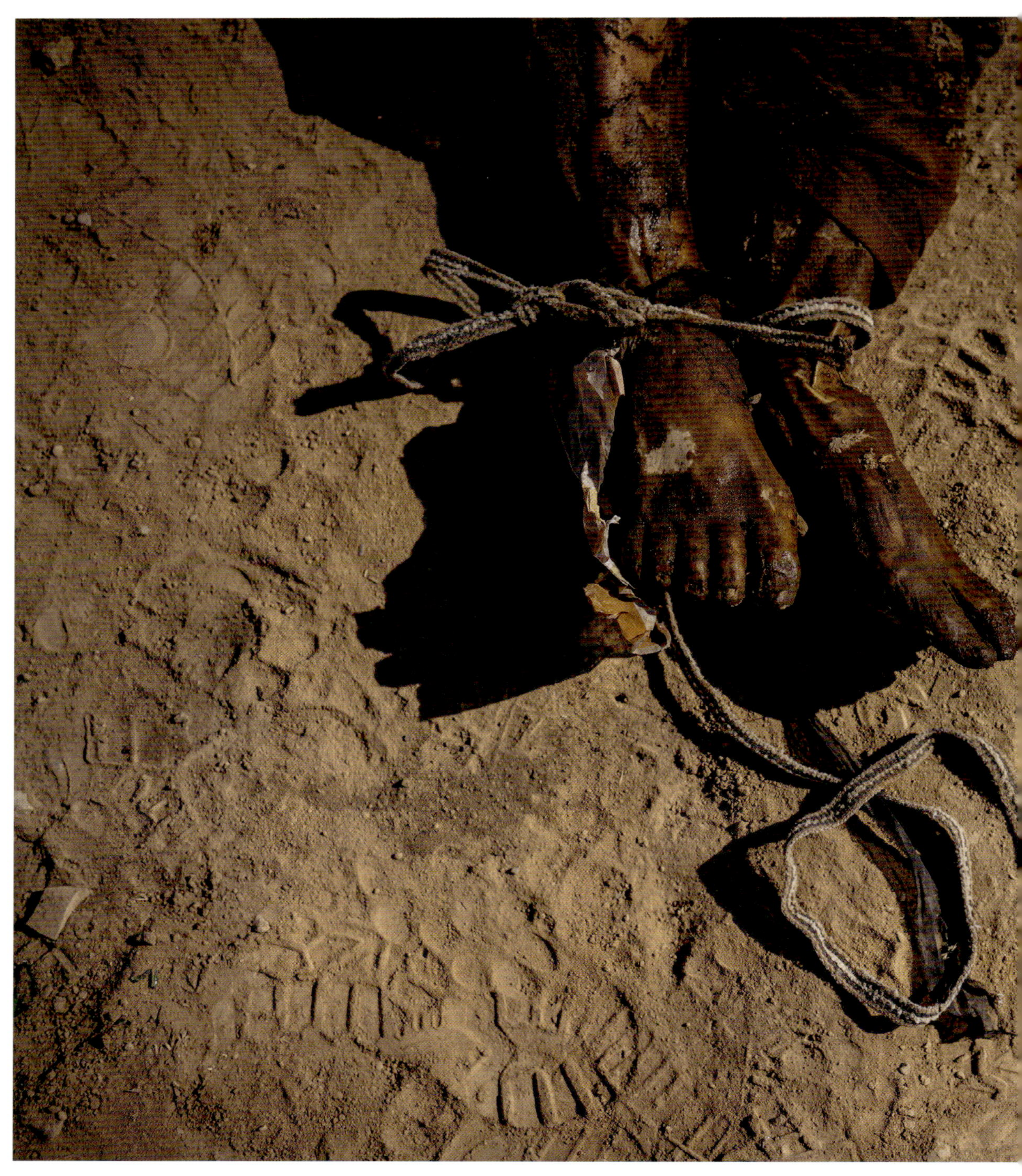

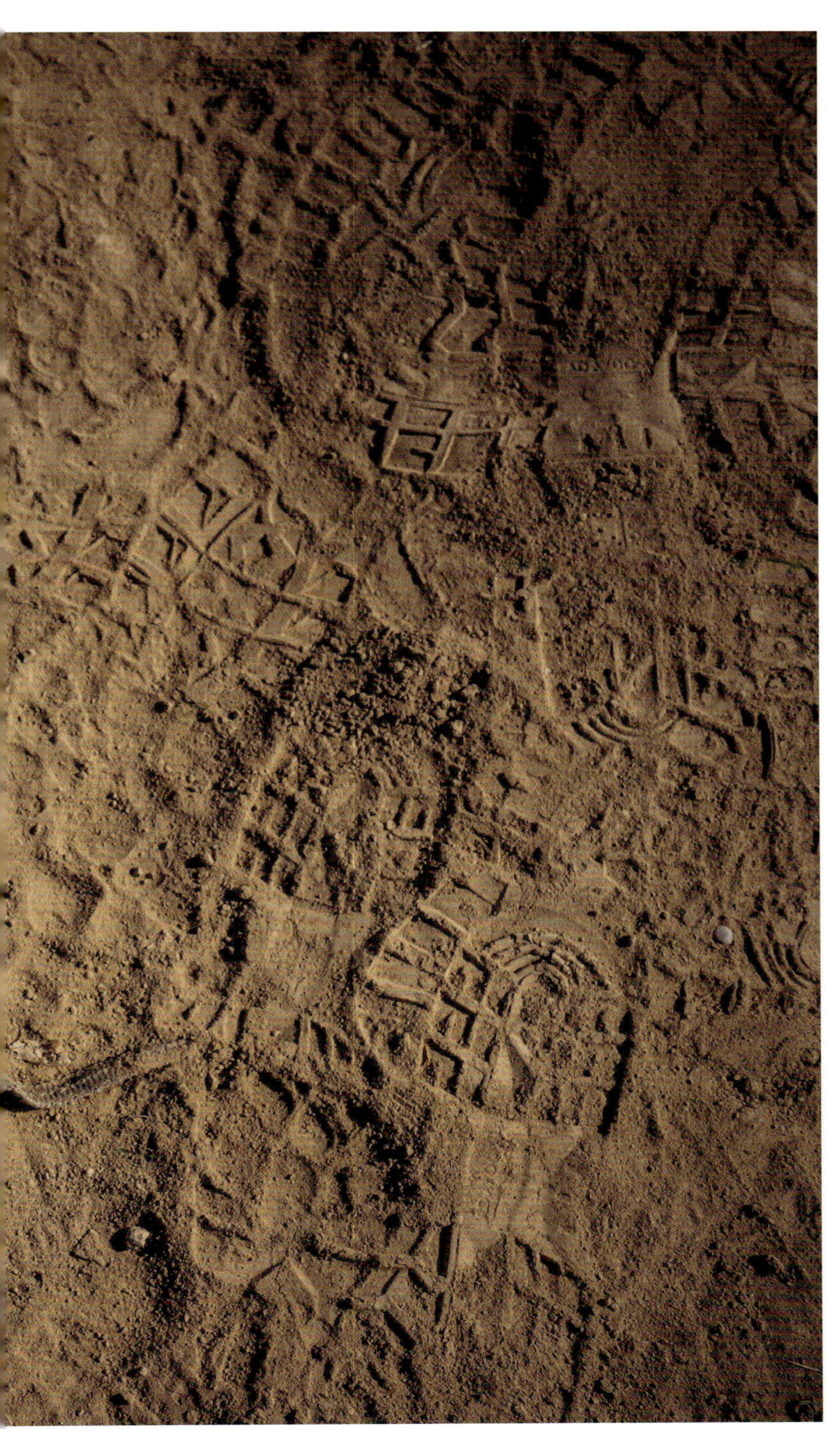

(*continued*) The UN High Commissioner for Refugees (UNHCR) states that more than 96,800 people were displaced in Mosul between October and December, while around one million civilians remained trapped in the city, running low on food and drinking water and facing increasing retaliation by IS fighters. *This spread*: A partially decomposed body with its feet bound together at a mass grave discovered in the old spa resort of Hamam al-Alil, south of Mosul. (*continues*)

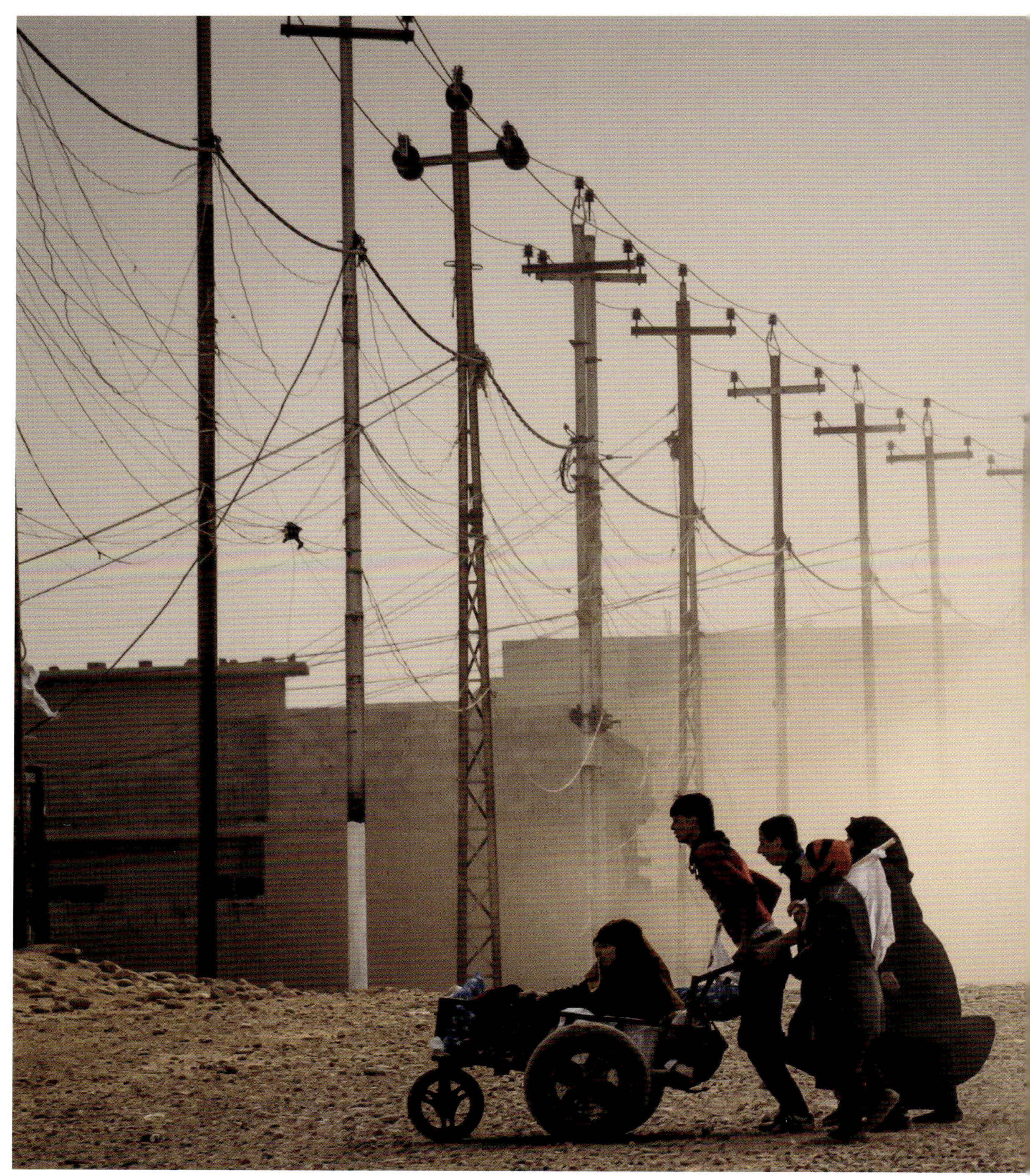

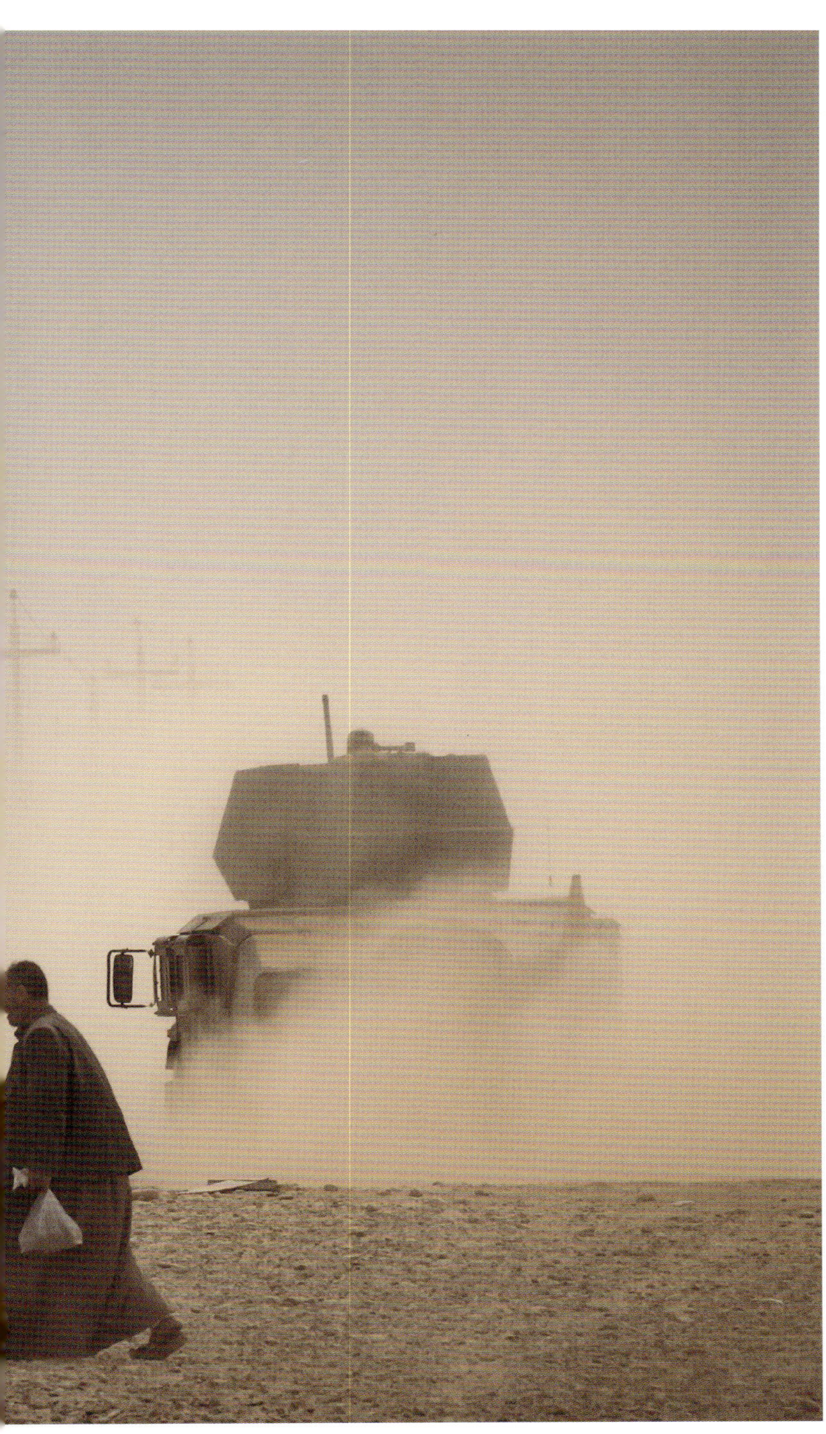

(*continued*) The Iraqi strategy of asking civilians to remain in their homes was aimed at averting a humanitarian crisis set off by hundreds of thousands fleeing, and at facilitating resistance to IS from within the city. As the number of people caught up in the battle escalated, and fears of IS retaliation grew, many preferred to face the risks of leaving. *This spread*: Residents of Mosul flee the city in November.

Alessio Romenzi

Italy /
3rd Prize General News

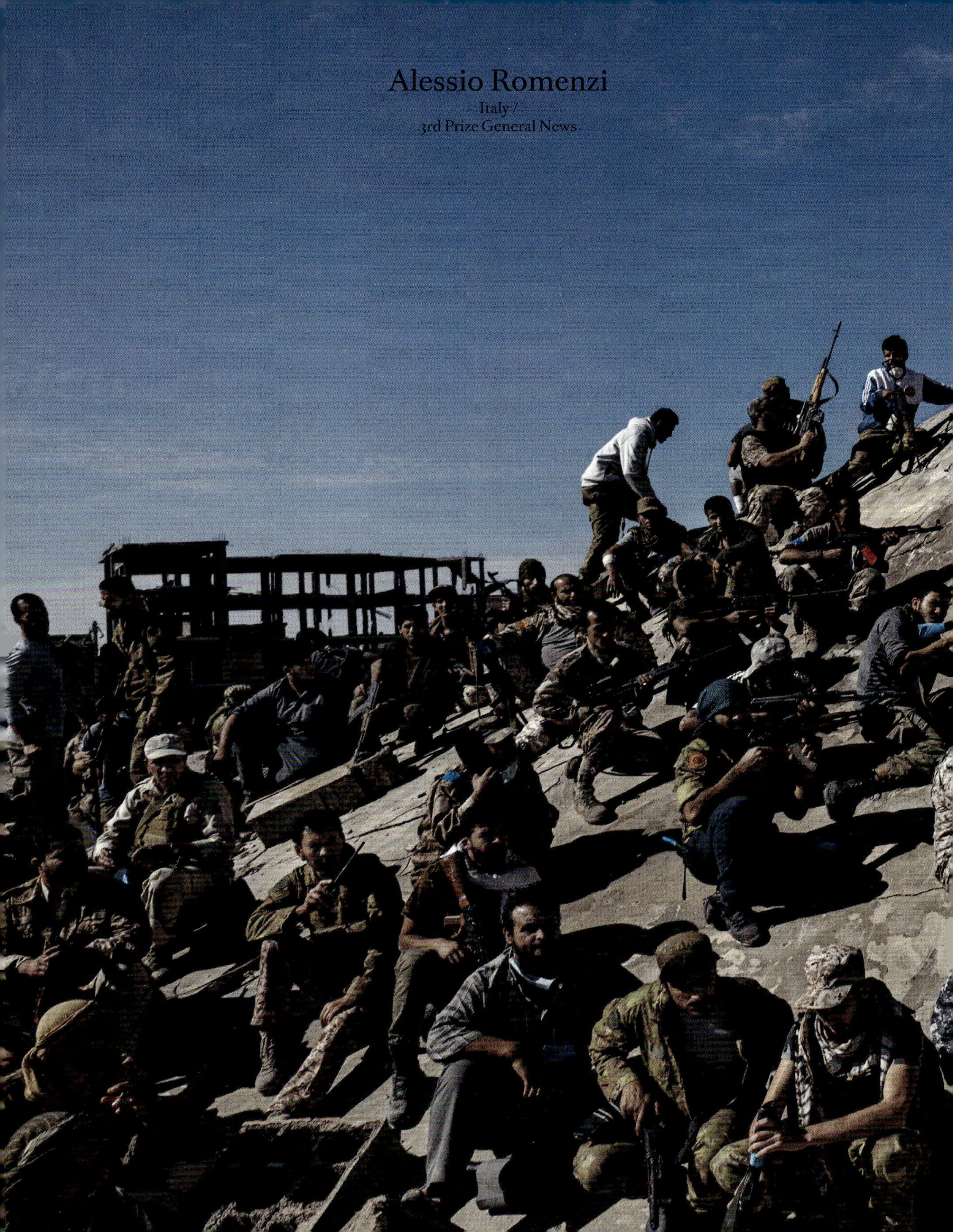

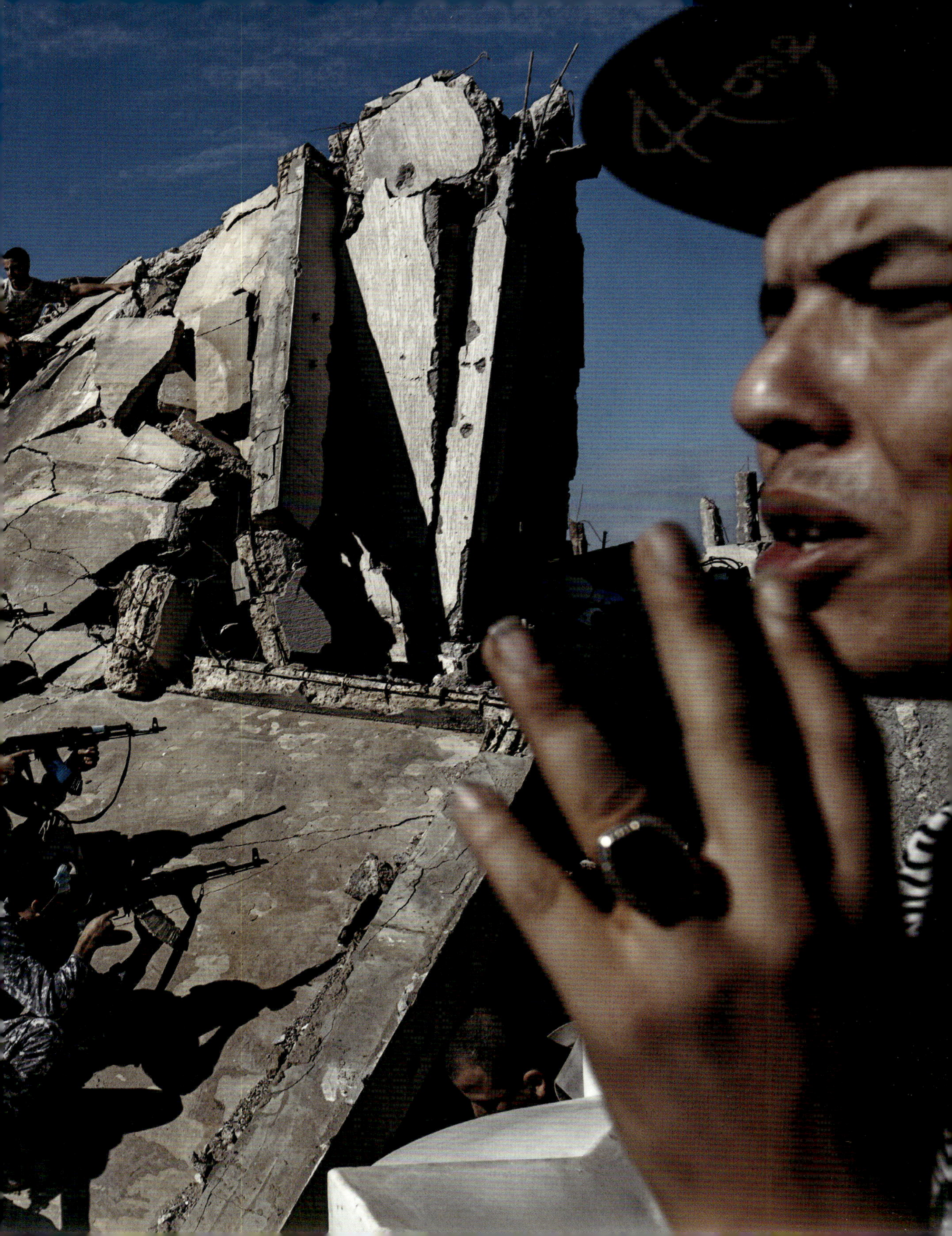

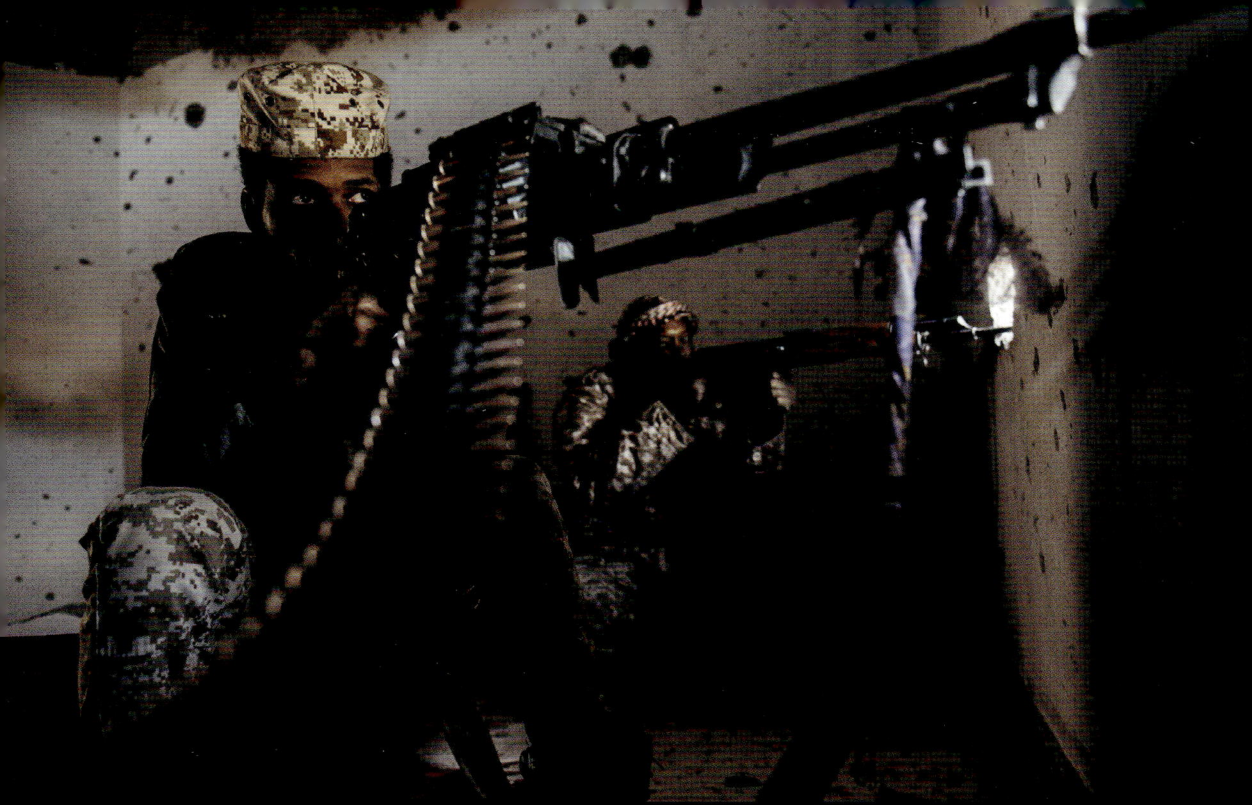

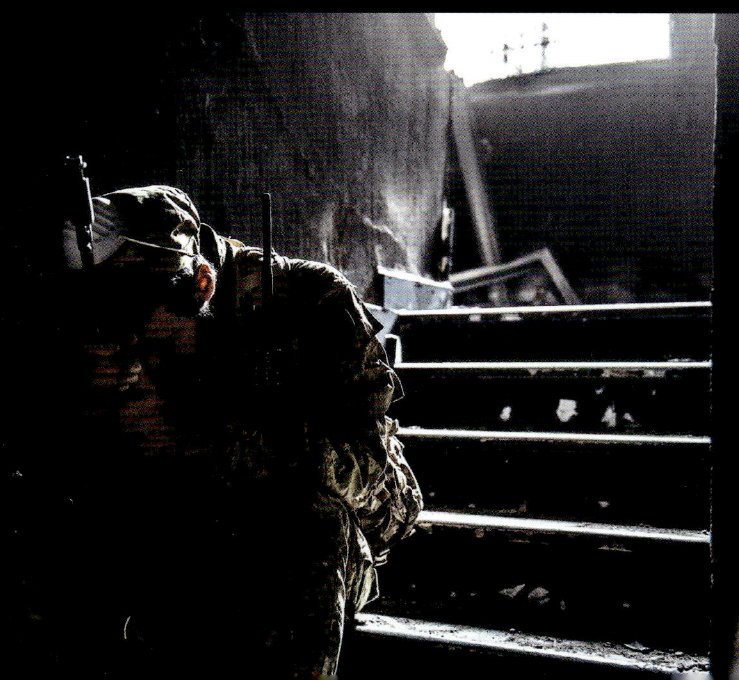

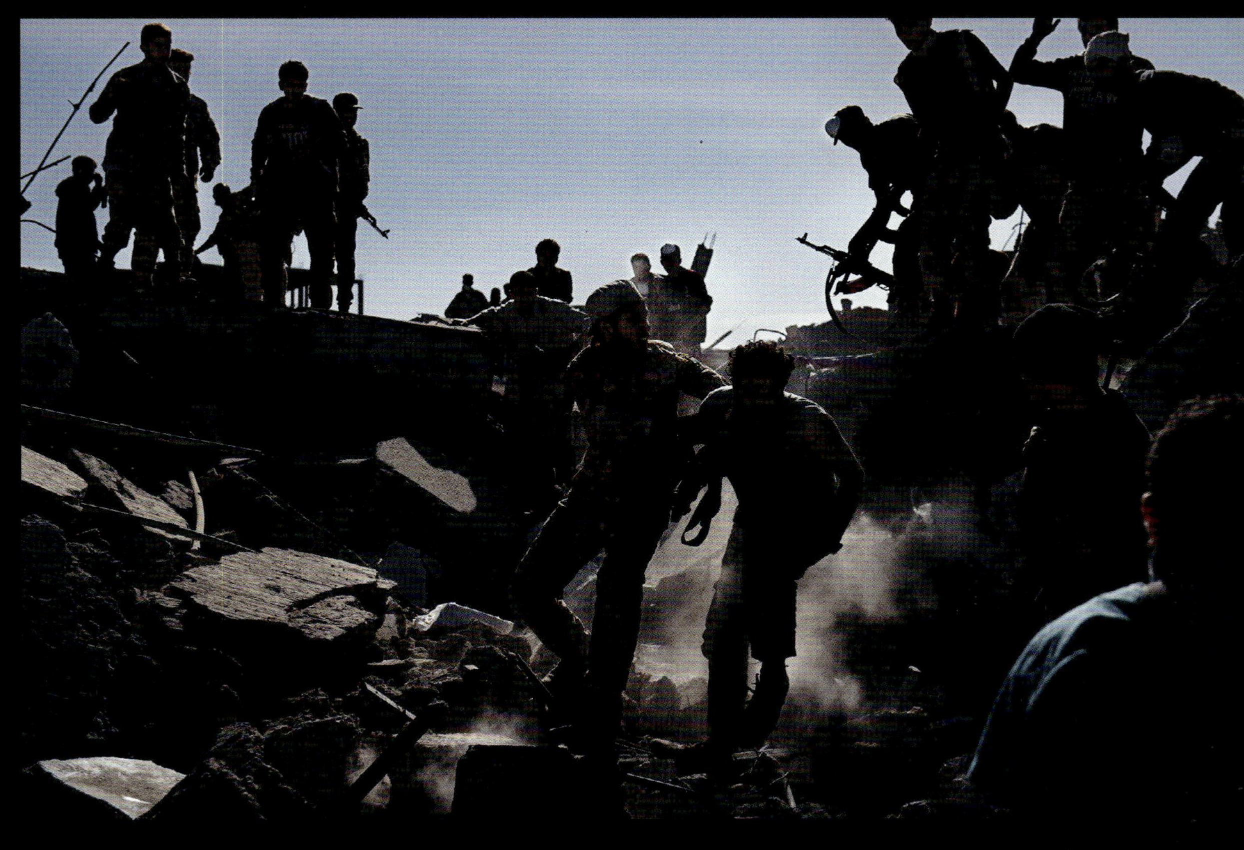

Military forces affiliated to Libya's Government of National Accord (GNA) launched an offensive to retake the coastal city of Sirte in May. The Islamic State group (IS) had gained control of the city a year earlier. IS emerged as a growing force in Libya in the political vacuum that resulted following the overthrow of President Muammar Gaddafi, and Sirte had become one of IS's three major strongholds, alongside Raqqa in Syria and Mosul in Iraq. The GNA offensive lasted until December, benefiting from US air support after August. According to a UN Security Council report, IS lost almost all of the territory it controlled in the area, although small groups remained active throughout the country. *Previous spread*: GNA-affiliated forces take position in an advance on IS, on 26 November. *Facing page, top*: Fighters take aim at IS positions in the Al Jiza neighborhood. *Below*: A GNA-affiliated fighter rests during the battle for Al Jiza. *This page*: An IS militant is captured by GNA-affiliated fighters. He was later found dead. *Following spread*: GNA-affiliated fighters walk through a room in the Ouagadougou congress complex, on 15 August. The complex became an impromptu IS fortress during the conflict.

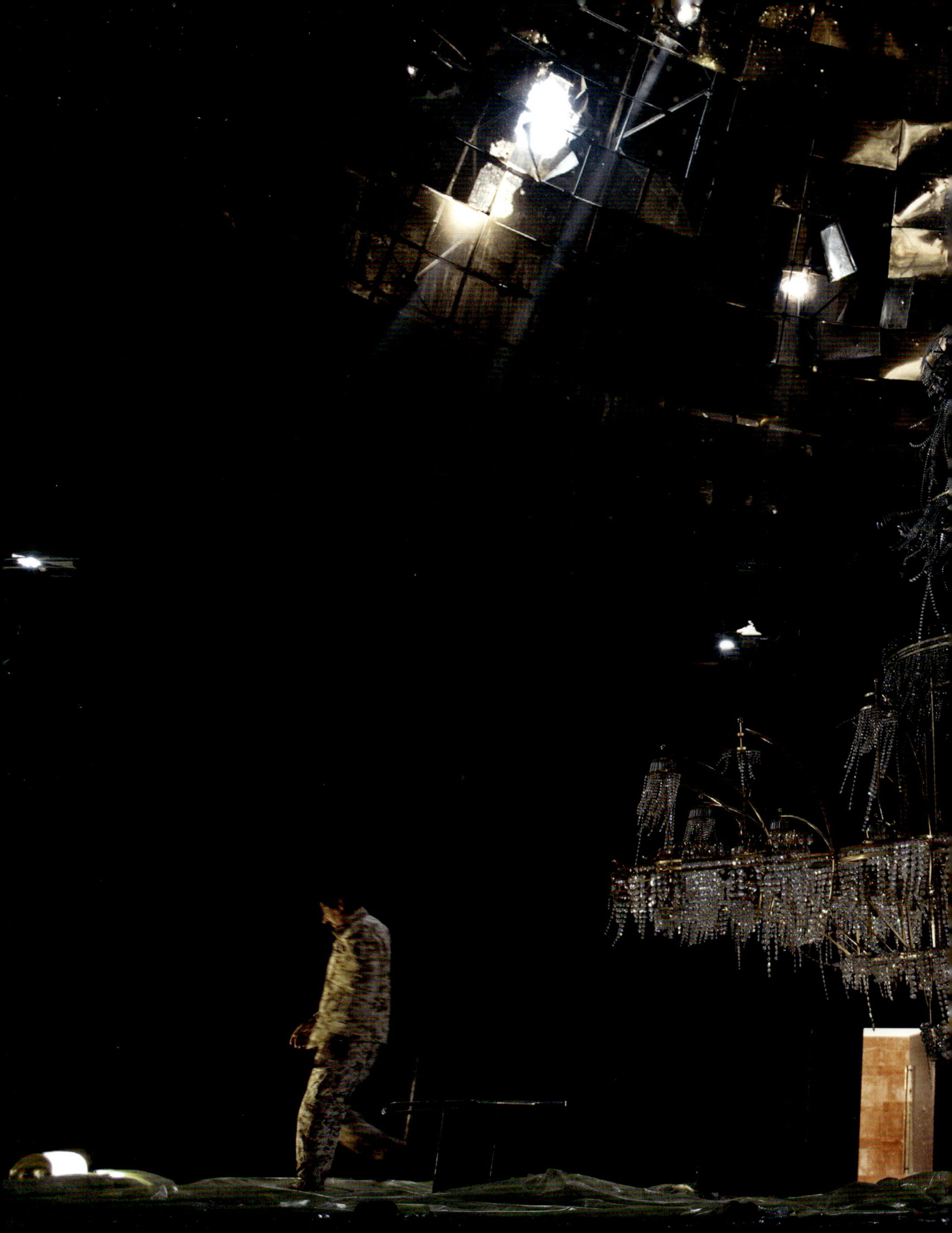

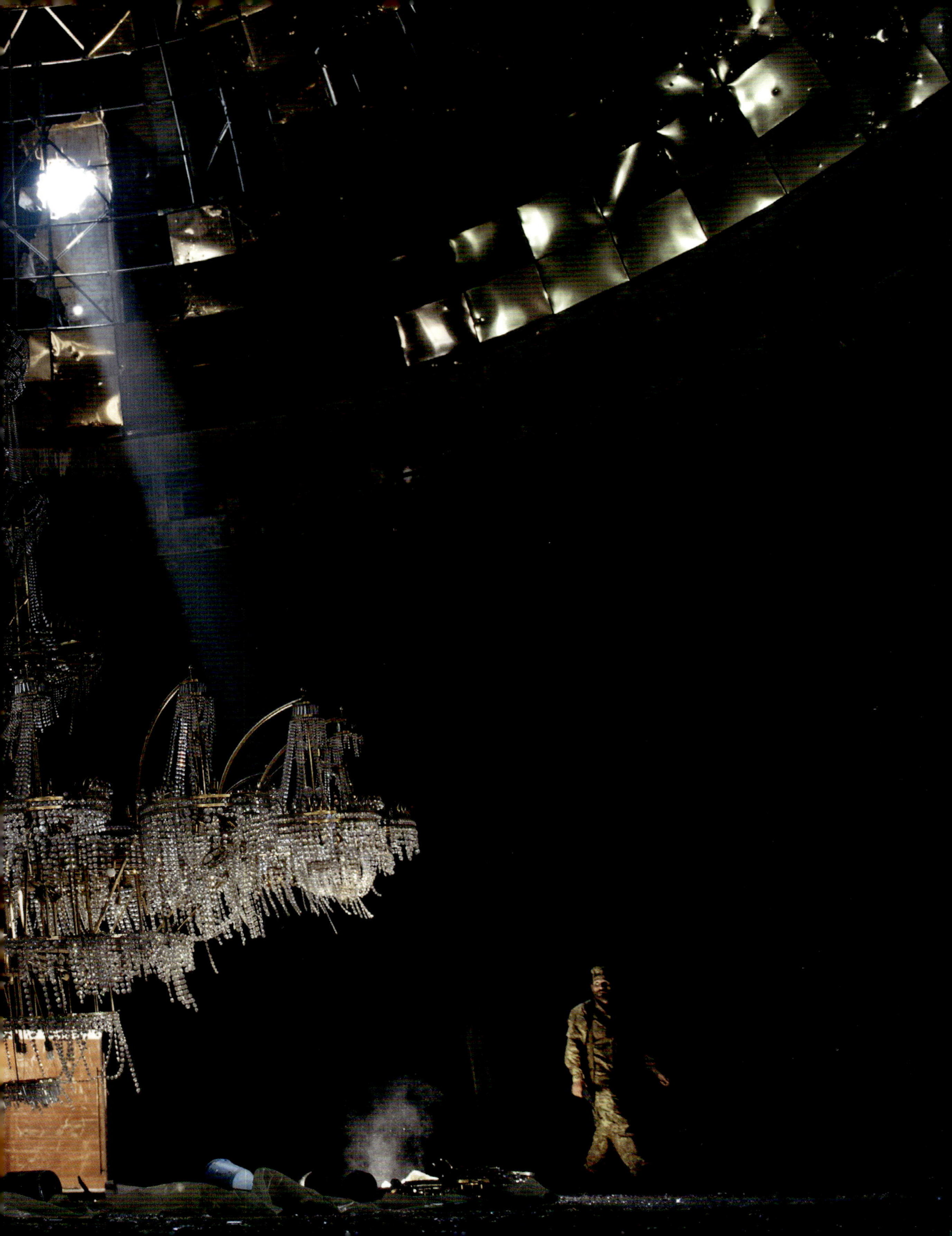

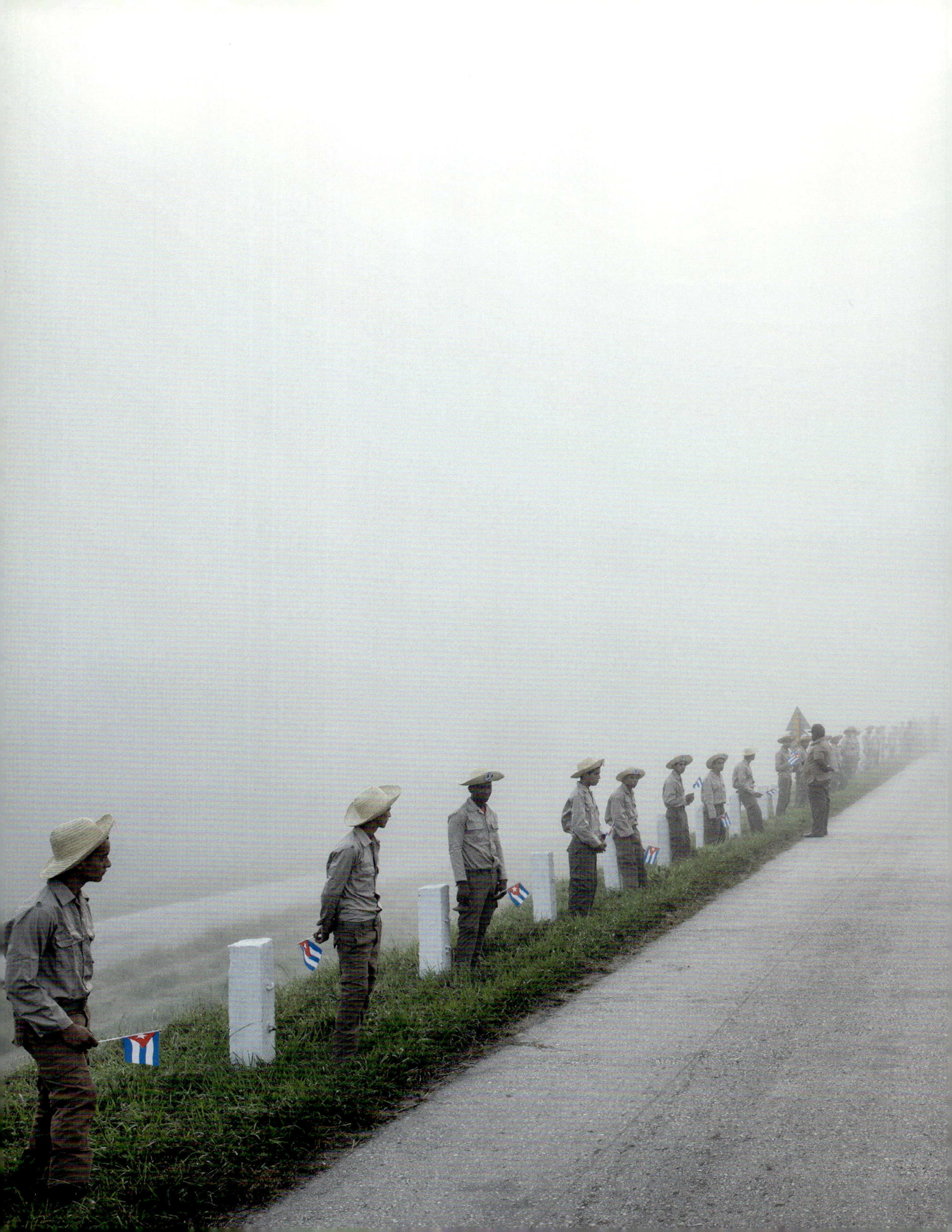

Tomás Munita

Chile, for *The New York Times* /
1st Prize Daily Life

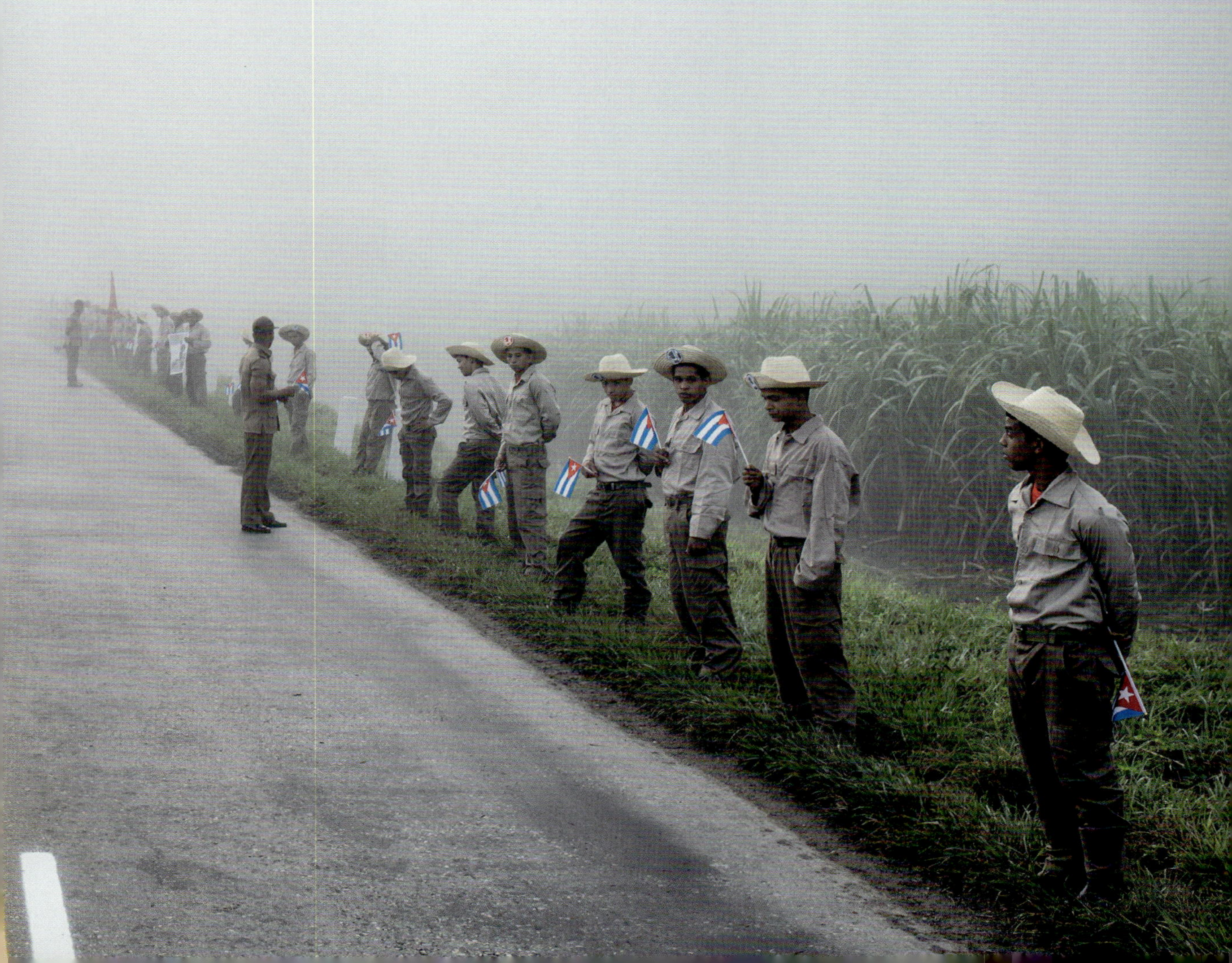

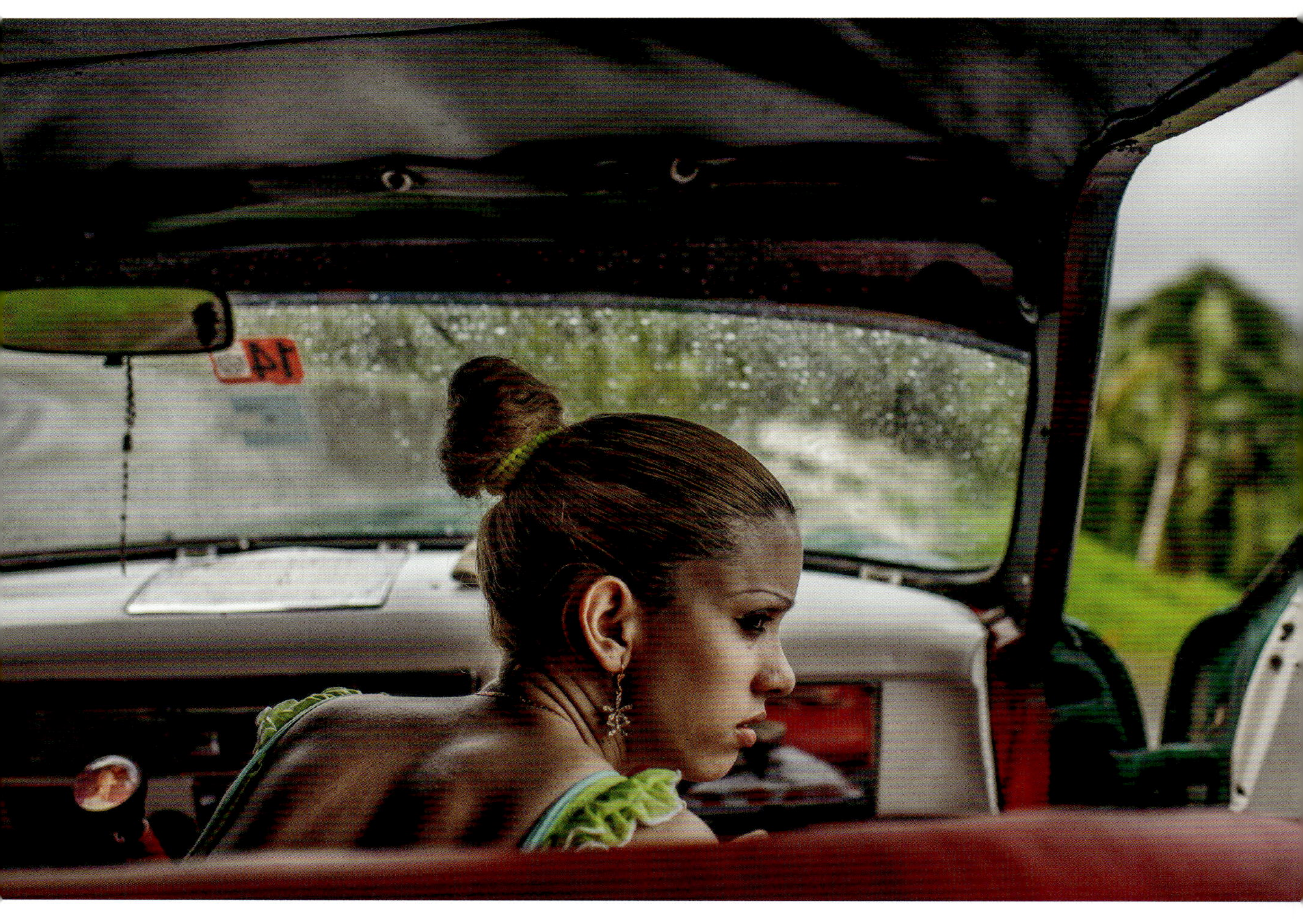

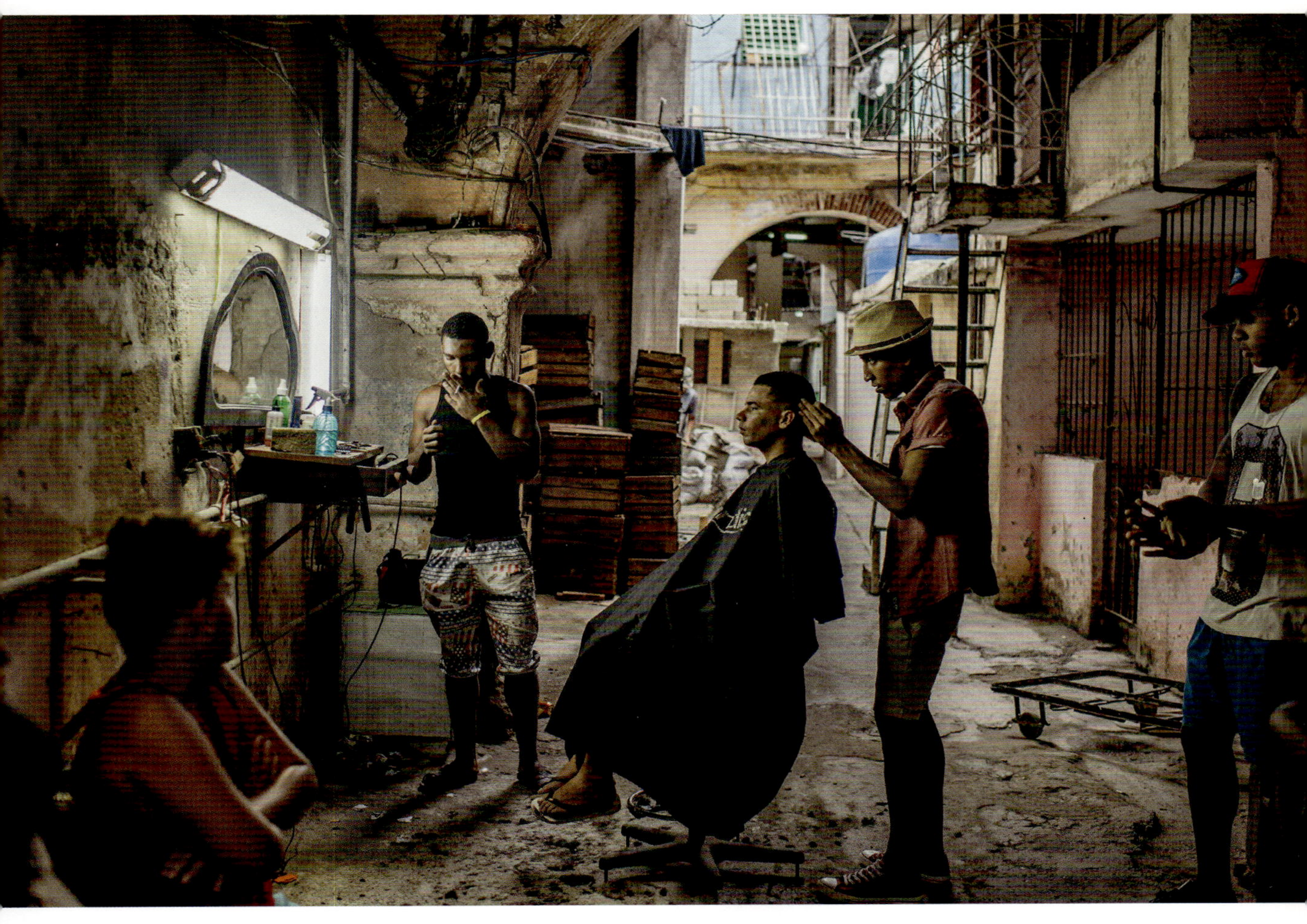

Fidel Castro, Cuba's former president and leader of the Communist revolution, died on 26 November. Mourning was fervent and public across the country. Castro's ashes were taken on a route that retraced, in reverse, the steps of his victorious march from Santiago to Havana in 1959. Thousands turned out to watch the procession pass. Castro left a Cuba with much-admired education and healthcare systems, but one where a longstanding US economic embargo had led to shortages of basic supplies and widespread disrepair. *Previous spread*: Members of Ejército Juvenil del Trabajo, a youth auxiliary wing of the Revolutionary Armed Forces, wait along the road to Santiago de Cuba at dawn for Castro's funeral procession to pass. *Facing page*: A woman shares a taxi ride to Santiago de Cuba. *Above*: A barber's shop in Old Havana. *Next spread*: A home in Santiago de Cuba. *Two spreads forward*: Castro's funeral procession passes through Santa Clara, central Cuba.

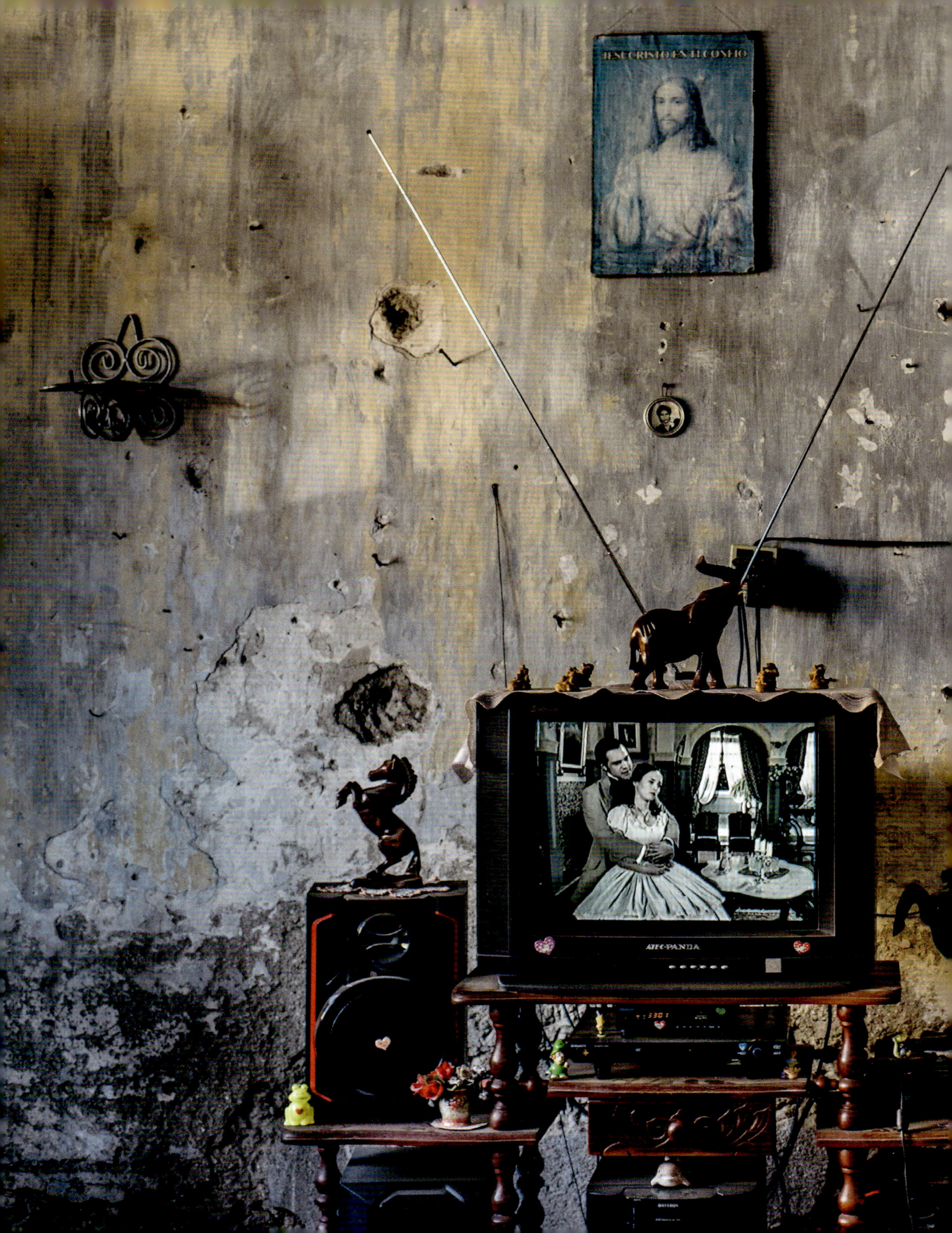
JESUCRISTO EN TI CONFIO

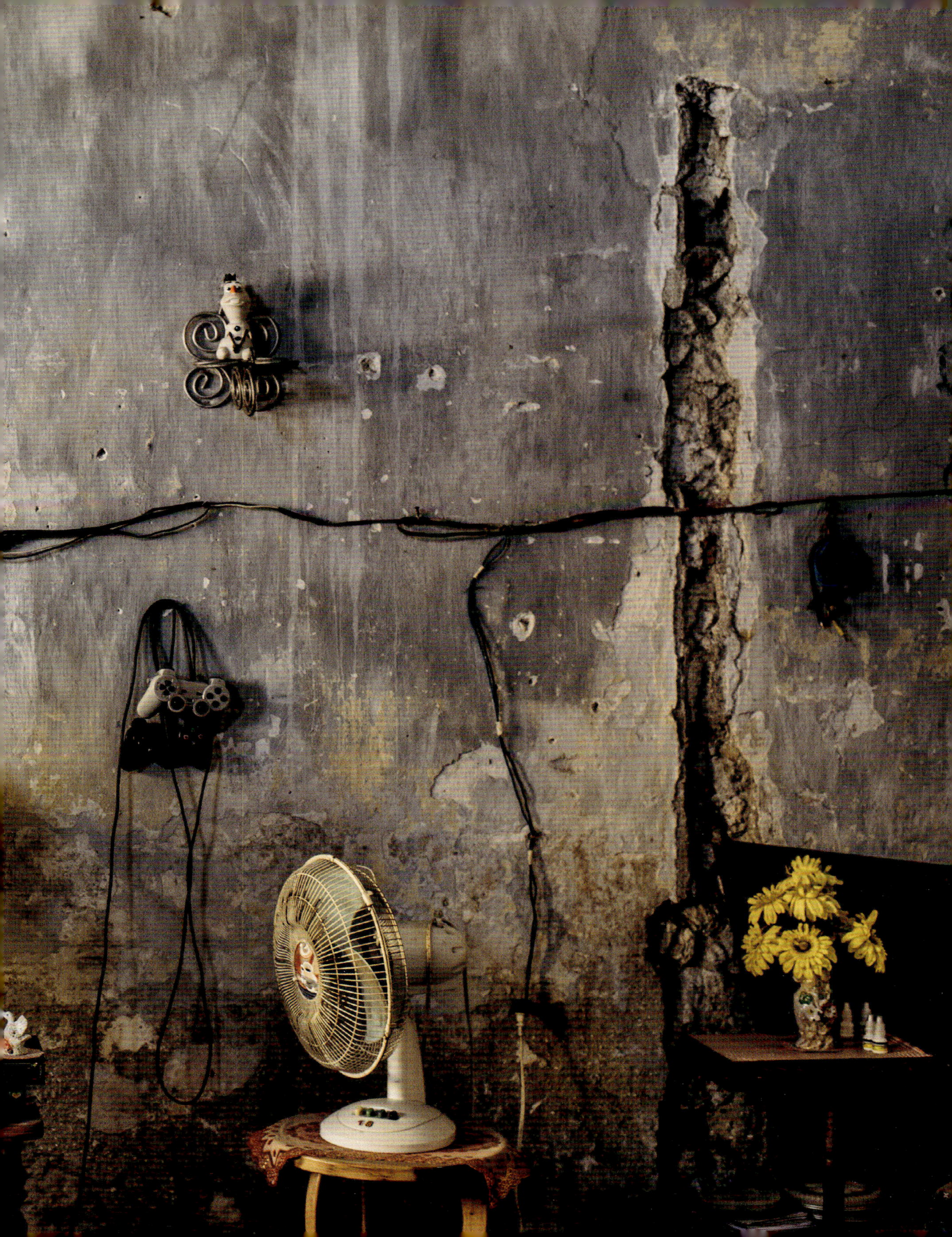

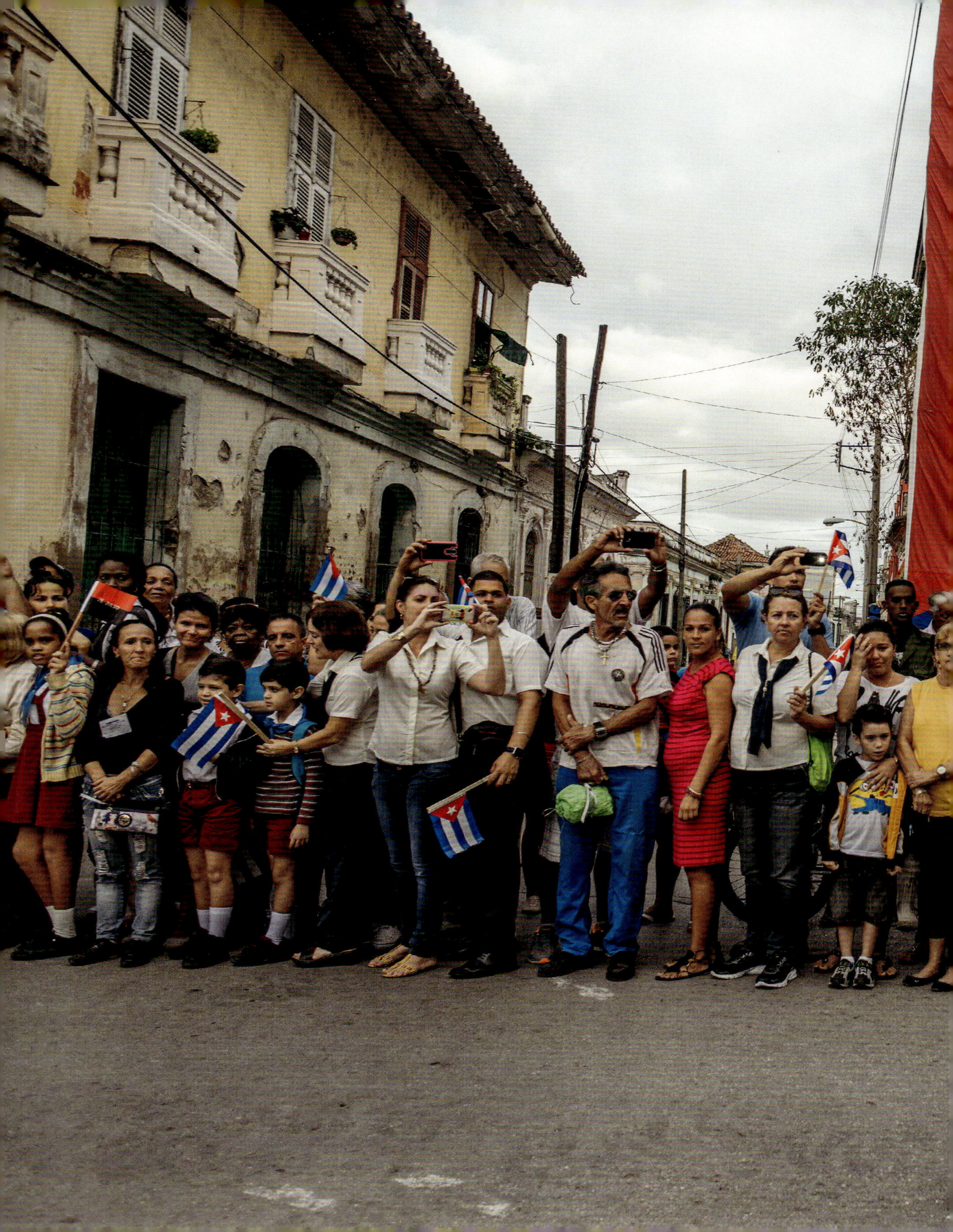

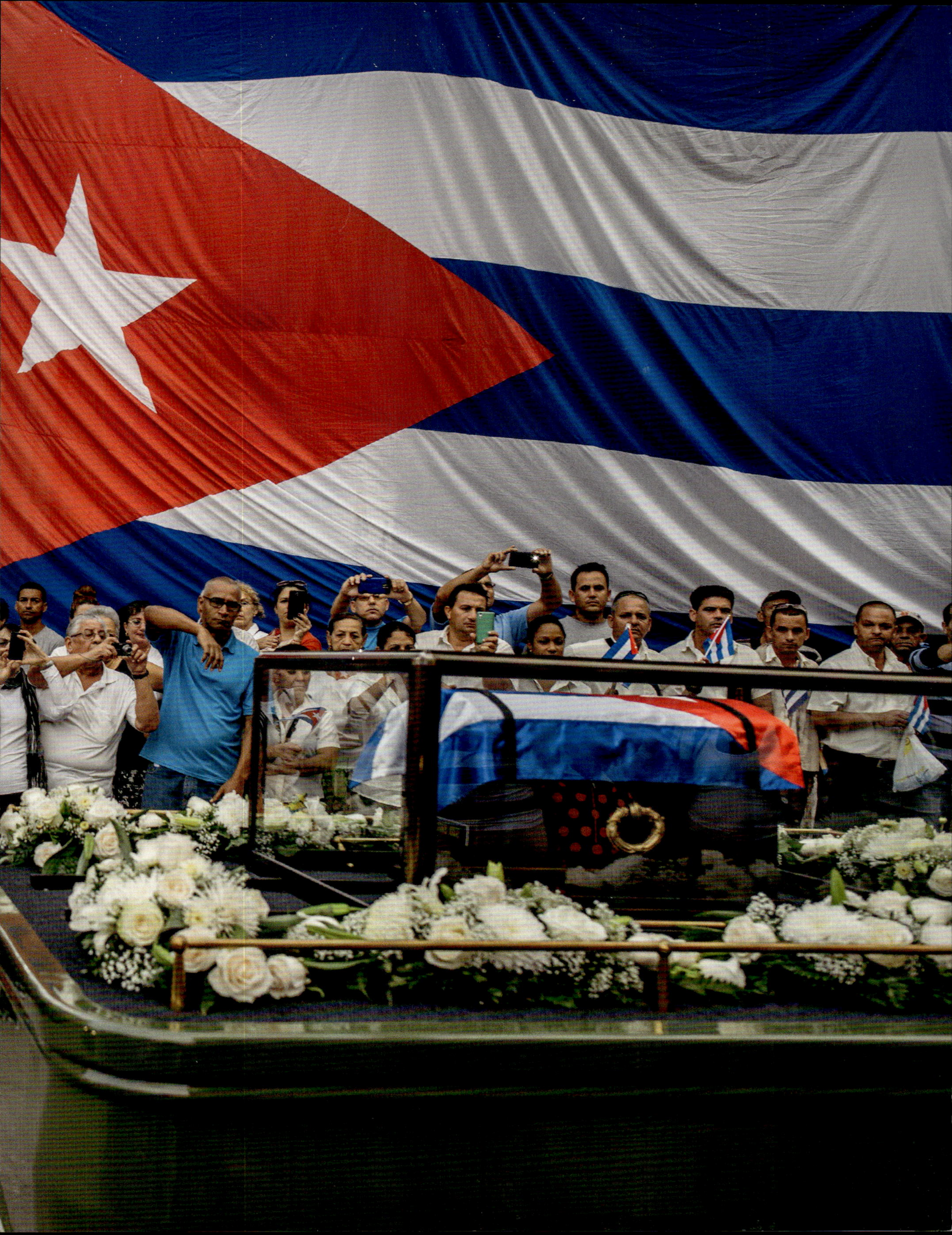

Elena Anosova

Russia /
2nd Prize Daily Life

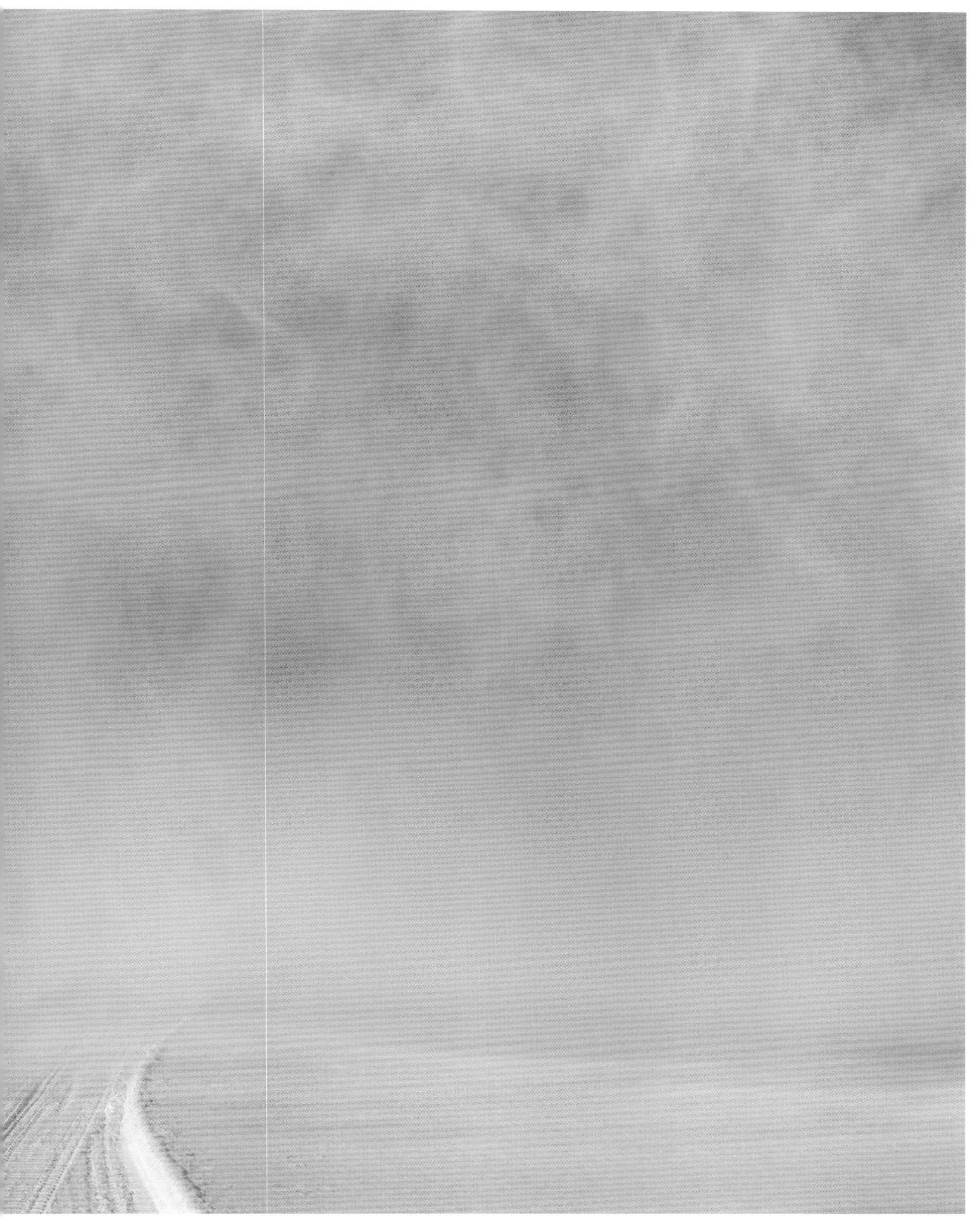

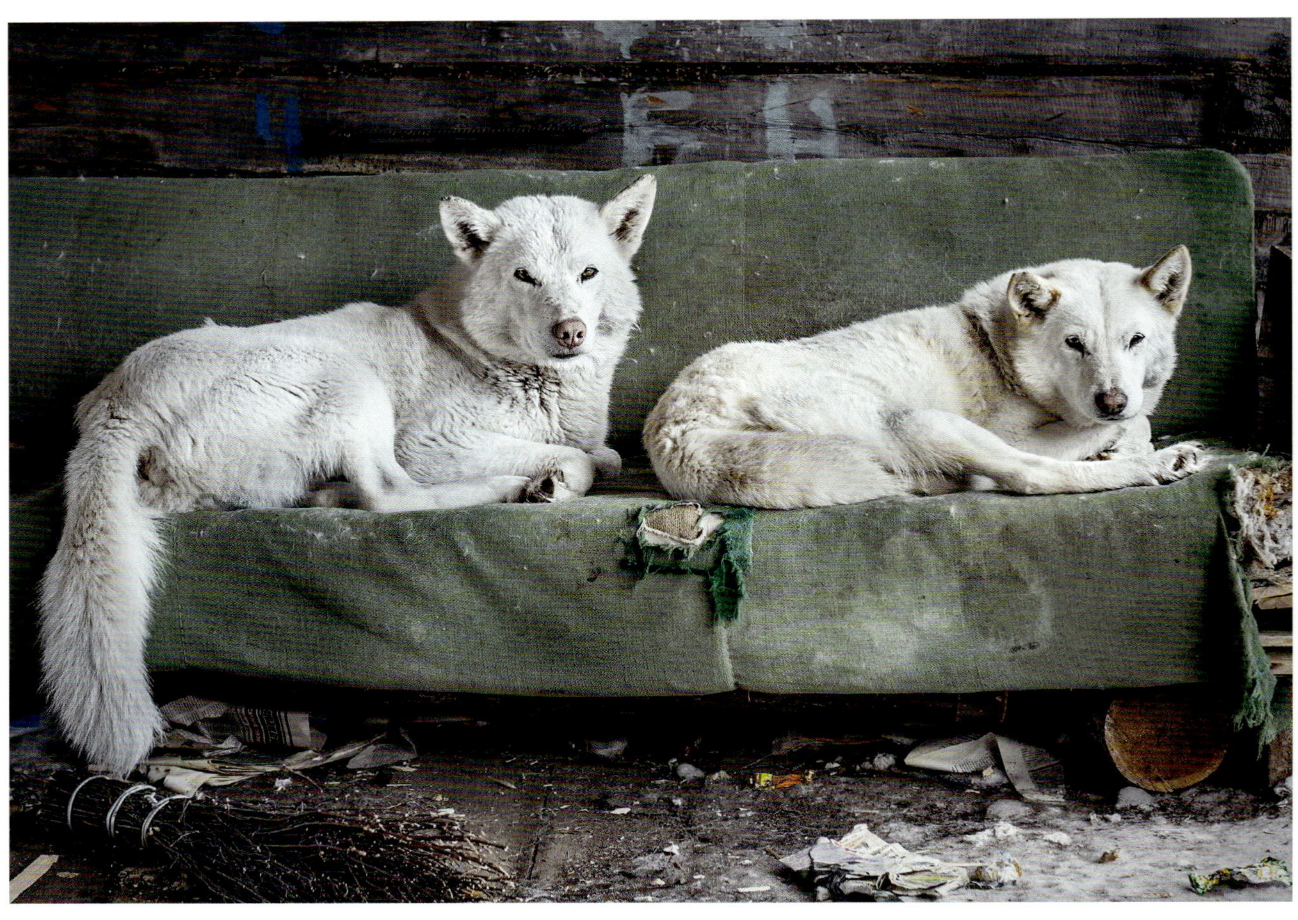

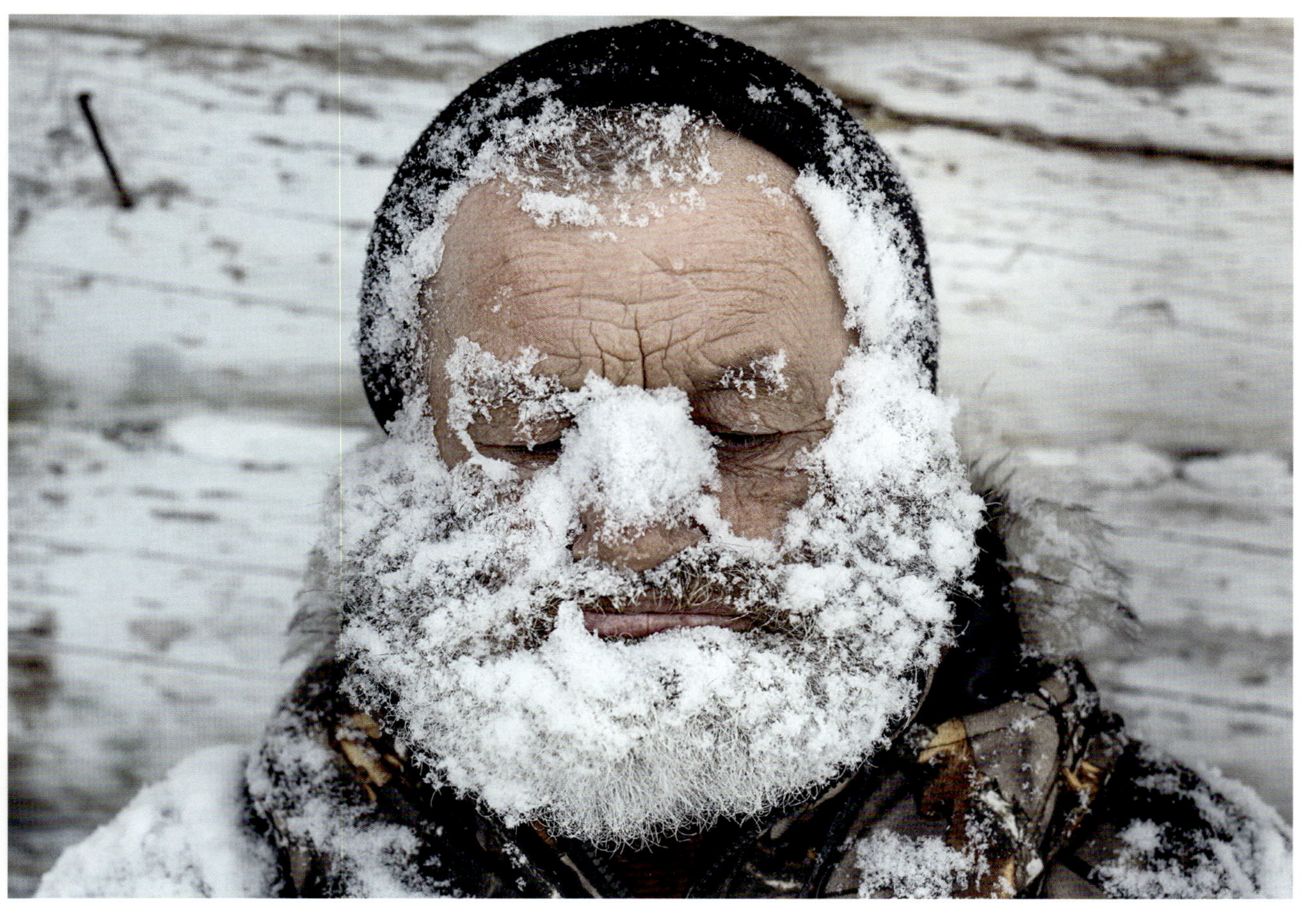

Life in a small settlement near the Nizhnyaya Tunguska River, in the far north of Russia, is one of extreme isolation. Change over the centuries has been gradual. About 100 adults live in the settlement; there are no roads and the nearest town is 300 kilometers away. *Previous spread*: Snowmobile tracks stretch across the snow. People also use skis and horses for transportation. *Facing page*: Dogs sleep outside all year round. Local crossbreeds are known for their hunting skills. *Above*: A local hunter washes his face with snow. (*continues*)

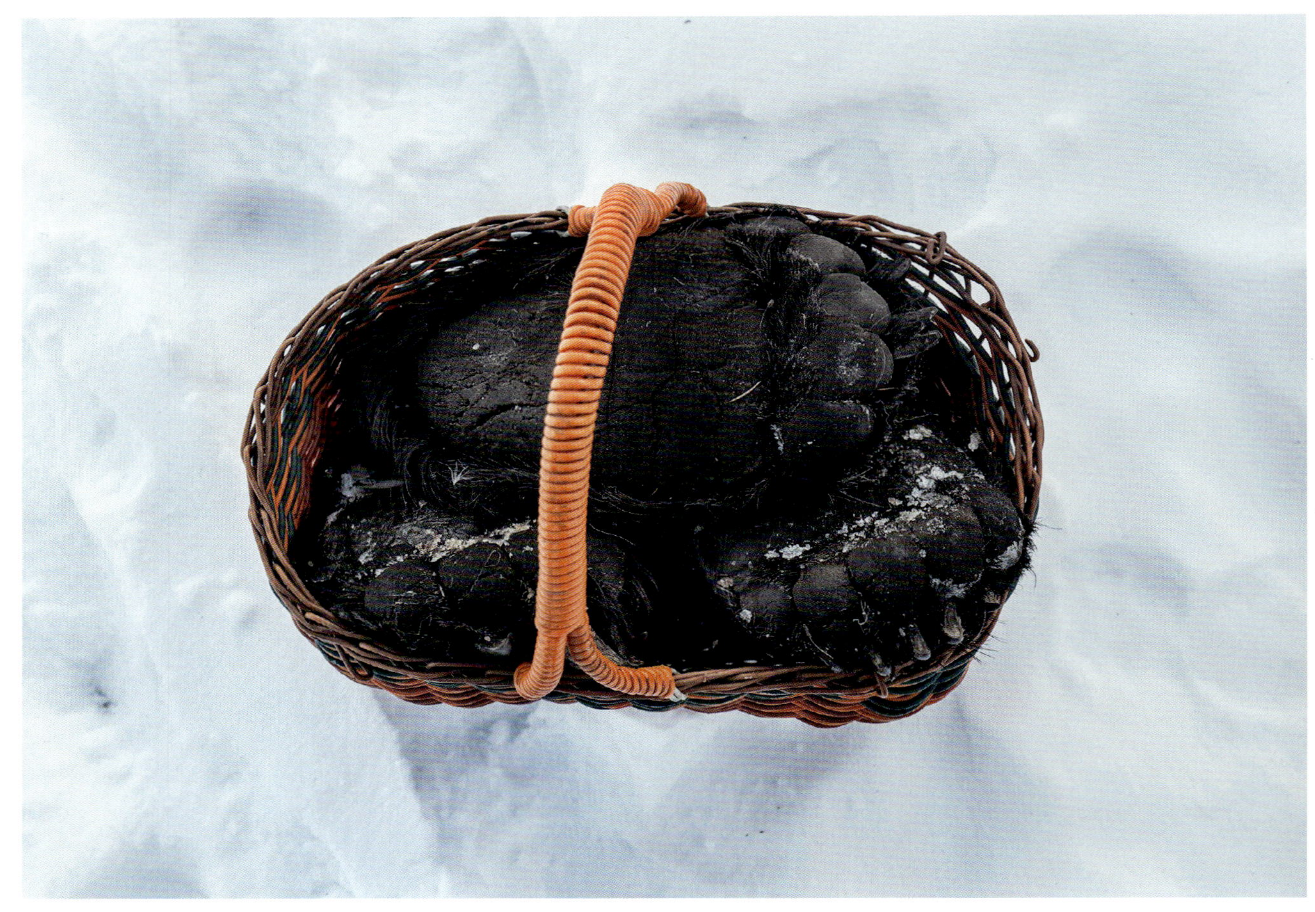

(*continued*) Electricity, supplied by a diesel generator, is available only in the mornings and evenings. Temperatures in winter average -45° Celsius. Hunting and the fur trade form a significant part of the local economy. *Above*: The paws of a rogue bear. Bears are not usually hunted as their meat is often infected and not fit for human consumption, but the paws are valued in Chinese medicine. *Facing page*: The head of a moose defrosts on the table in preparation for New Year festivities. Moose lips are considered a delicacy. *Following spread*: A bearskin is stretched out on a wall. The animal was killed after prowling the village at night, and entering the house.

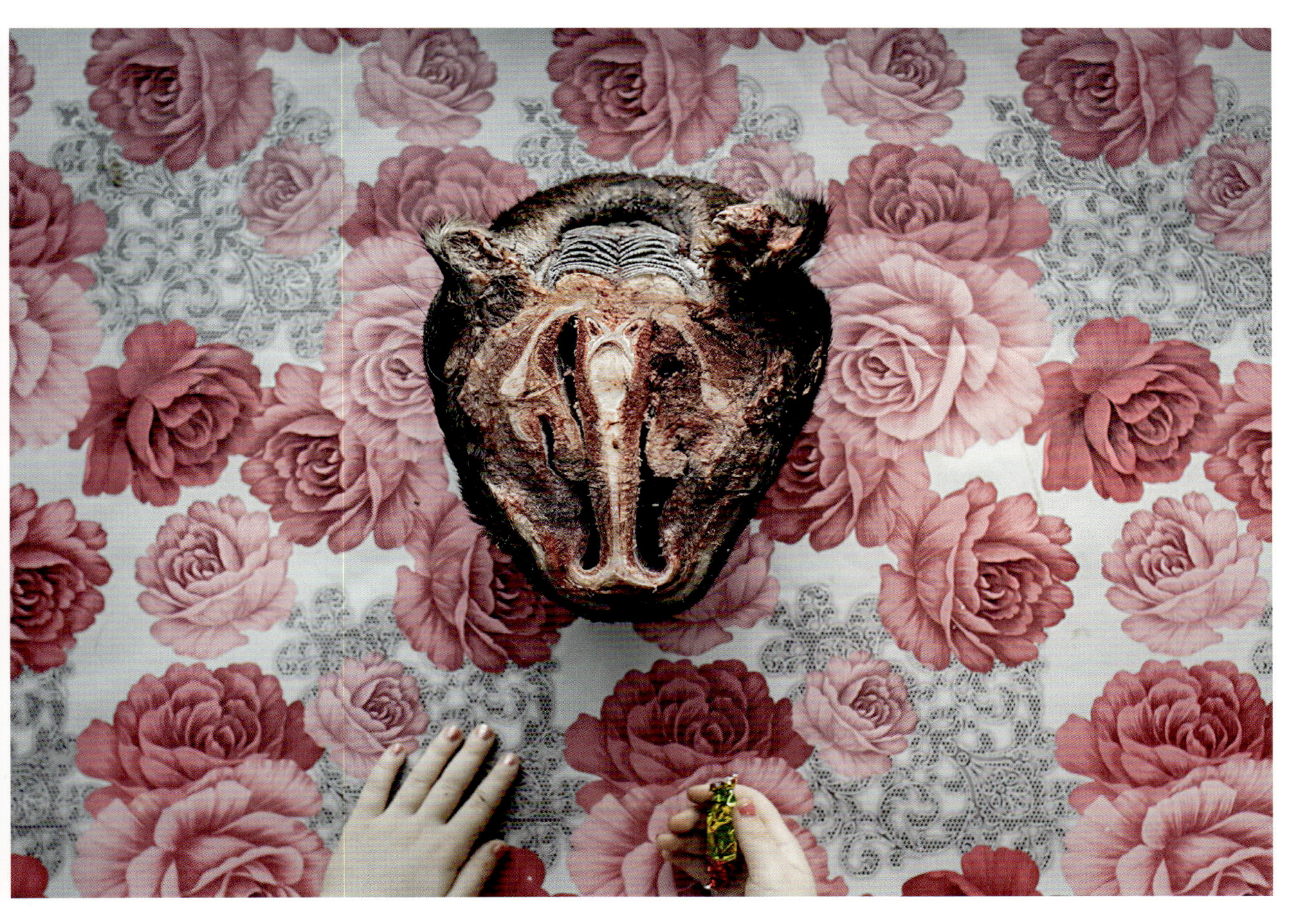

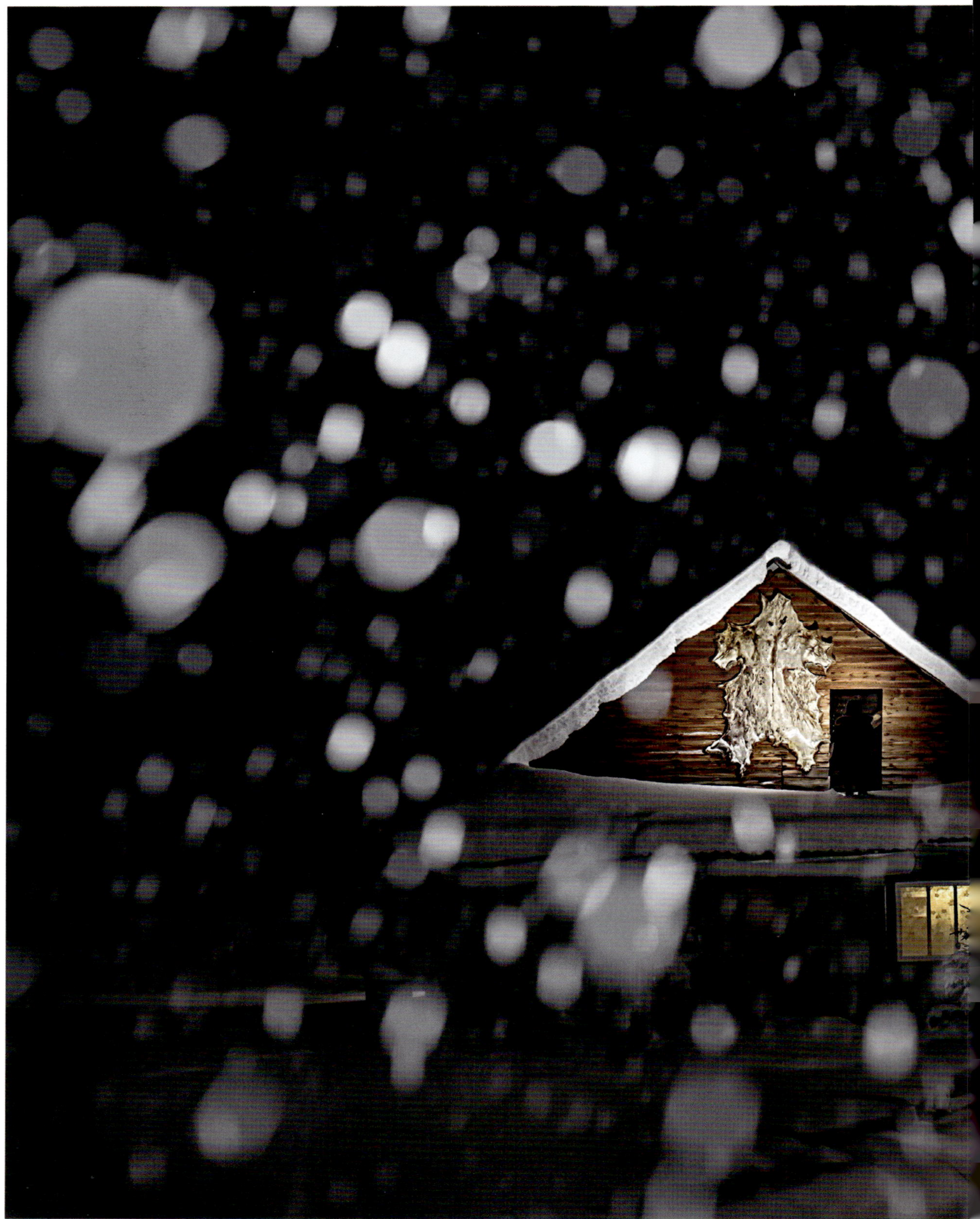

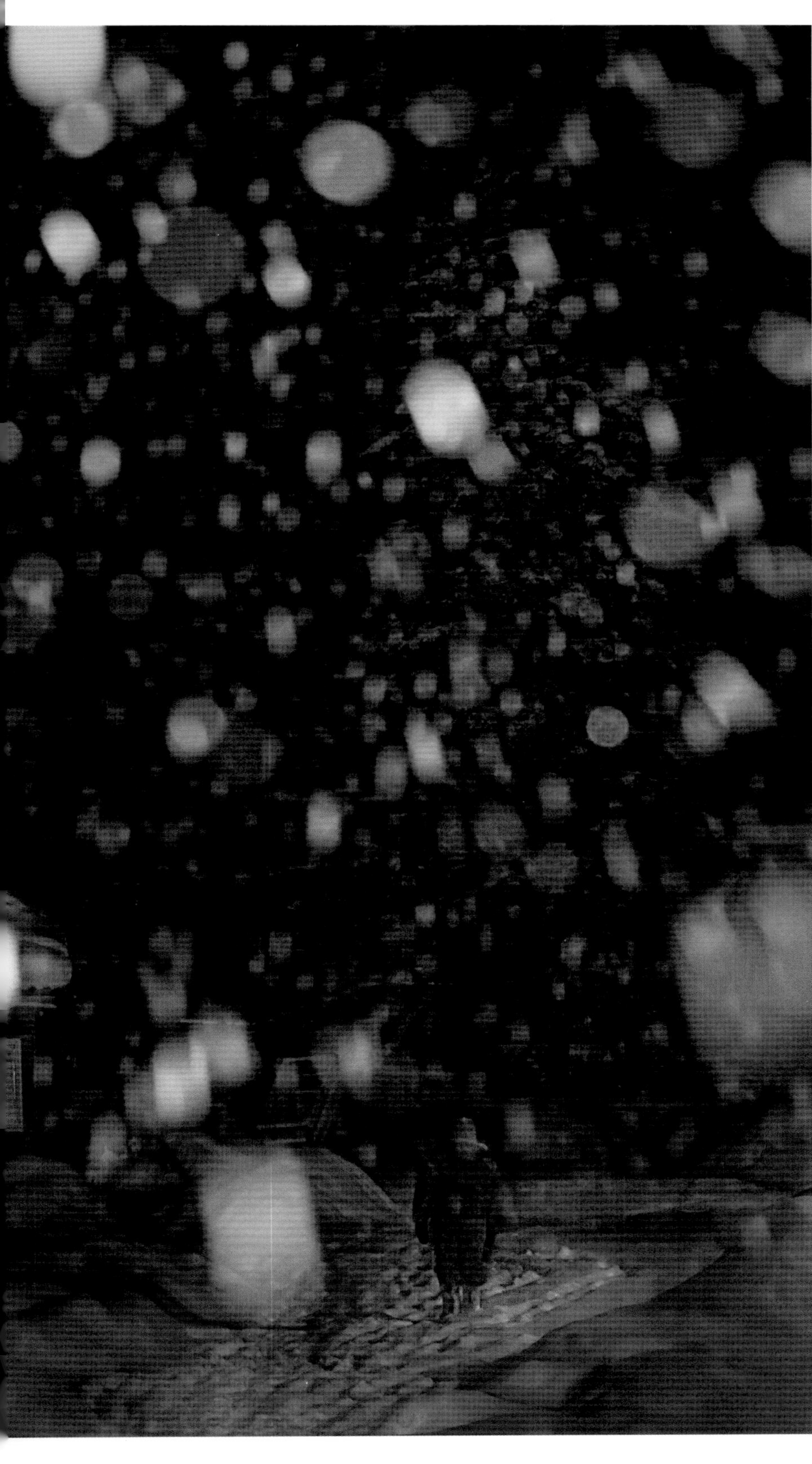

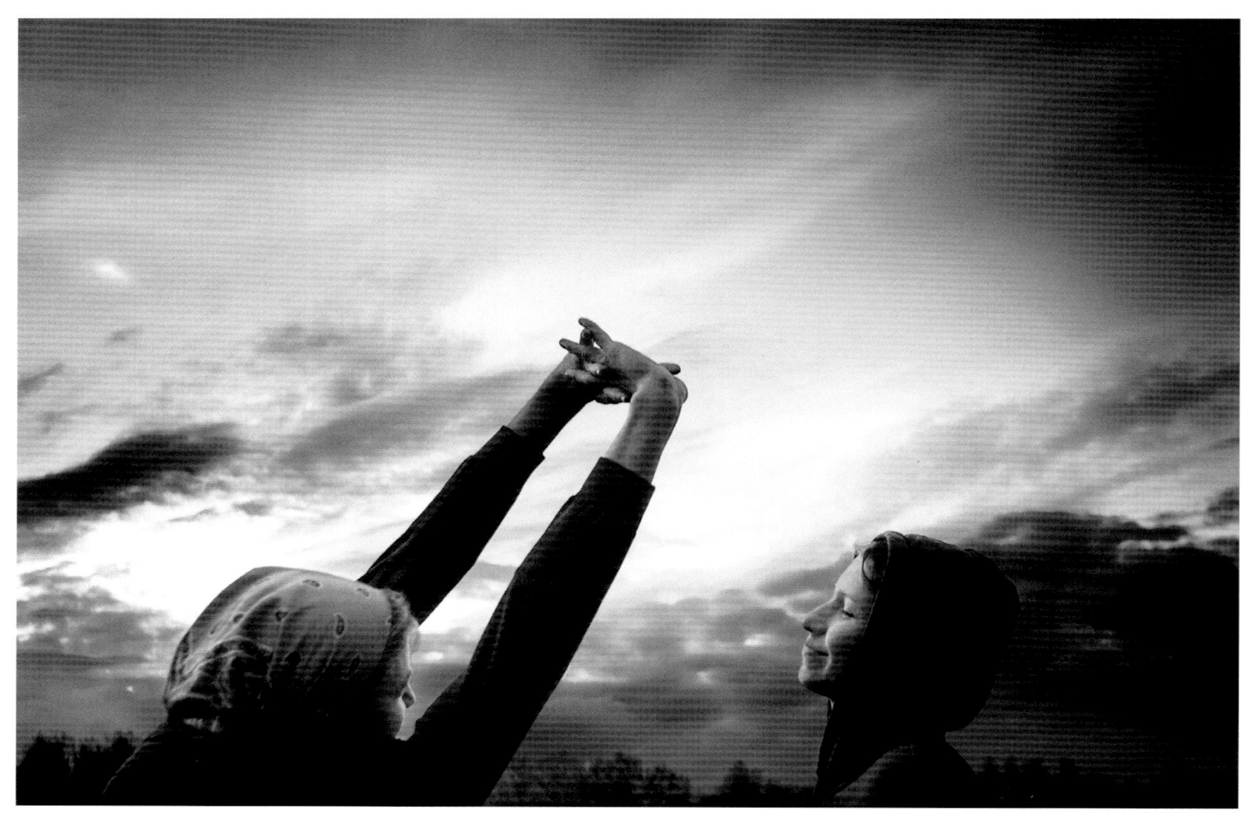

Francesco Comello

Italy /

3rd Prize Daily Life

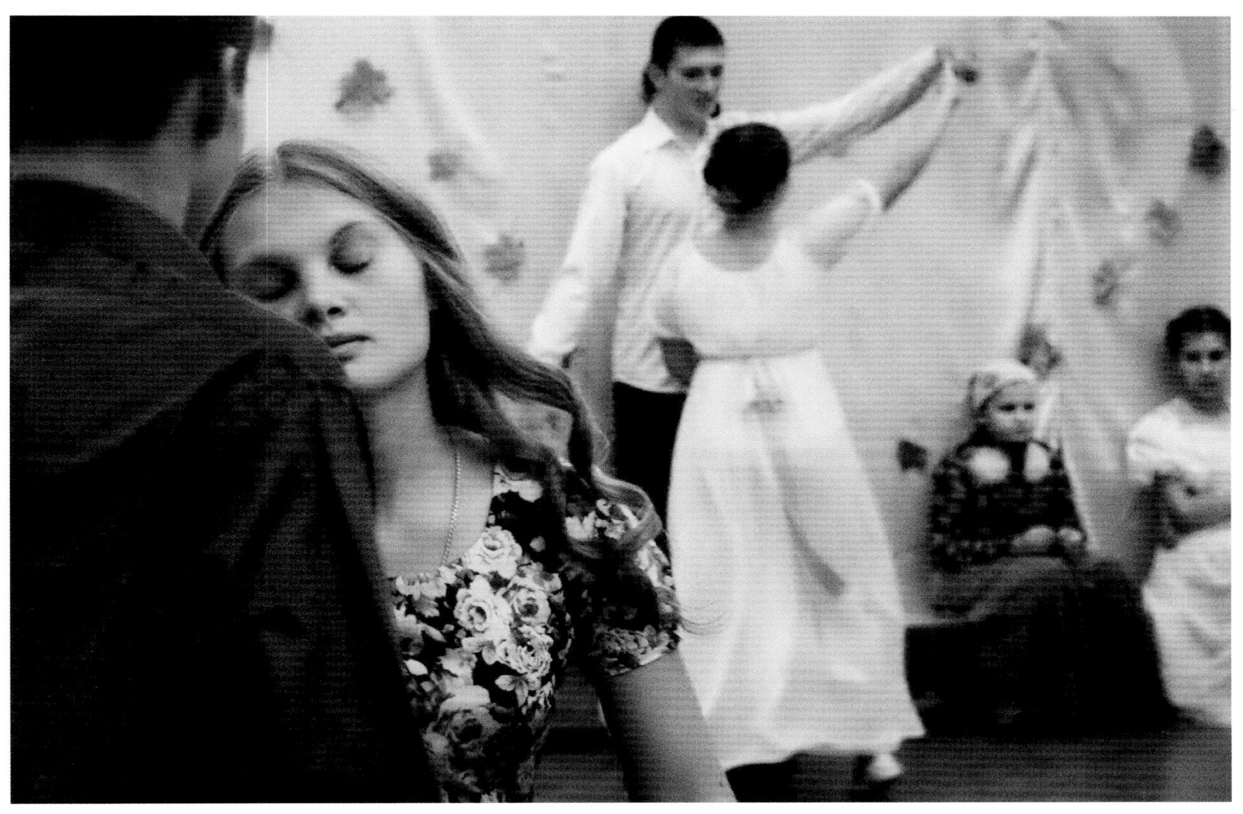

The Isle of Salvation is a reclusive spiritual and educational community on the busy road between Moscow and Yaroslavl in Russia. It was founded in the 1990s by an orthodox priest, and initially comprised some 30 people, dedicated to living a holy life. *Facing page*: Maria and Alexandra help harvest potatoes. They have become inseparable friends. *Above*: The community holds an autumn ball, for which the women sew their own dresses. (*continues*)

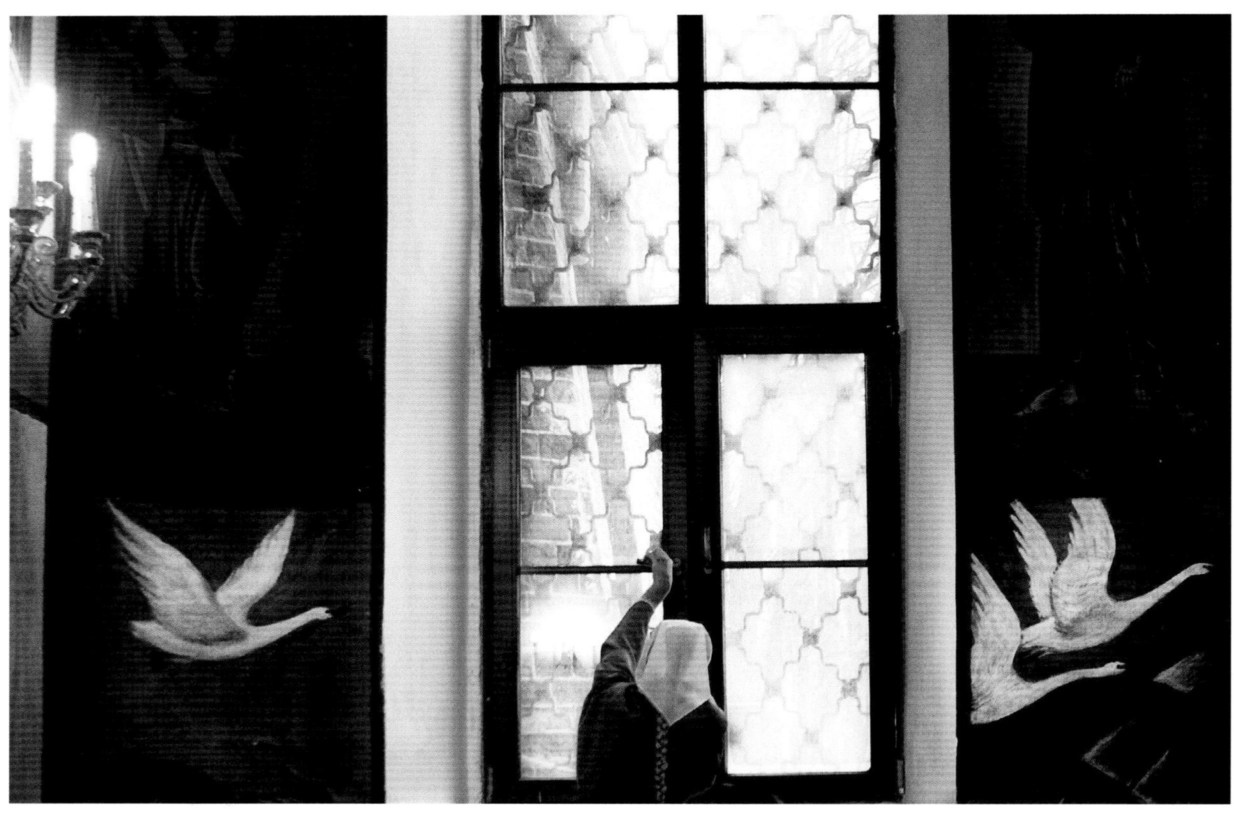

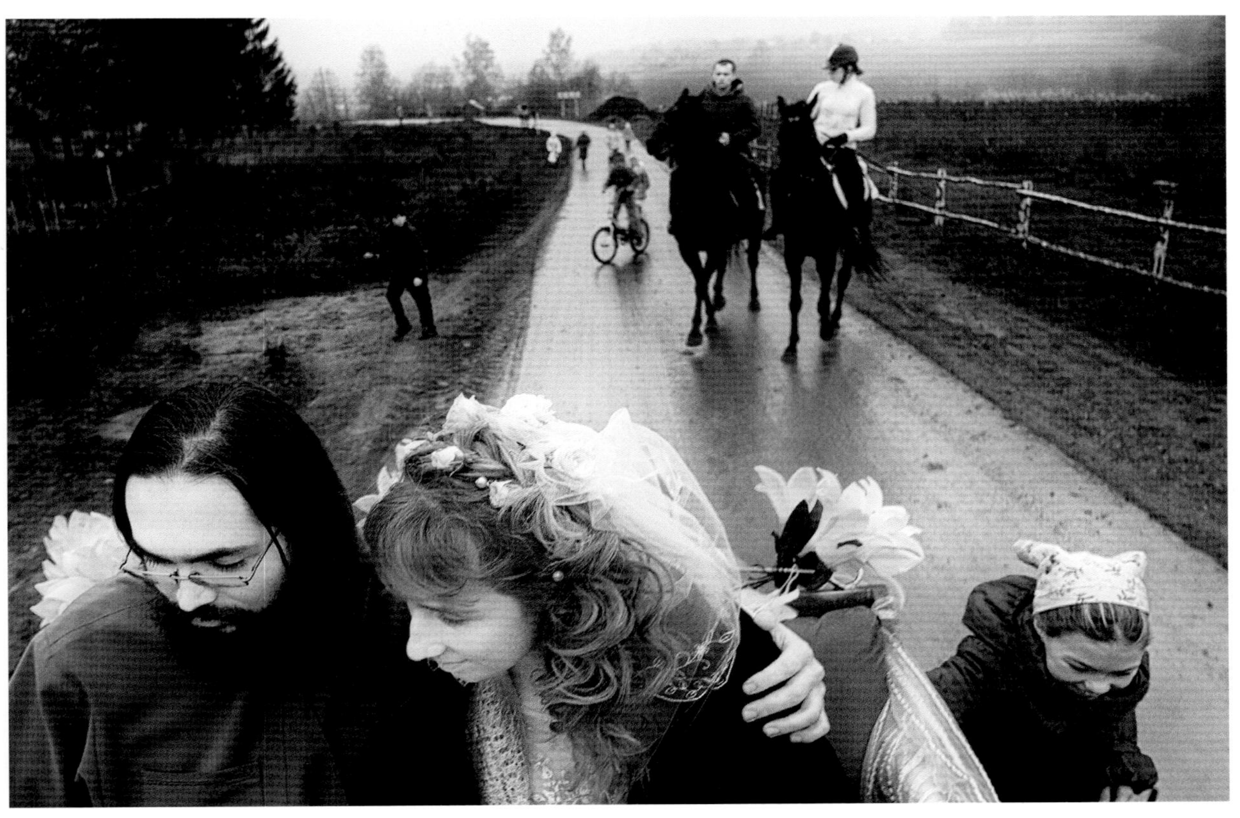

(*continued*) The community now looks after children with family or social problems. Around 300 boys and girls are cared for by the Isle of Salvation. *Facing page*: The community church, rebuilt in the 1990s, was partially destroyed during the Soviet era. *Above*: Vladimir and Vittoria, both former residents, return to the Isle of Salvation to be married. (*continues*)

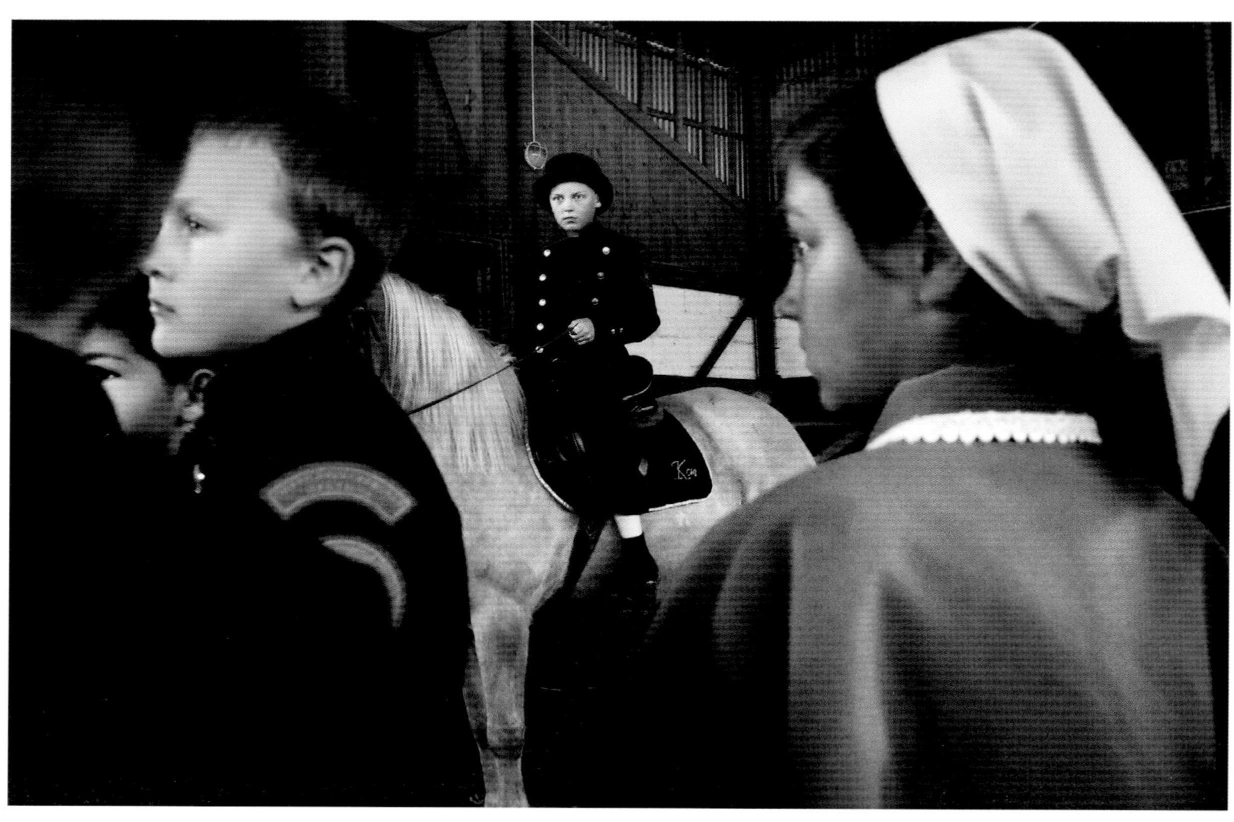

(*continued*) There is no TV, no internet and no money in circulation—all are deemed society's evils. The focus is on God and fatherland and on spiritual and physical development. People work the land, study and dance. *Facing page*: The community keeps around 30 horses. Students have daily riding lessons with Cossack instructors. *Above*: A view of the village.

Michael Vince Kim

USA /
1st Prize People

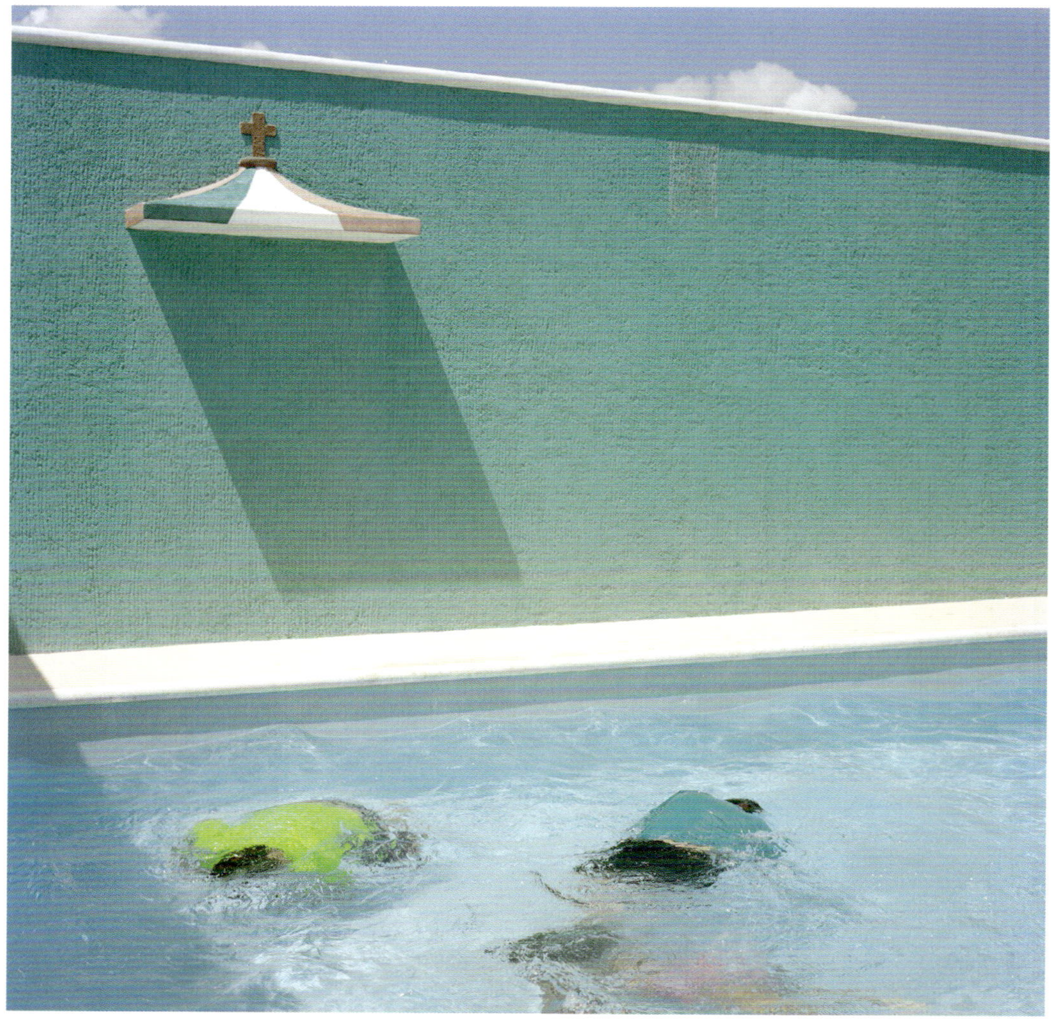

In 1905, around 1,000 Koreans arrived in Mexico aboard the *SS Ilford*. They alighted in Salina Cruz in the state of Oaxaca, and then traveled by steamboat to Progreso, on the Yucatán Peninsula. The Koreans had departed an impoverished country and were promised future prosperity, but were destined instead to be indentured laborers—a form of bonded contract labor in which they were forced to work for low wages for four or five years. *Above*: Young Korean-Mayans play around in the pool at the 90th birthday party of a second-generation relative. *Facing page*: The coastal town of Progreso. (*continues*)

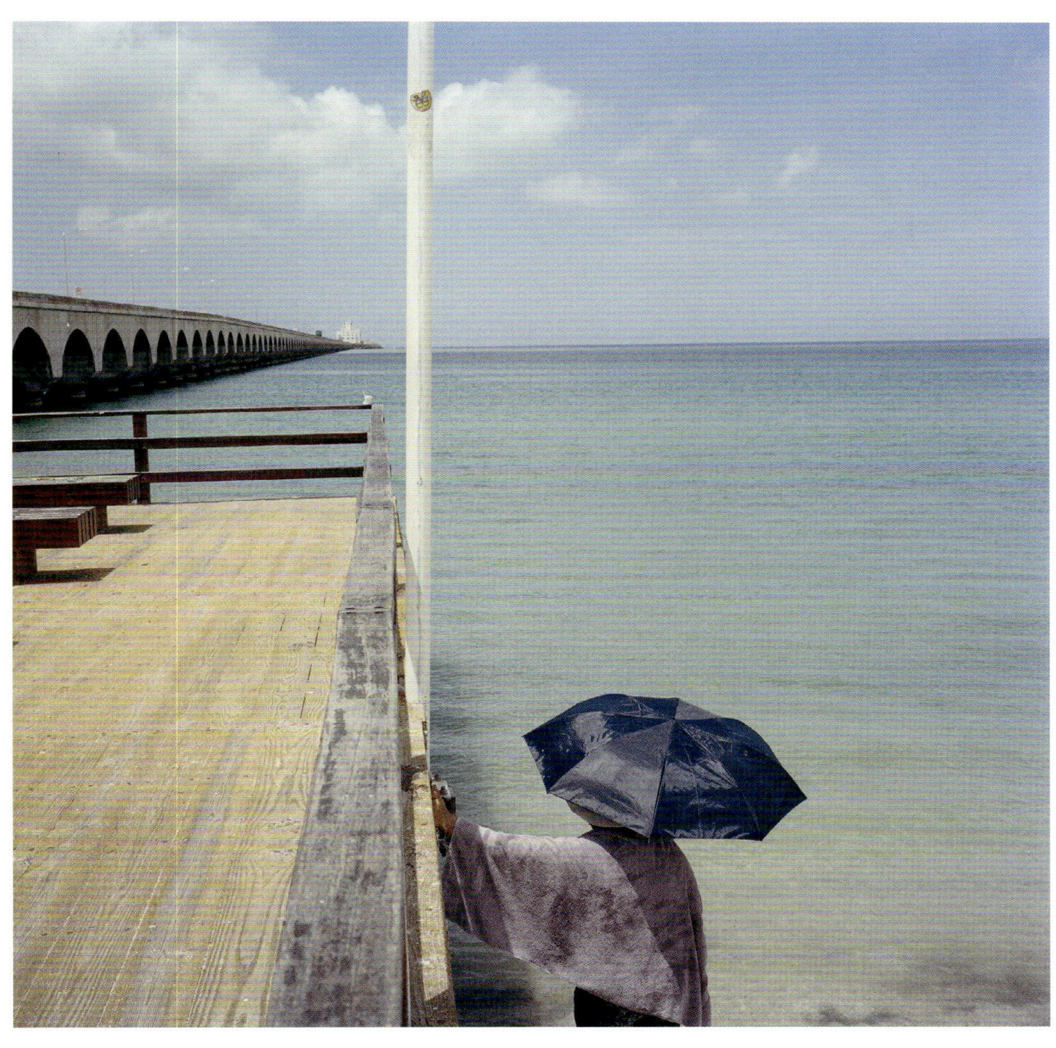

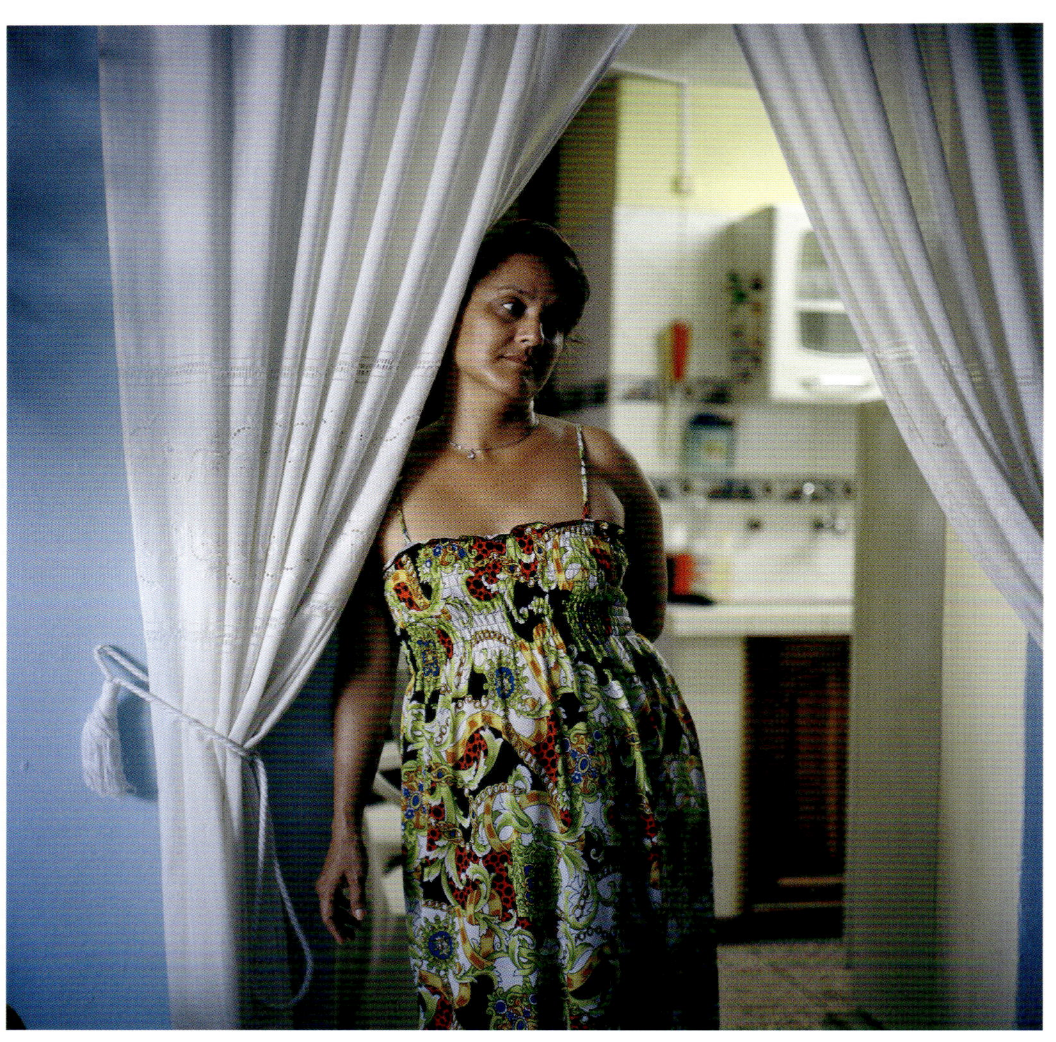

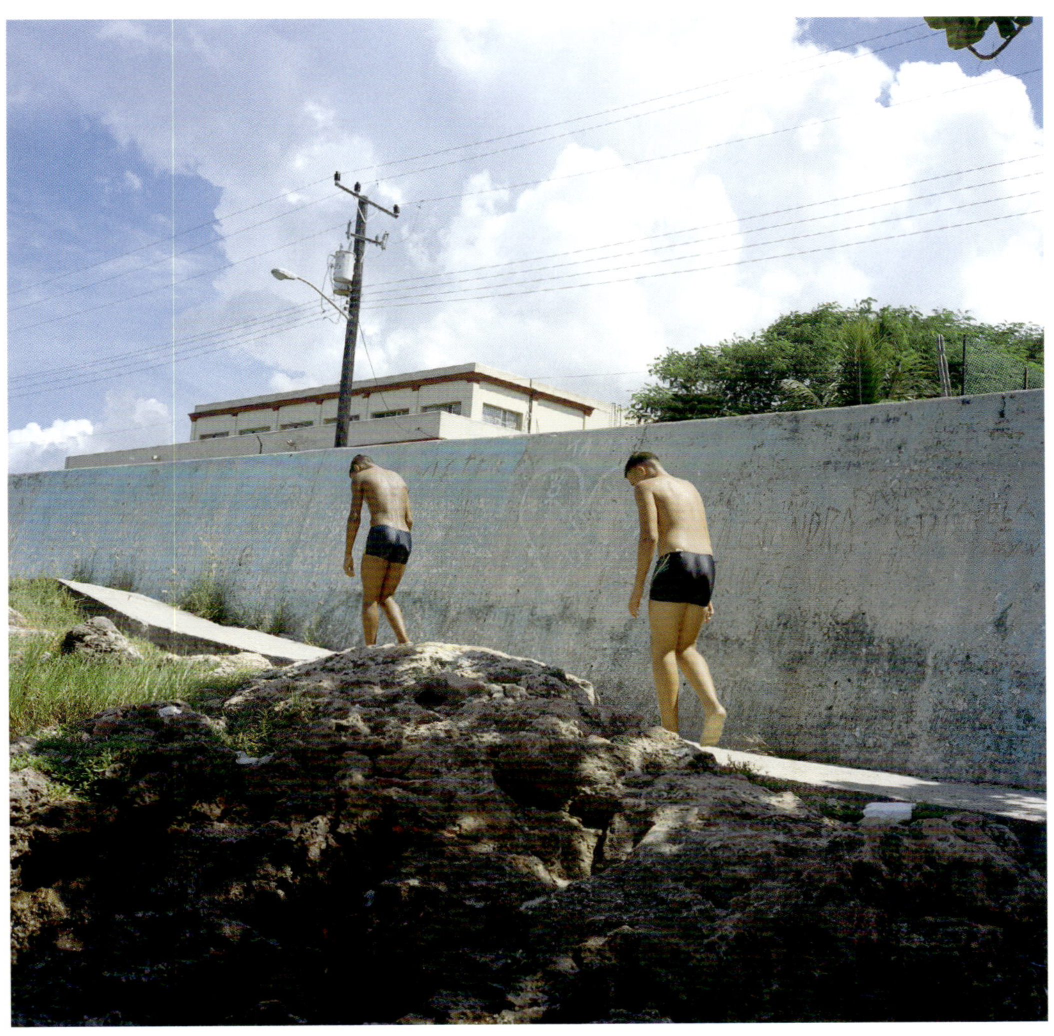

(*continued*) The immigrants were set to work on henequen plantations. Henequen, a variety of agave plant used in rope making, generated vast revenues for Mexico. Most laborers expected to return to their homeland, but by 1910 Korea had been incorporated into the Japanese Empire, and so many decided to stay in Mexico. With the decline in demand for henequen after World War I, a number of Koreans went on to seek work elsewhere in Mexico and in Cuba. *Facing page*: Sandra Posada Lee, a Korean-Cuban, at home in Matanzas, Cuba. *Above*: Swimming lessons on the beach at Matanzas. (*continues*)

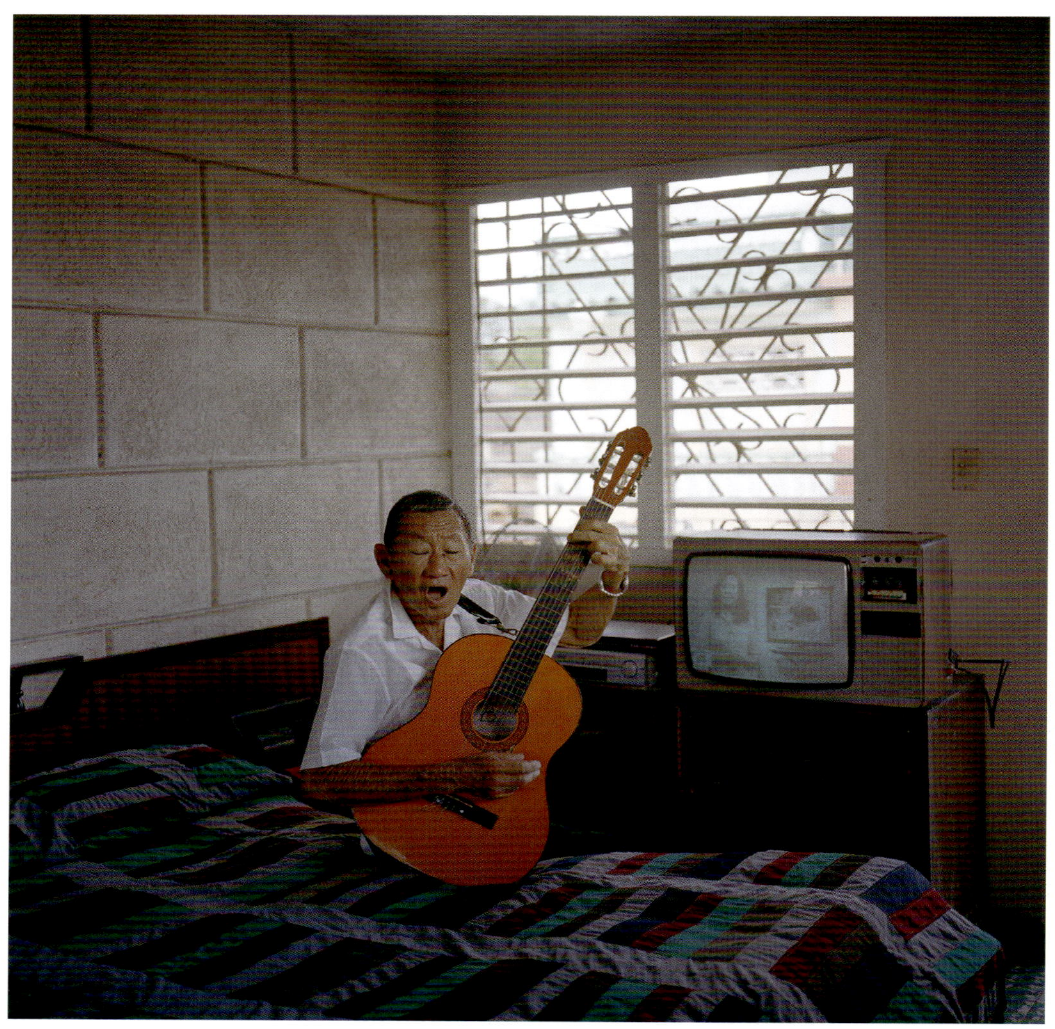

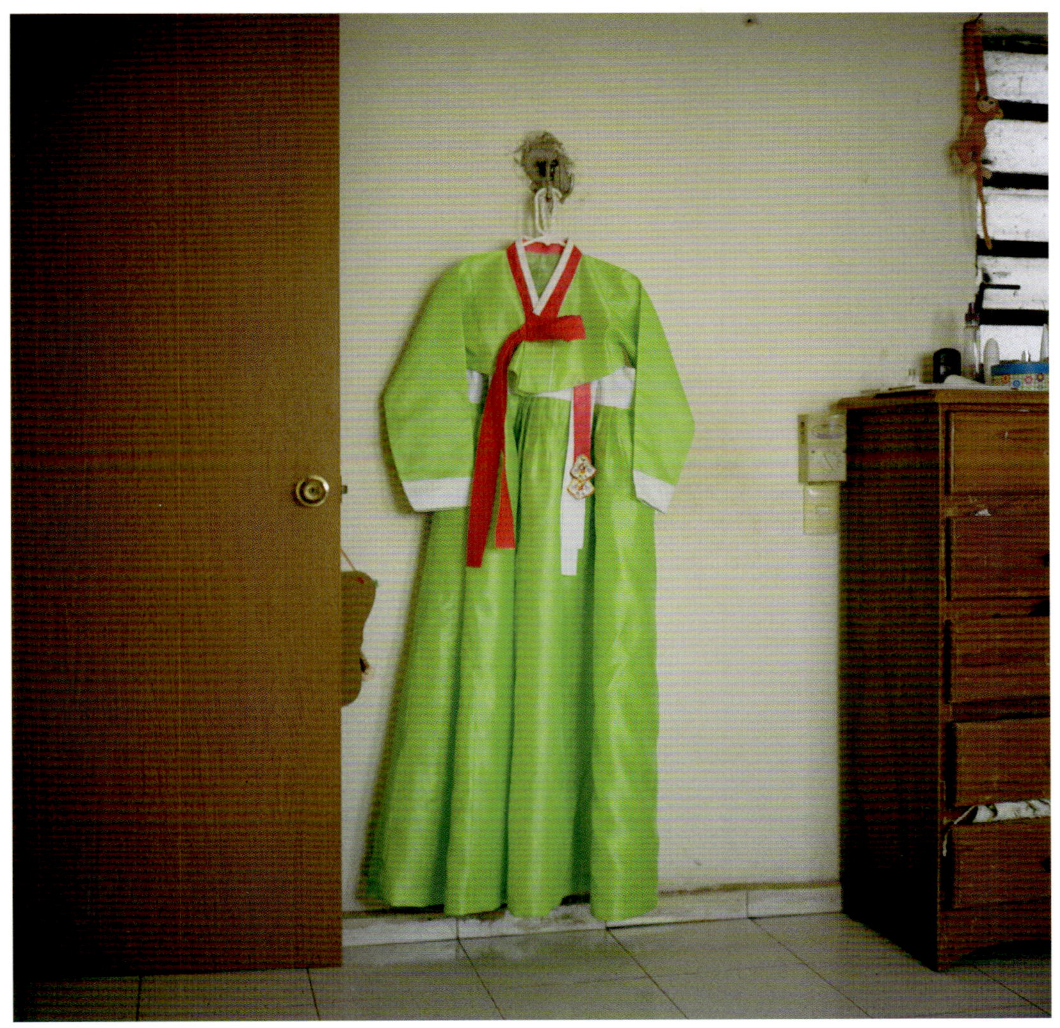

(*continued*) Most of the original Korean immigrants were men, and many went on to marry local Mayan women. *Facing page*: Cecilio Pak Kim, a Korean-Cuban musician, in Cárdenas, Cuba. *Above*: Traditional Korean clothing, belonging to a Korean-Mayan. (*continues*)

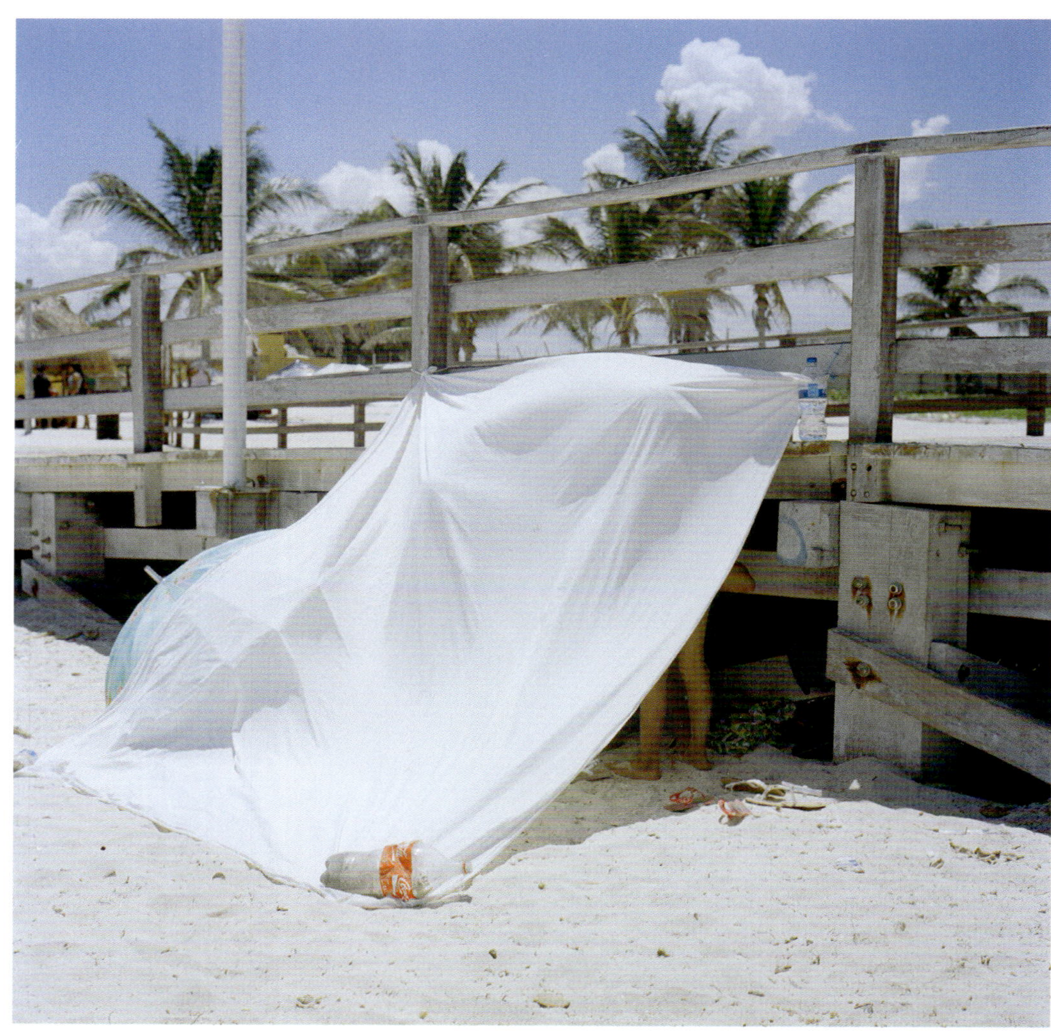

(*continued*) Second-generation Korean-Mexicans often lost their parents' language and traditions. More recently, young people of Korean descent are proving eager to pick up again on their cultural heritage. *Above*: A beach at Progreso, where immigrant Koreans first arrived on the Yucatán Peninsula. *Facing page*: Cecilio Pak Kim, a Korean-Cuban musician, in Cárdenas, Cuba.

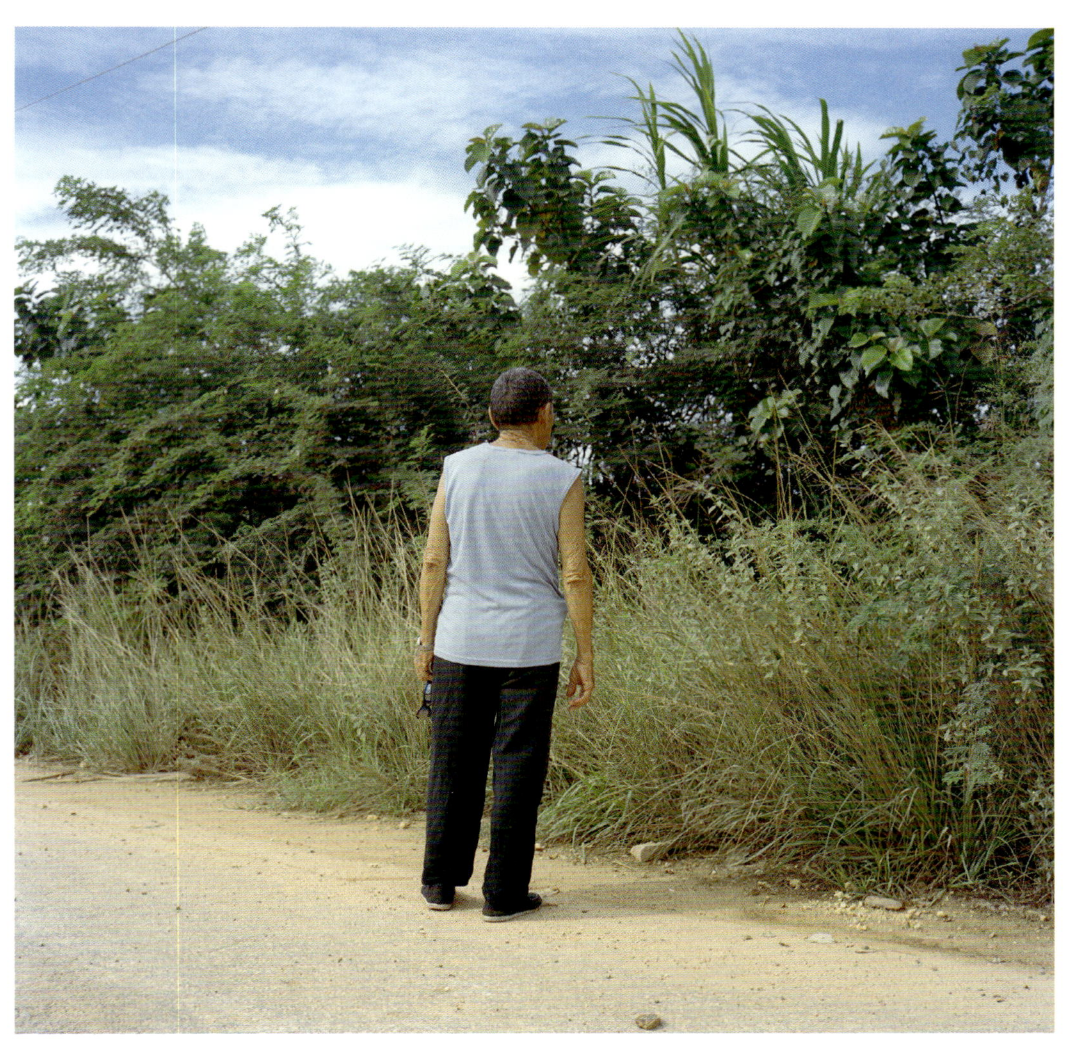

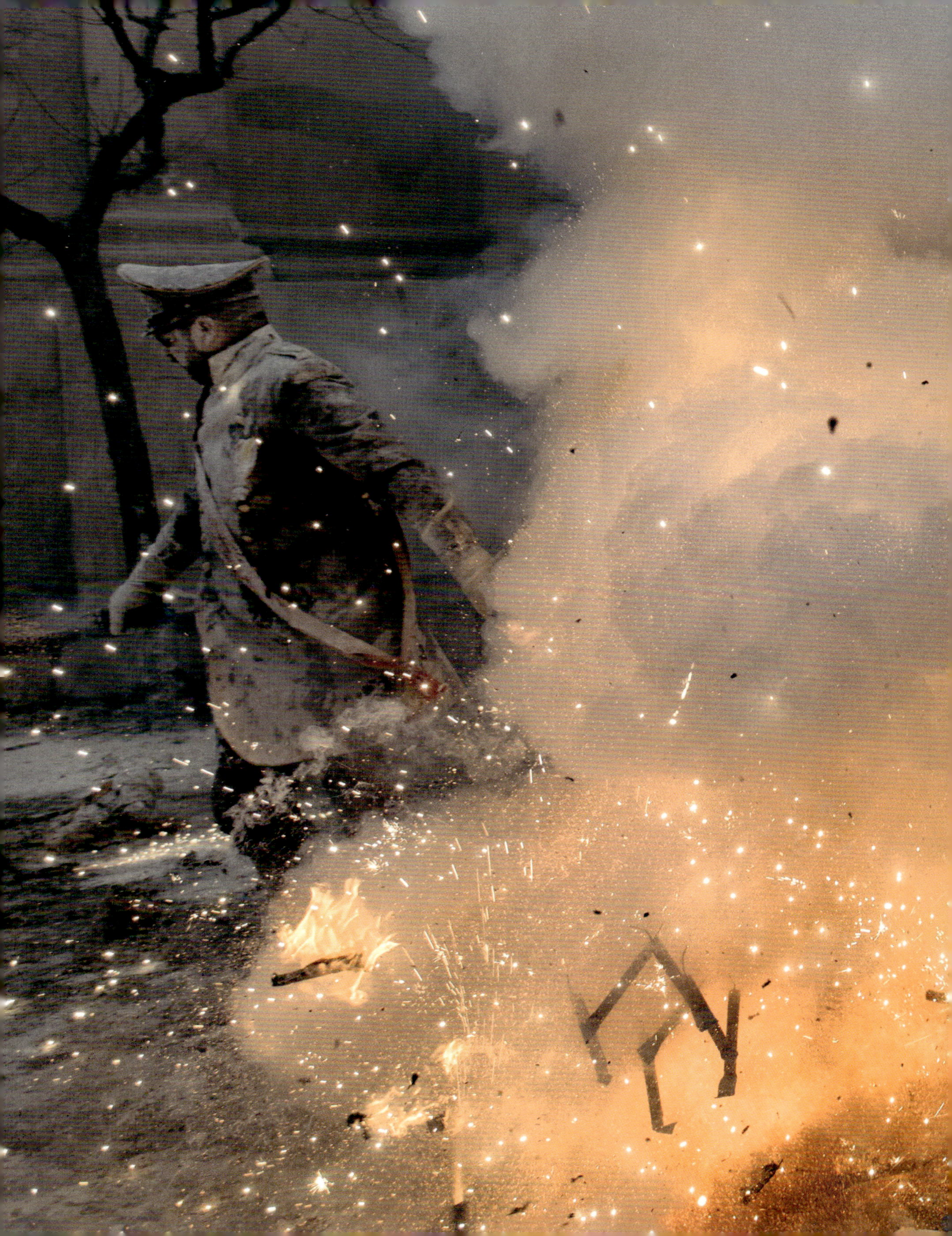

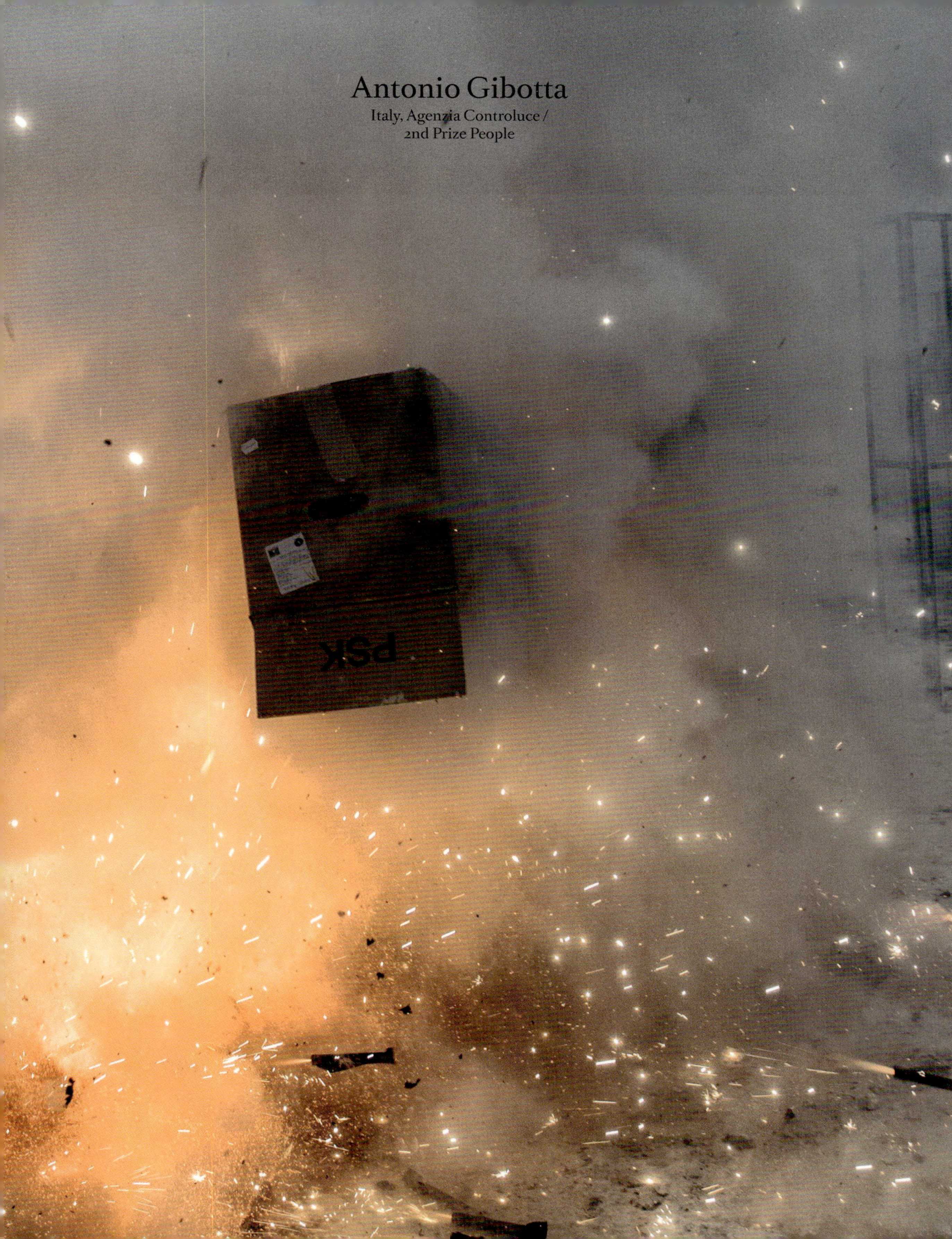

Antonio Gibotta
Italy, Agenzia Controluce /
2nd Prize People

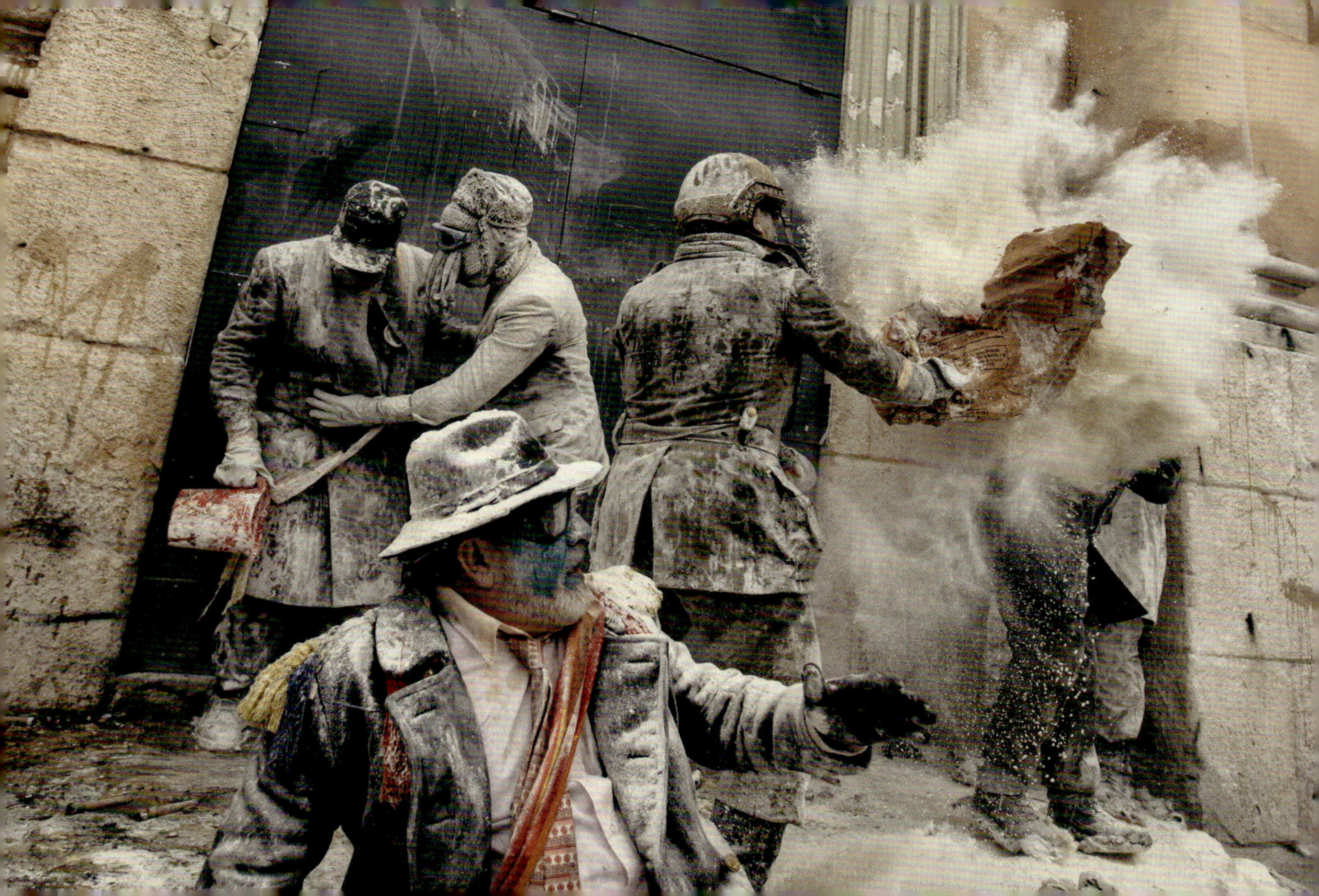

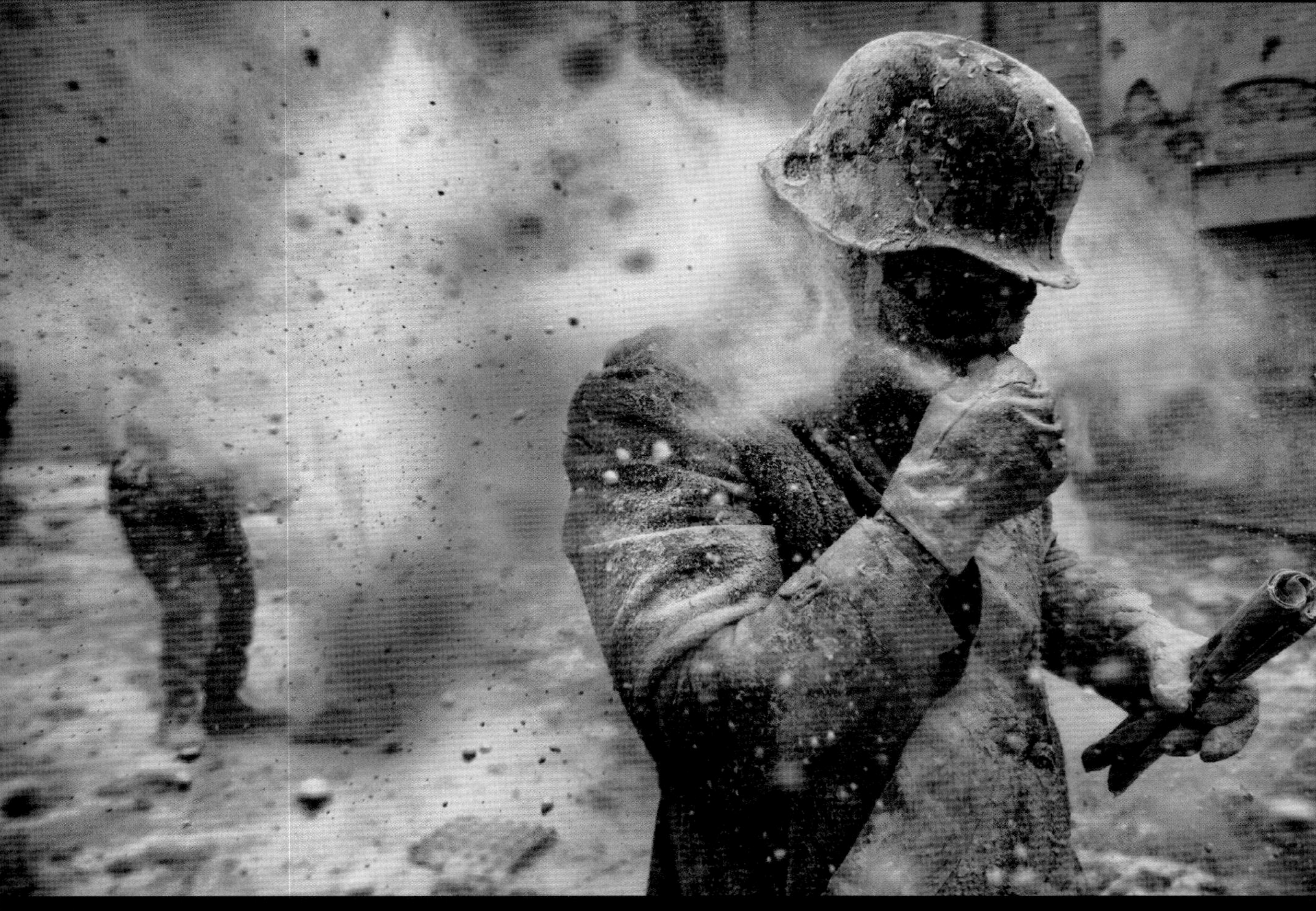

Each year on 28 December, residents of Ibi in Spain stage a mock military coup, pelting each other with flour and eggs and letting off firecrackers. A group of men, 'Els Enfarinats' (The Floured Ones) take control of the town, pronouncing ridiculous laws and fining citizens who infringe them. Another group, 'La Oposicio' (The Opposition) tries to restore order. At the end of the day, the fines are donated to charity. Reputedly 200 years old, the festival was revived in 1981 after long lying dormant.

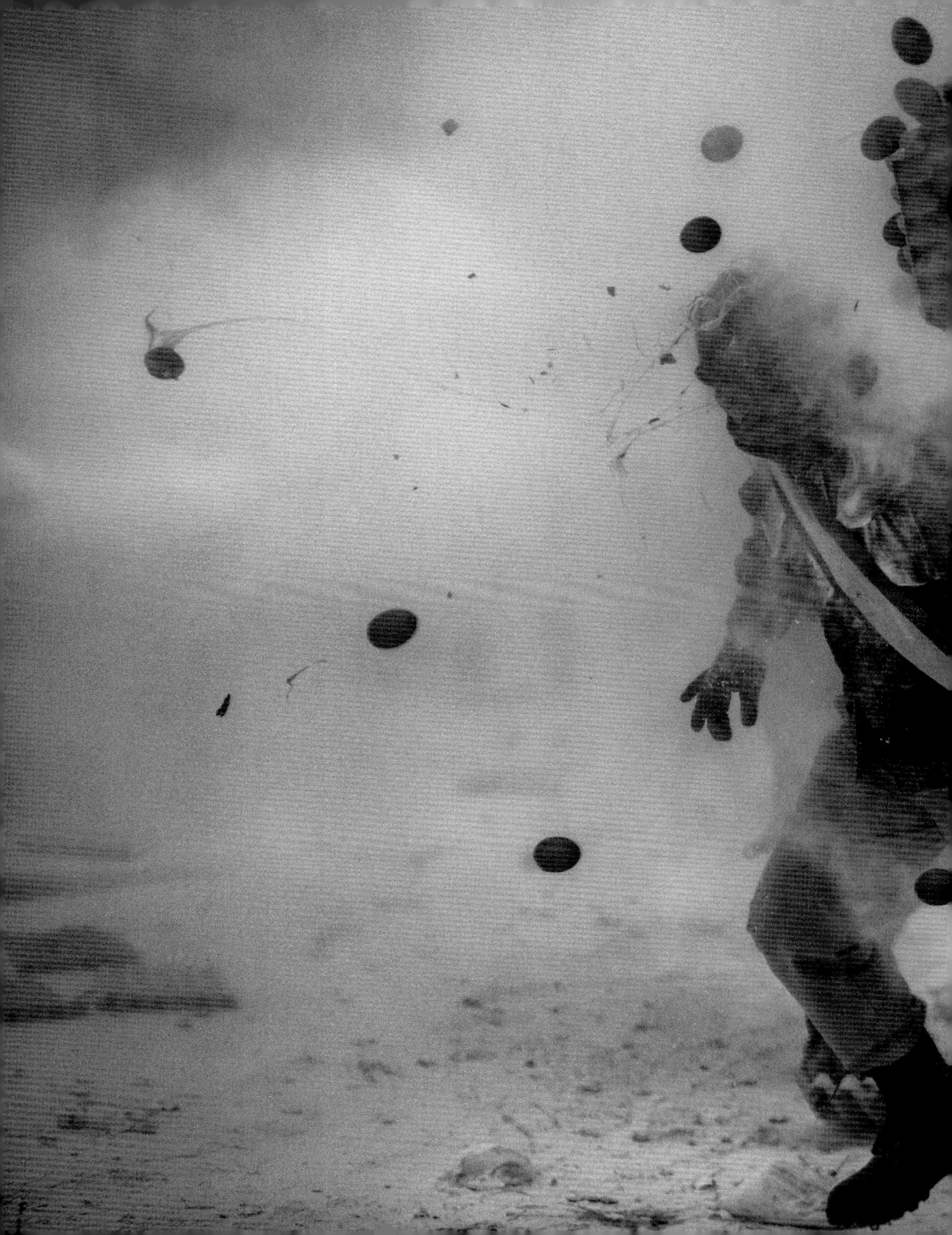

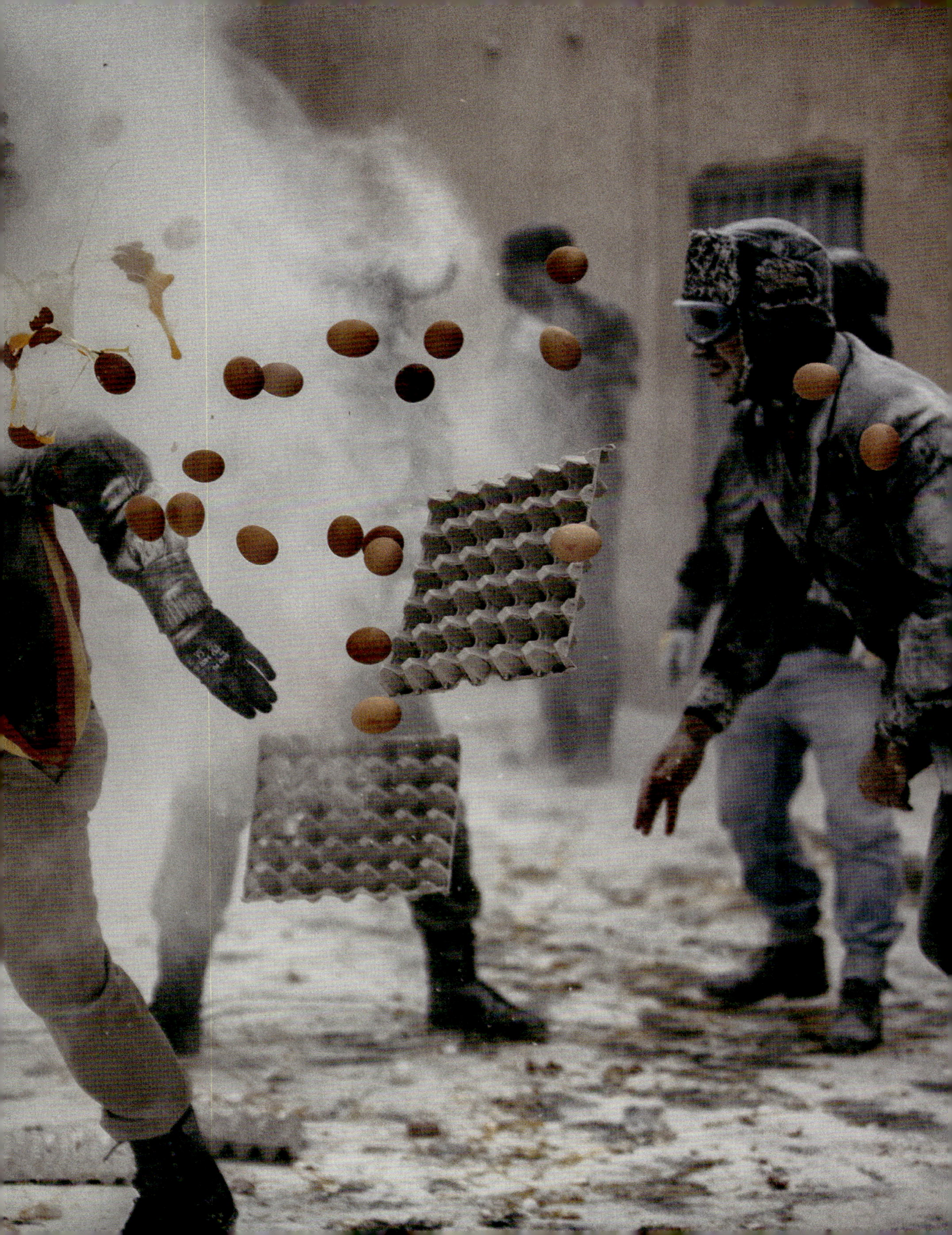

Jay L. Clendenin

USA, *Los Angeles Times* /
3rd Prize People

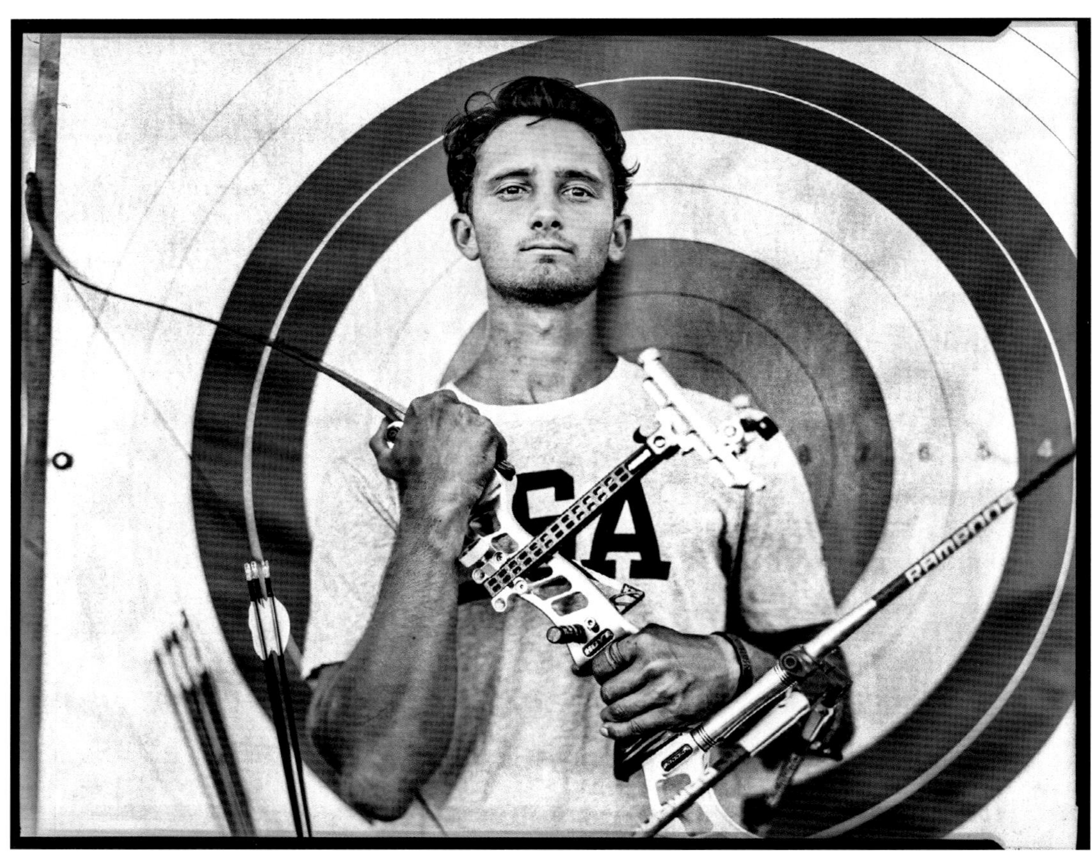

Californian Olympians, headed for the 2016 Rio Olympics, pictured some weeks prior to the event. Zach Garrett, at the Olympic Training Center in Chula Vista, California. This was his first Olympics. Together with others in the US archery team, he brought home a silver medal.

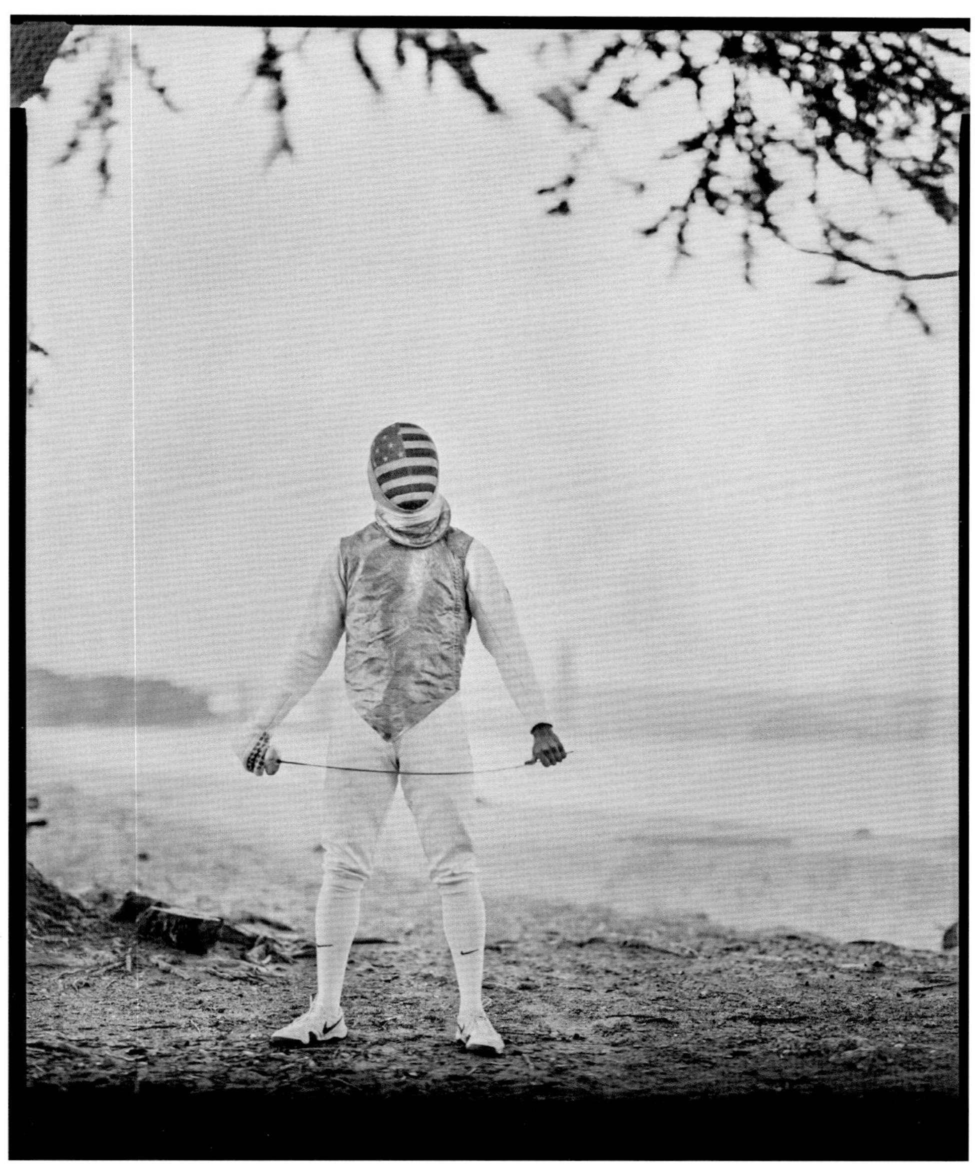

Foil fencer Alexander Massialas, near Chrissy Field, San Francisco. He won a silver medal: a milestone as American men had won no individual fencing medals since 1984, and no silvers since 1932.

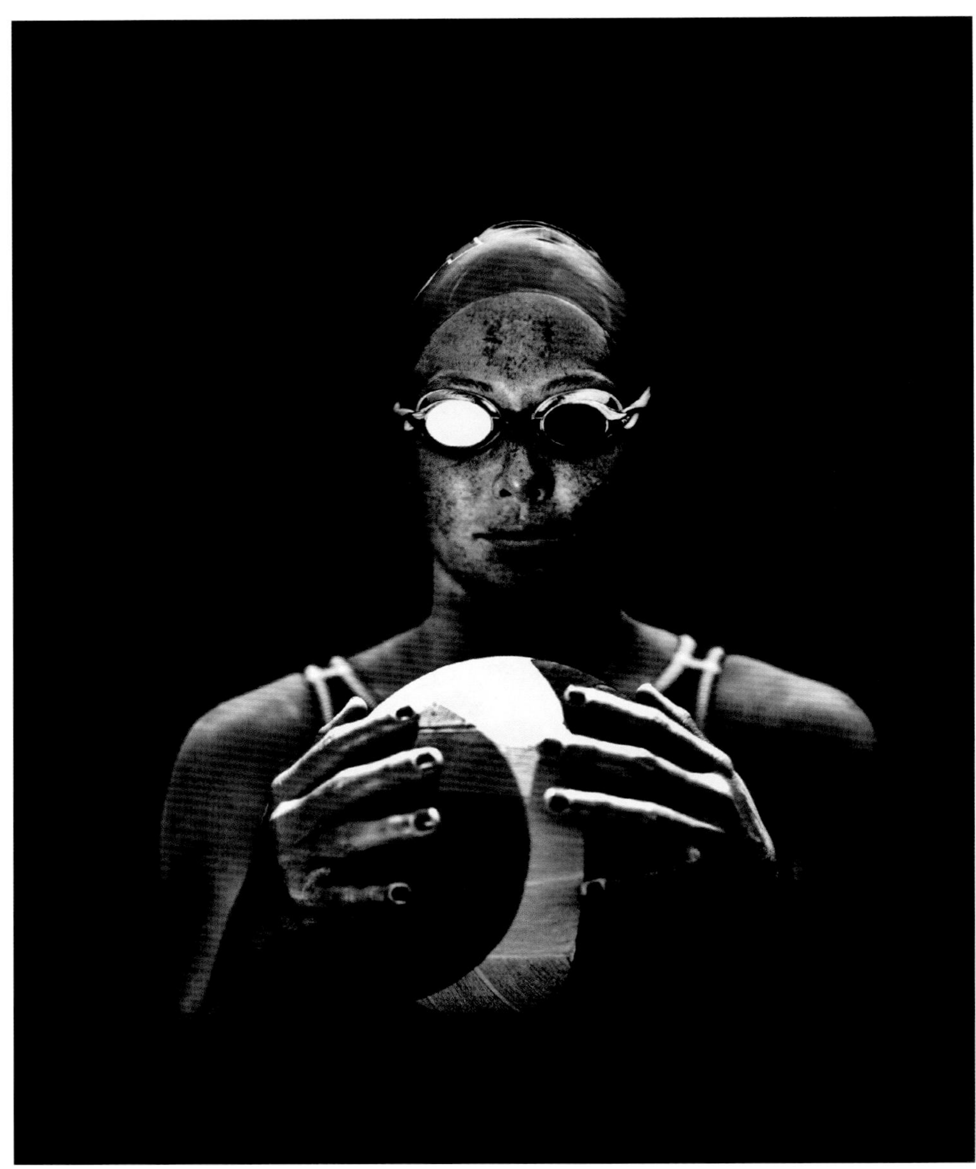

Courtney Mathewson, at the Joint Forces Training Base pool, Los Alamitos, California. She had been part of the US women's water polo team that won gold in the 2012 Olympics. The 2016 team went on to do the same, making it the first back-to-back gold in water polo history.

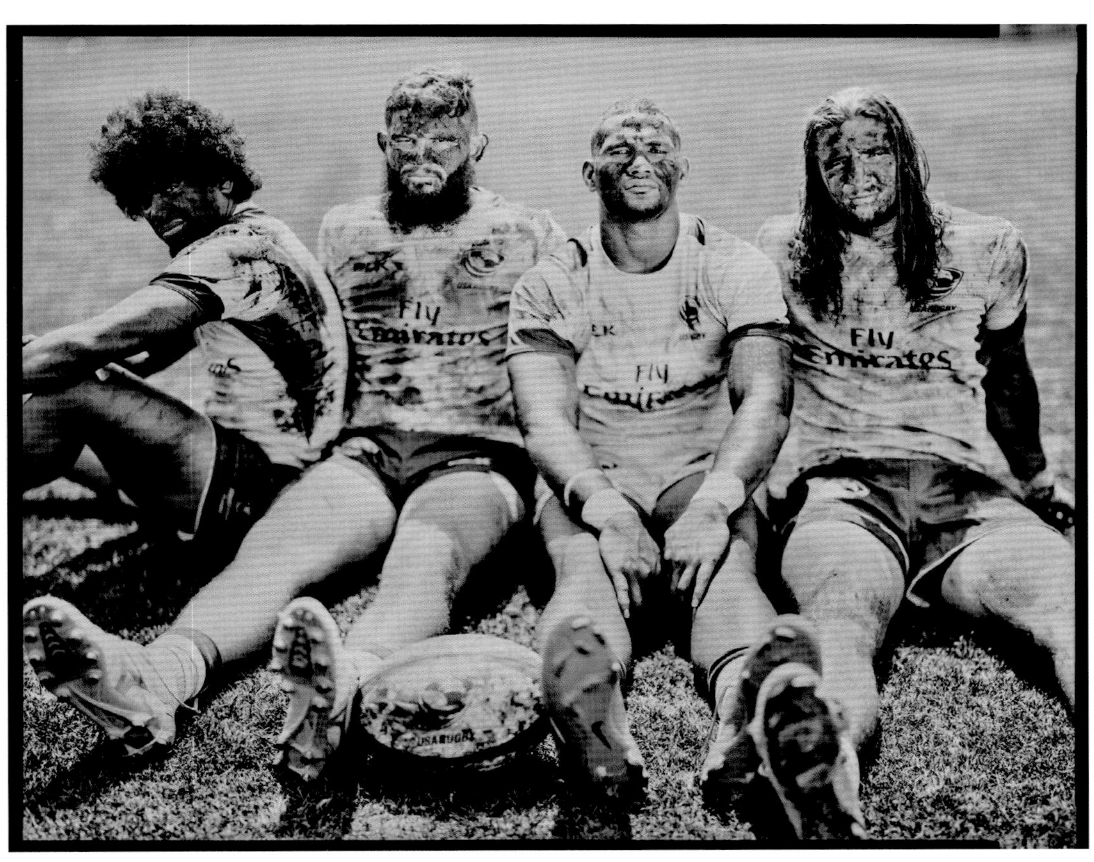

Folau Niua, Danny Barret, Martin Iosefo and Garrett Bender (left to right) formed part of the US men's rugby sevens team. Men's rugby sevens made its Olympic debut in Rio.

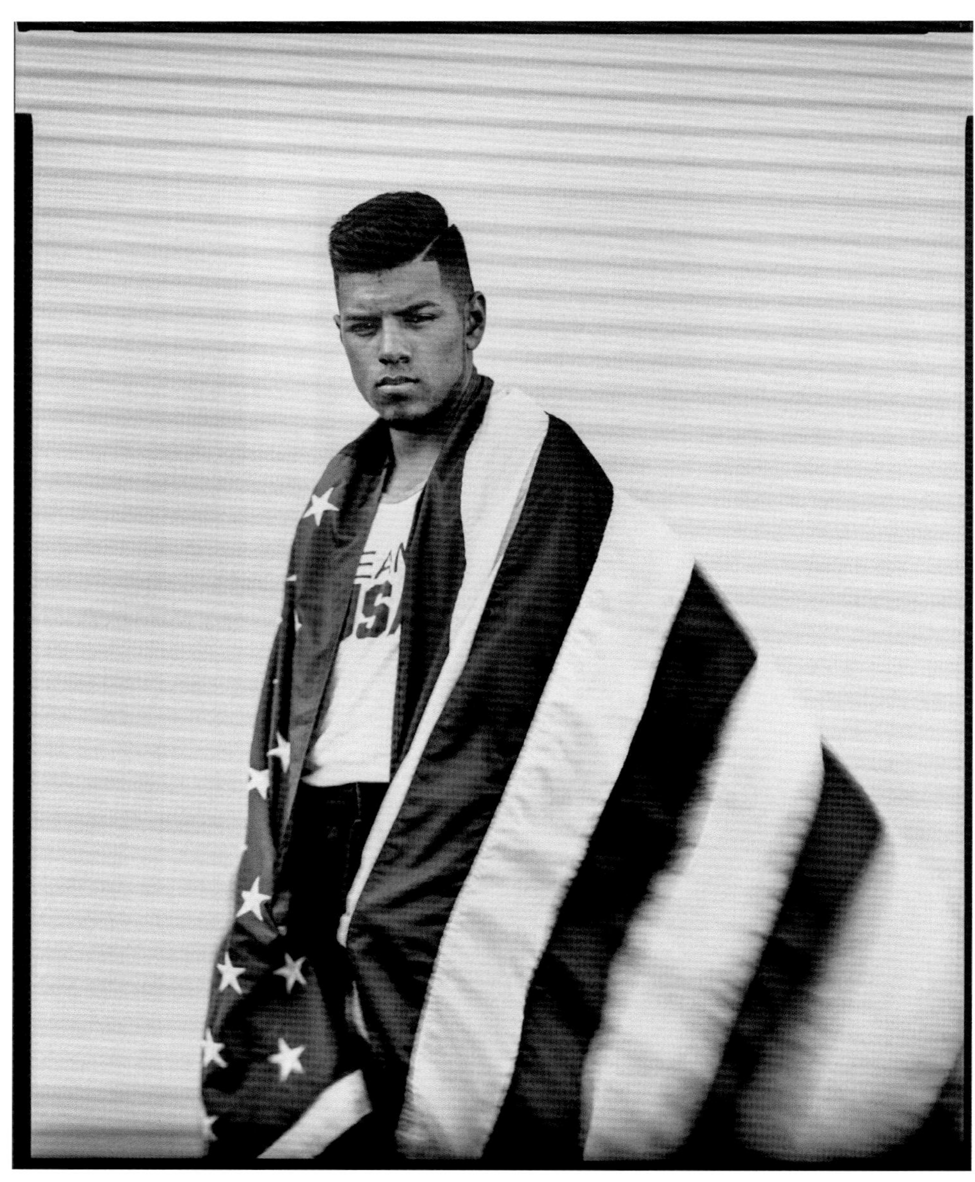

Carlos Balderas, at his family gym in Santa Maria, California. He competed as a lightweight boxer, reaching the quarterfinals.

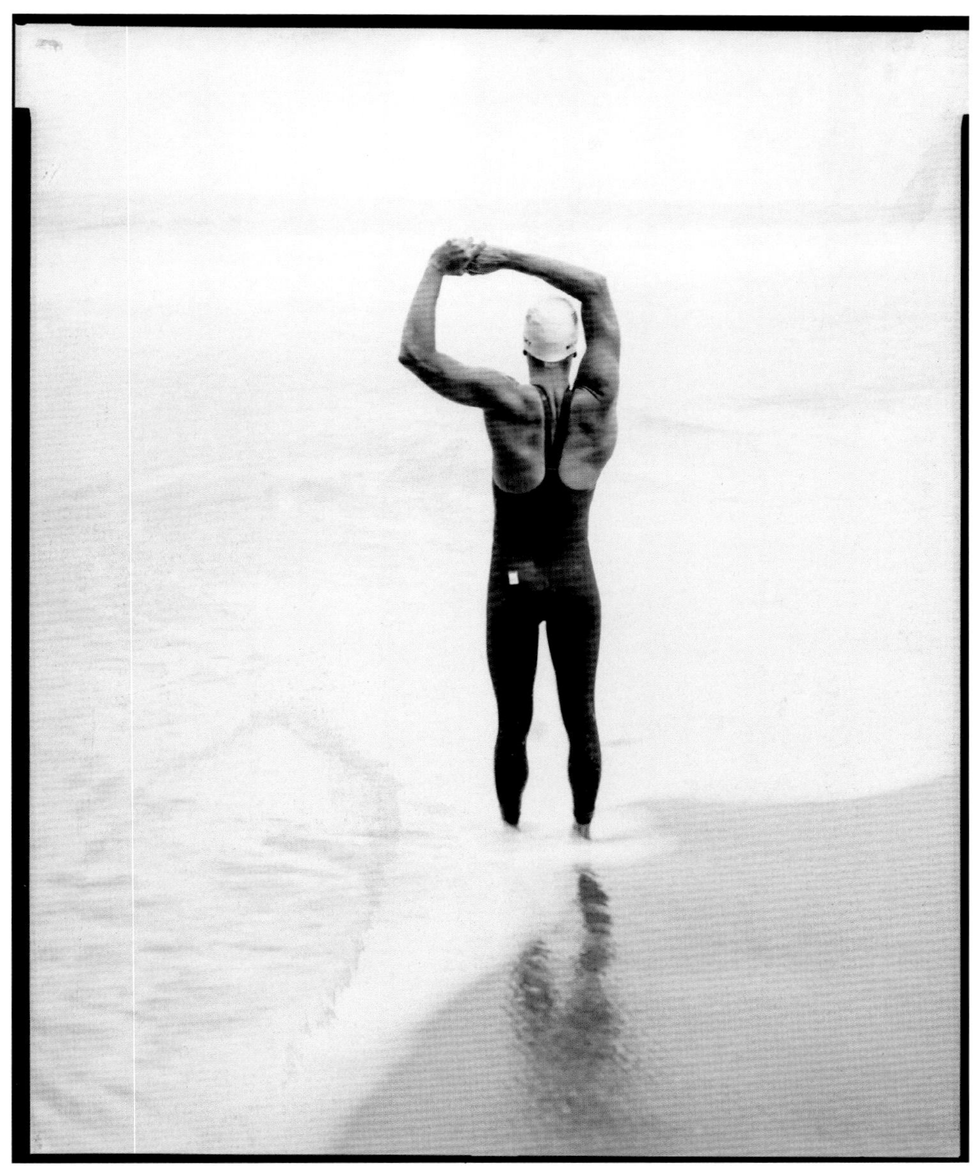

Swimmer Jordan Wilimovsky, on the beach at Santa Monica, California. He is the first American to have competed in both indoor and outdoor swimming events at the Olympics, coming fourth in the 1,500 meters and fifth in the men's marathon in the waters off Fort Copacabana.

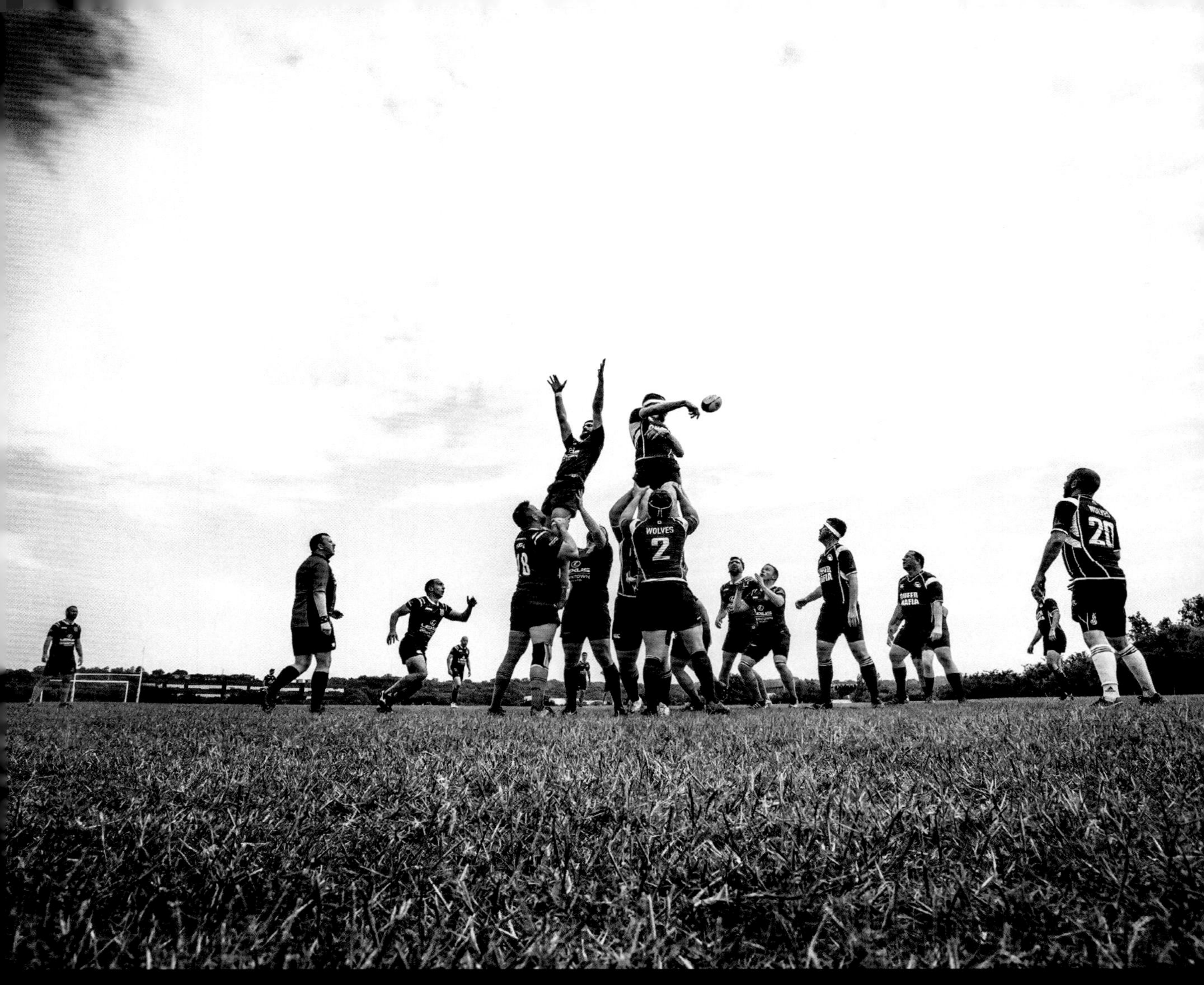

Giovanni Capriotti

Italy /
1st Prize Sports

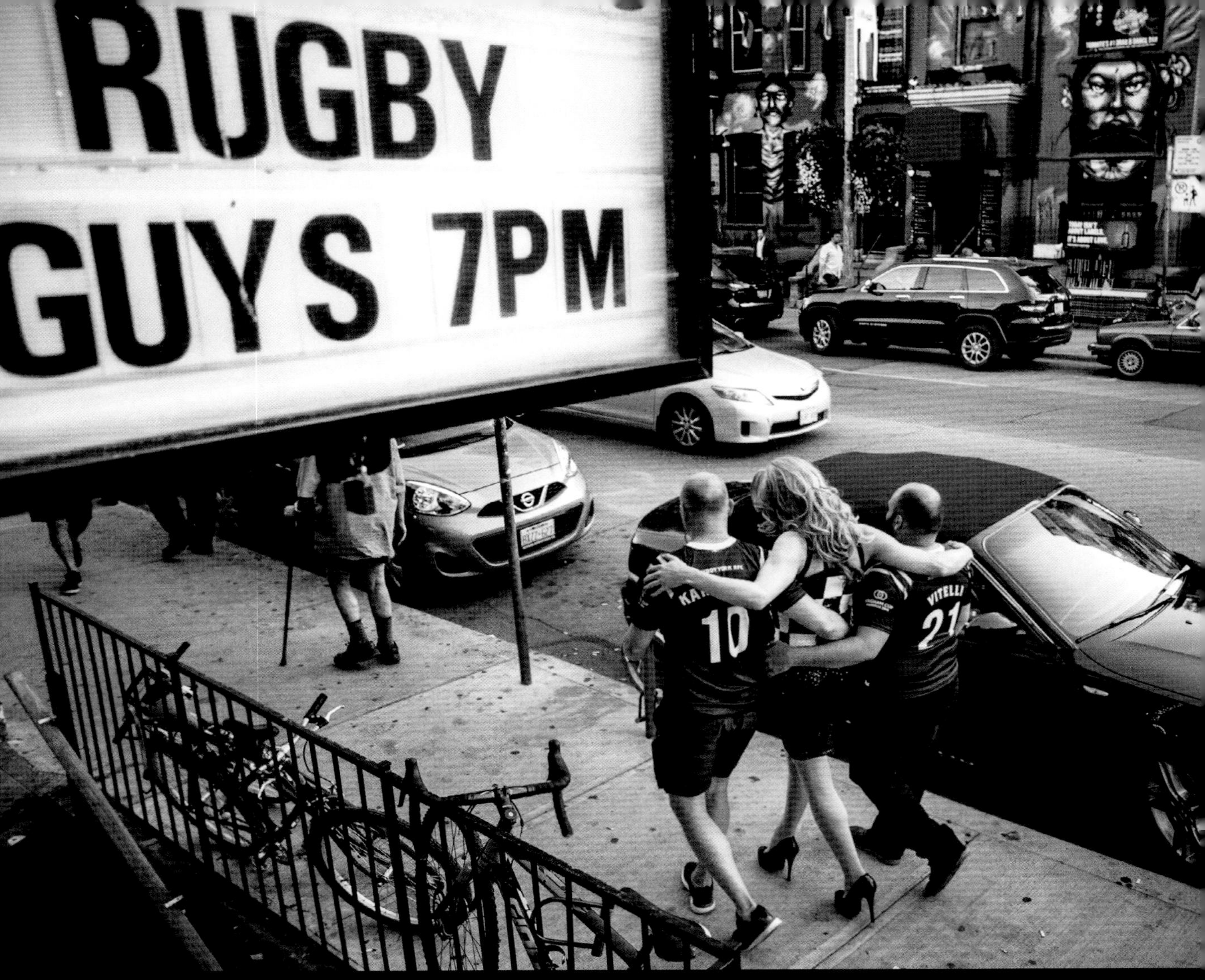

Muddy York Rugby Football Club, established in 2003, is the first gay-friendly rugby team in Toronto, Canada. It was set up to resist the idea that gay men were not suitable for a heavily masculine sport like rugby, and to counter the stereotypes surrounding gay athletes. *Facing page*: Muddy York competes with the Ottawa Wolves in Nashville, Tennessee, USA, in a match during the Bingham Cup, an international competition featuring gay rugby teams. *Above*: Muddy York's captain Jimmy Karttunen (left) and teammate Carlo Vitelli (right) walk with drag queen Demanda Tension, along Church Street in Toronto's gay village. *(continues)*

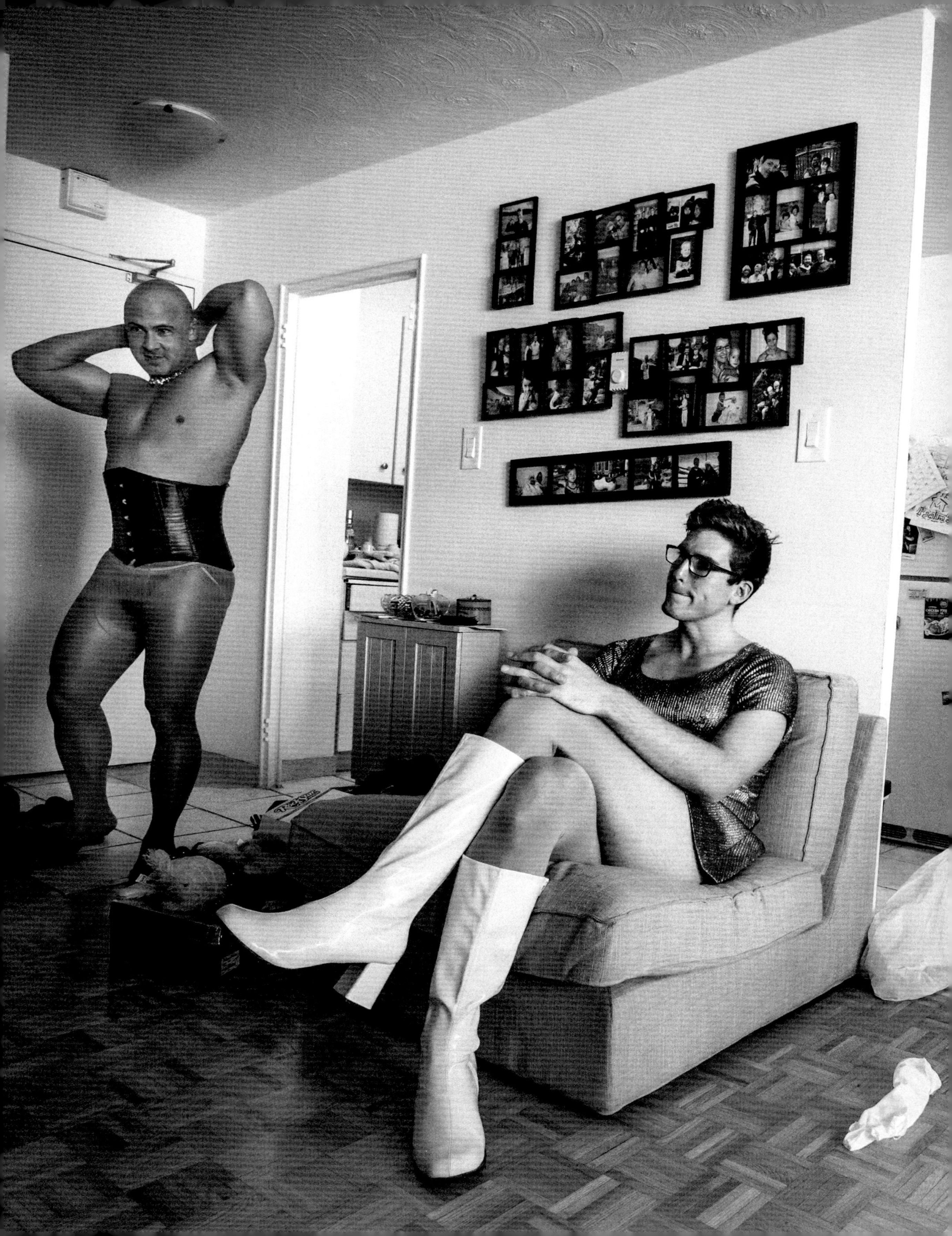

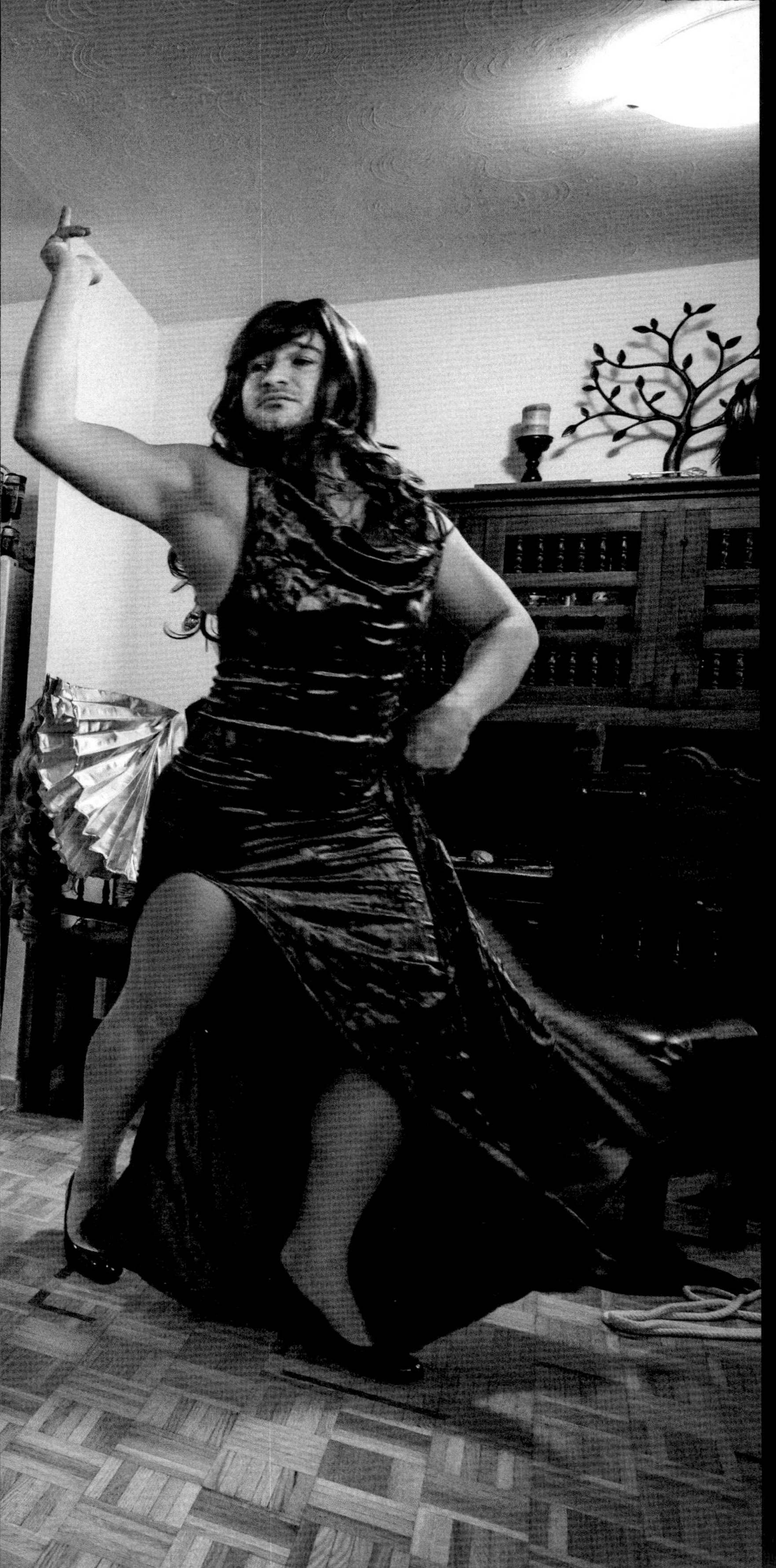

(*continued*) Canada is now host to three gay-oriented teams, after the Montreal Armada joined the Ottawa Wolves and Muddy York. A fourth, the Vancouver Rogues, dissolved after players felt they had brought sufficient awareness to issues of inclusion, and now play on mixed teams. *Left*: Muddy York players Michael Smith (left), Devin McCarney (center) and John-Paul Markides rehearse for their performance at the team's annual fundraiser drag show. (*continues*)

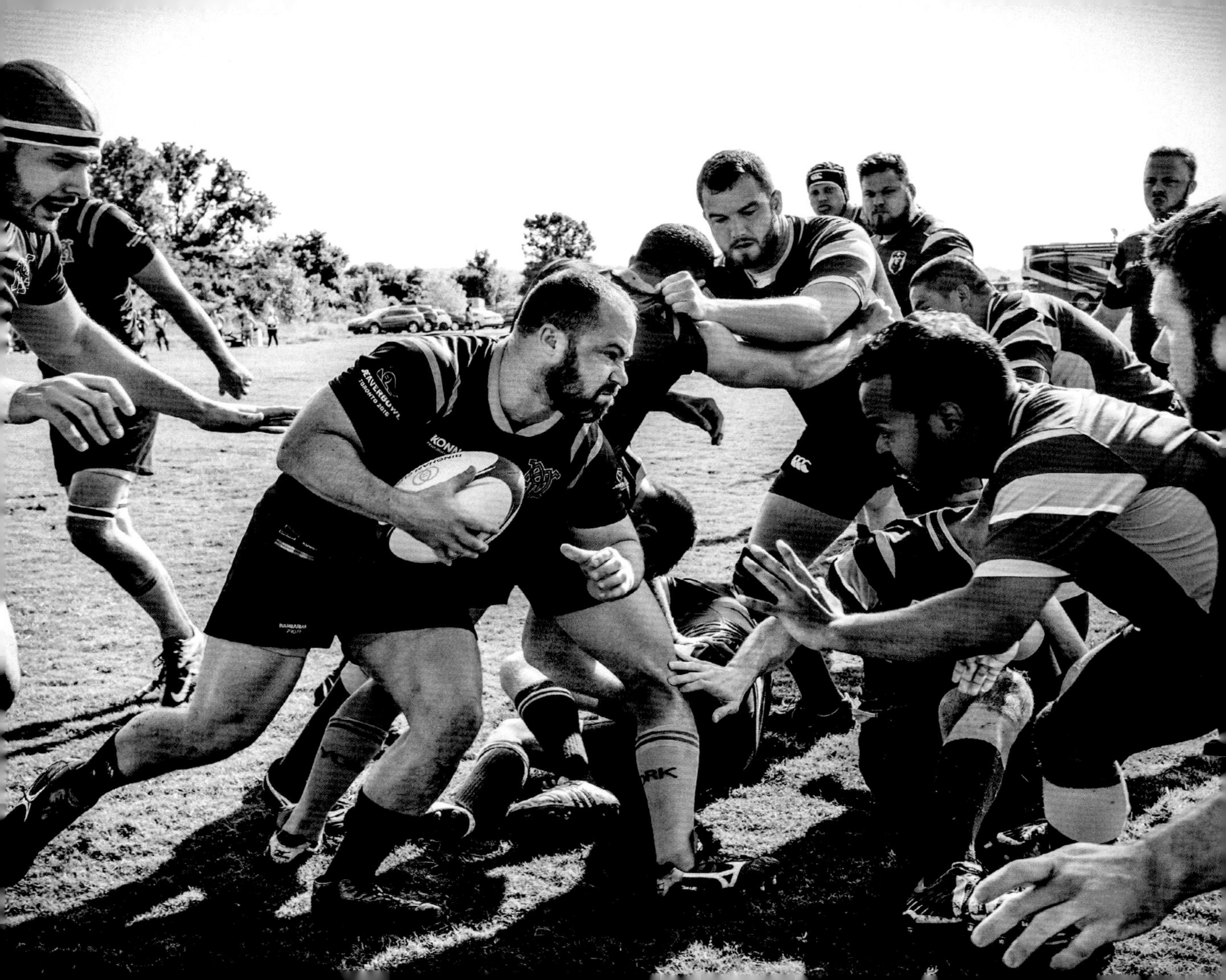

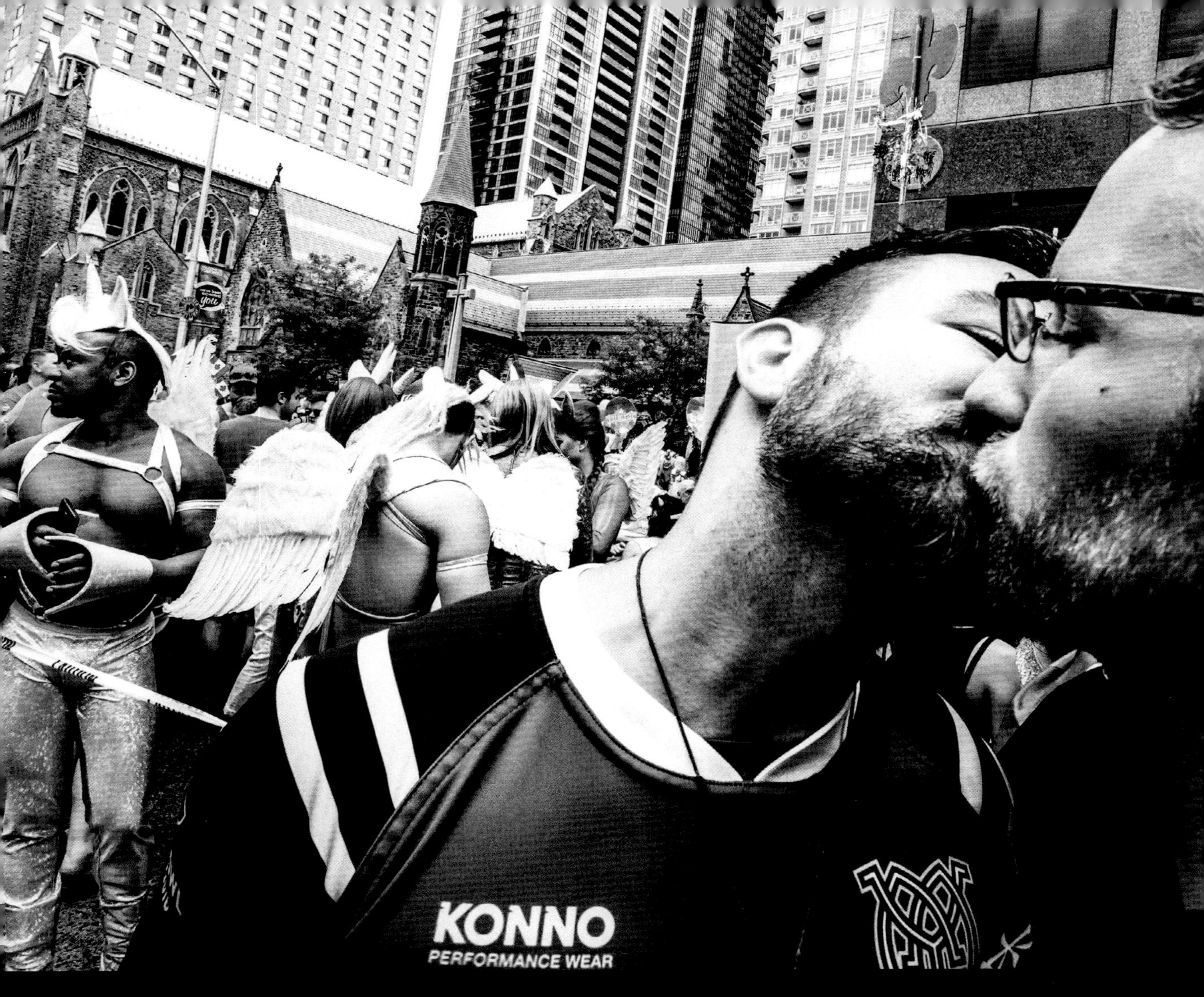

(*continued*) Muddy York RFC competes against mainstream teams in the Toronto Rugby Union, and travels to play against other gay teams. *Facing page*: Muddy York's Michael Smith carries the ball in a match against the Nashville Grizzlies, during a semi-final of the Hoagland Shield, in Nashville, Tennessee, USA. The Grizzlies won 15-0. *Above*: John-Paul Markides (left) kisses his partner, Muddy York teammate Kasimir Kosakowski, during the Pride Toronto parade, on 3 July.

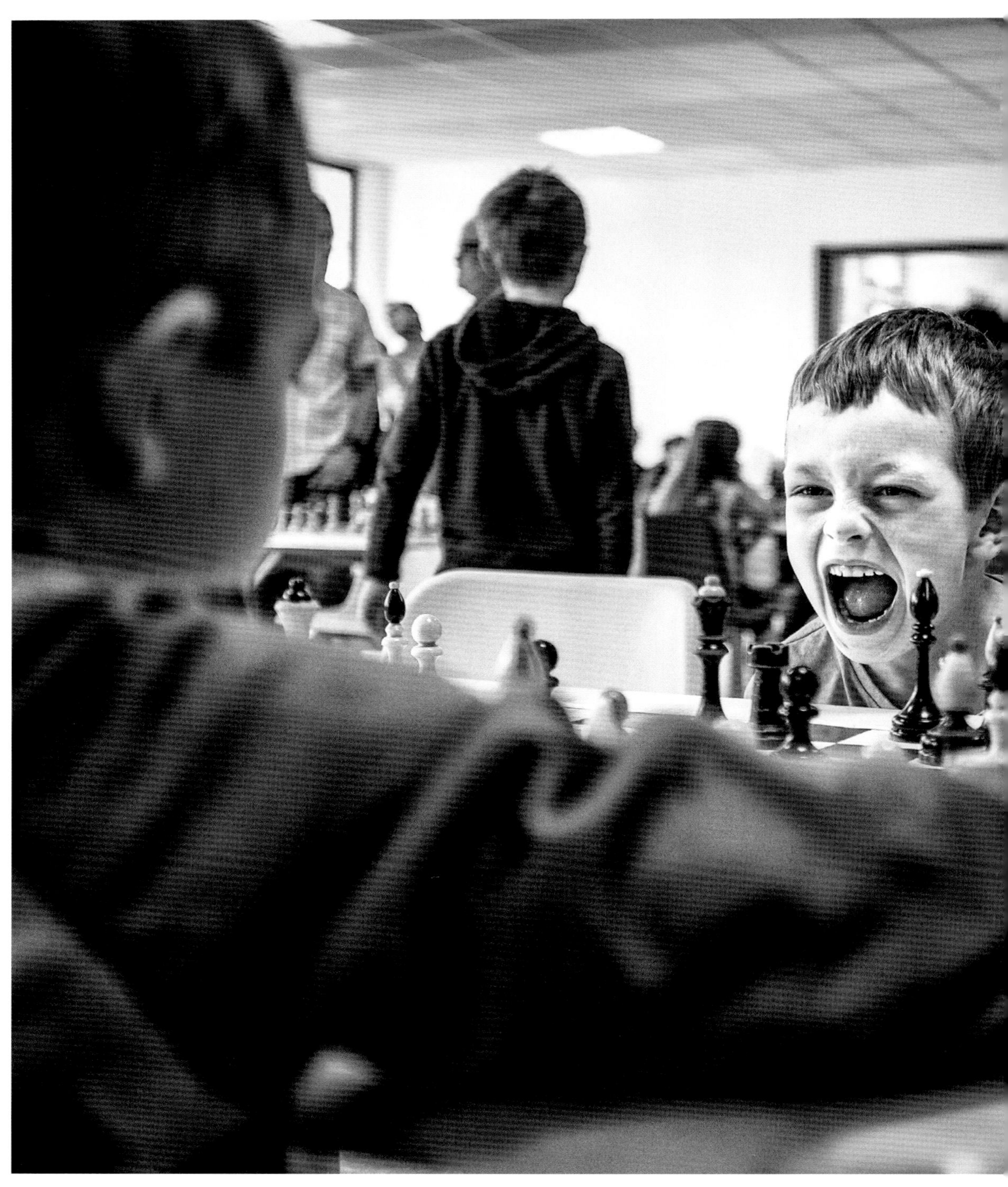

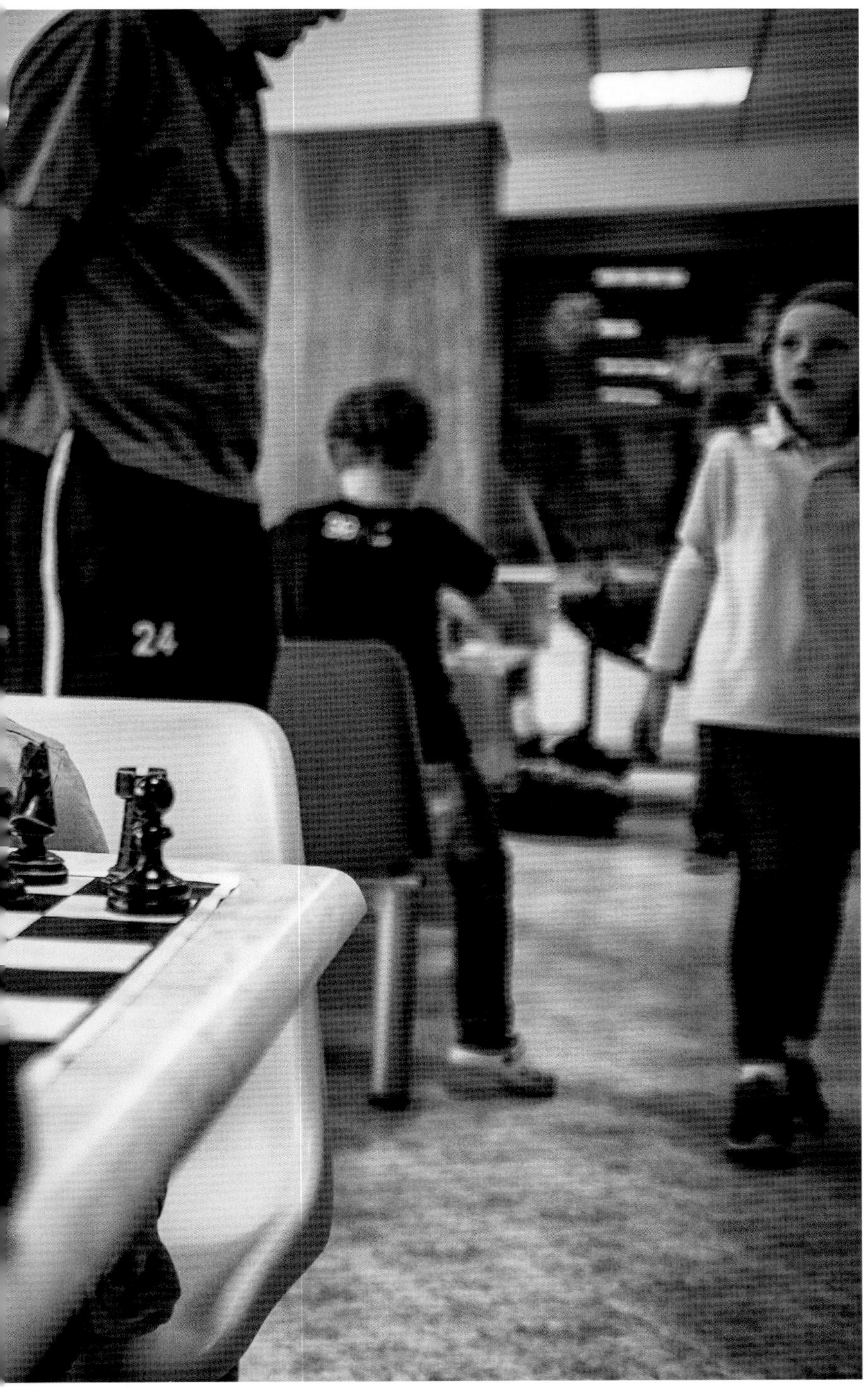

Michael Hanke

Czech Republic /
2nd Prize Sports

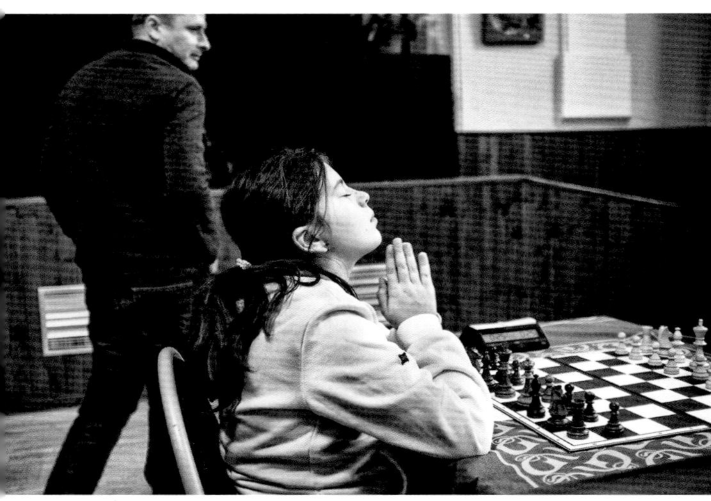

Youth chess tournaments remain popular in the Czech Republic, despite competition from computer games. The national chess federation currently has around 15,000 members, of which 3,000 are under 15. A special 'Chess for Schools' project aims to introduce chess into the classroom in primary and secondary schools. Far from its reputation as a sedate pursuit, chess playing can involve a high degree of tension. *Previous spread*: Emotions run high at a tournament at Kamenice, Czech Republic. *This page, top*: The moments before the start of a new round, in Zdice. *Below*: A father gives his son advice, in Zdice. *Facing page, top*: Parents and trainers watch the course of a game, in Slaný. *Middle*: Players who have completed their games watch the final round of one of the games still being played, in Zdice. *Below*: A game in progress in Slaný.

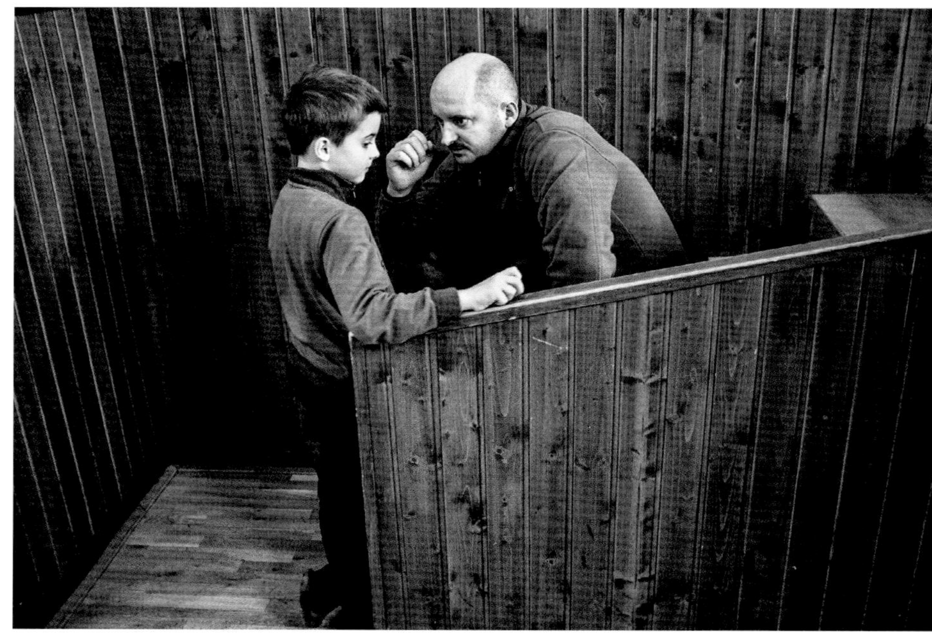

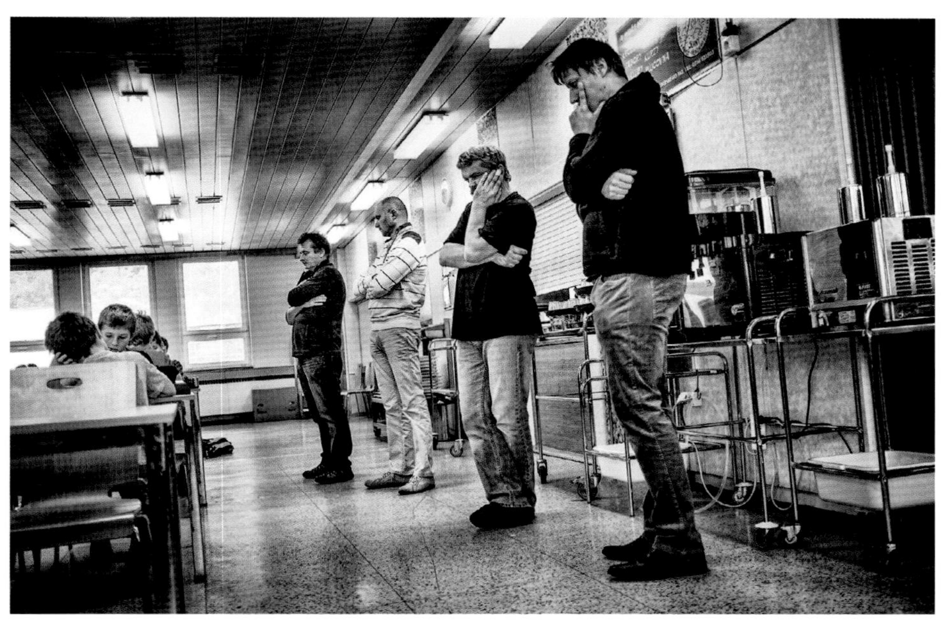

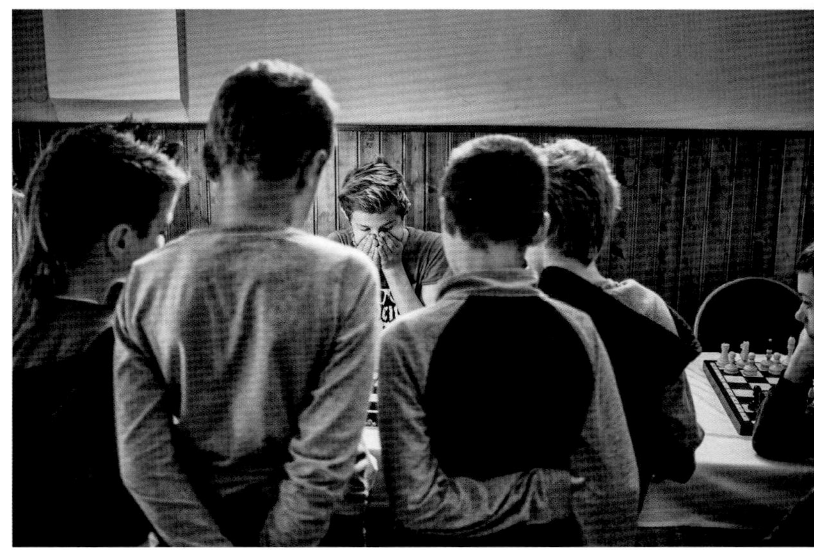

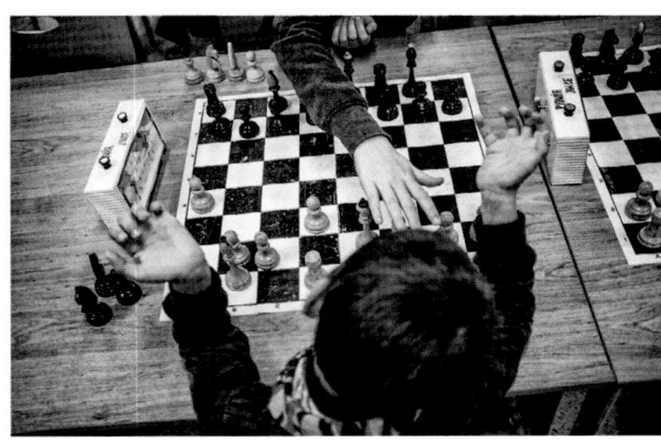

Darren Calabrese

Canada /
3rd Prize Sports

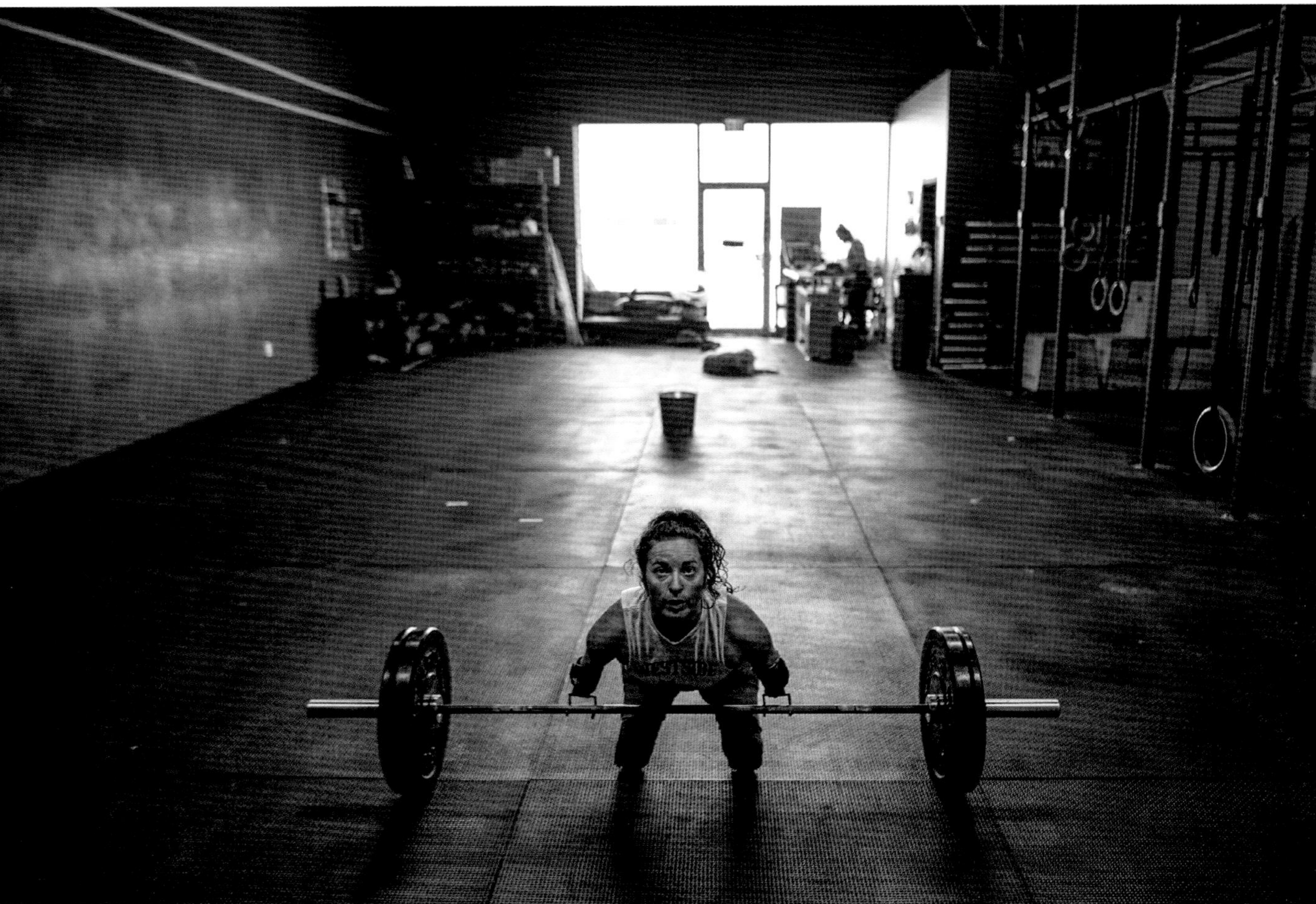

Lindsay Hilton, from Halifax, Nova Scotia, Canada is dedicated to CrossFit, despite having been born with no arms or legs. CrossFit is a fitness regime that draws on such sports as high-intensity interval training, weightlifting and gymnastics. Hilton participates in grueling workouts using equipment she has had adapted using everyday hardware materials. *Above*: Hilton pauses to focus between deadlift reps. *Facing page*: Hilton hangs from an adapted bar for a series of butterfly pull-ups. (*continues*)

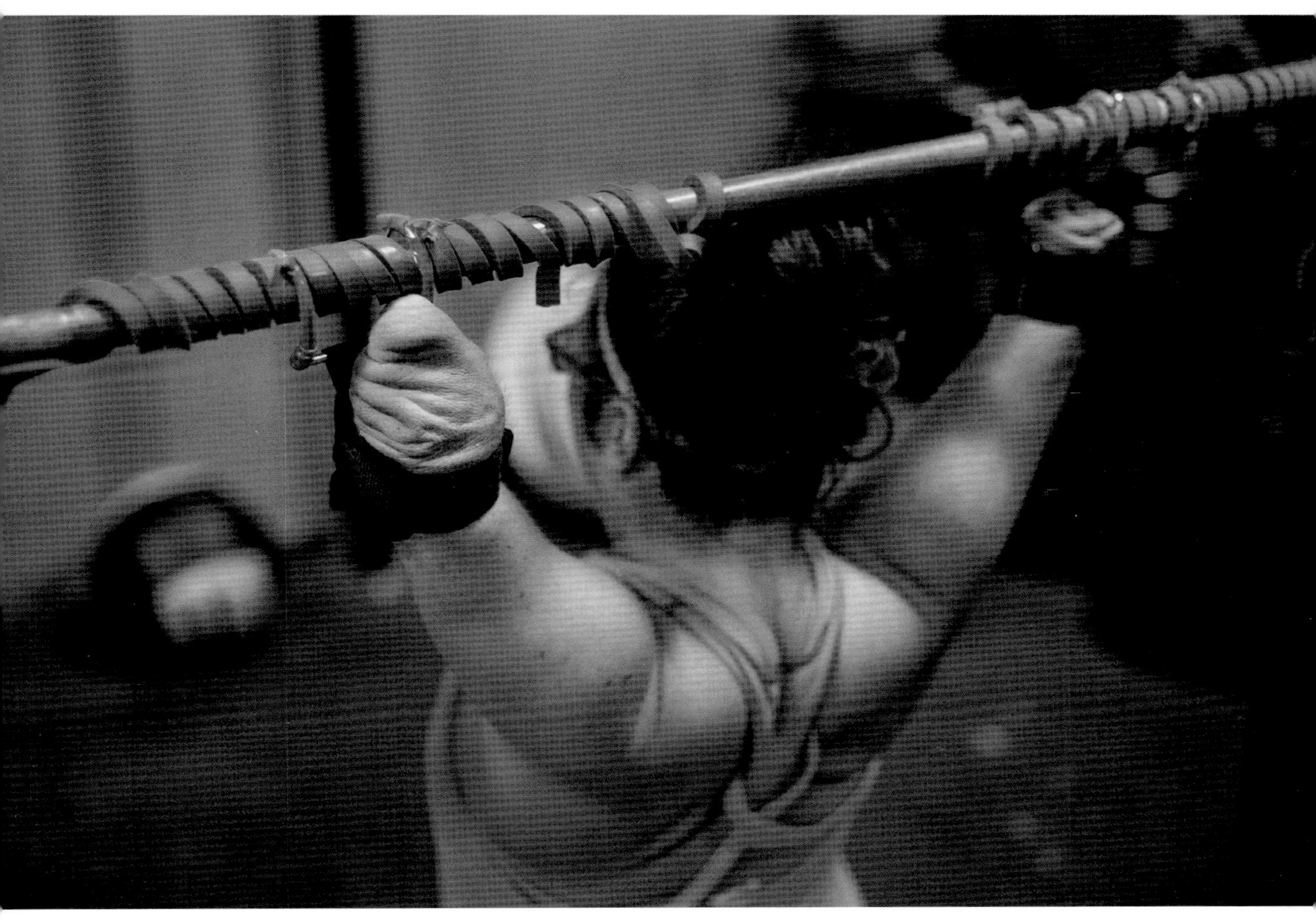

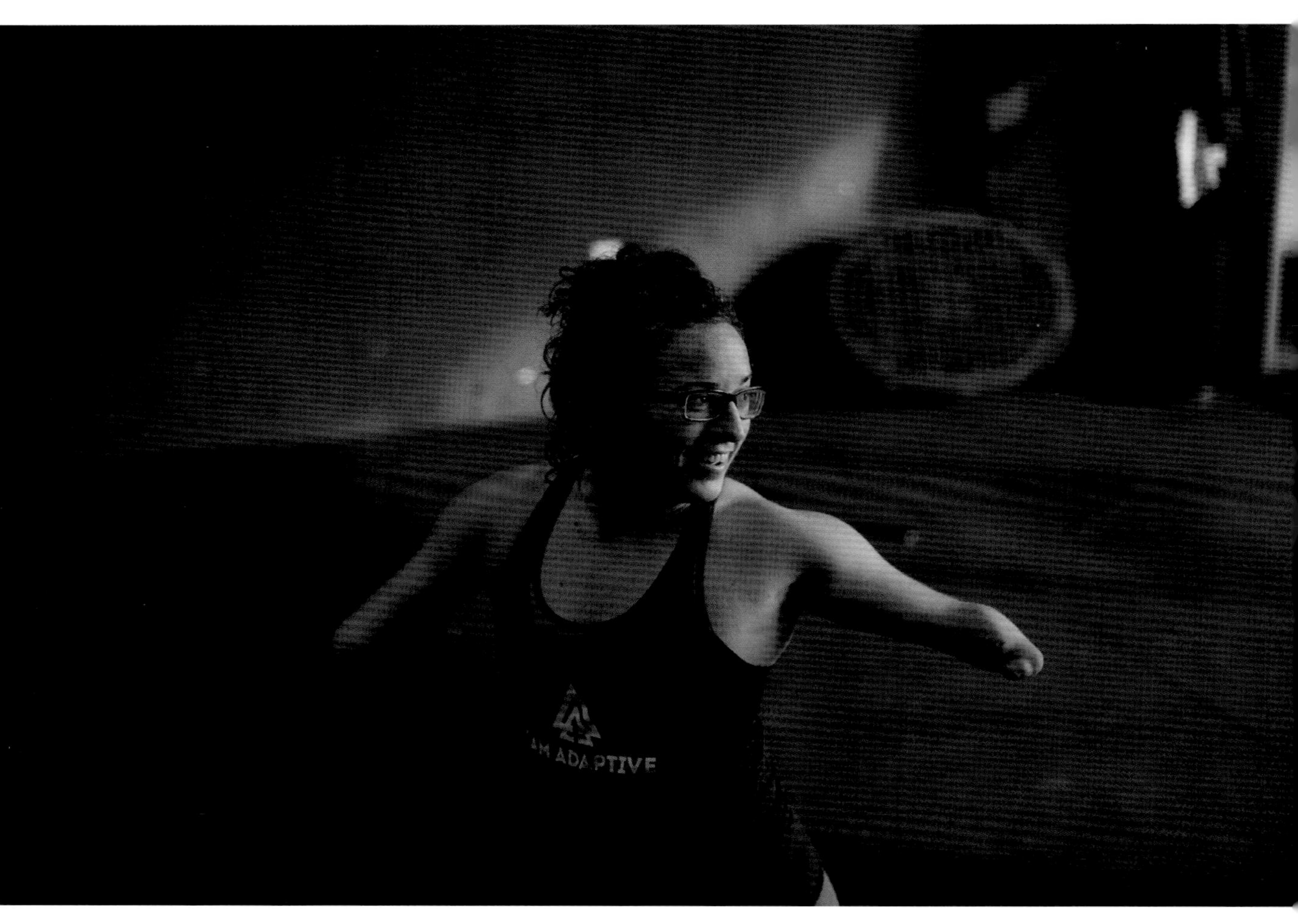

(*continued*) Hilton juggled her intensive training regime with work, life and coaching commitments in order to qualify for the Adaptive Seated RX division of the international CrossFit fitness festival. She finished in the top five in the category. *Above*: Hilton trains on Thanksgiving Sunday for the competition. *Facing page*: Hilton rests with her boyfriend Matt Melanson, whom she met playing rugby, another of her sporting passions.

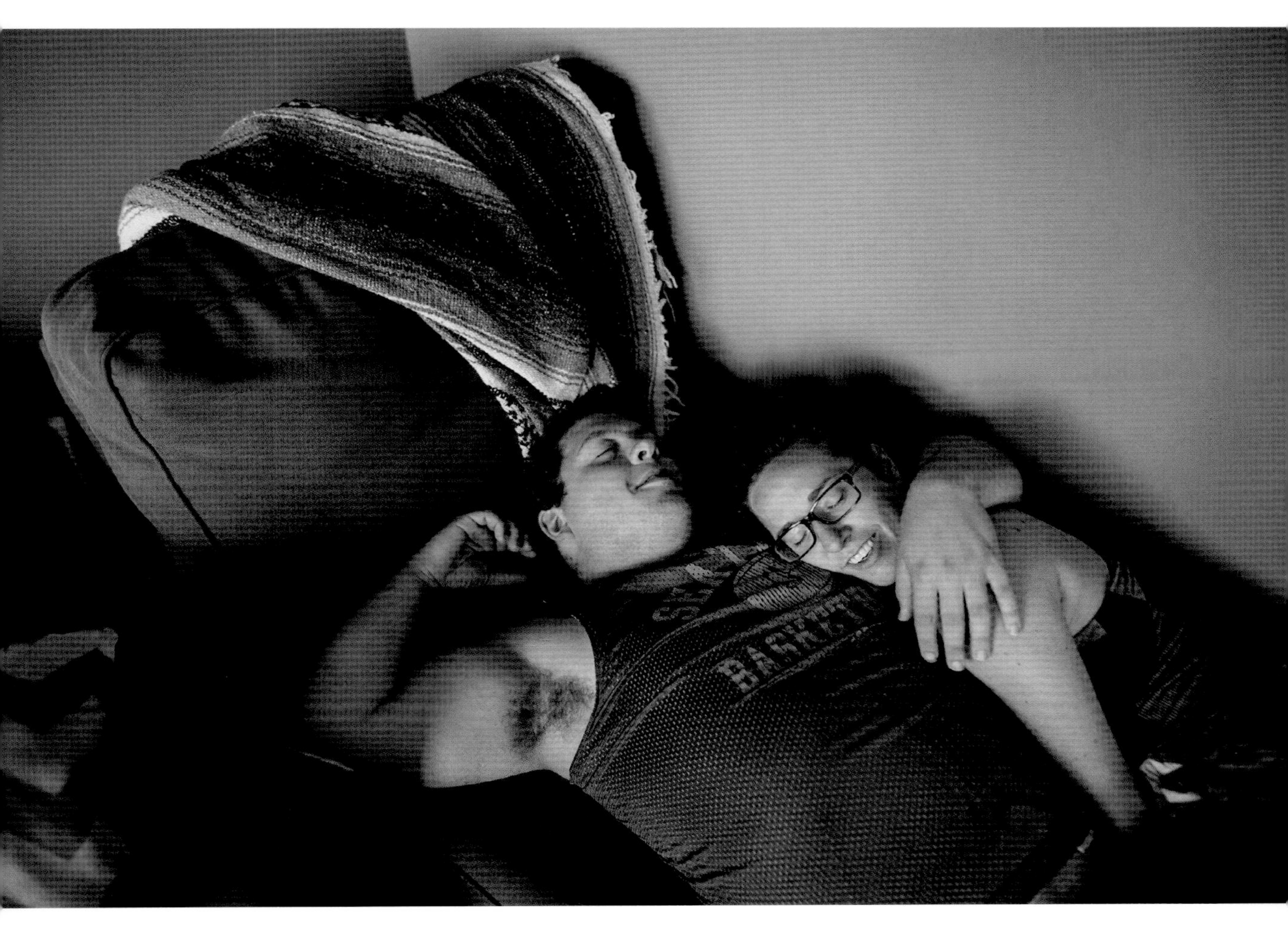

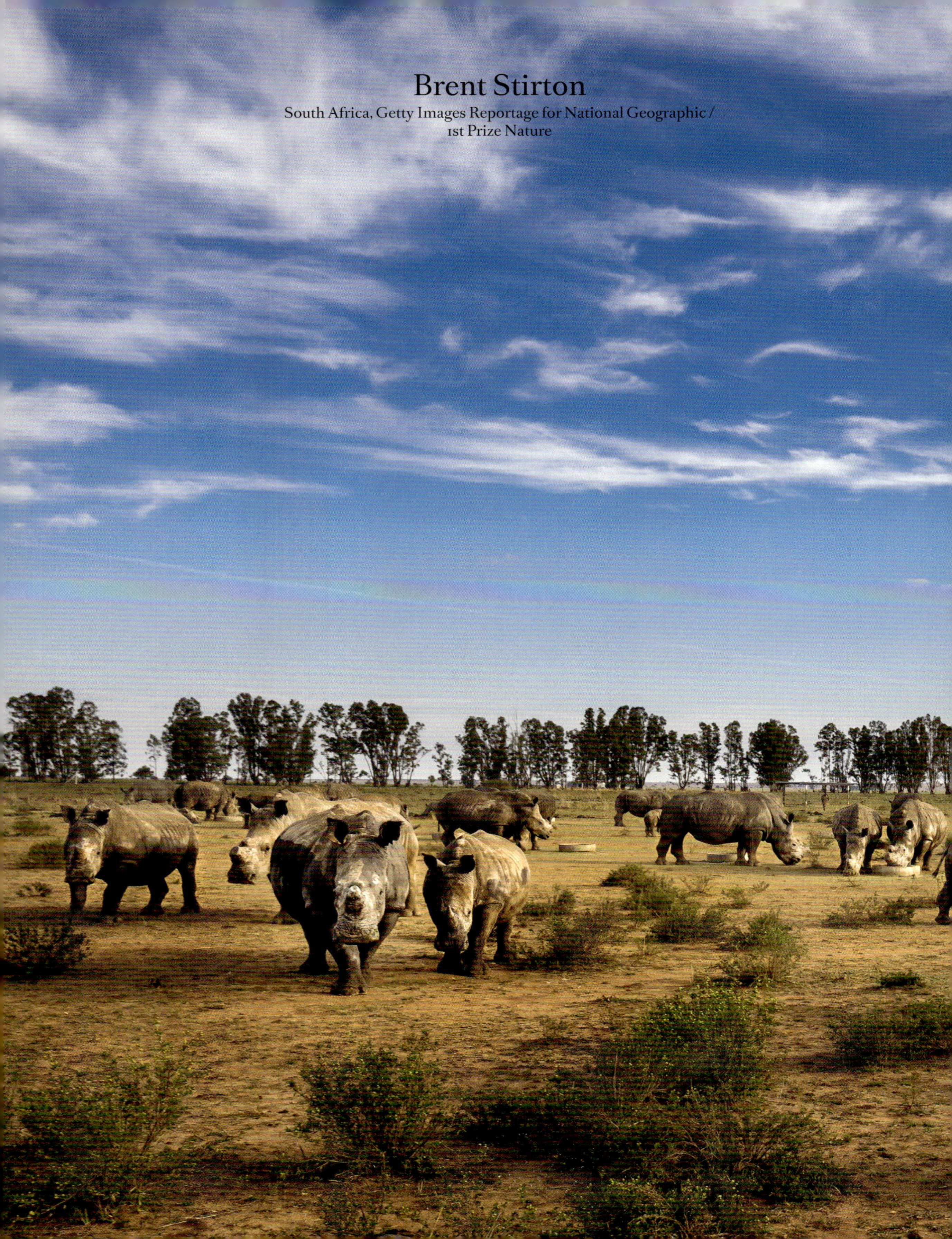

Brent Stirton

South Africa, Getty Images Reportage for National Geographic / 1st Prize Nature

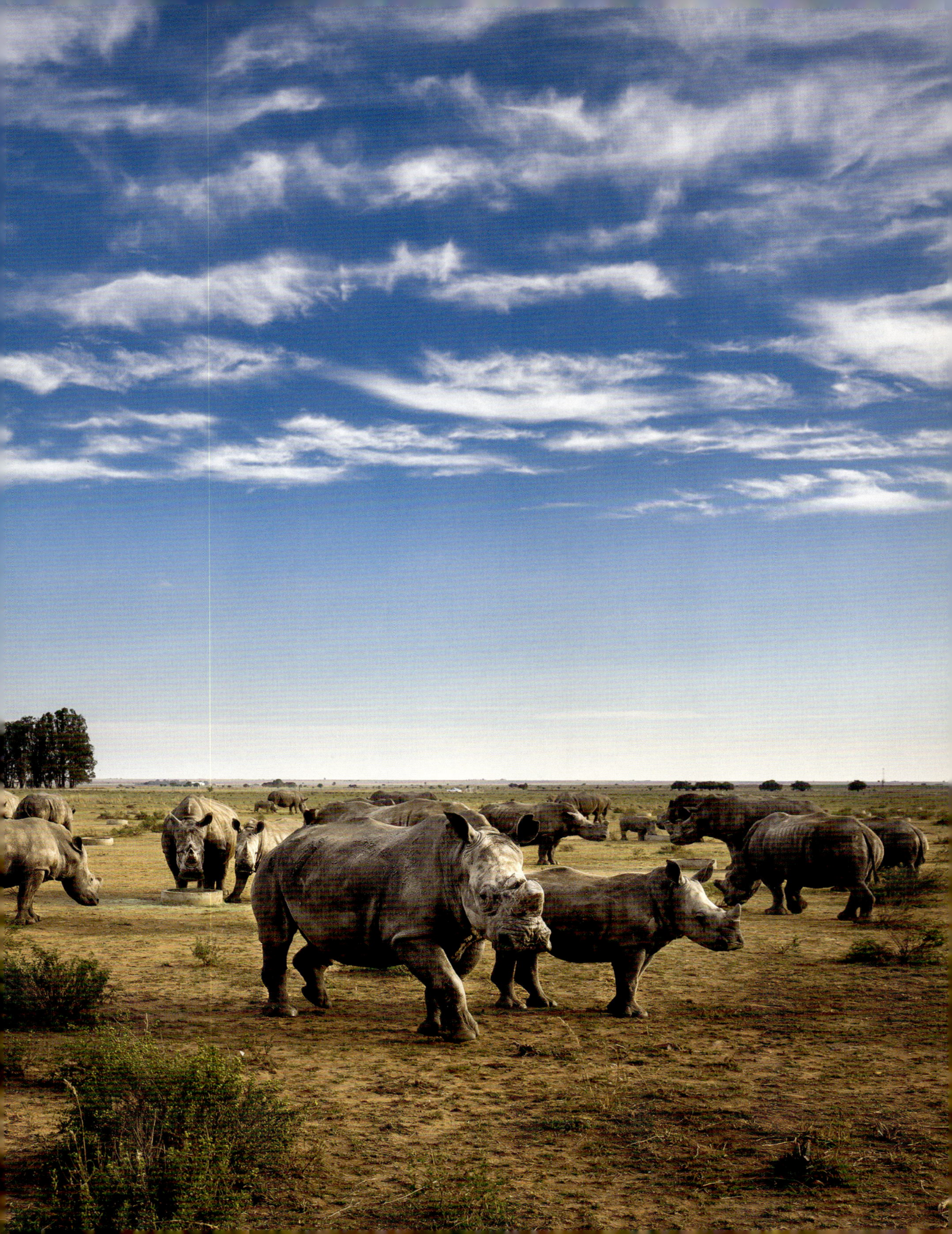

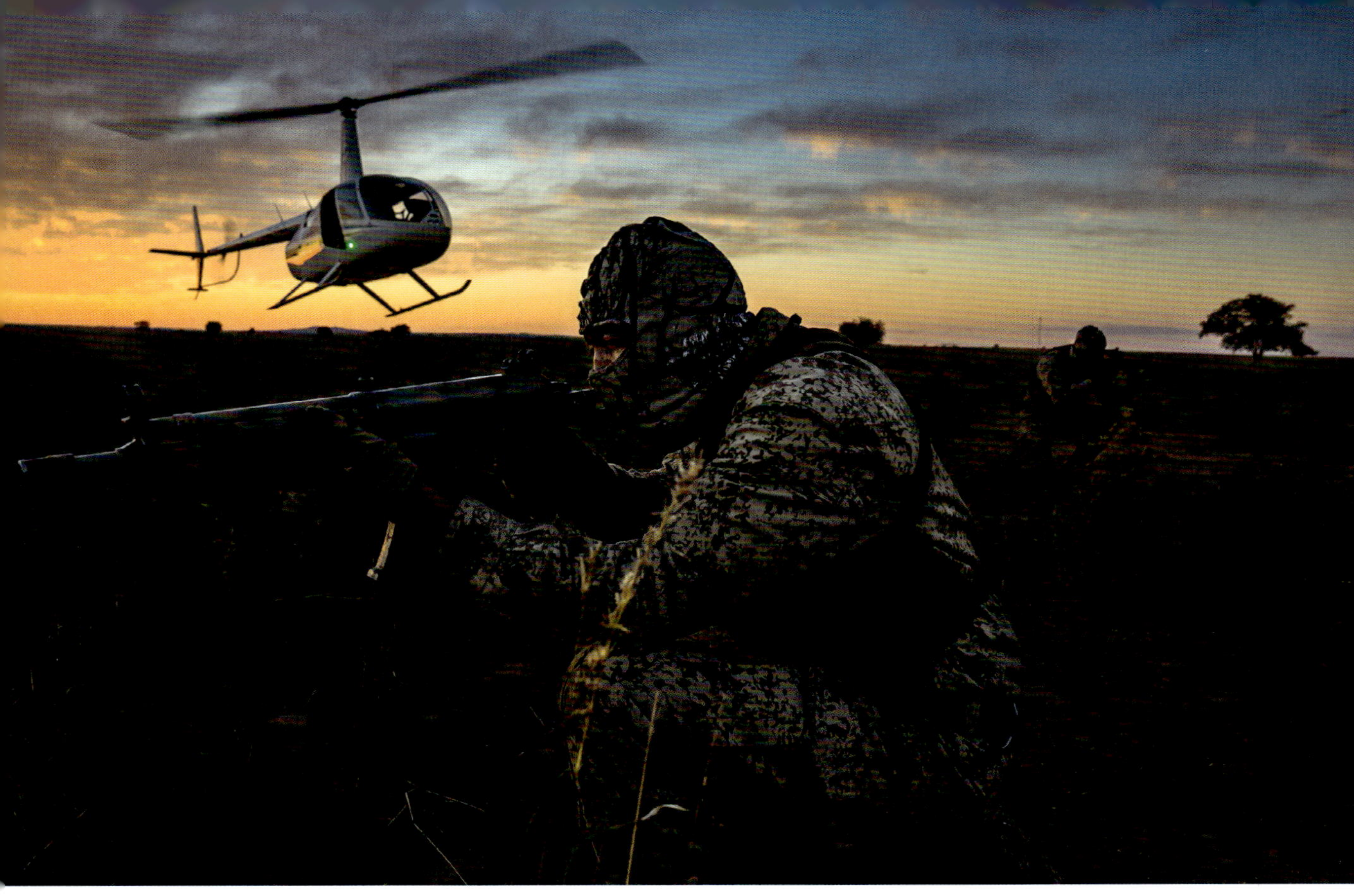

Demand in Asia for rhino horn—traditionally valued for its medicinal properties—is rising steeply, as increasing prosperity in the region means more people can afford to pay the extremely high prices involved. This puts growing pressure on a species already threatened with extinction. In 2007, South Africa, home to 70 percent of the world's rhinos, reported losing just 13 to poachers; by 2015 that had risen to 1,175. Unlike elephant tusks, rhino horn grows back when cut properly. Rhino rancher John Hume is among those attempting to end the international ban on trading in rhino horn, and to farm rhinos commercially, a move fiercely opposed by conservationists, who say a legal trade could doom rhinos. *Previous spread*: Dehorned rhino graze on John Hume's ranch. He reputedly has five tons of horn in storage. *Above*: A security team deploys on Hume's ranch. *Facing page, top*: Authorities arrest a man believed to have been assisting poachers, in Mozambique, near South Africa's Kruger National Park. *Below*: Dorota Ladosz comforts a baby rhino after surgery, at a sanctuary in Mbombela, South Africa. The orphaned animal had been attacked by hyenas. *Next spread*: A black rhino, poached for its horn, is found dead at Hluhluwe Umfolozi Game Reserve, South Africa.

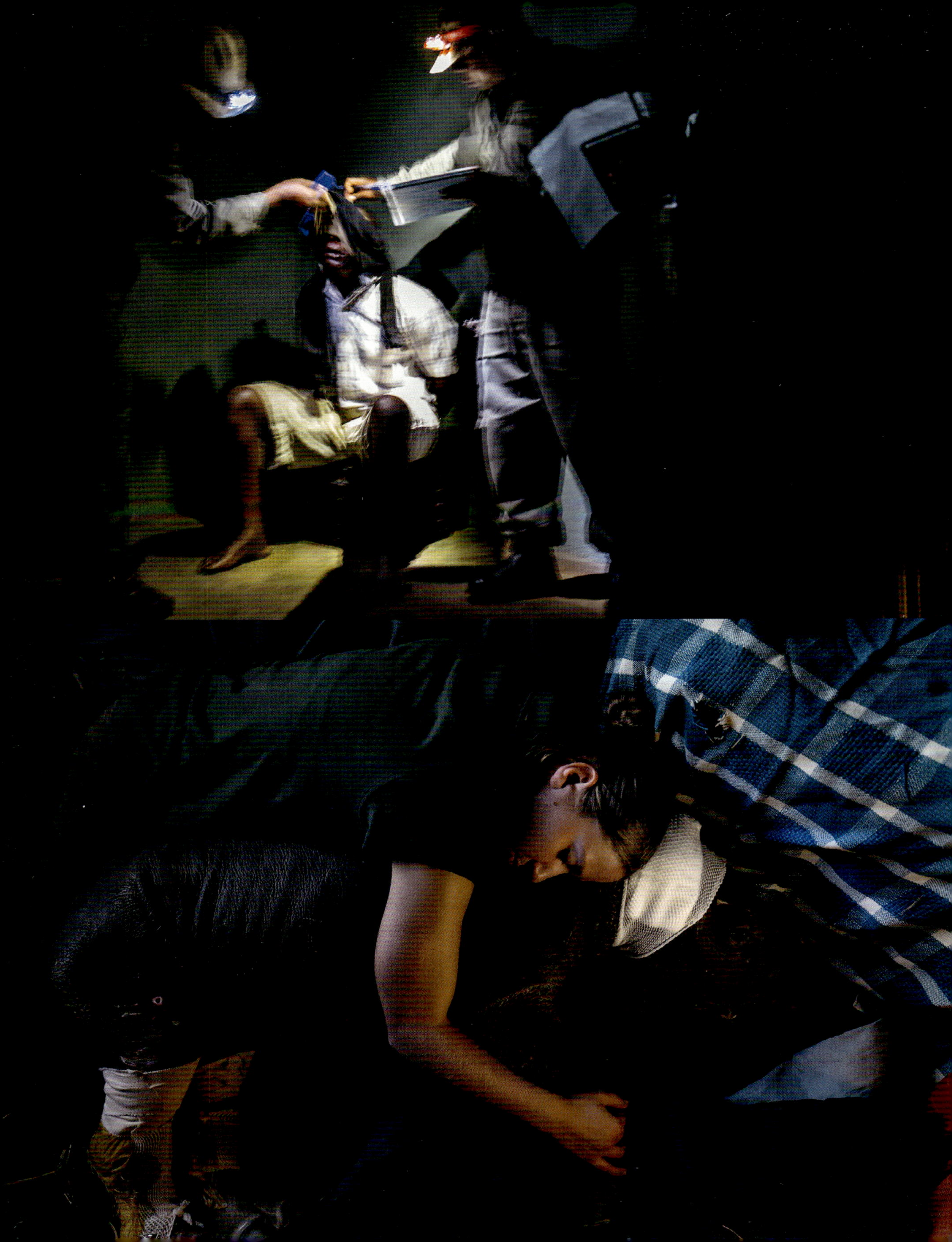

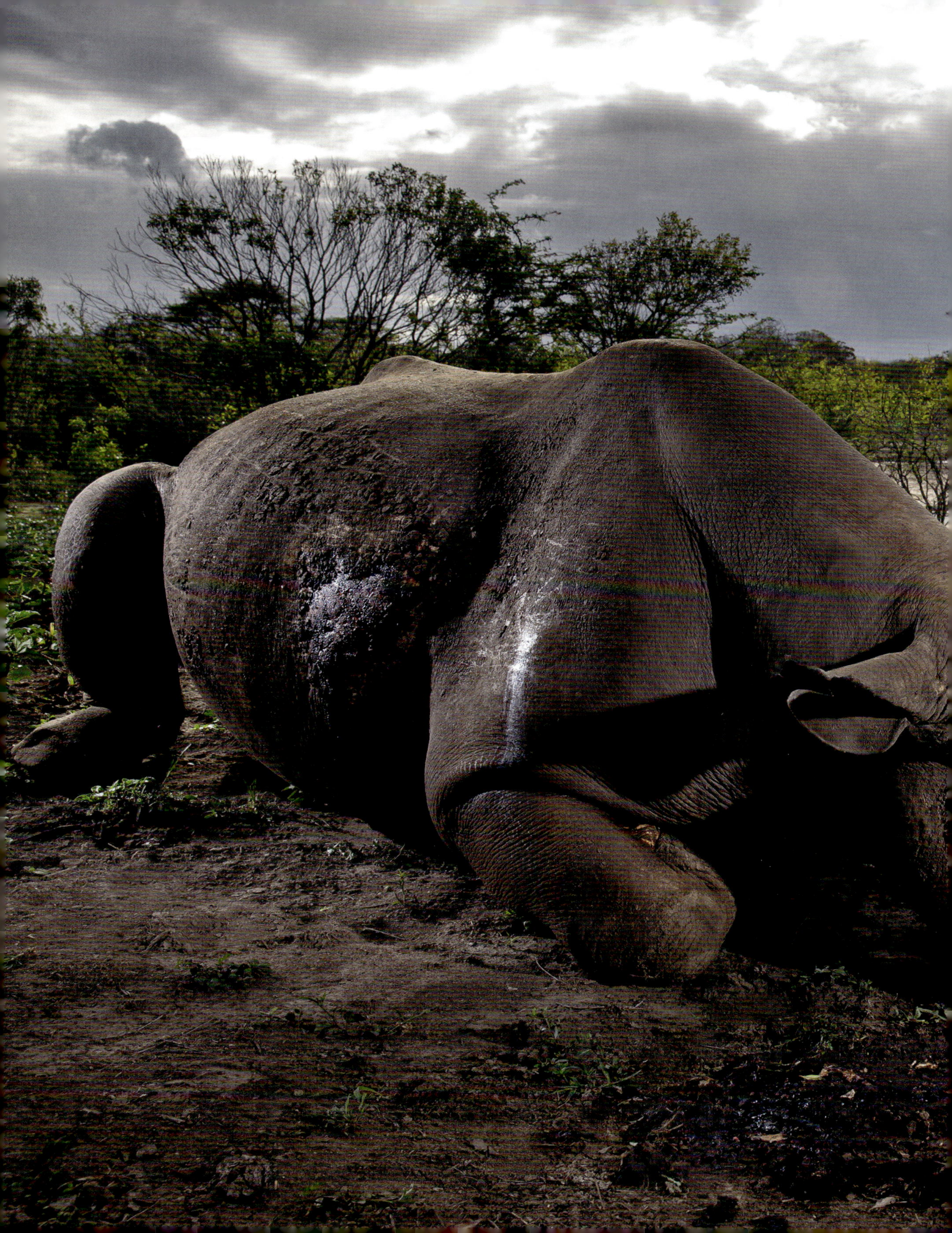

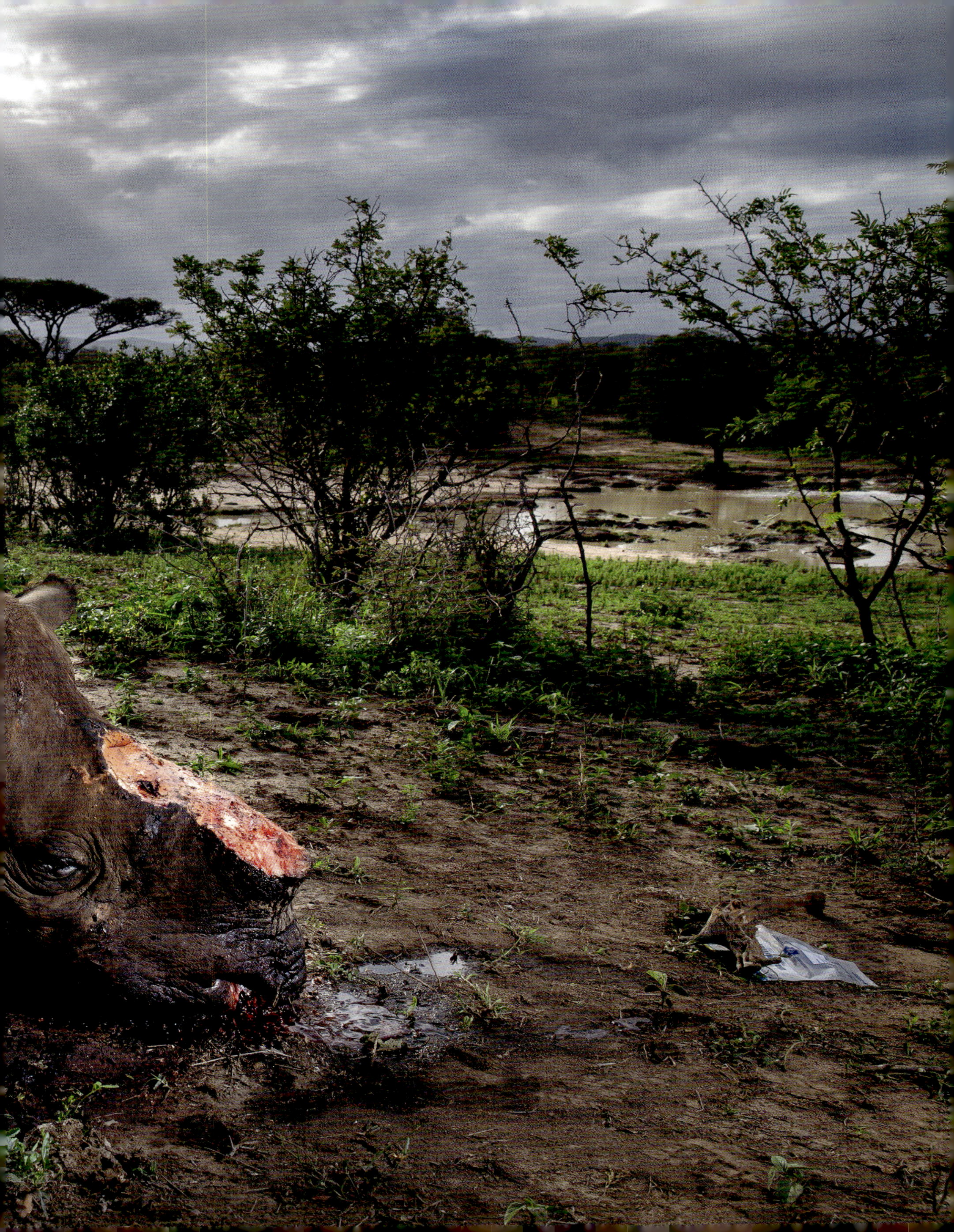

Ami Vitale

USA, for National Geographic /
2nd Prize Nature

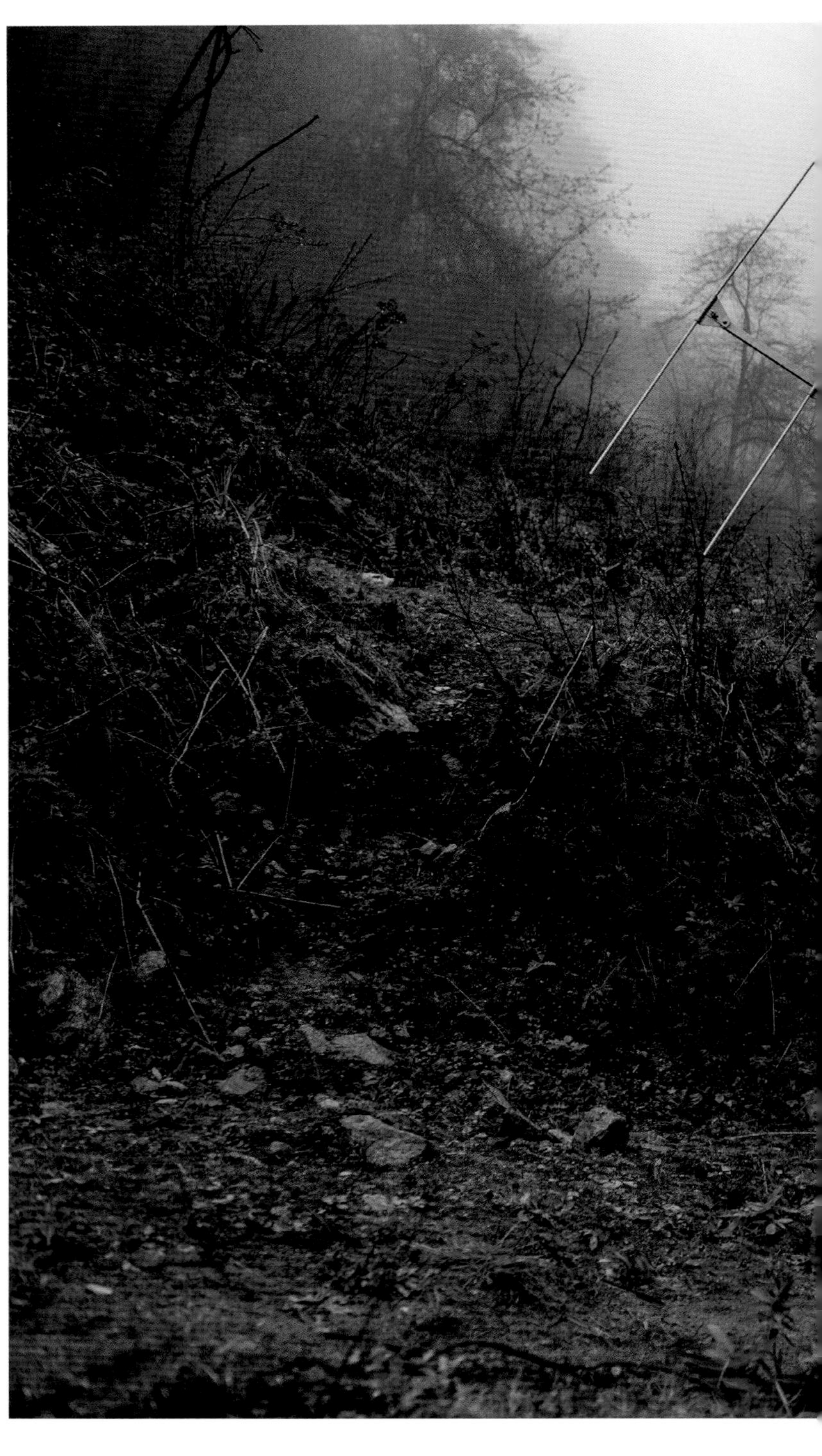

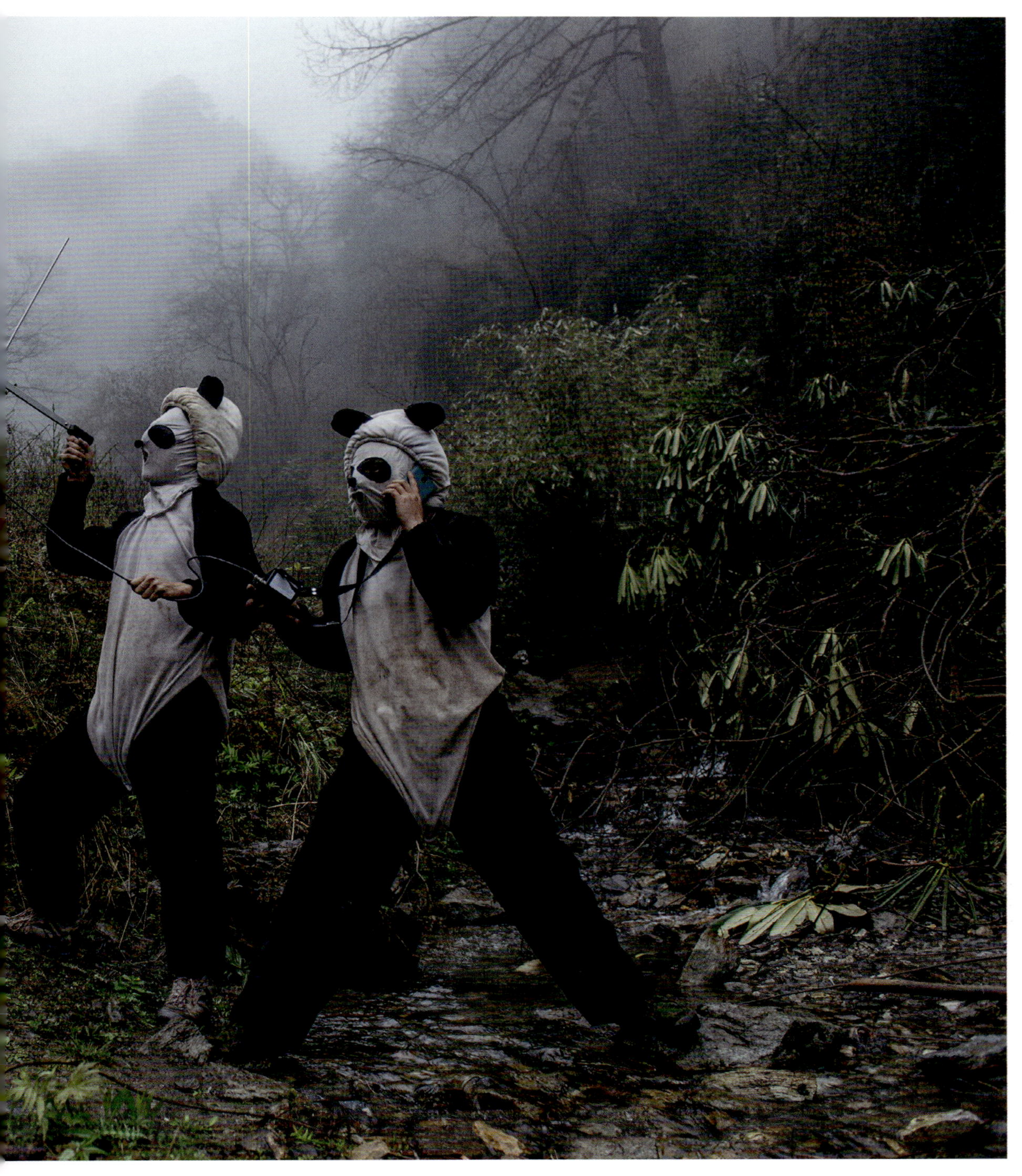

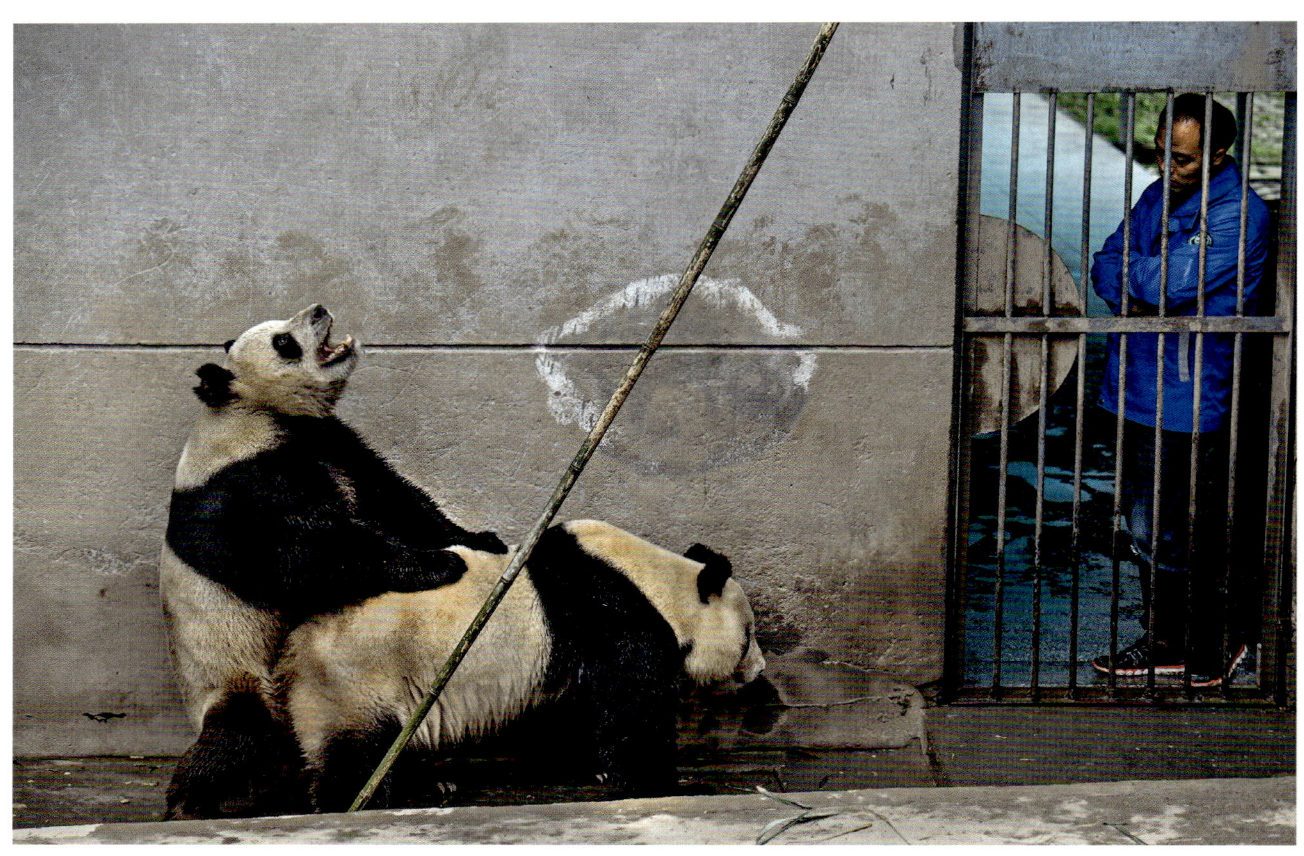

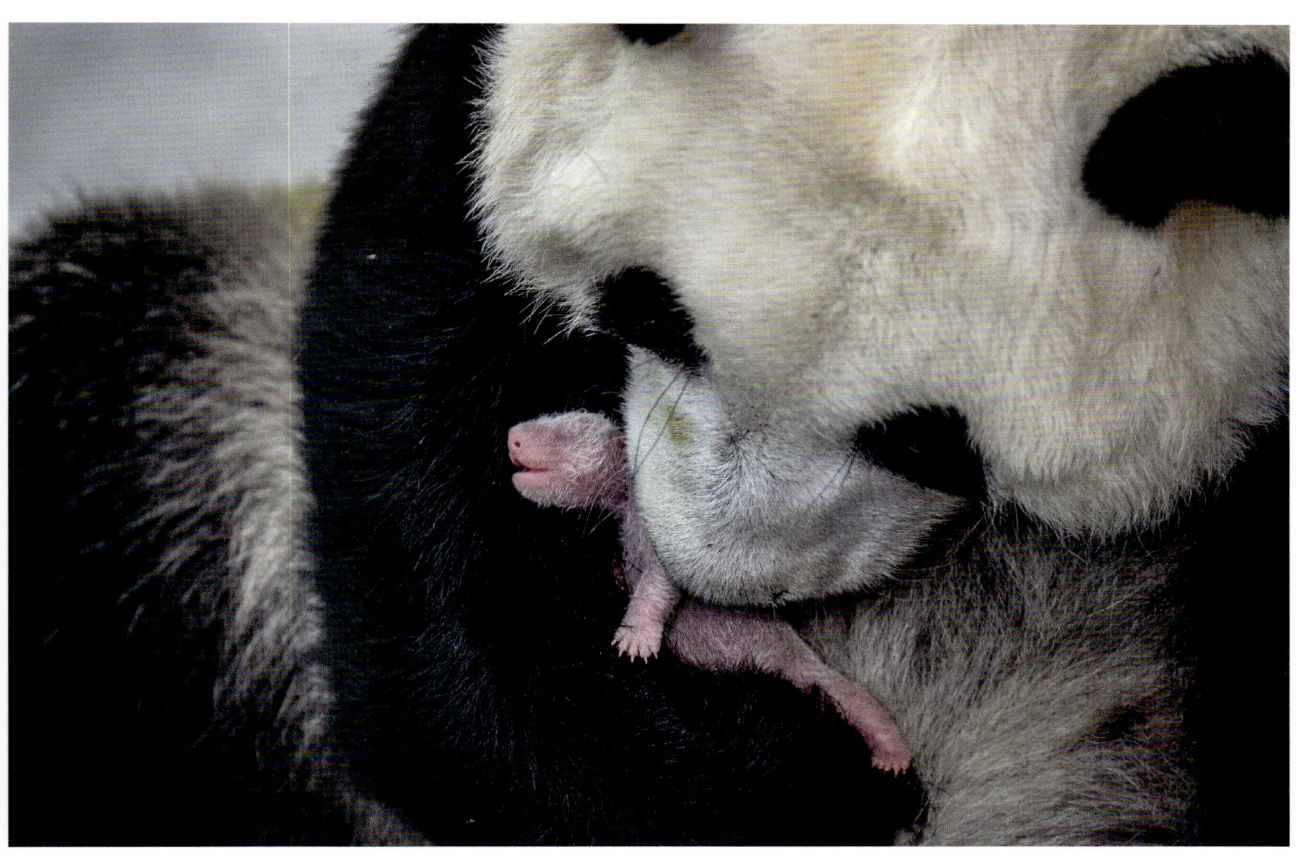

Once endangered, the giant panda is now considered vulnerable, meaning at lower risk of extinction. China's efforts to eliminate poaching and to protect the panda's habitat played a large role in increasing numbers. *Previous spread*: Panda keepers listen for radio signals from a collared panda, in training to be released into the wild, at Wolong Reserve, Sichuan, China. *Facing page*: Bears mate, watched by a keeper, at Bifengxia Panda Base, Sichuan. *Above*: Min Min tends to her new-born cub, at Bifengxia. (*continues*)

(*continued*) Two-thirds of the world's wild pandas live in nature reserves in the bamboo-rich forests above the Sichuan Basin. The original decline of the species was attributed in part to the disappearance of bamboo, the panda's principle food, as forests were converted to farmland. China's restoration of the animal's habitat has led to an increase in geographic range, and animals bred in captivity are now being reintroduced to the wild. *Right*: A keeper wears a panda suit in the hope of keeping bears about to be released into the wild as free as possible from human contact.

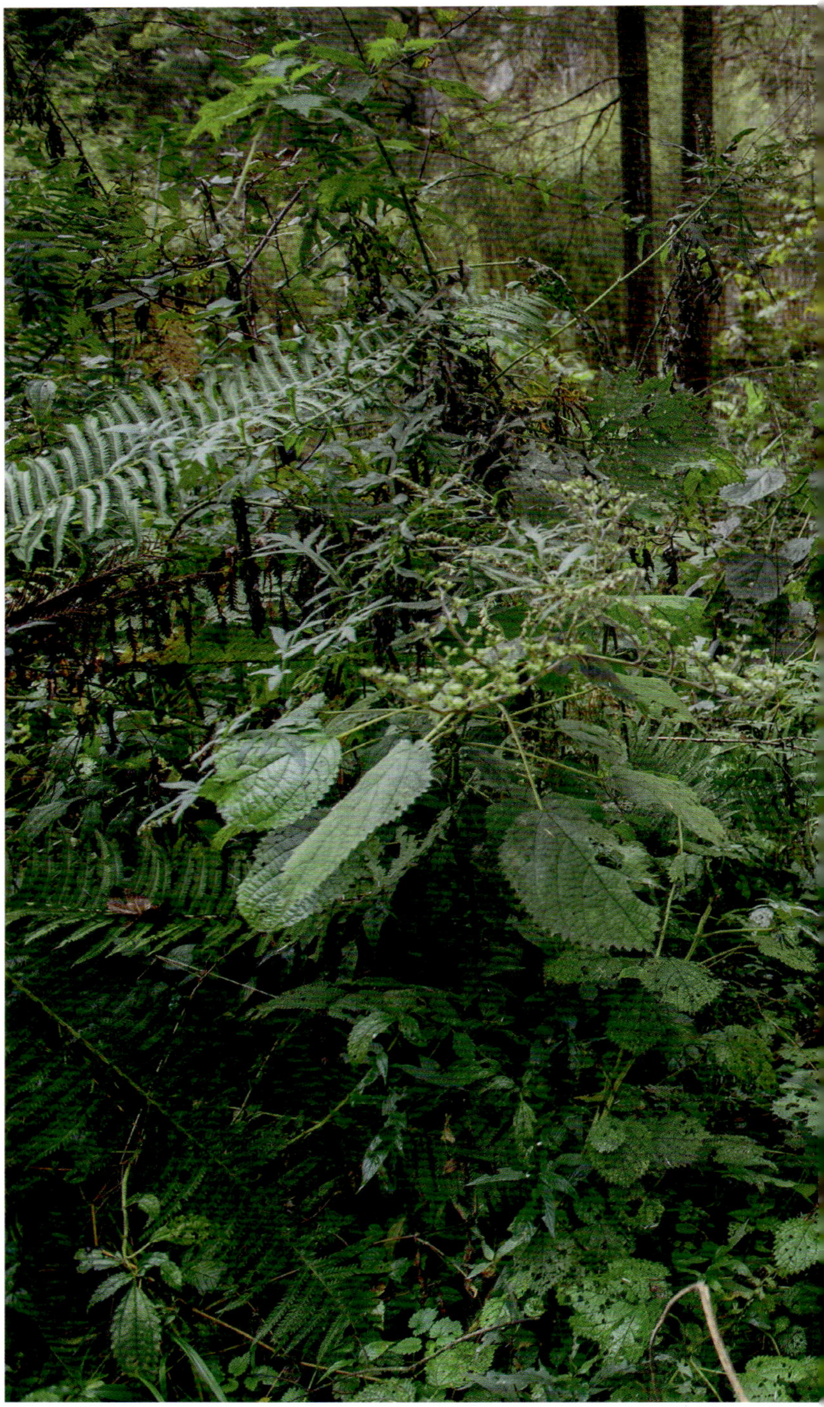

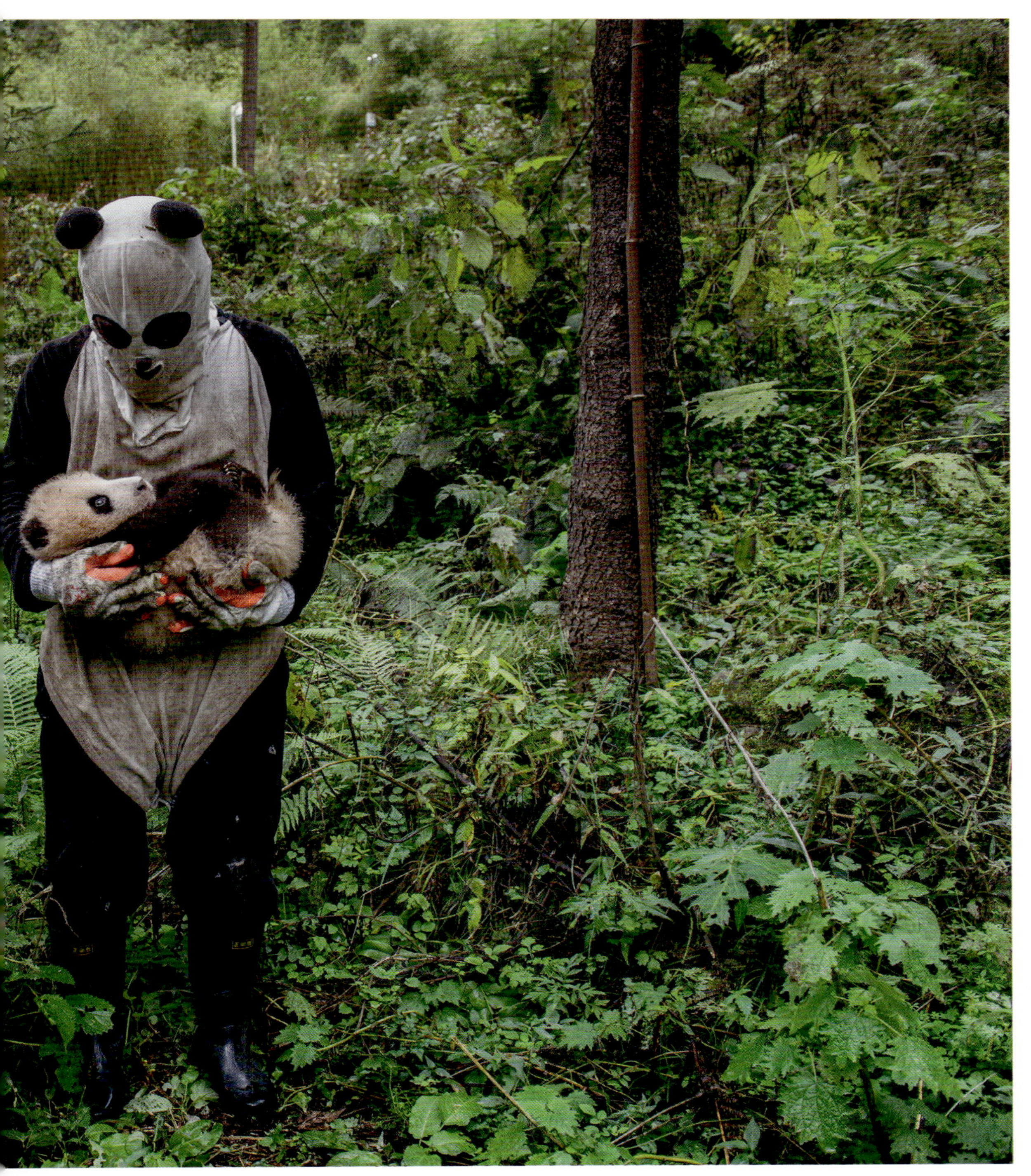

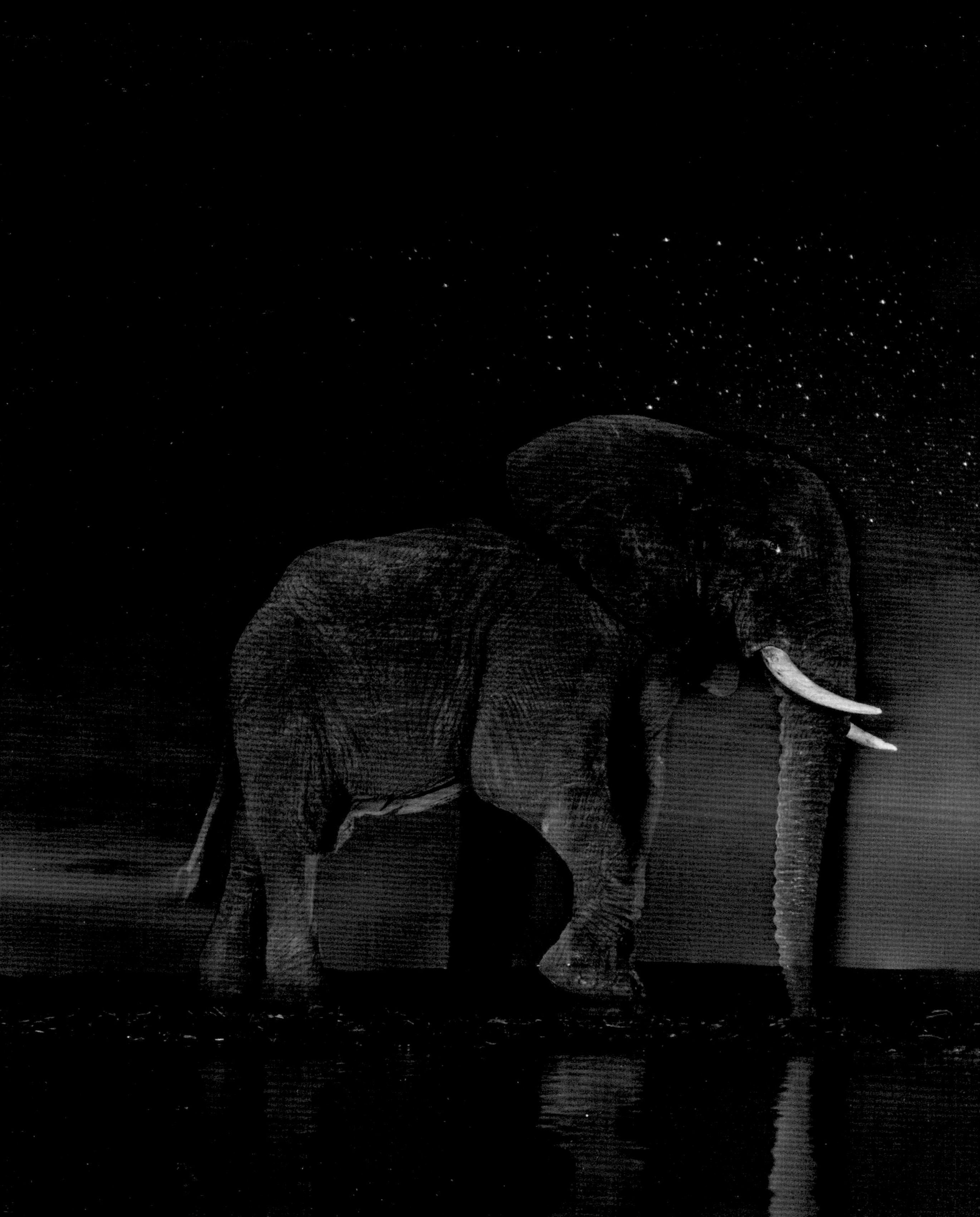

Bence Máté

Hungary /
3rd Prize Nature

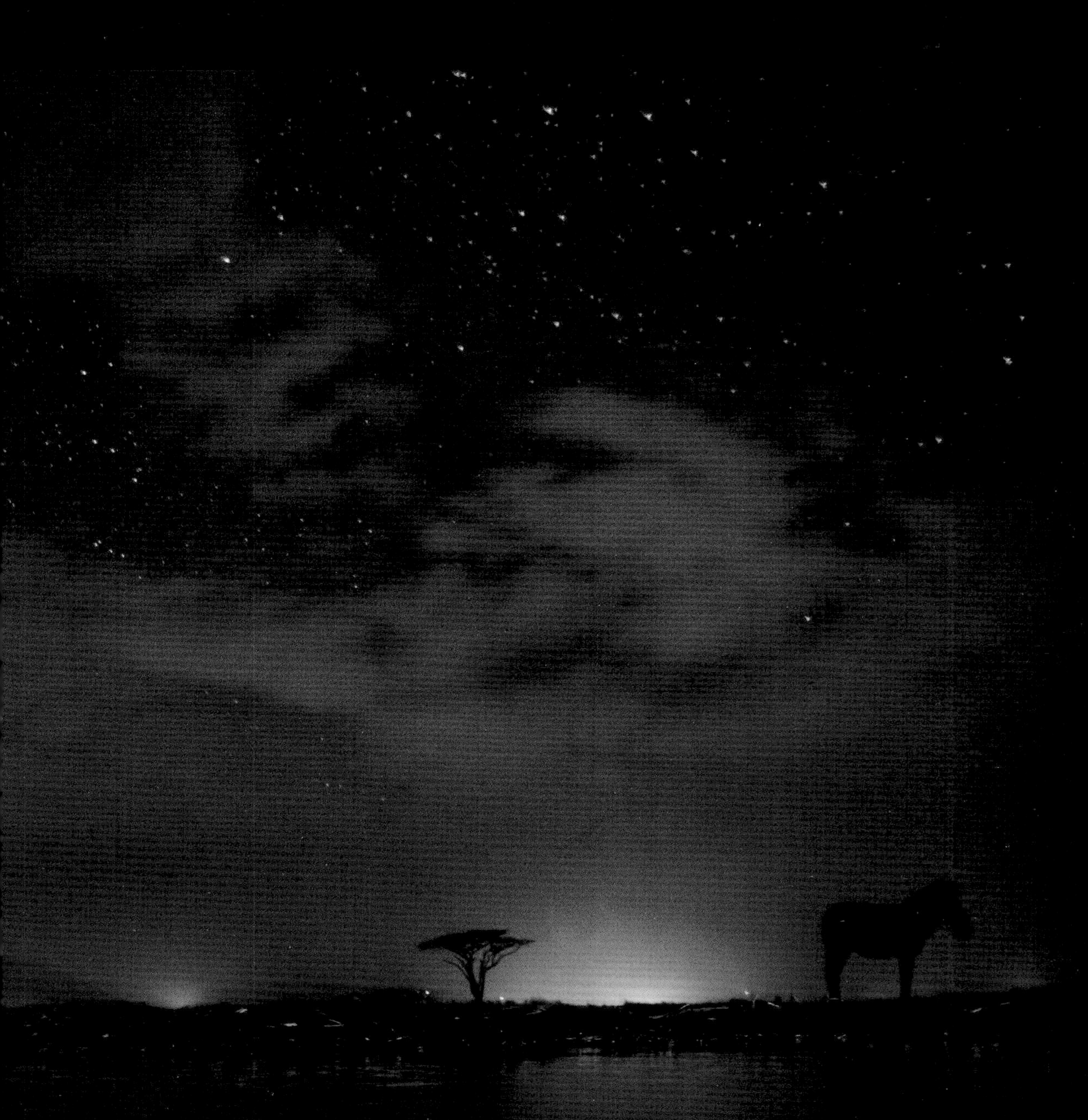

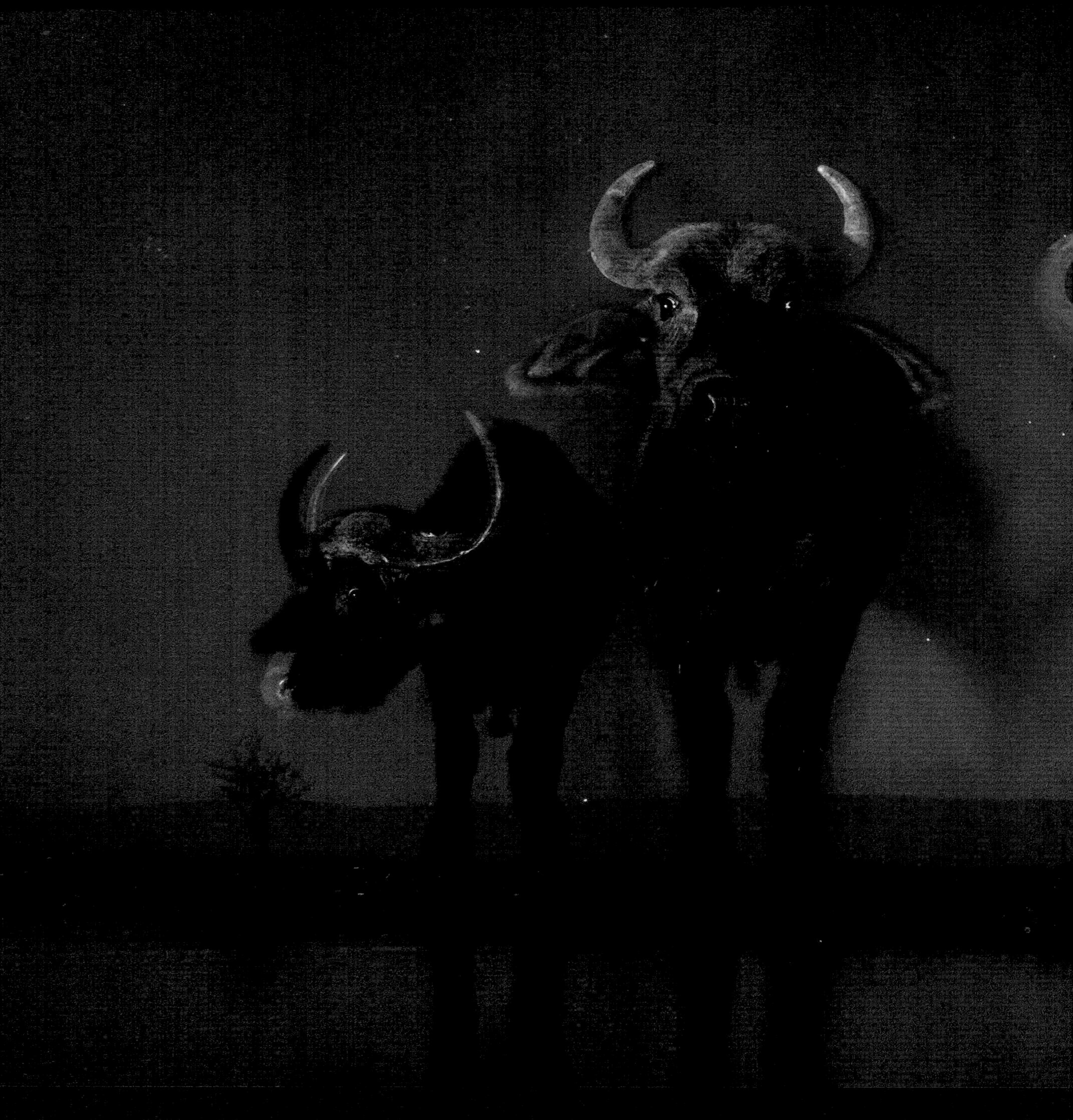

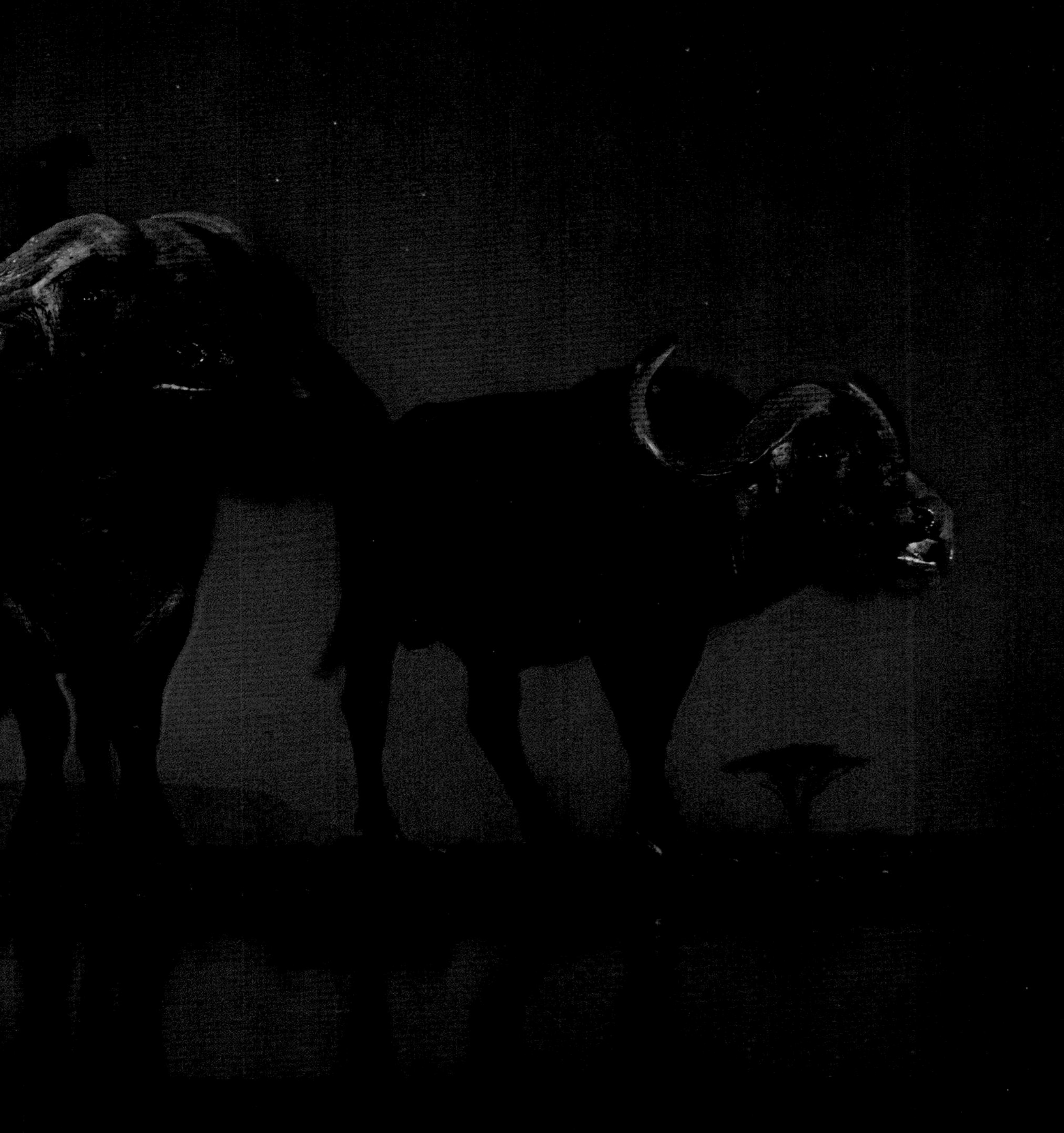

Animals pictured at night in their natural habitats. *Previous spread*: An elephant and zebra at a watering hole in Zimanga Private Game Reserve, Mkuze, South Africa. *Above*: Buffalo at the Zimanga reserve. *Following spread*: A hippo at a watering hole in Zimanga.

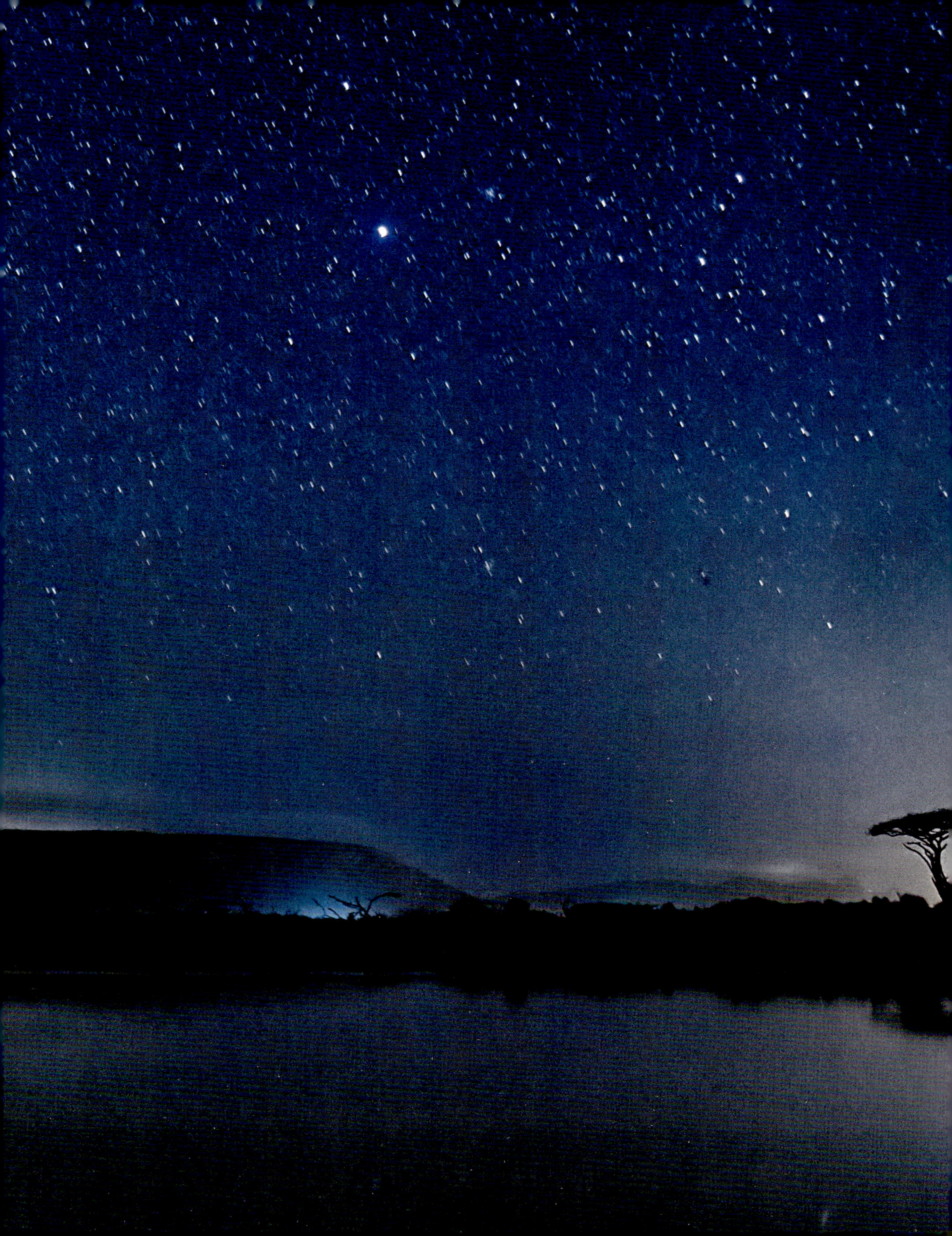

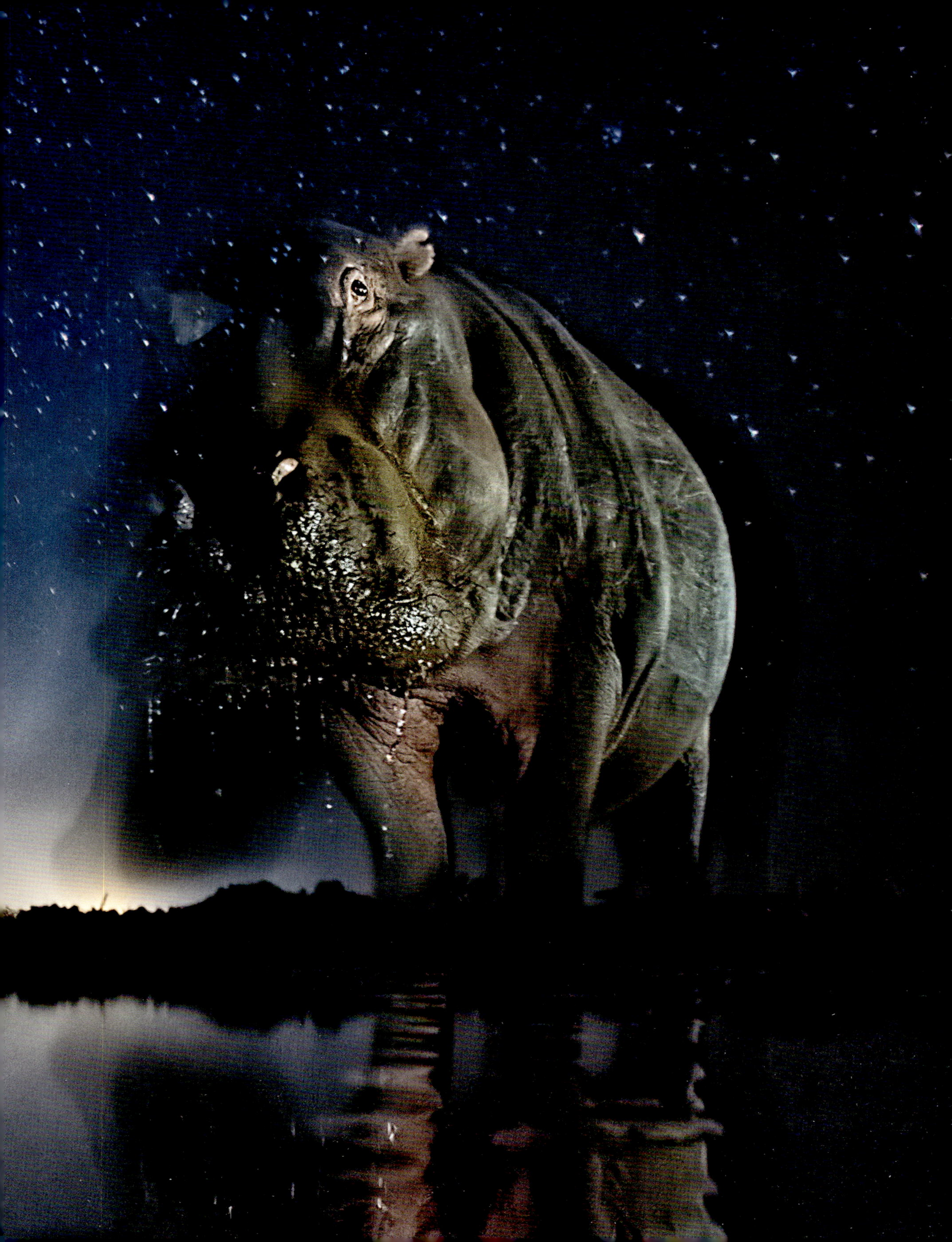

The 2017
Long-Term Projects

Valery Melnikov

Russia, Rossiya Segodnya /
1st Prize

Black Days of Ukraine

Donetsk and Luhansk are two self-proclaimed, pro-Russian 'People's Republics' in the Donbass region in easternmost Ukraine. A 2001 government census showed that 74.9 percent of the population in the Donetsk region and 68.8 percent of the Luhansk region have Russian as a mother tongue. In April 2014, a month after Russian forces had entered Crimea in southern Ukraine, pro-Russian separatists seized parts of Donetsk and Luhansk. The Ukrainian government launched a military operation in response, and over the course of the summer the conflict escalated into full-scale hostilities. In August 2014 (and again in February 2015) Russian forces gave active support in training and equipment to the rebels. A ceasefire was signed in September 2014, but was repeatedly violated before breaking down completely.

The photographer first went to Luhansk in the early summer of 2014, and witnessed conditions change as hostilities intensified. He believes that the most important side to any conflict is the third one: that of the ordinary people caught up in the violence. Civilians in Luhansk and Donetsk had to survive often without running water or electricity, under repeated shelling, experiencing the destruction of their homes and the deaths of friends and relatives.

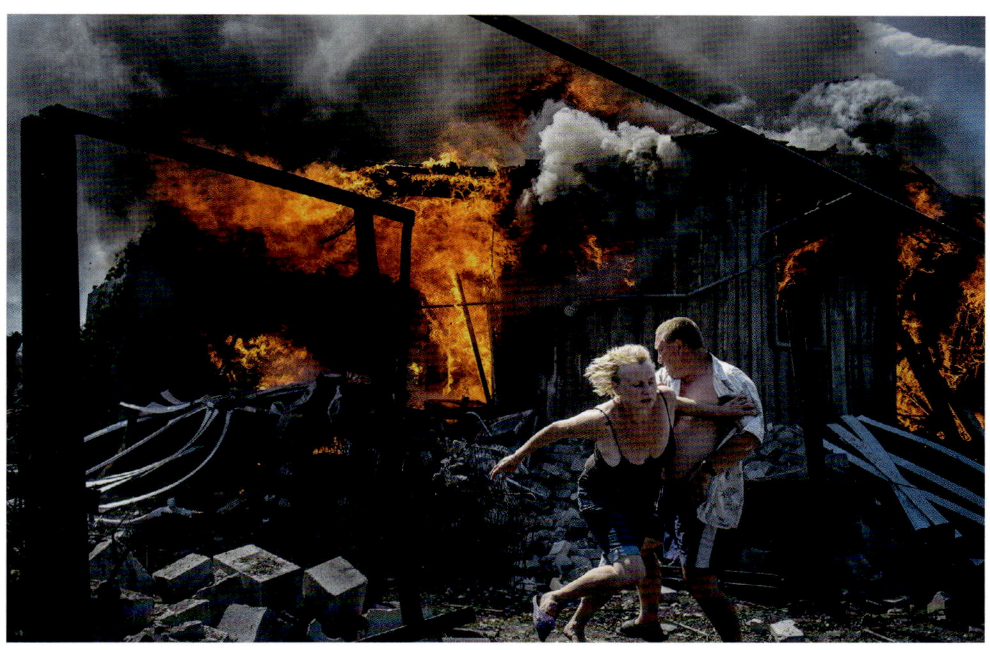

Top: Civilians escape from a fire in a house hit during an air attack, in the village of Luhanskaya, Luhansk, in July 2014. *Below*: A refugee family and baby look out through the window of a bus, at a checkpoint on the border between Ukraine and Russia. *Next spread*: A house destroyed during an air attack on the village of Luhanskaya, about 27 kilometers out of Luhansk city.

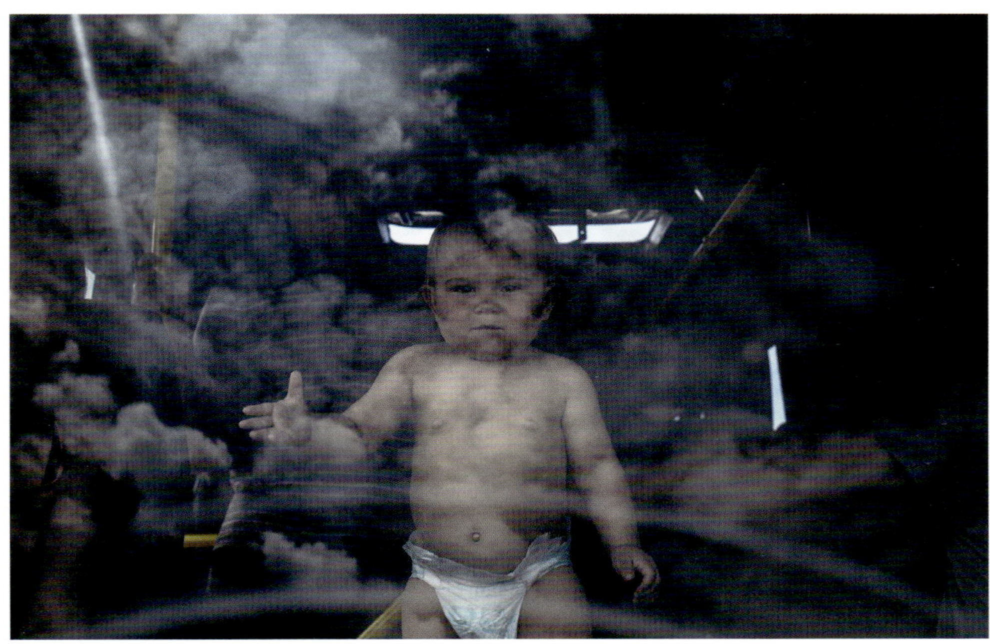

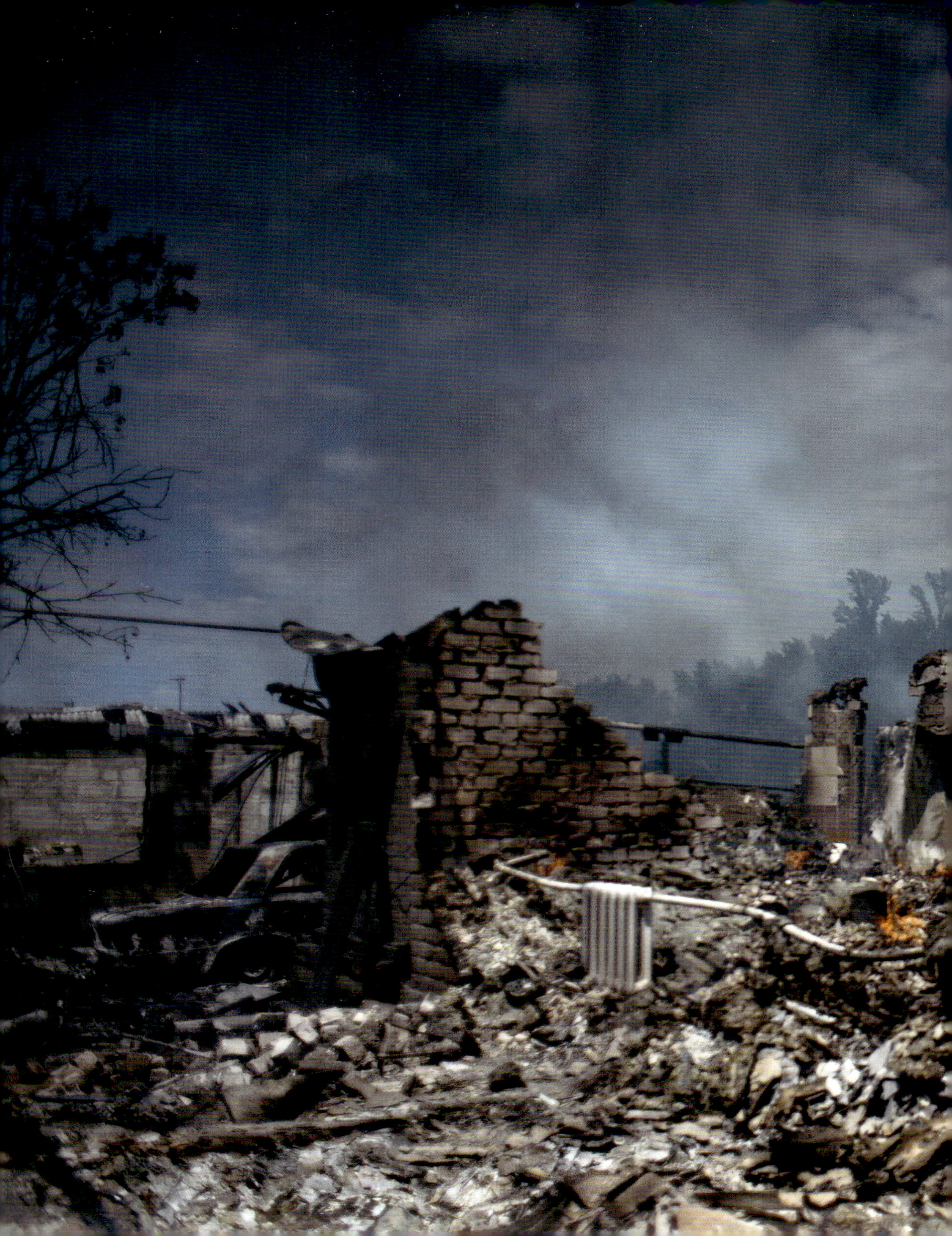

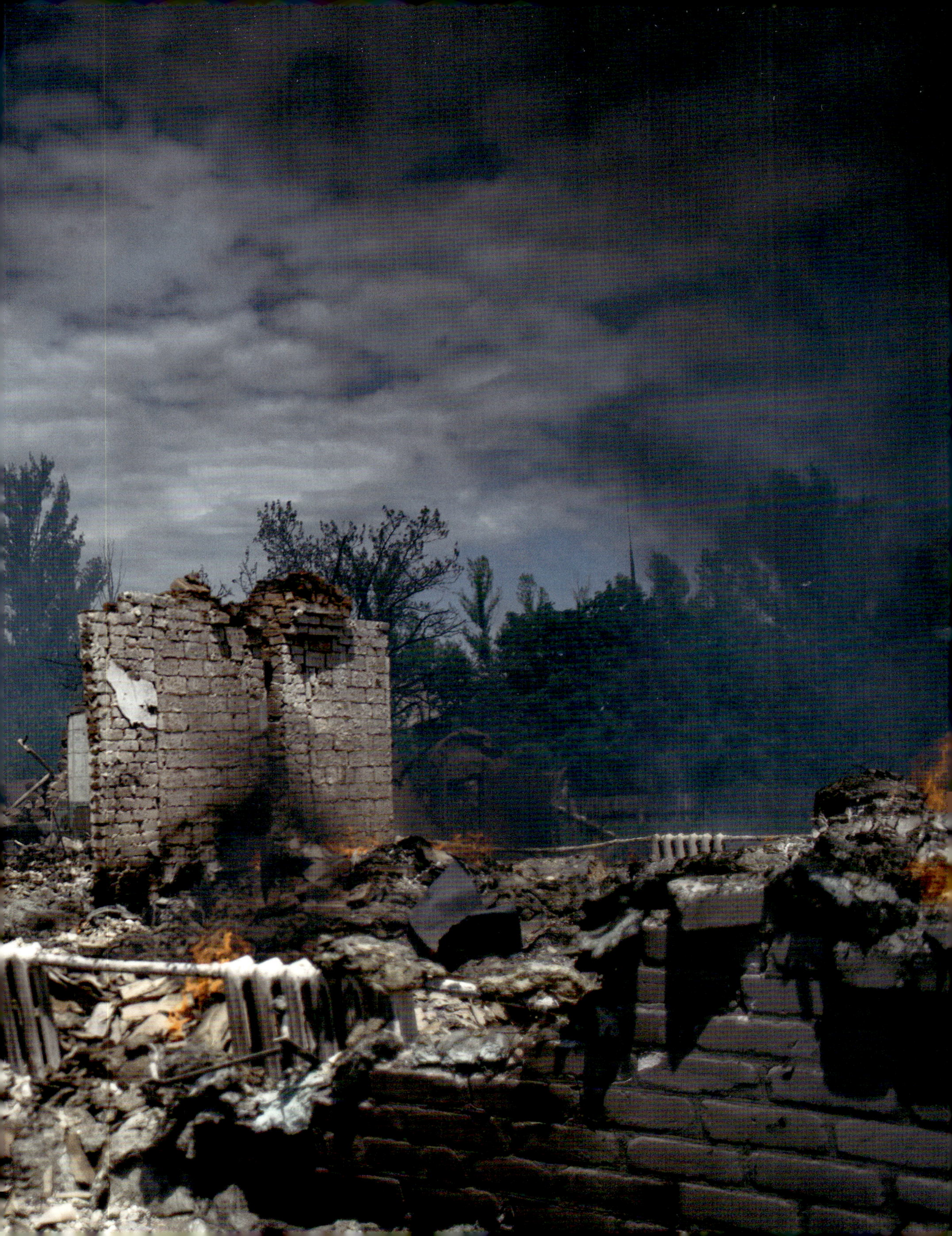

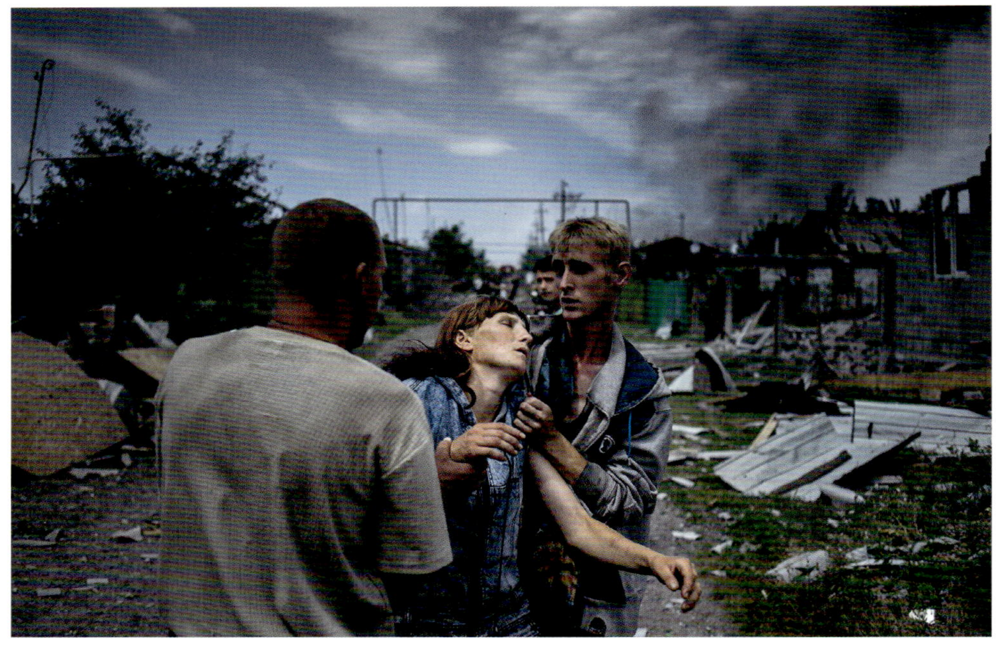

Top: Citizens help each other in Luhanskaya, Luhansk, after an air attack in July 2014. *Below*: A youth in Donetsk handles a gun. The conflict in the region gave rise to a patriotic youth movement. A youth club set up by separatist authorities in Donetsk glorifies the Soviet past and aims to develop the newly declared republic.

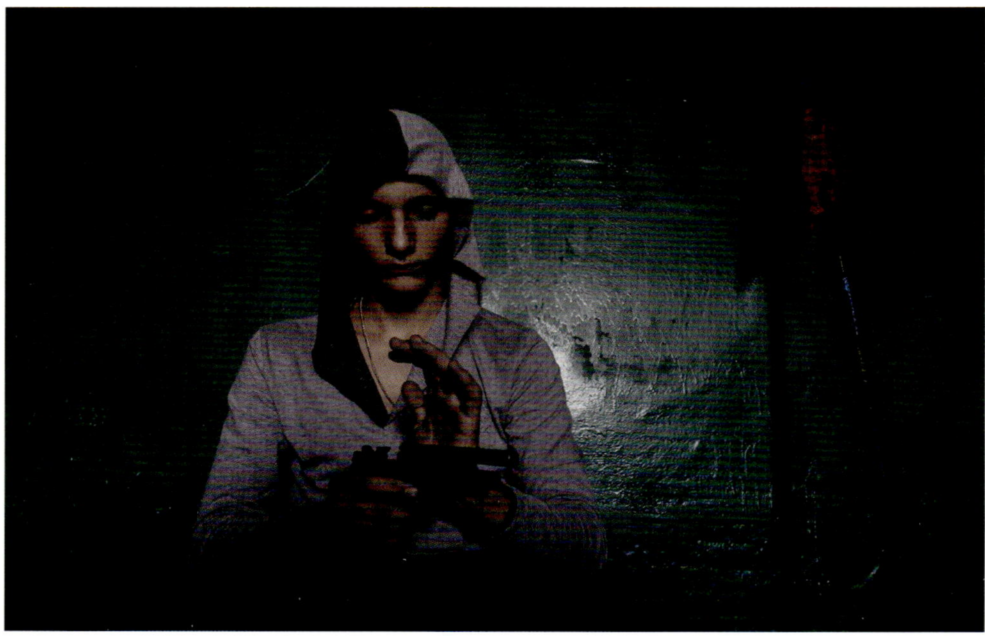

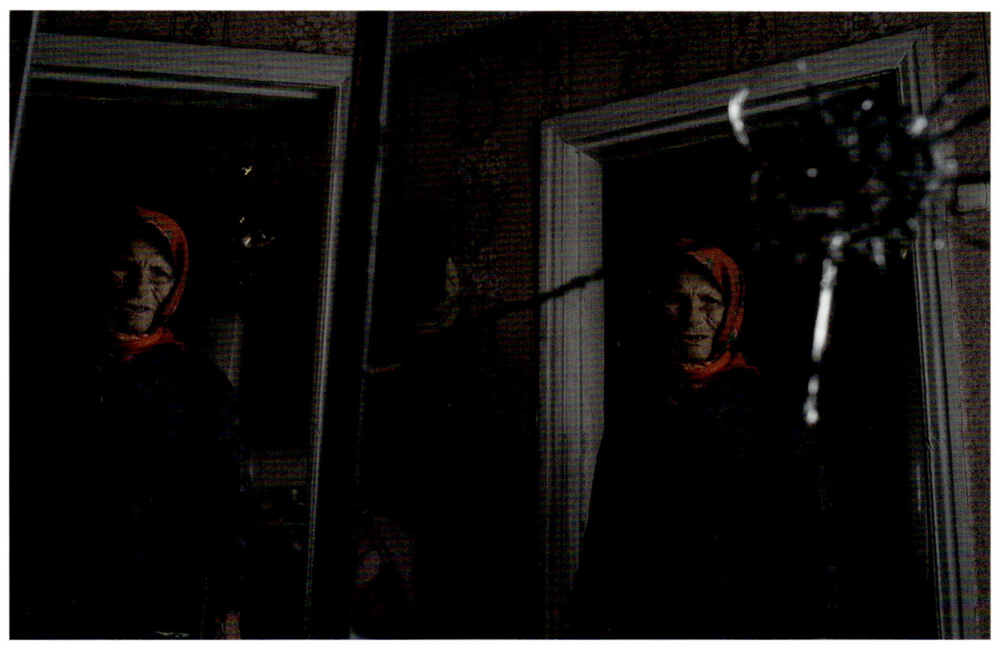

Top: Raisa Shipulya (85), one of the last residents of the devastated village of Zhelobok, stands in her house in September 2015. *Below*: A woman escapes from a fire during an artillery attack on the Krasnodon highway, Luhansk. *Next spread*: Buildings in the village of Veseloe, near Donetsk airport, burn following shelling in October 2015.

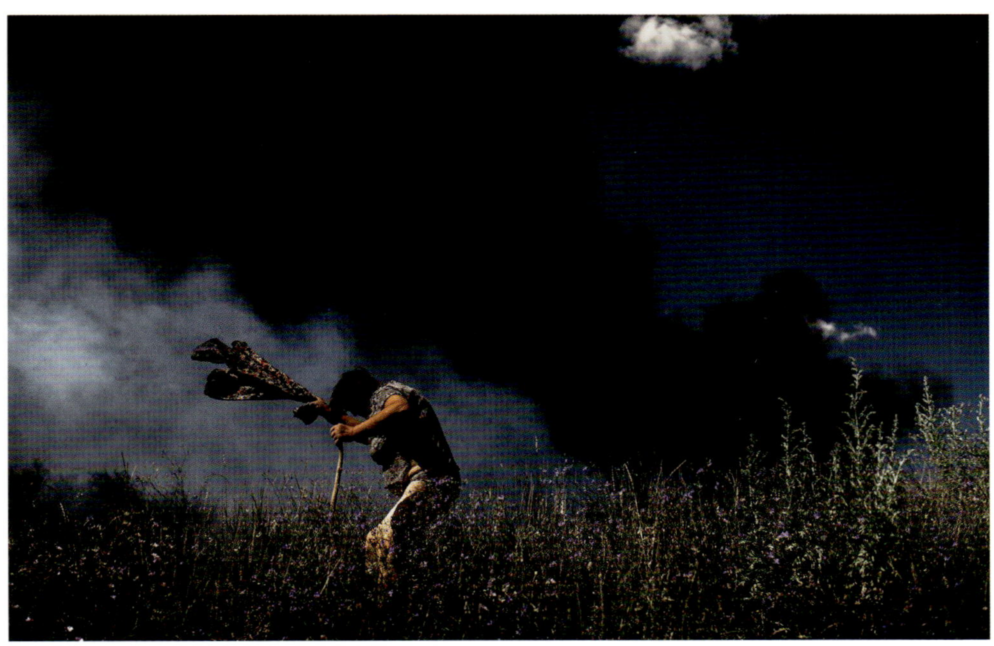

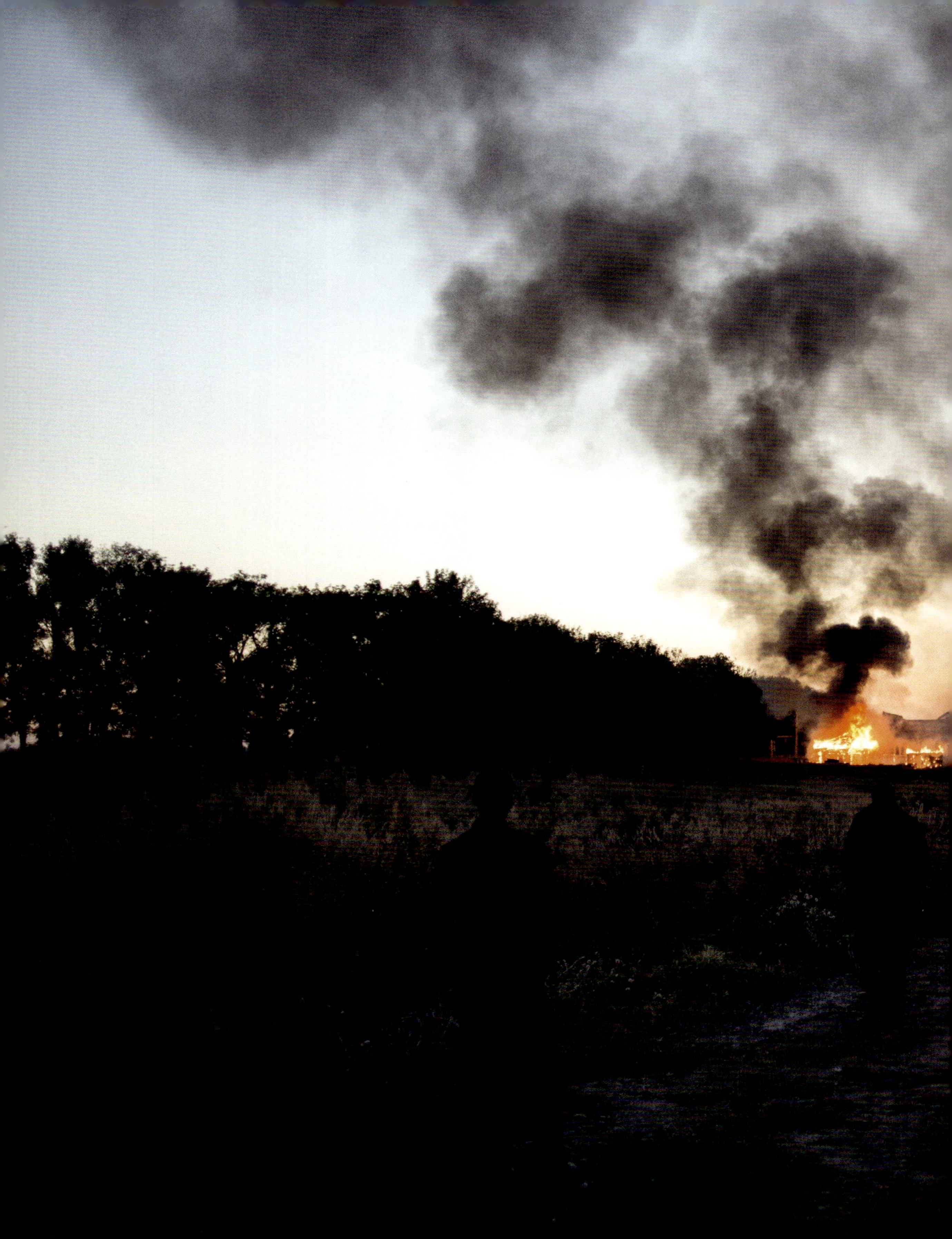

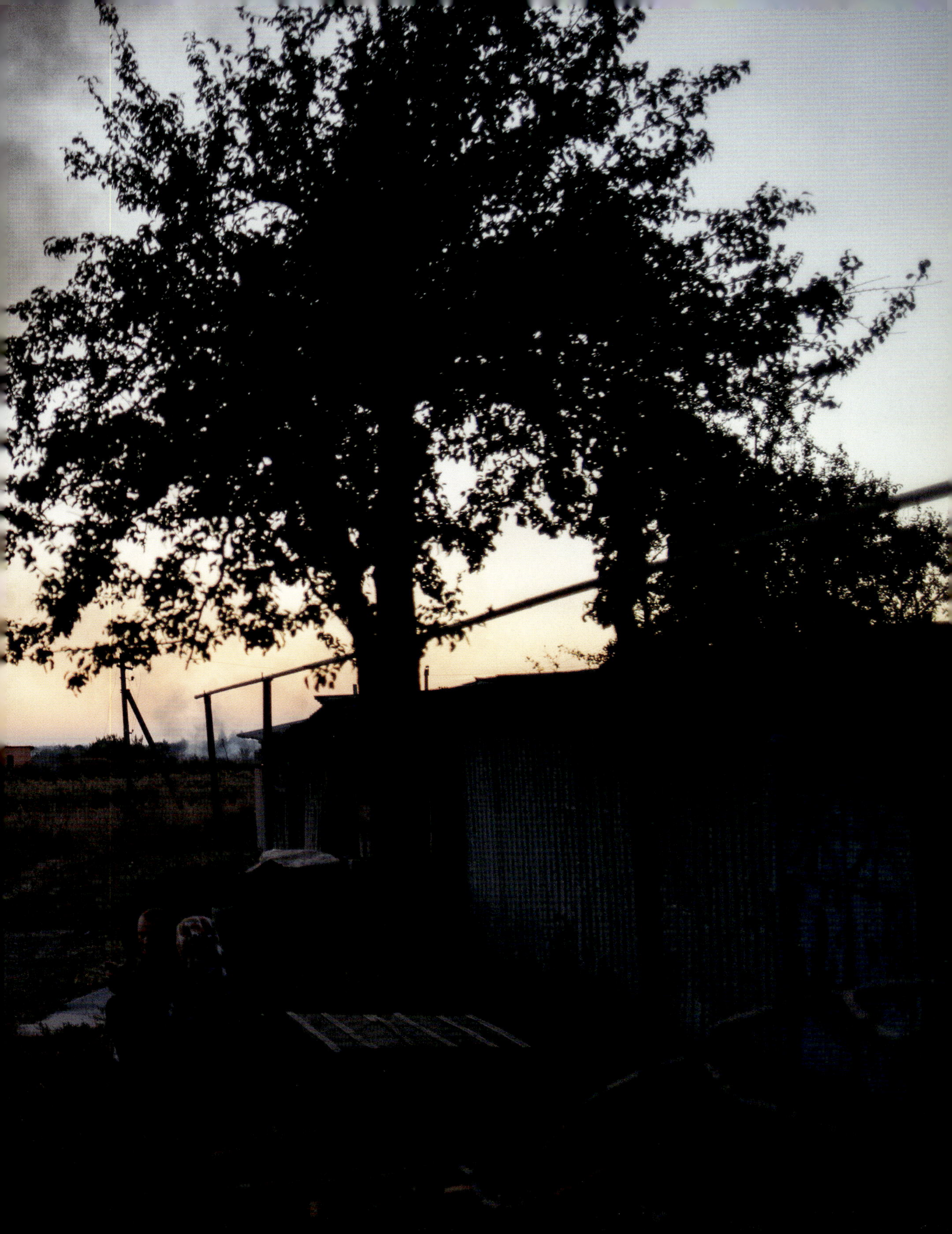

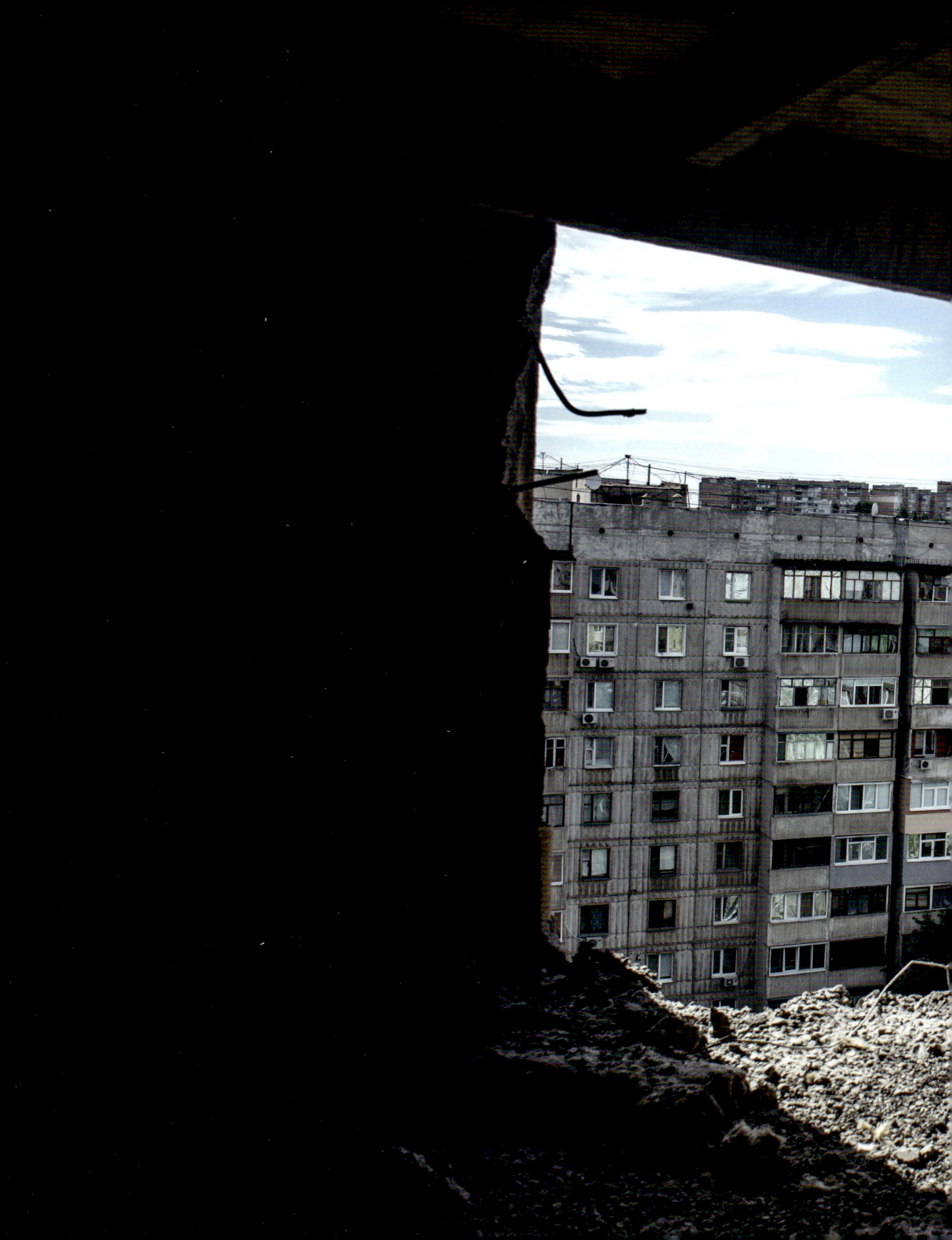

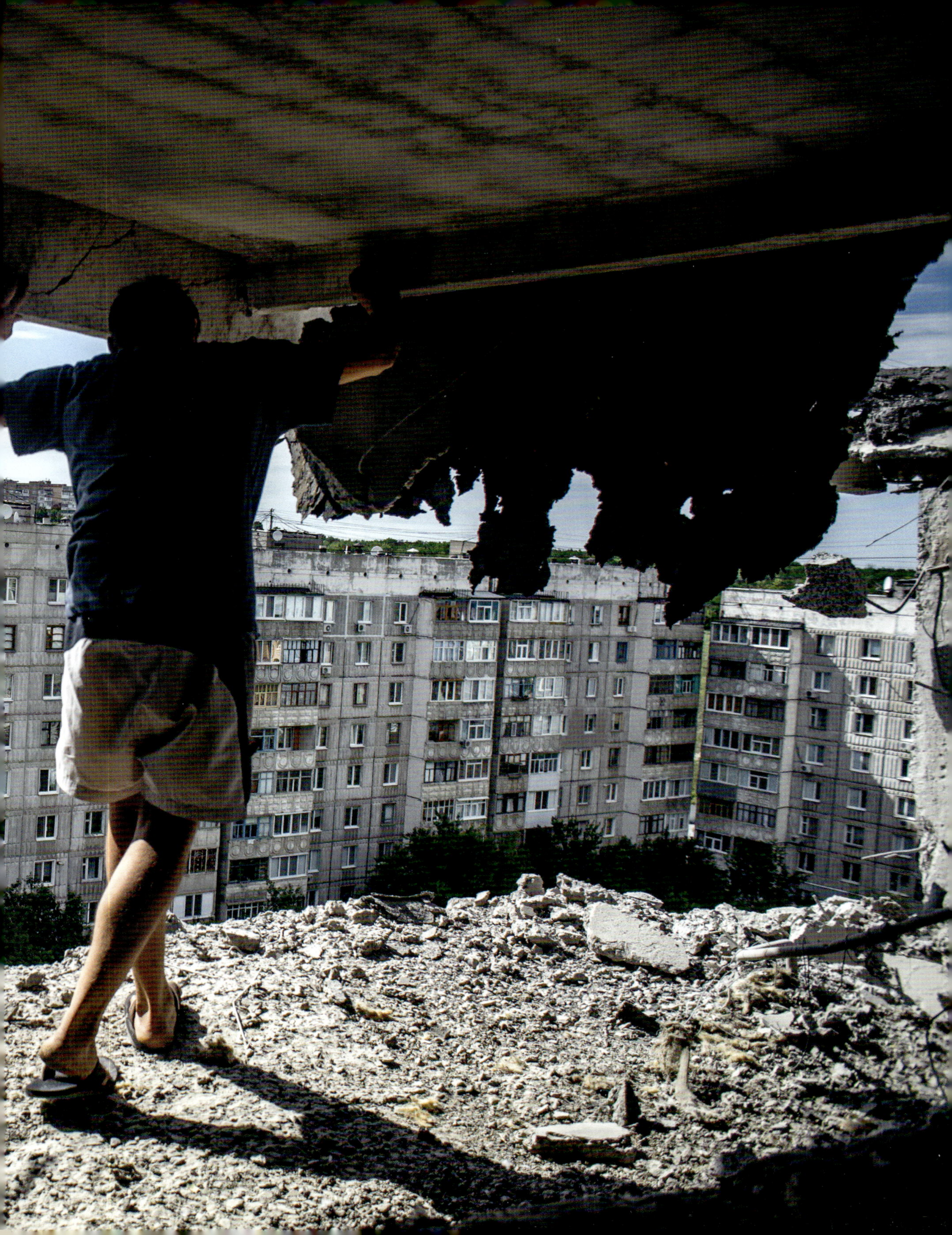

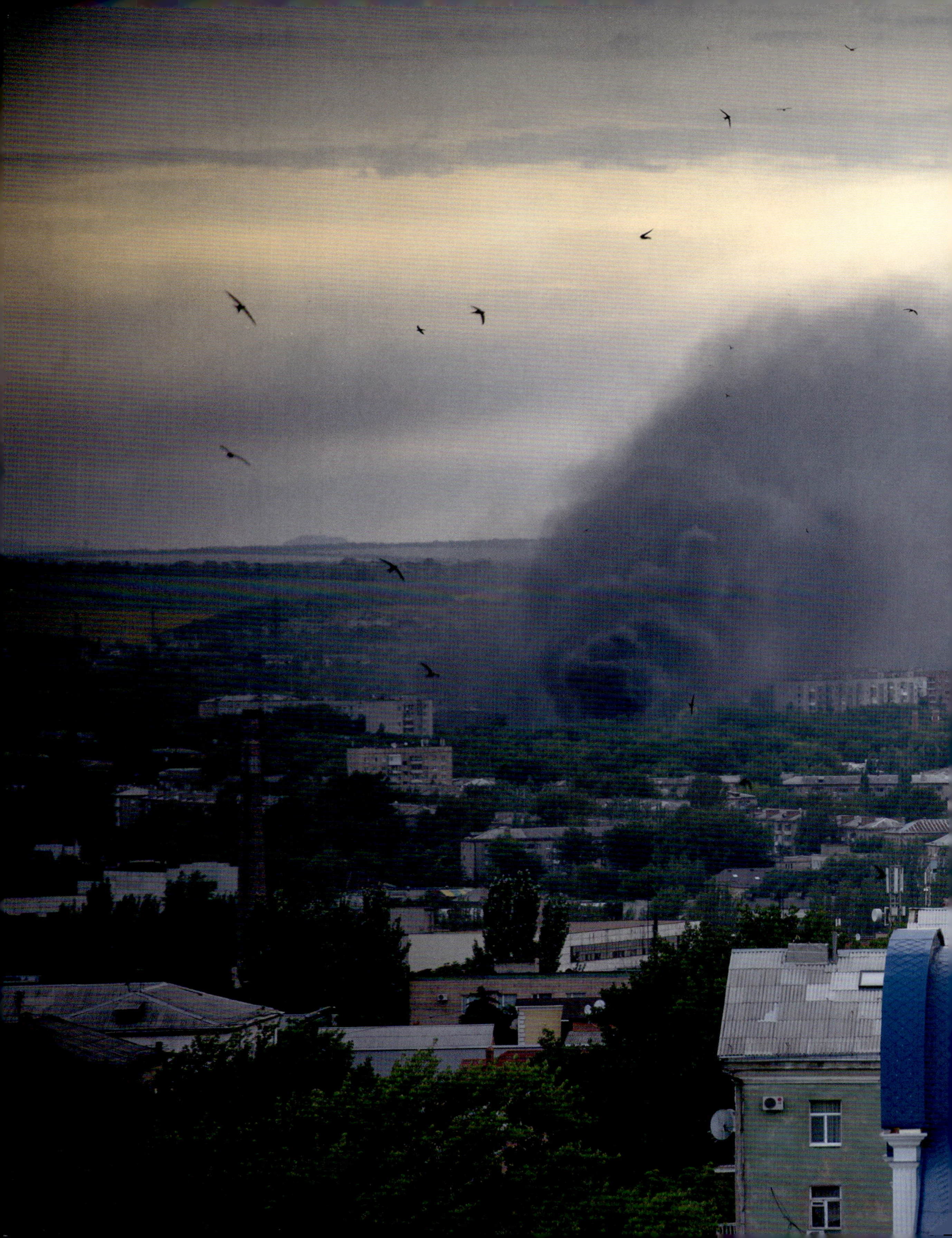

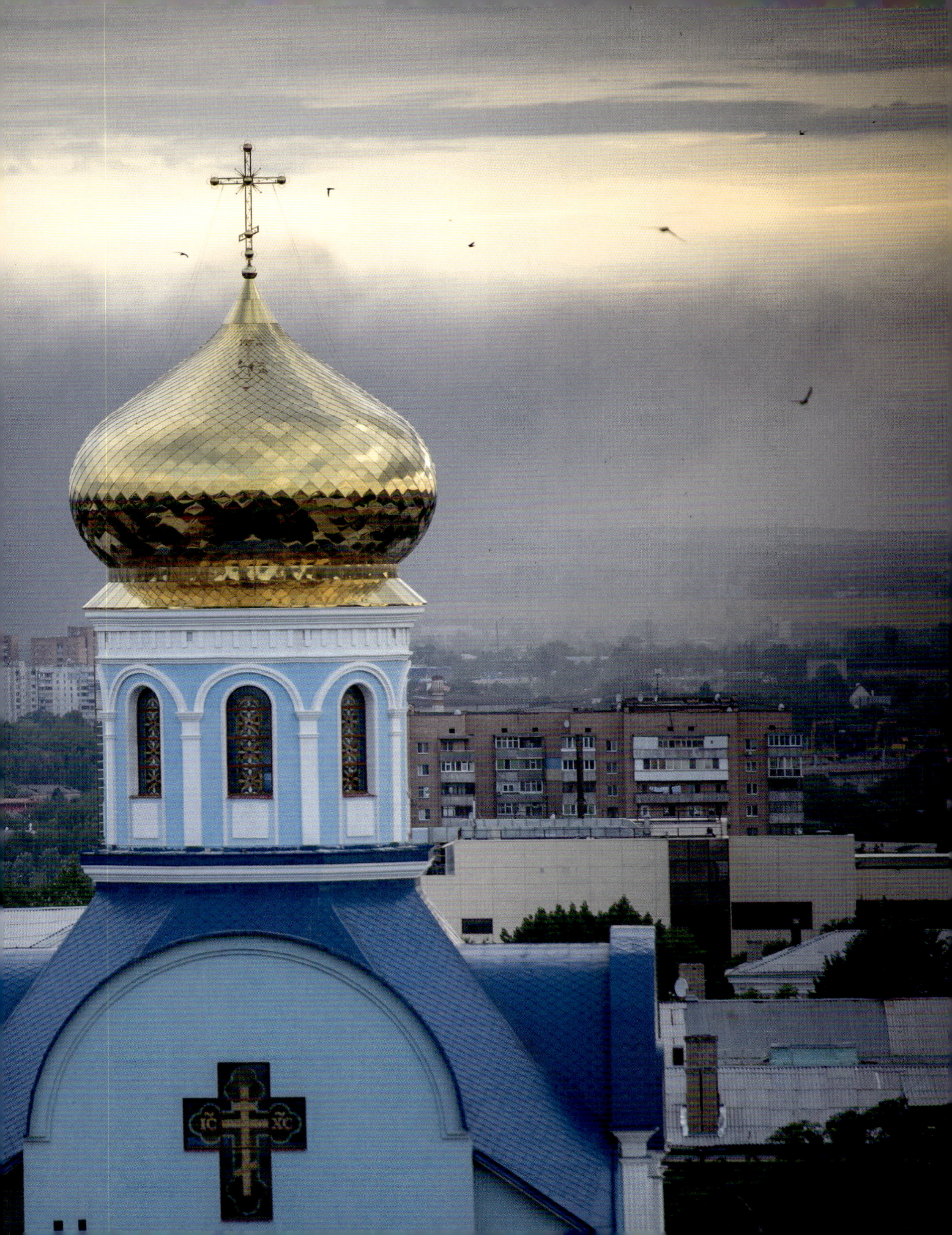
IC
XC

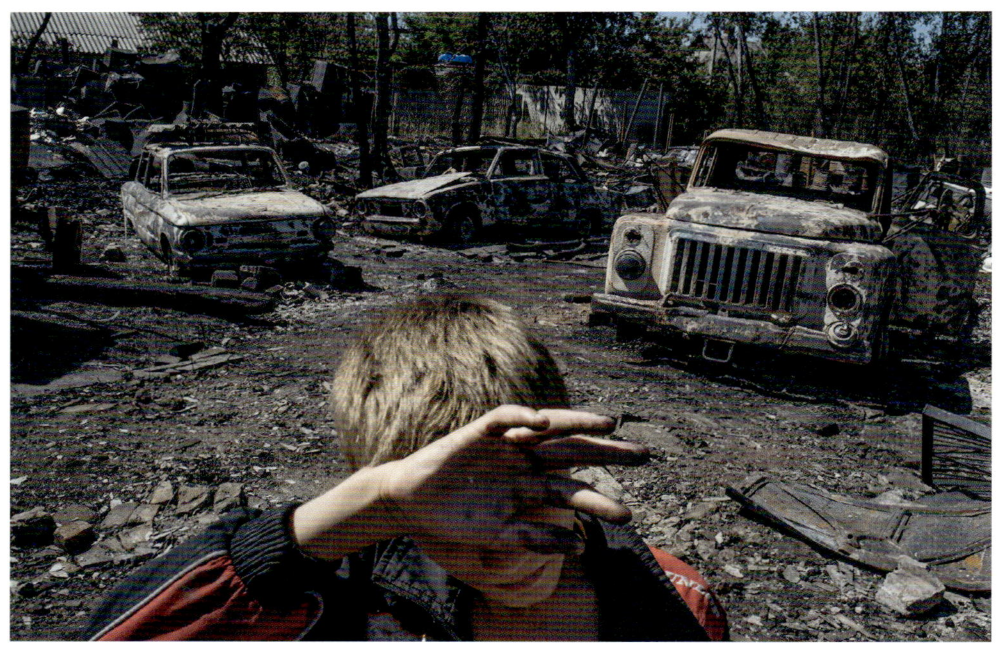

Two spreads back: A man inspects damage to a building in the Mirny district of the city of Luhansk. *Previous spread*: Buildings in Luhansk city burn during an artillery attack. *Top*: A villager walks past burnt-out cars in Lozovoe, Luhansk. *Below*: Ivan Ermilov (5), who was killed during shelling in Luhanskaya, lies in his coffin on 4 July 2014.

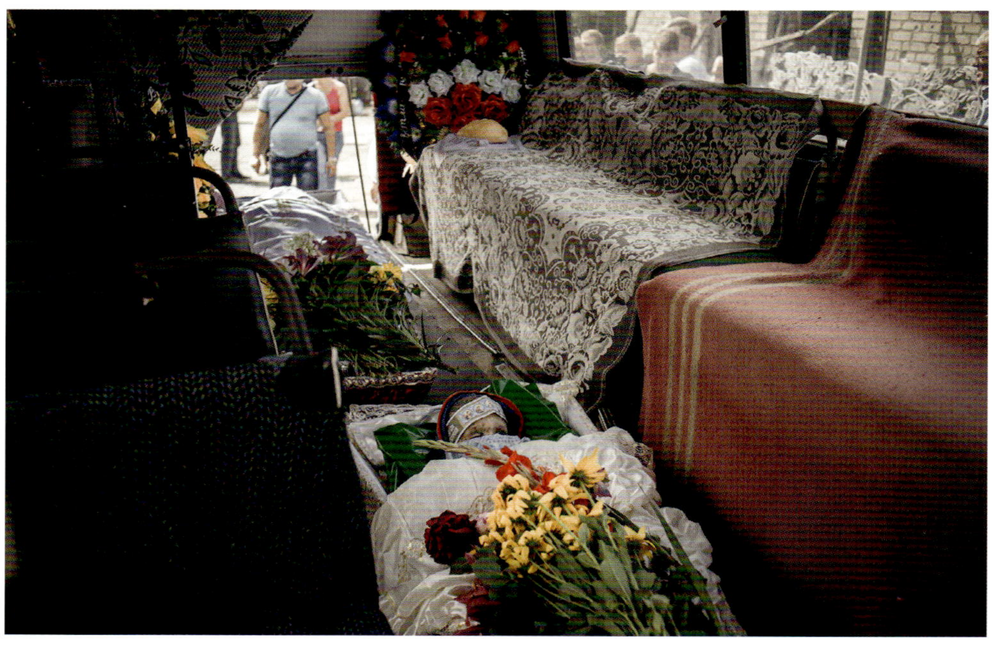

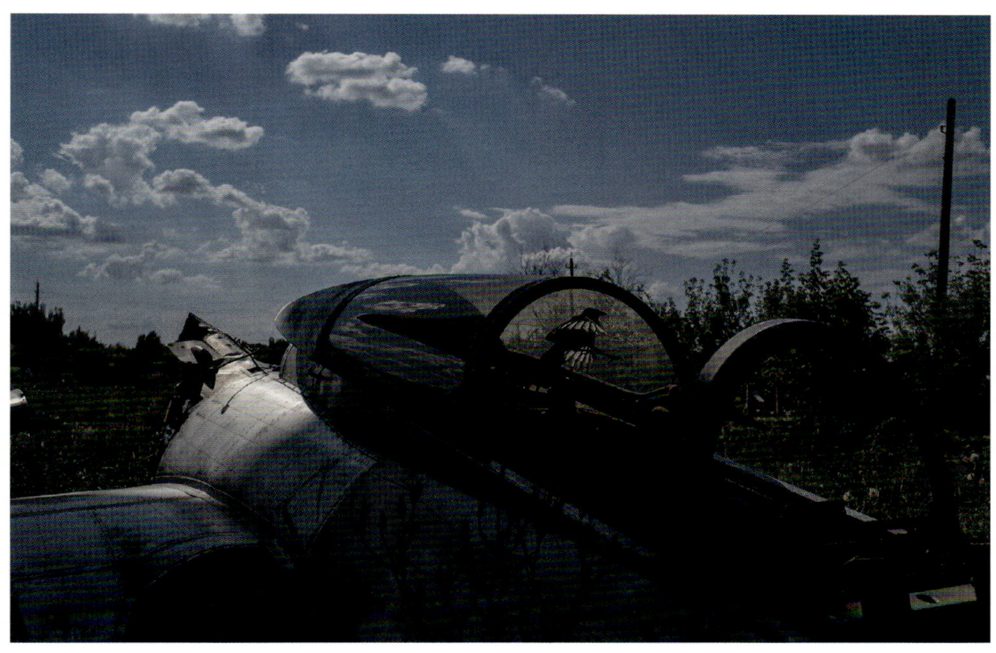

Top: A plane damaged in an artillery attack, in Luhansk. *Below*: A man waters flowers in the village of Spartak in July 2016. *Following spread*: A woman sits outside her house, hit by shelling on 17 July 2014, in Luhansk.

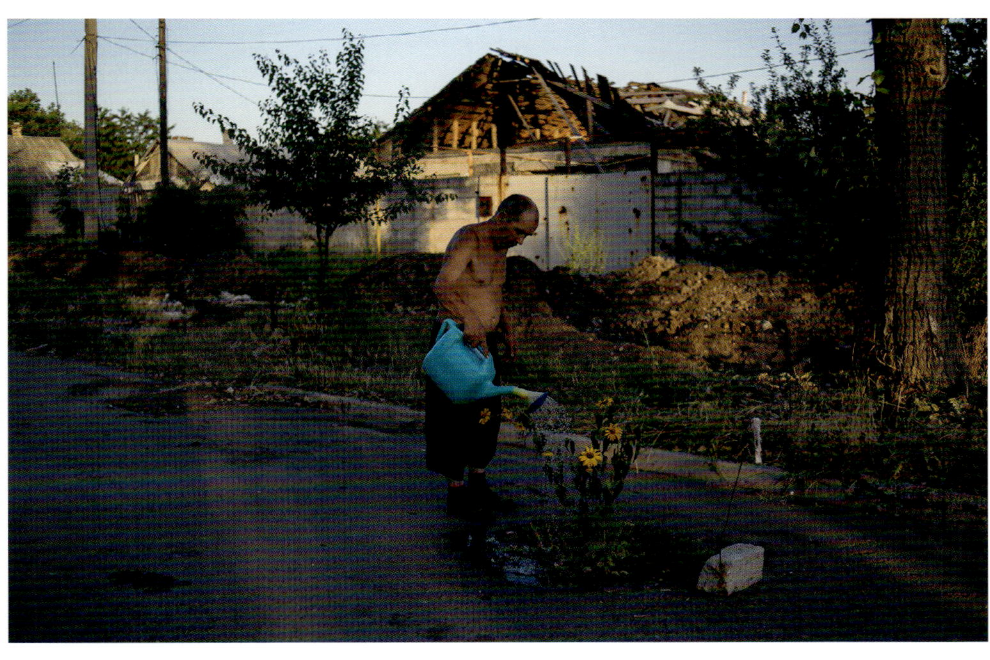

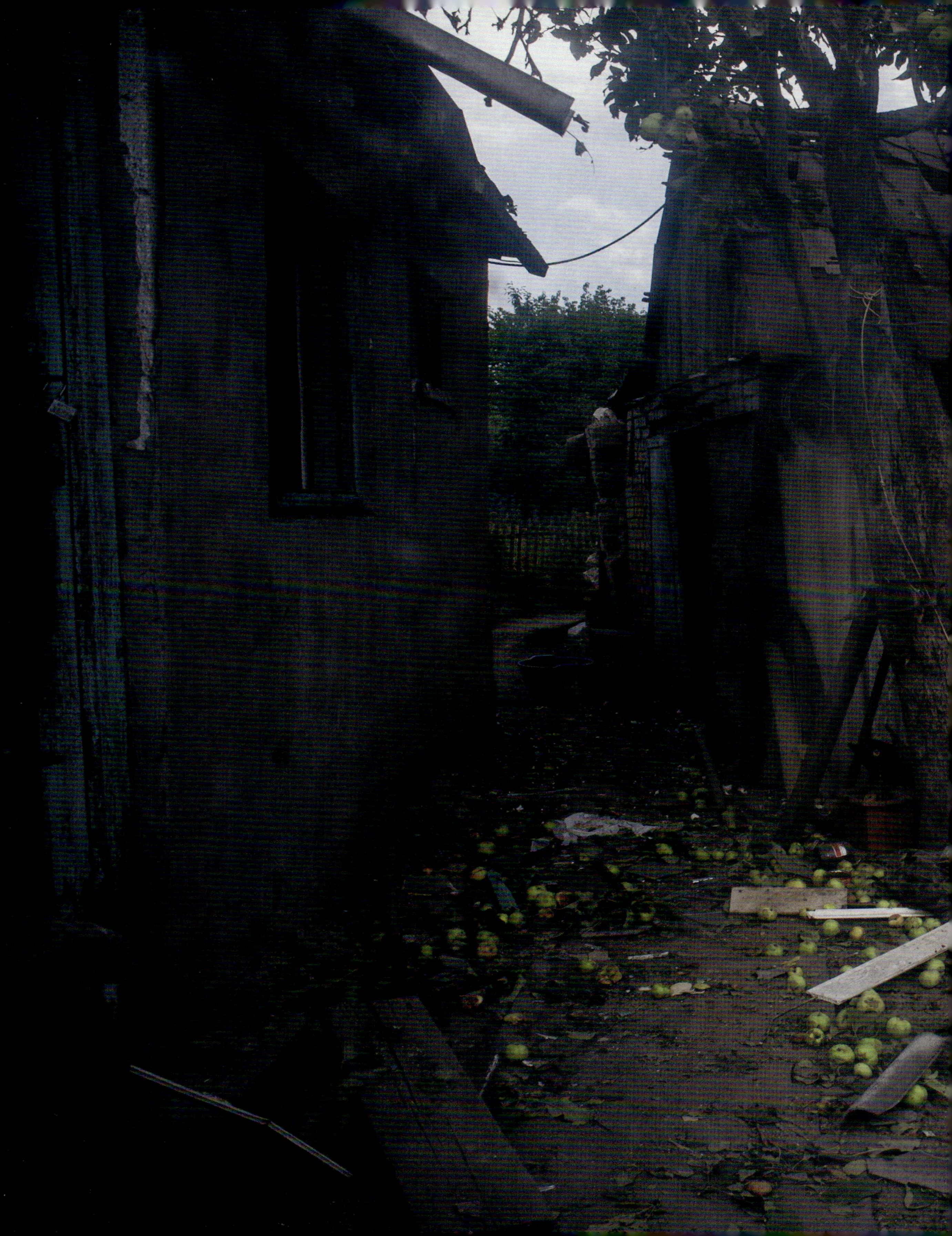

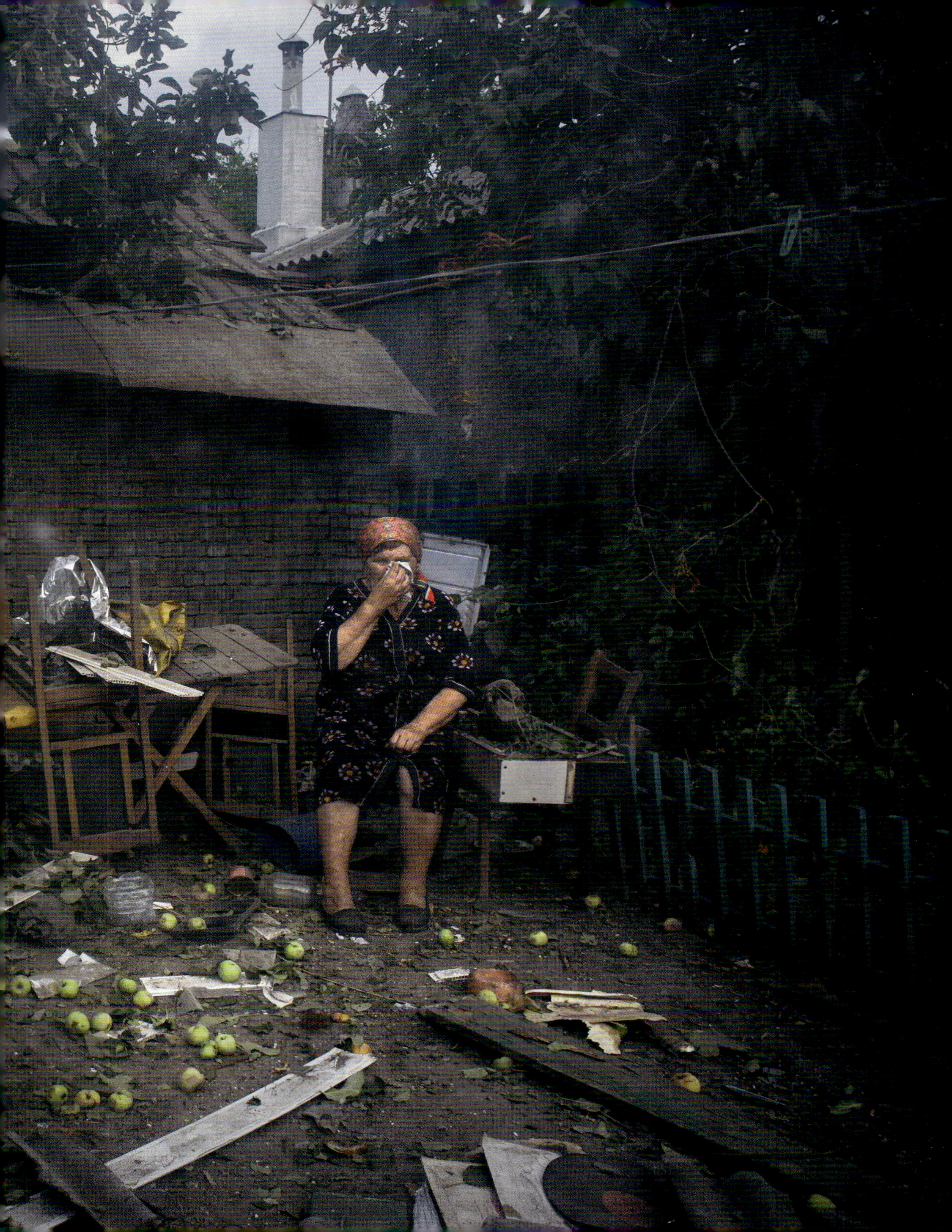

Hossein Fatemi

Iran, Panos Pictures /
2nd Prize

An Iranian Journey

Since the Islamic Revolution in Iran in 1979, the country has followed a strictly conservative theocratic line. Western cultural influences have been severely restricted. An estimated 60 percent of Iran's population is under 30 and have little knowledge of their country before the revolution, yet all the trappings of Western youth and modernity are now beamed into homes via the internet and (as yet still illegal) satellite television. Daily, millions of young people engage in activities that are officially illegal and can carry severe penalties. The Basij—a volunteer militia—polices public morals, on the lookout for such offences as women showing too much hair, or couples inappropriately holding hands.

The photographer was born and raised in Iran and has been photographing his country for 15 years. He aims to document parts of Iran's complex society, showing less-observed areas of daily life.

Facing page, top: Women are made up in a beauty salon. *Below*: A cleric and his family walk on Valiasr Street, one of Tehran's main commercial thoroughfares. *Next spread*: Young men and women in a swimming pool at a party in Tehran.

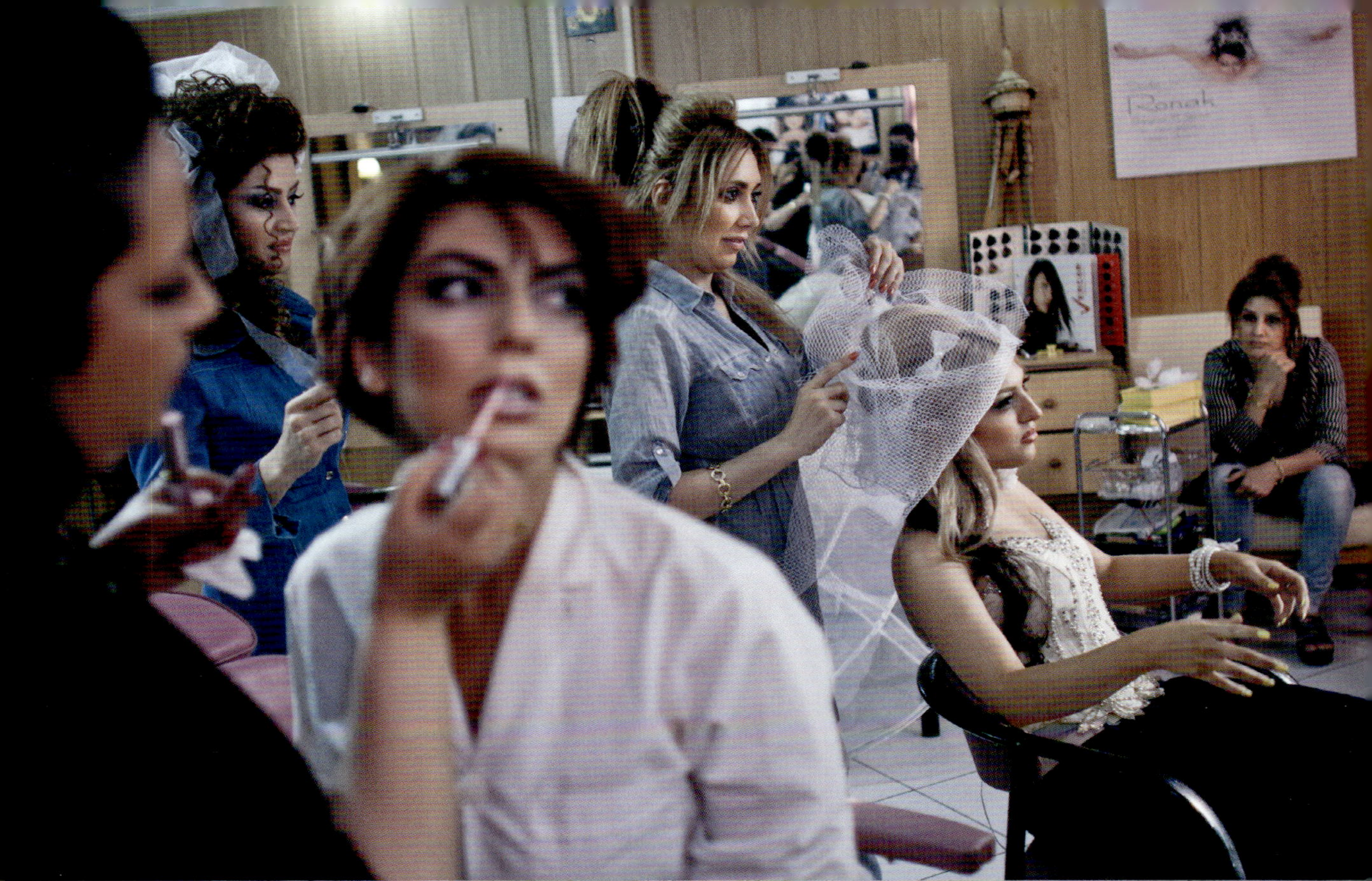

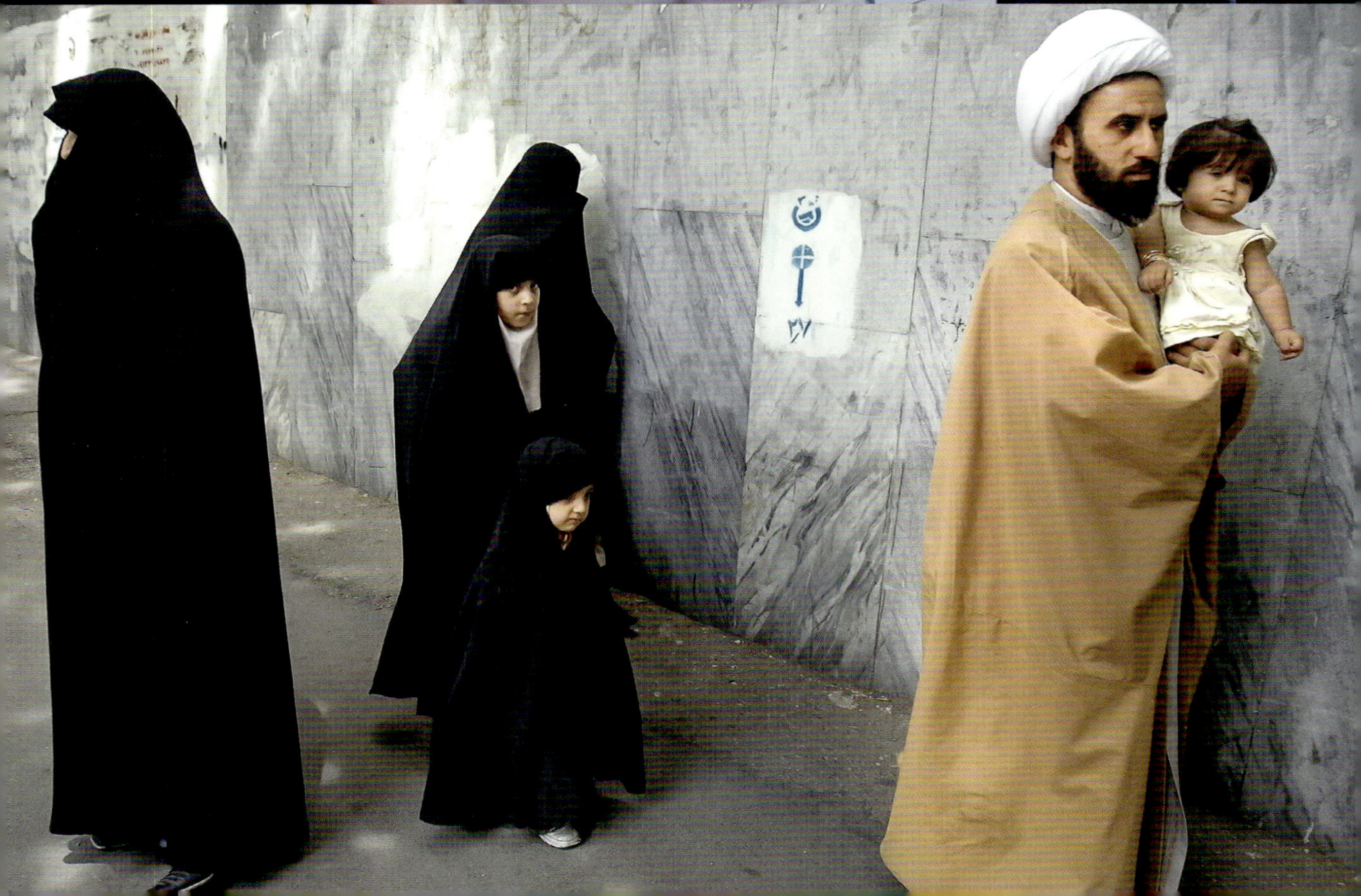

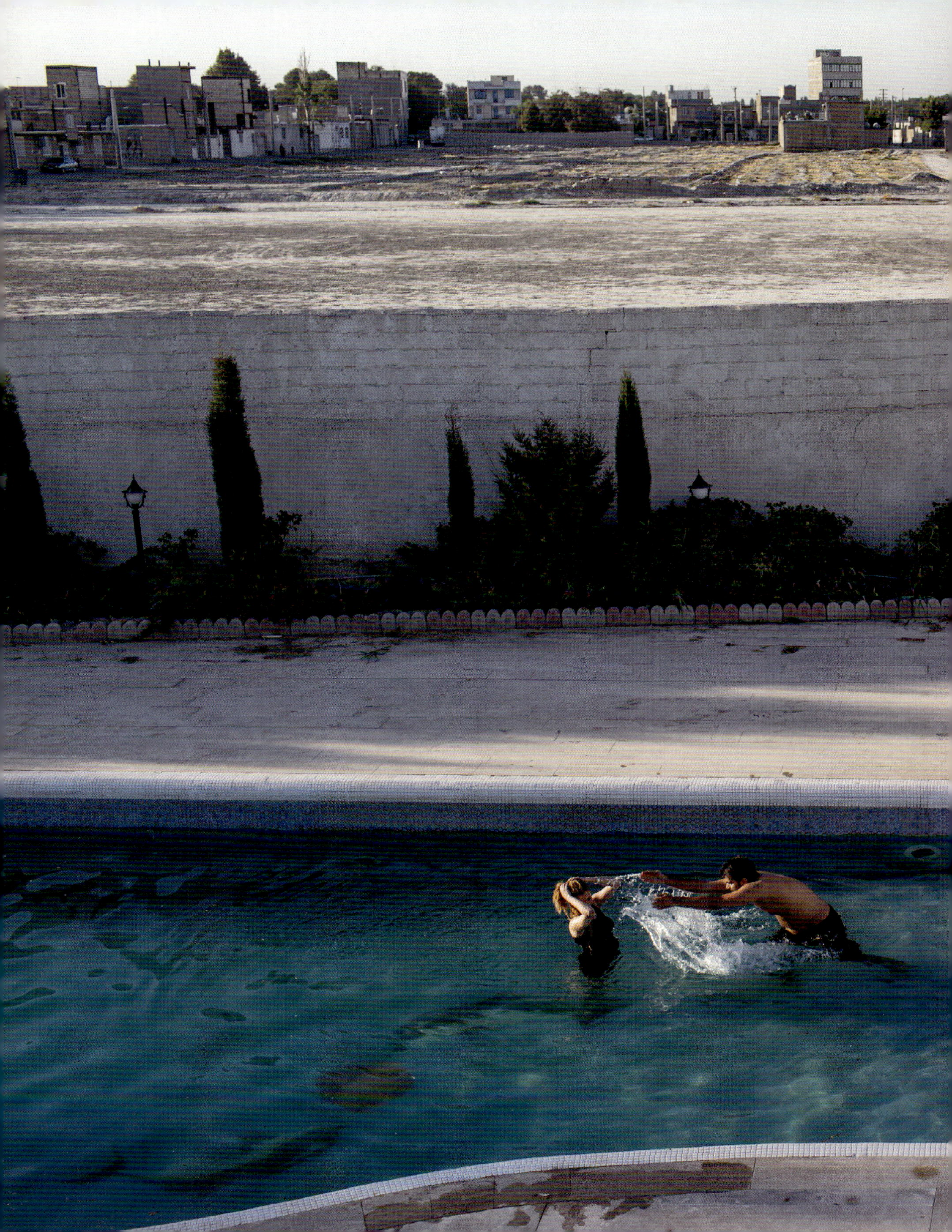

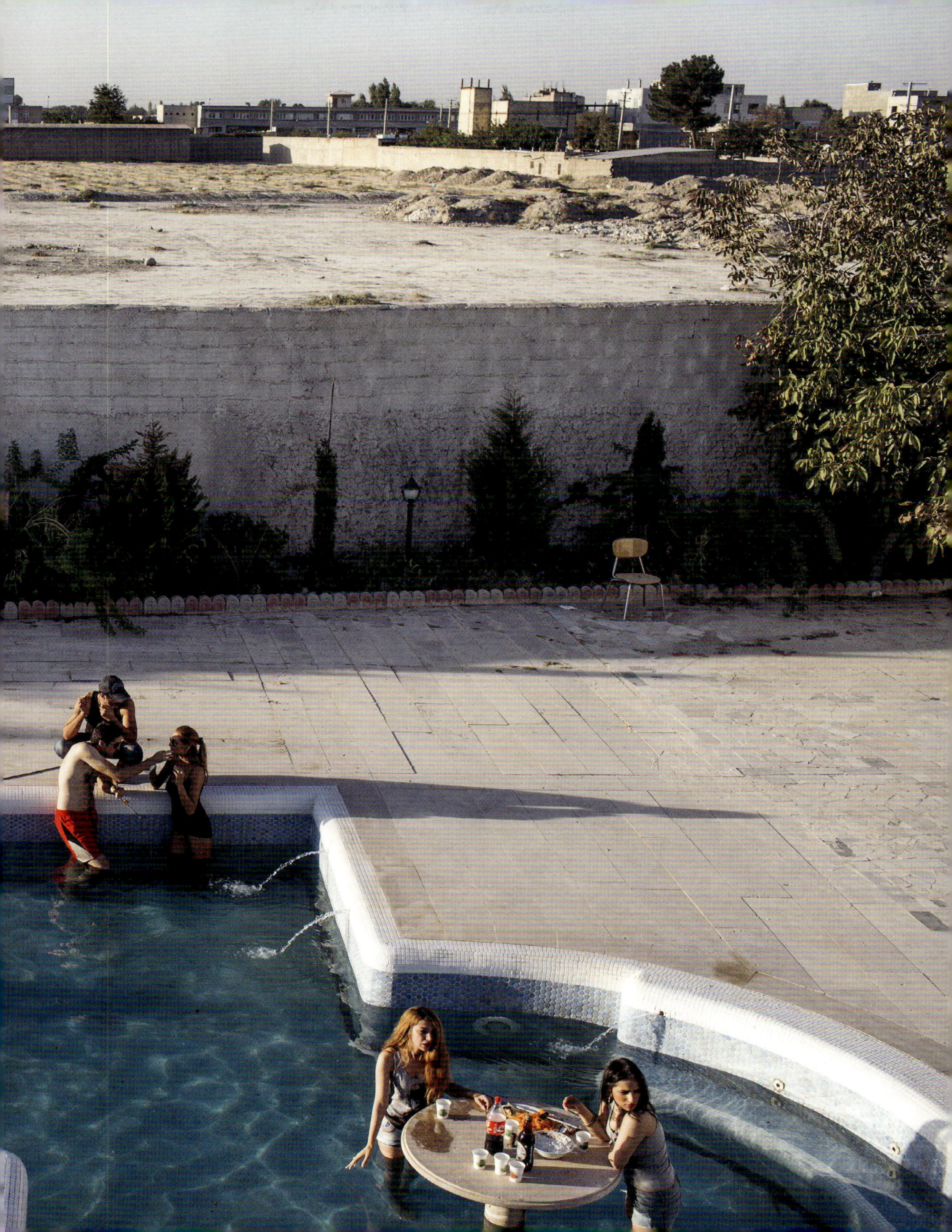

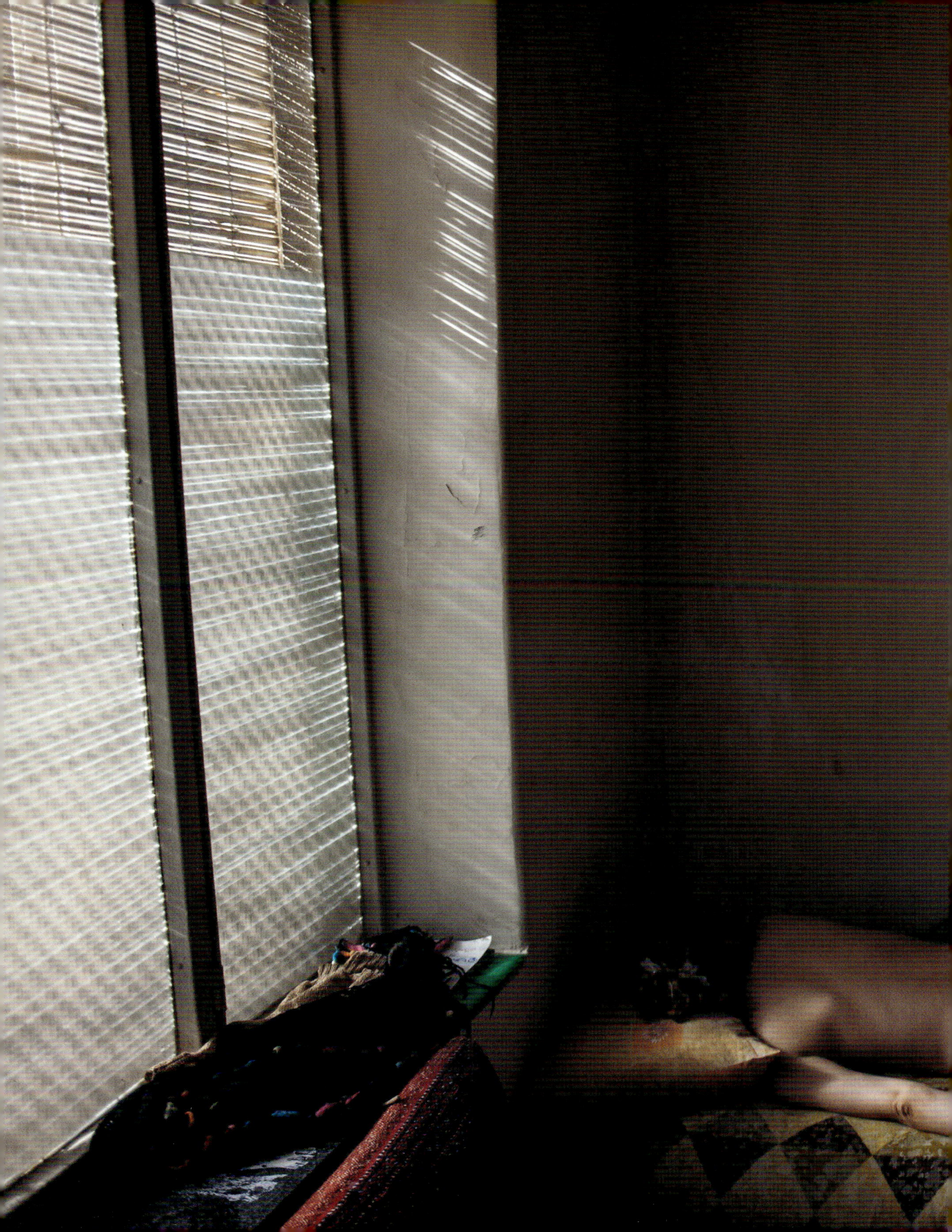

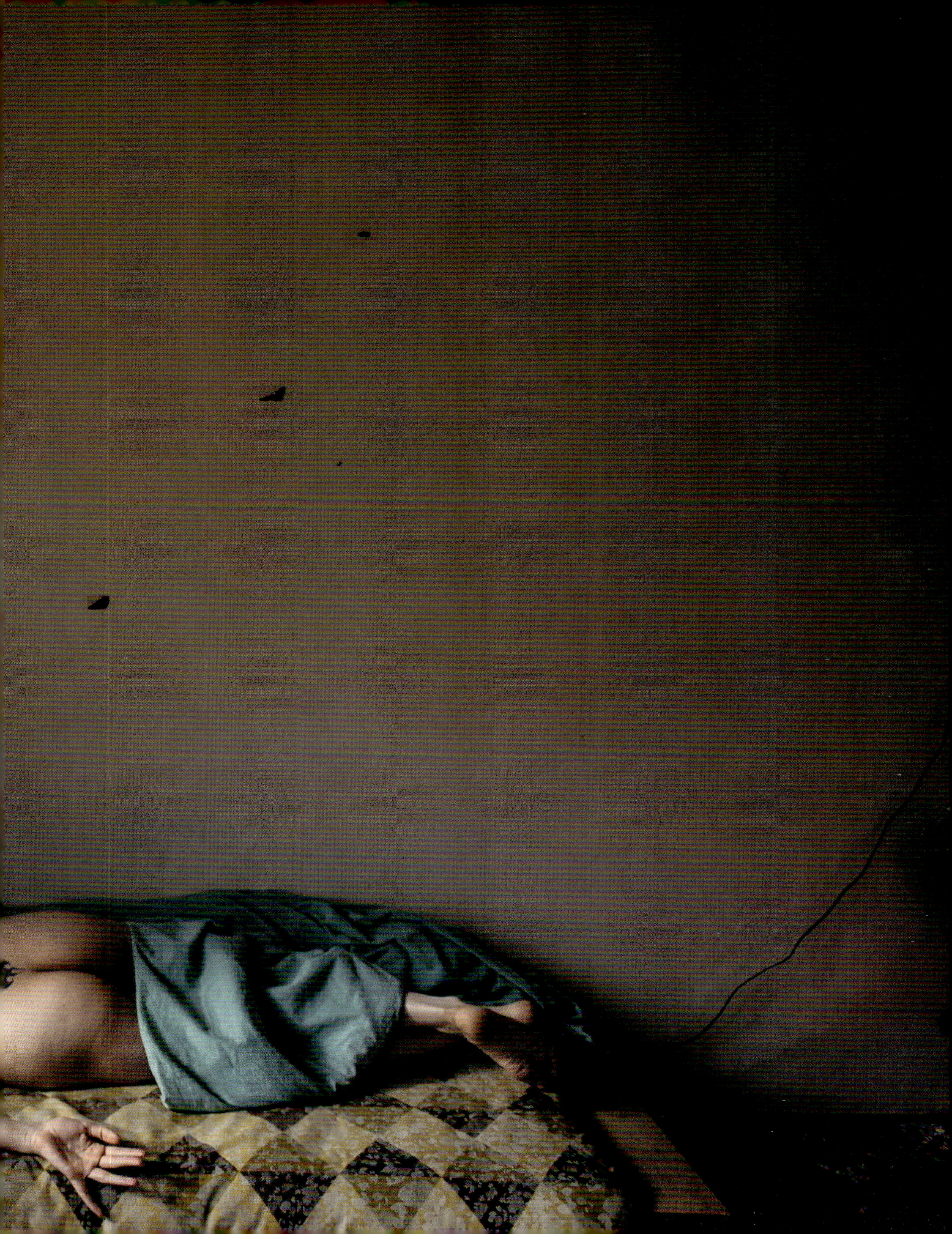

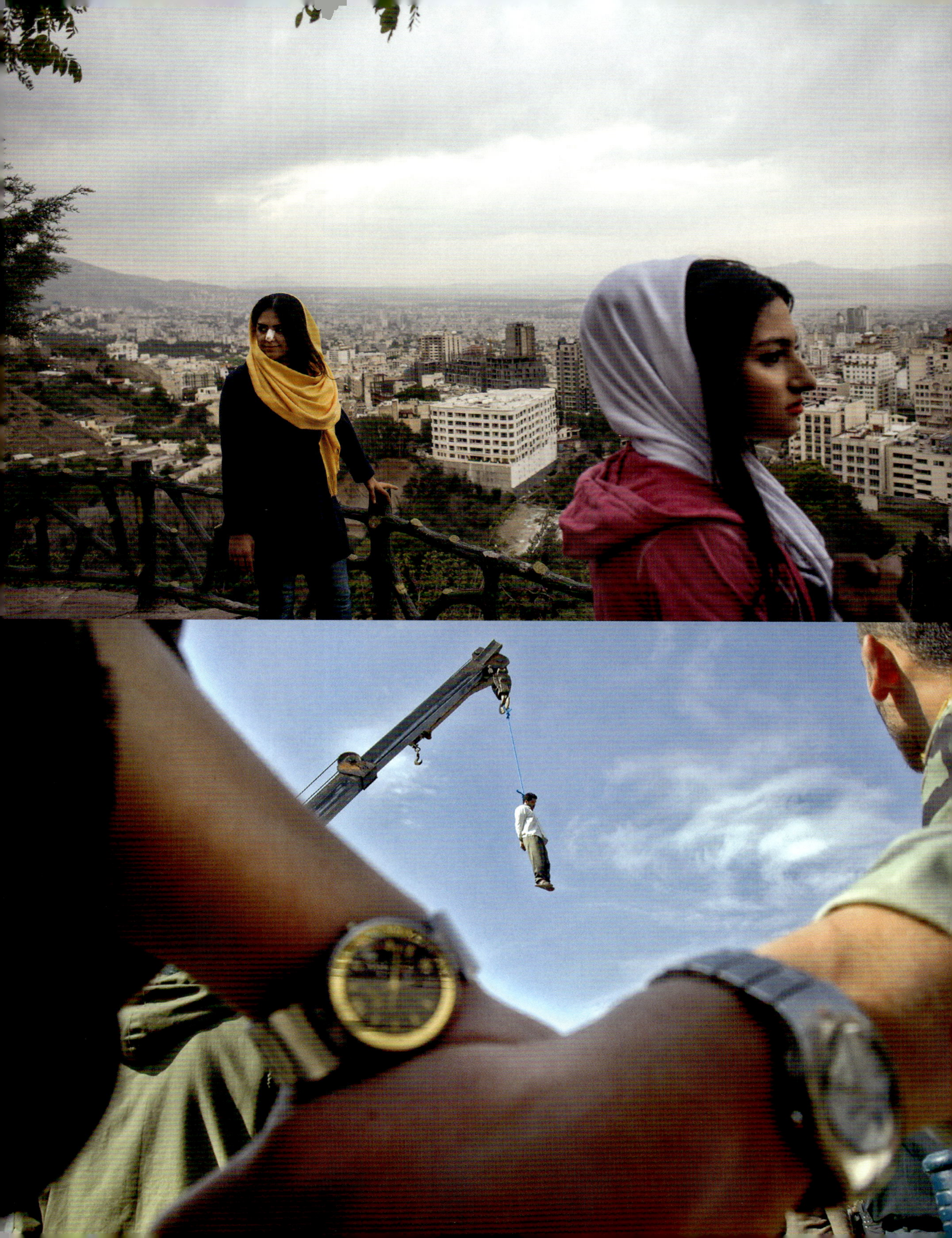

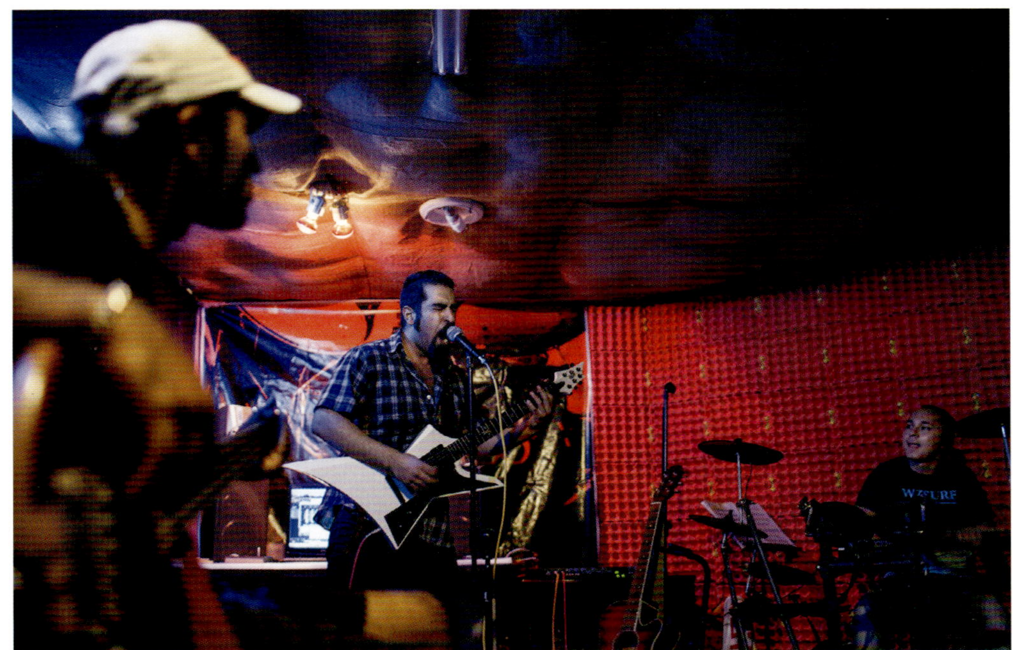

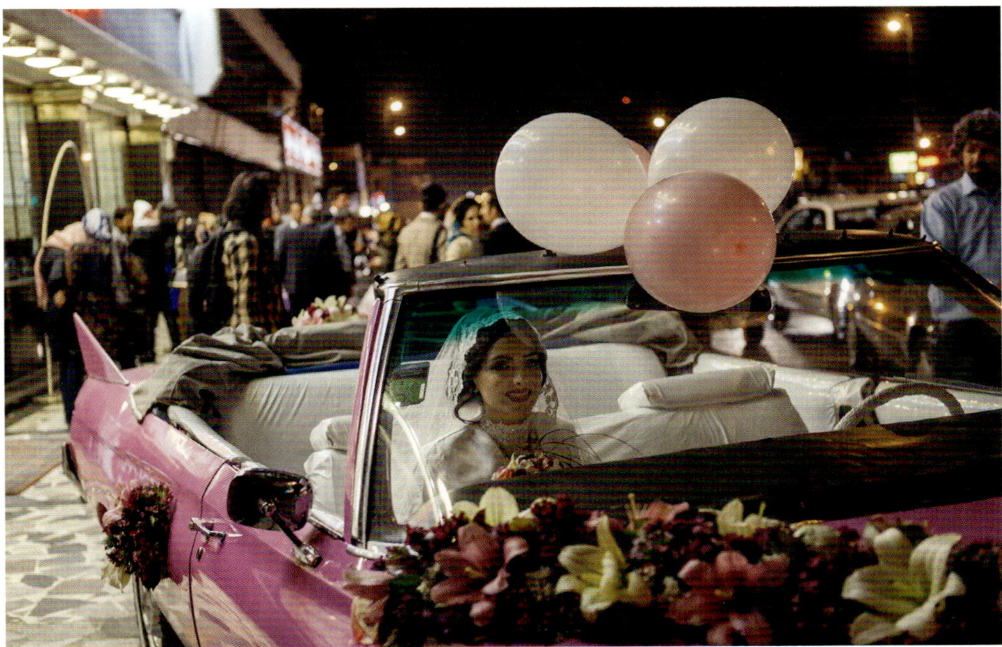

Previous spread: A sex worker lies on her bed. *Facing page, top*: Women on Bam-e Tehran, the 'Roof of Tehran', look out over the capital. One wears a dressing following plastic surgery. Iran has one of the highest rates of nose surgery in the world. *Below*: Serial killer Mohammad Bijeh is hanged after receiving a public flogging. *This page, top*: A rock band plays in Isfahan, central Iran. *Below*: Ashraf (30) sits in a classic car after her wedding and reception. *Next spread*: Female relatives of men killed in the 1980-88 Iran-Iraq War offer prayers at a memorial site near the Iraqi border.

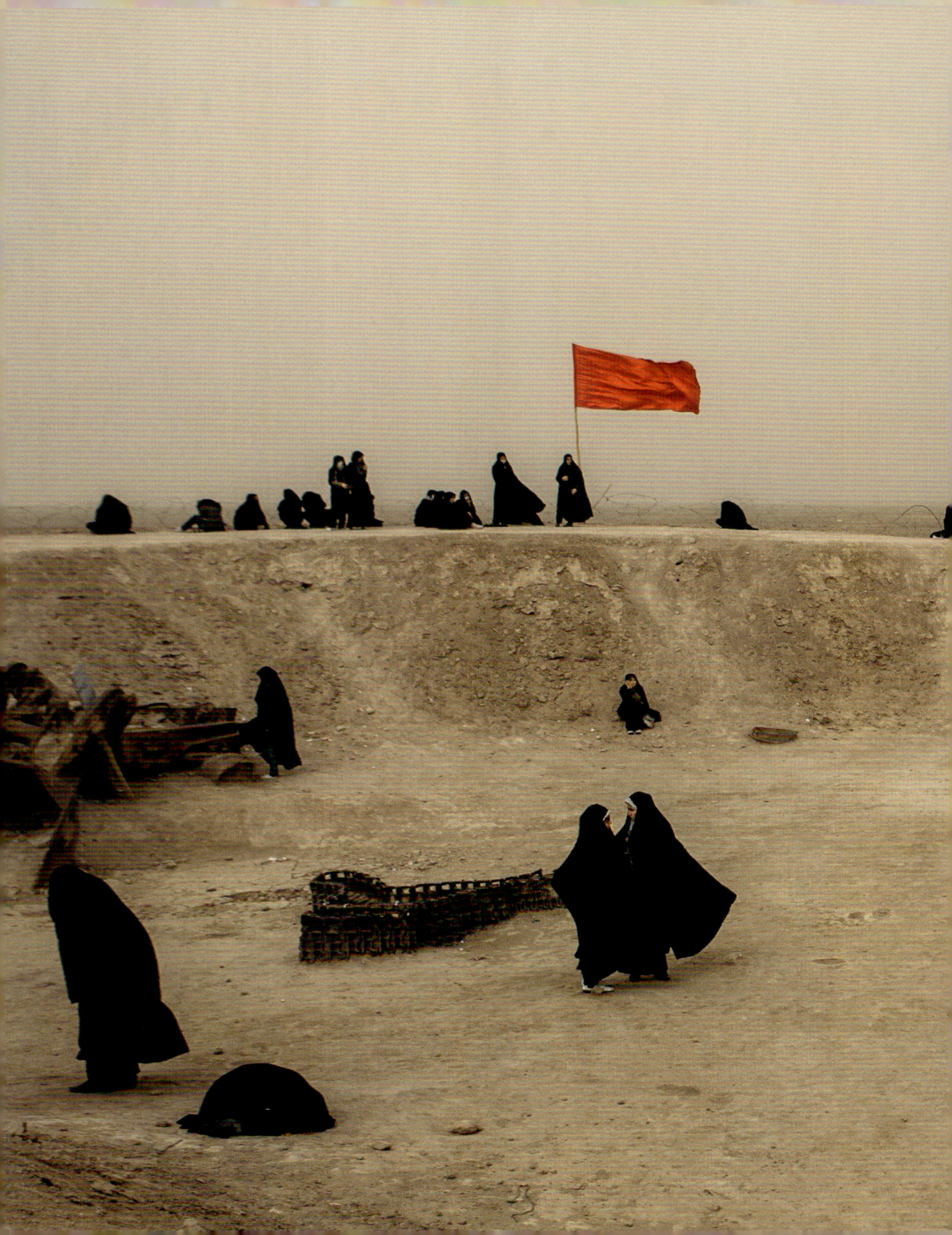

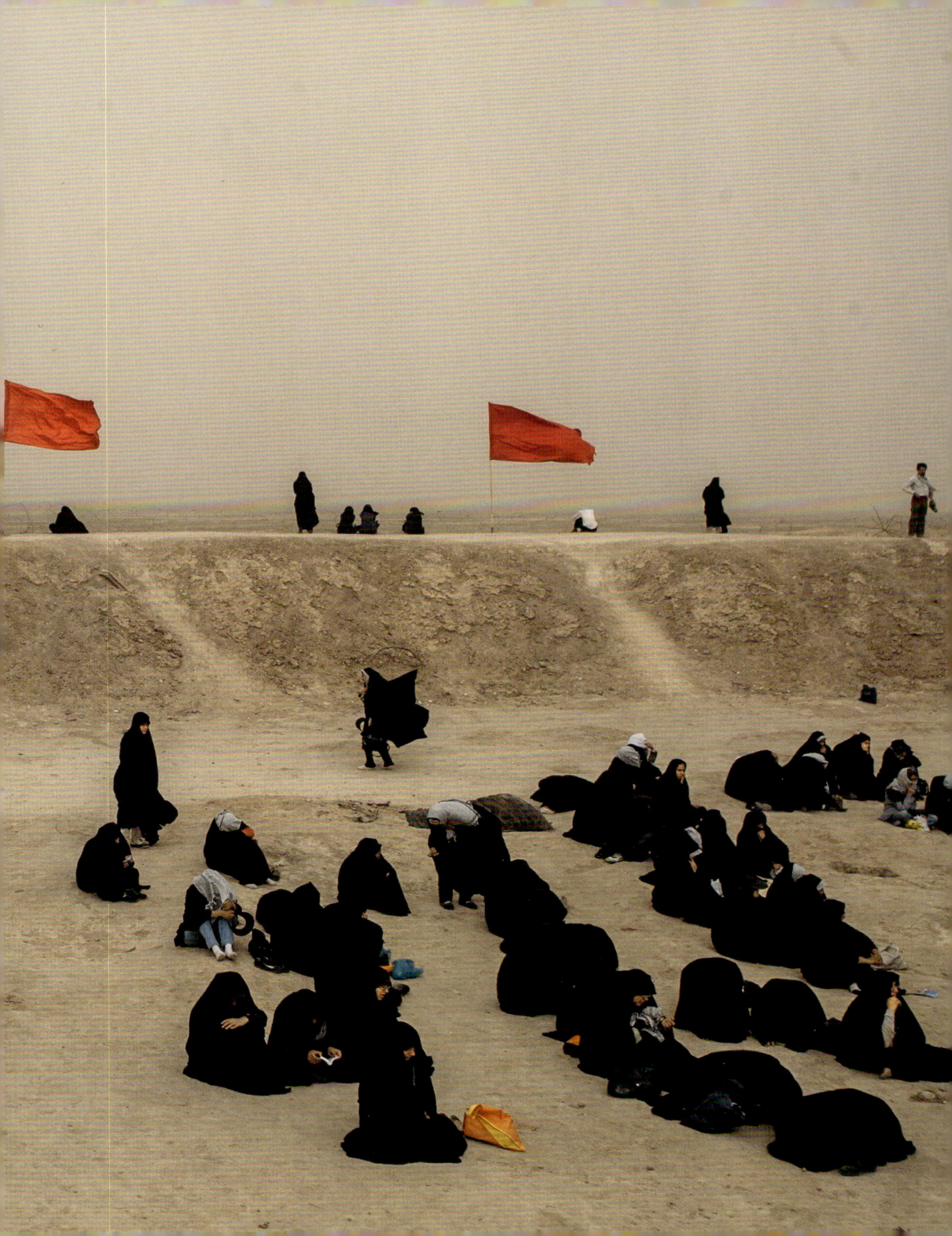

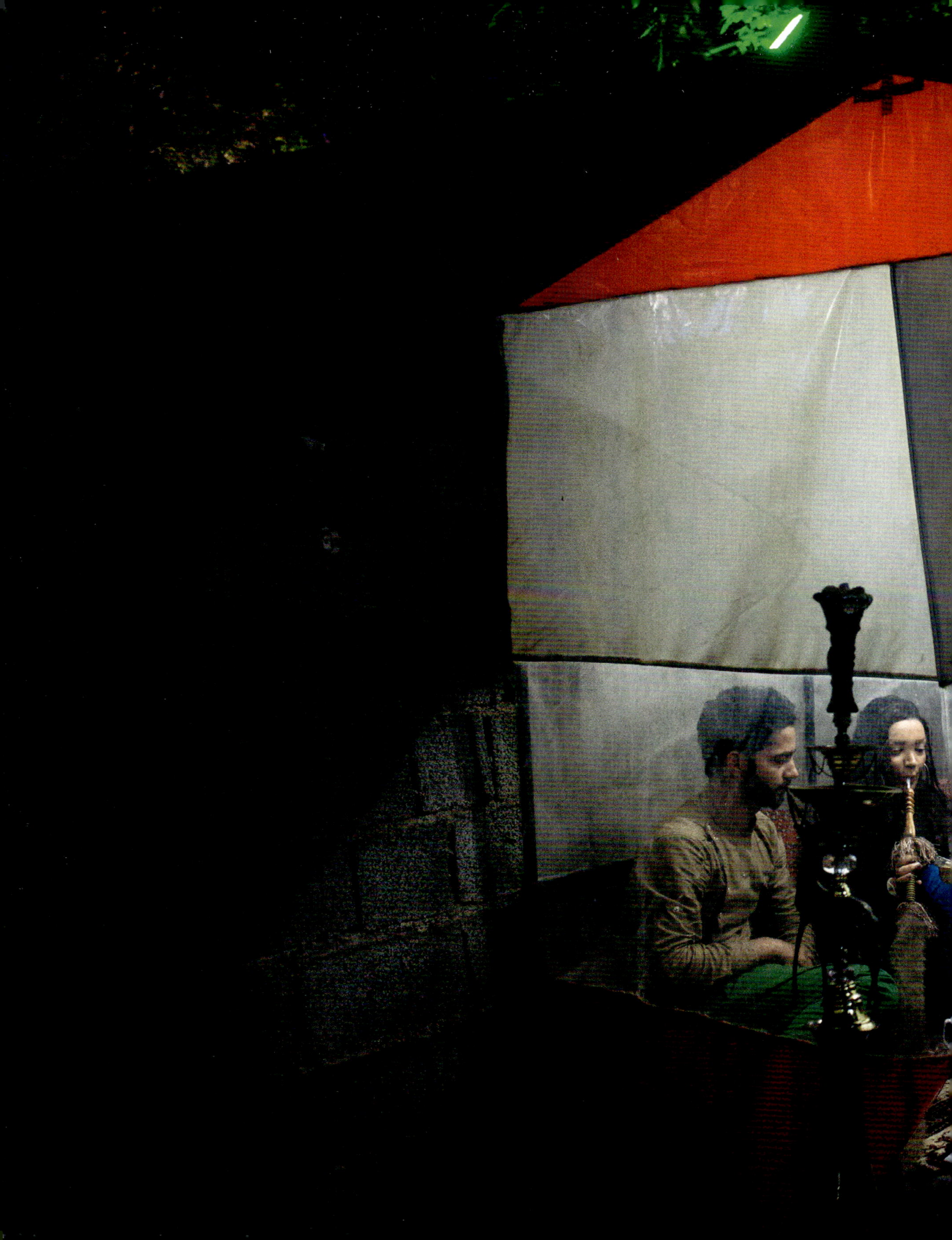

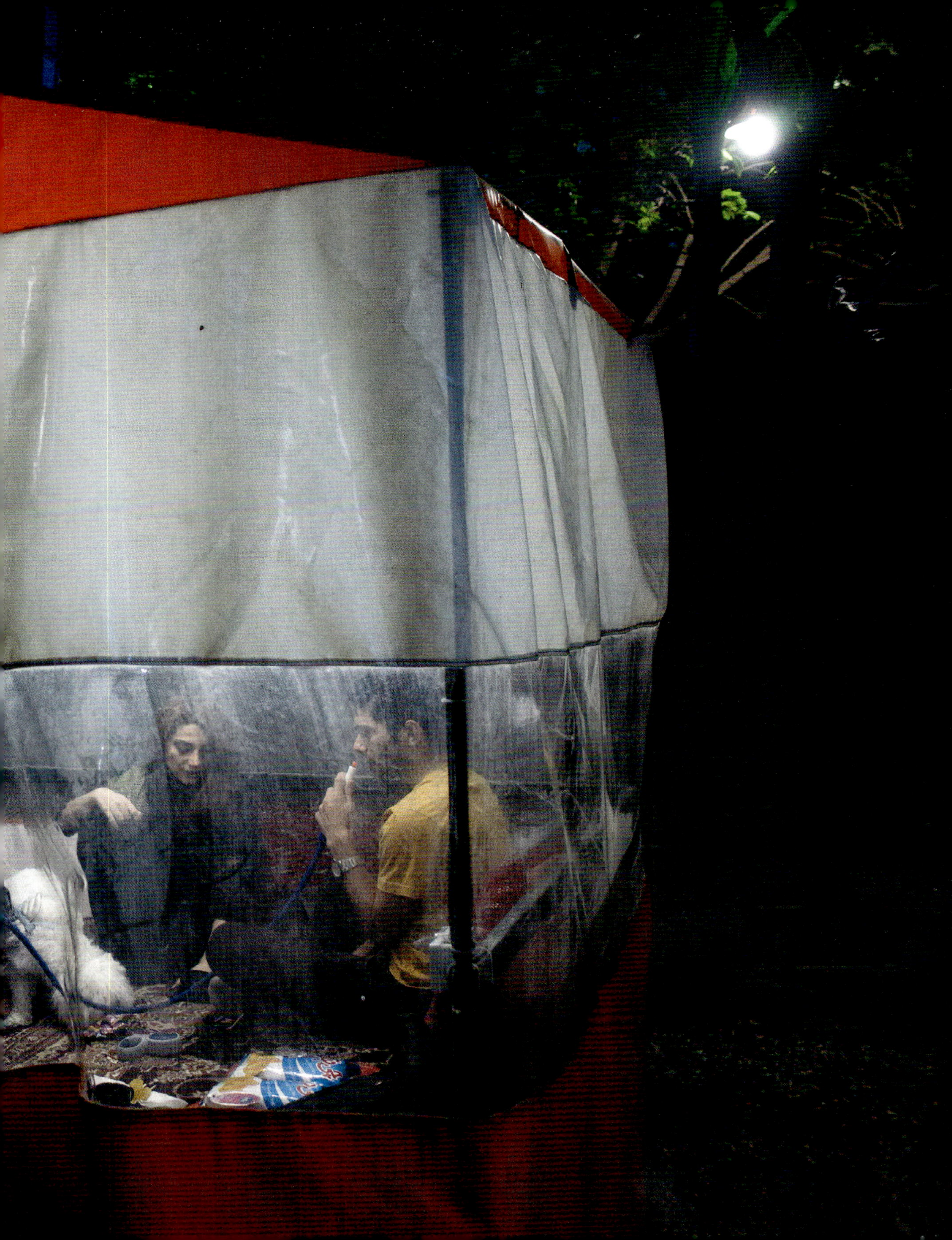

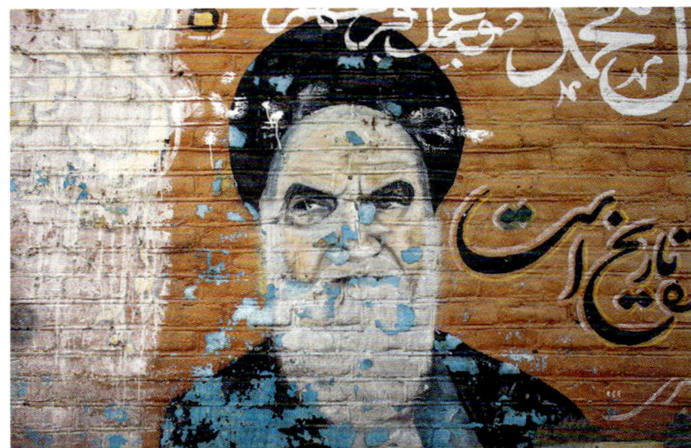

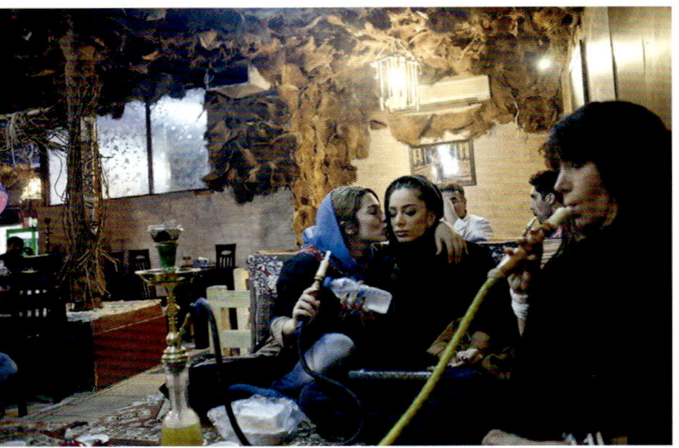

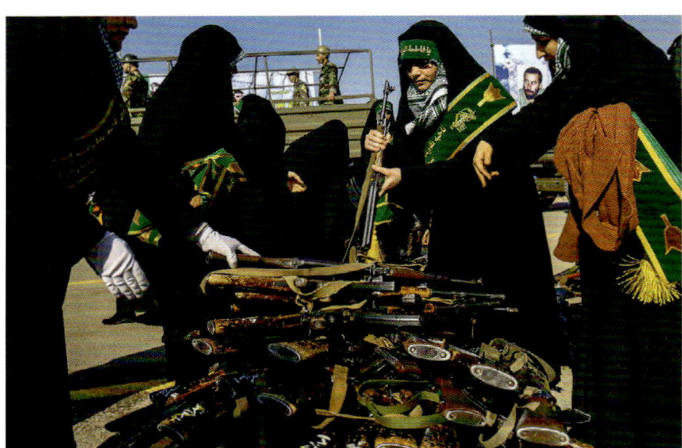

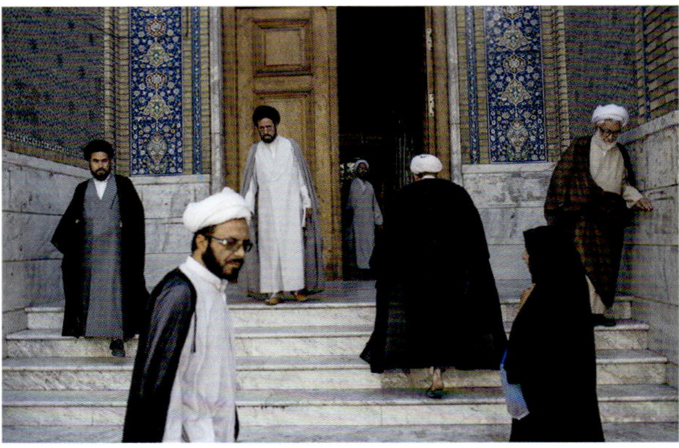

Previous spread: Two young couples sit in a tent smoking shisha. *This page, top left*: A mural of Ayatollah Khomeini, the figurehead of Iran's Islamic Revolution. *Top right*: Women smoke shisha in a Tehran café. *Below, left*: Women members of the Basij militia put away their guns after a ceremonial parade. *Right*: Clerics leave a mosque in the city of Qom, southwest of Tehran. *Facing page, top*: Siavash, a tattooist, smokes a cigarette. *Below*: A boy rides a bike in a housing estate in the Ekbatan district of Tehran.

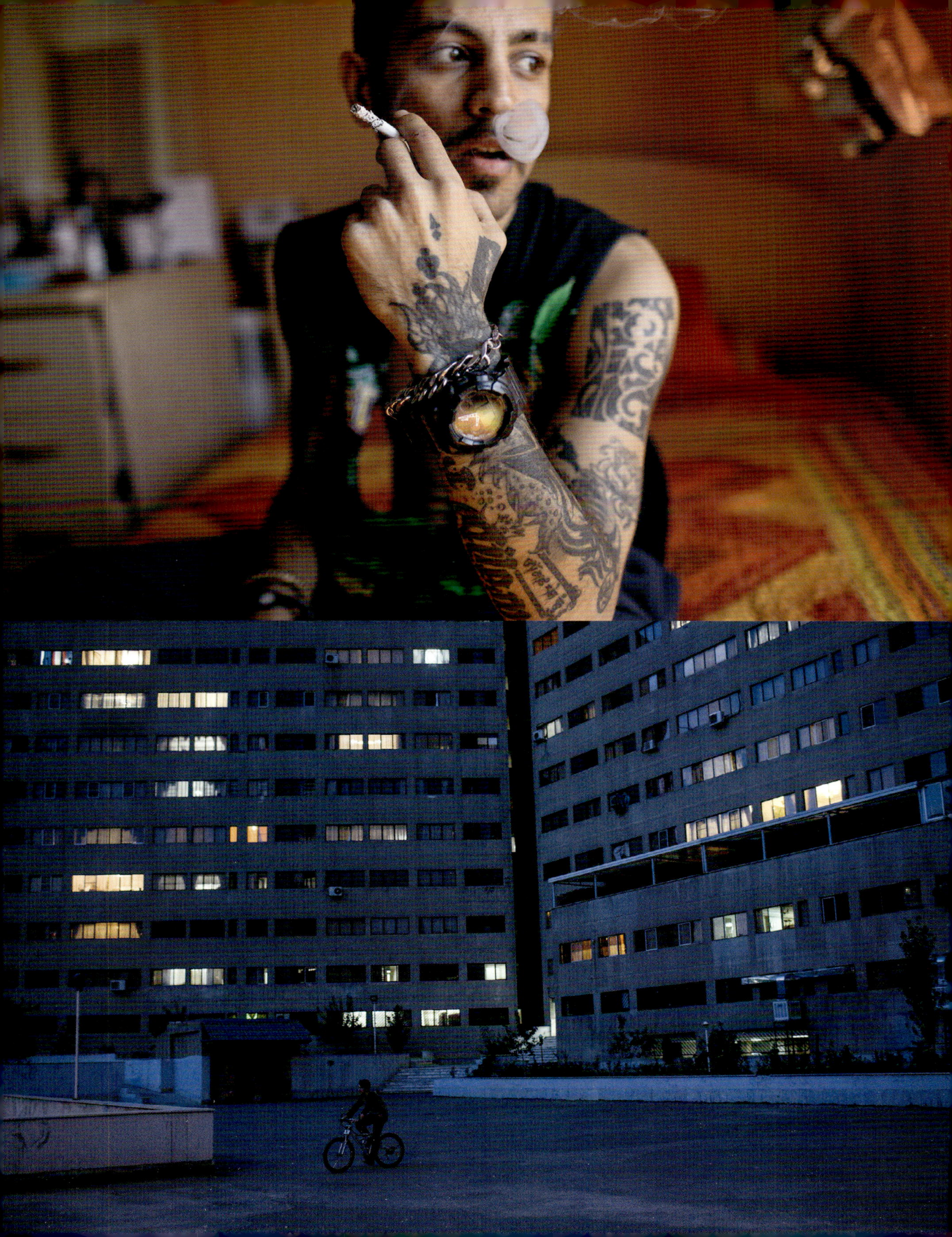

Markus Jokela

Finland, *Helsingin Sanomat* /
3rd Prize

Table Rock, Nebraska

Table Rock is a small rural community in the northeast part of Pawnee County, Nebraska, in the USA. It was named for a unique rock formation near the Nemaha River. In 1992, Table Rock had 308 citizens; in a 2015 census the population was 255. Most people living in Table Rock spend their whole lives there. Some try moving to larger places, but often return to raise their children in their hometown. As with many other Midwestern towns, work is difficult to find. Farms around Table Rock provide employment for some, others seek jobs in neighboring communities.

The photographer is interested in the mundane aspects of everyday life. He first went to Table Rock in 1992. He and a colleague had been commissioned to do a story on American life, and the colleague closed his eyes and put his finger on a point he thought was the middle of the map. That turned out to be Table Rock. In 2009, the photographer became curious about what was happening in the town and so returned. He made a few further visits in the years that followed. For the most part, little had changed.

Facing page, top: Libby Kalina collects her mail, on a September morning in 1992. *Below*: Matt Schaardt takes the school bus from his home farm to Table Rock School, in 1992. The school closed in 2016. *Next spread*: Mary Lou Waters, Myron Kent and Sheriff Schulze outside the Table Rock Tavern.

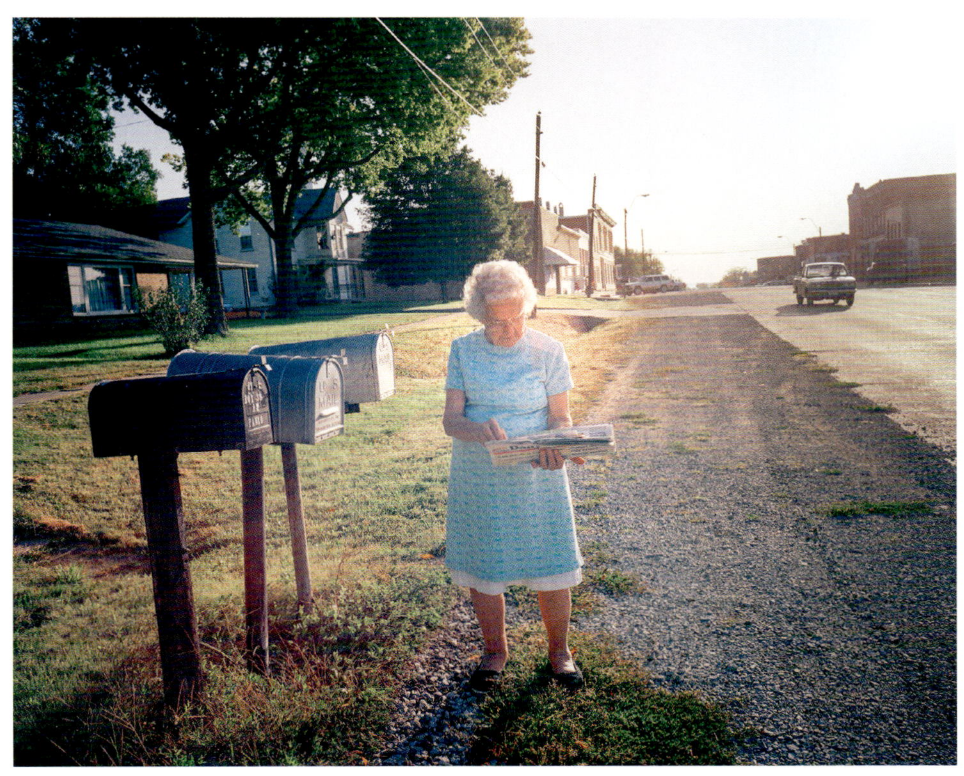

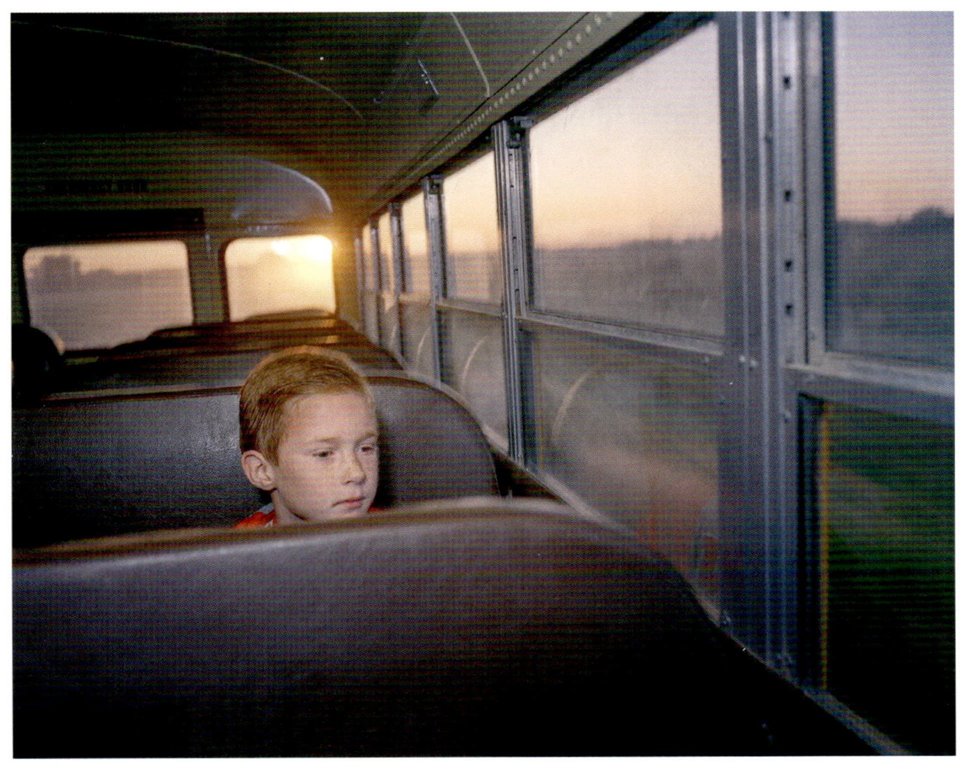

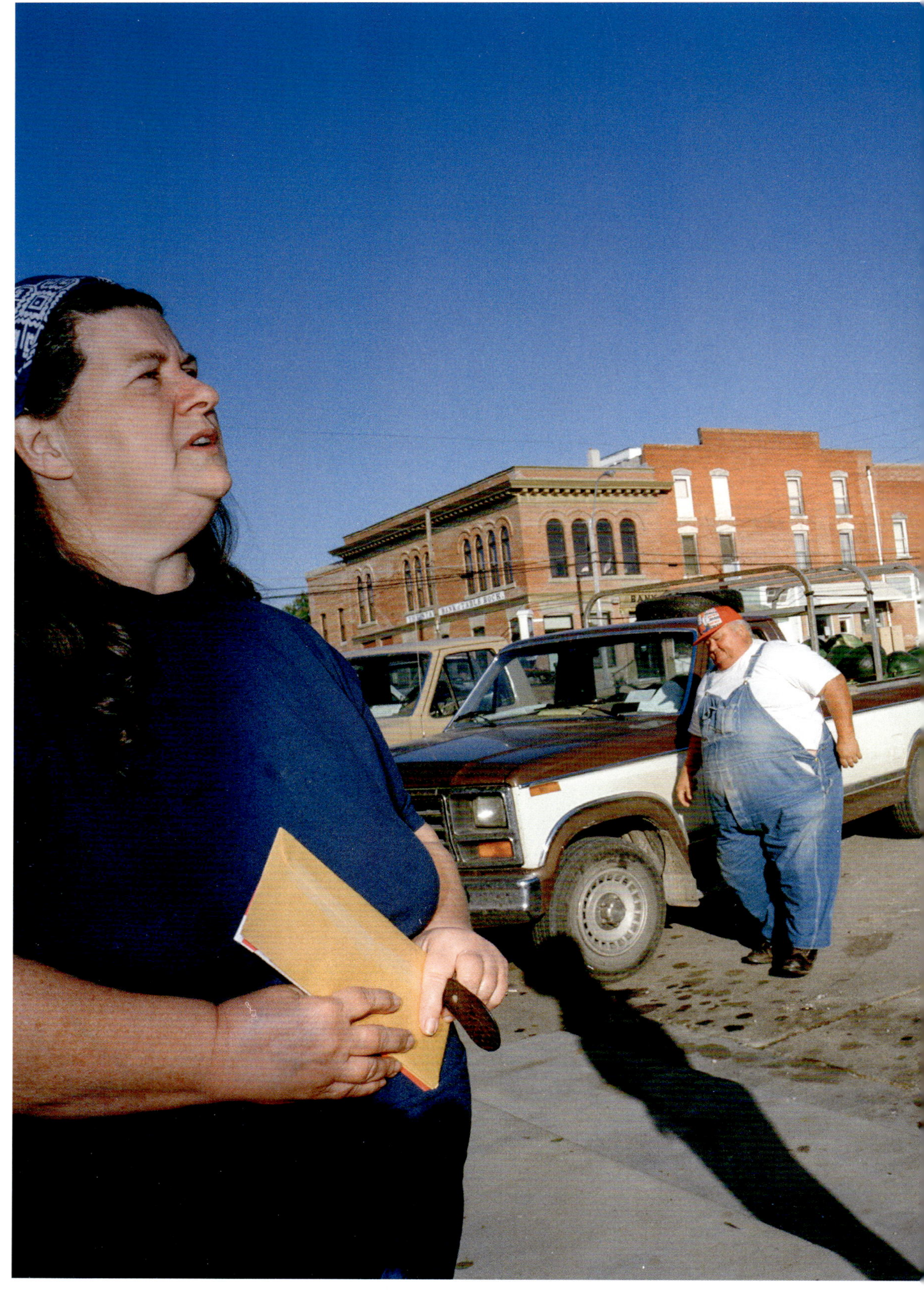

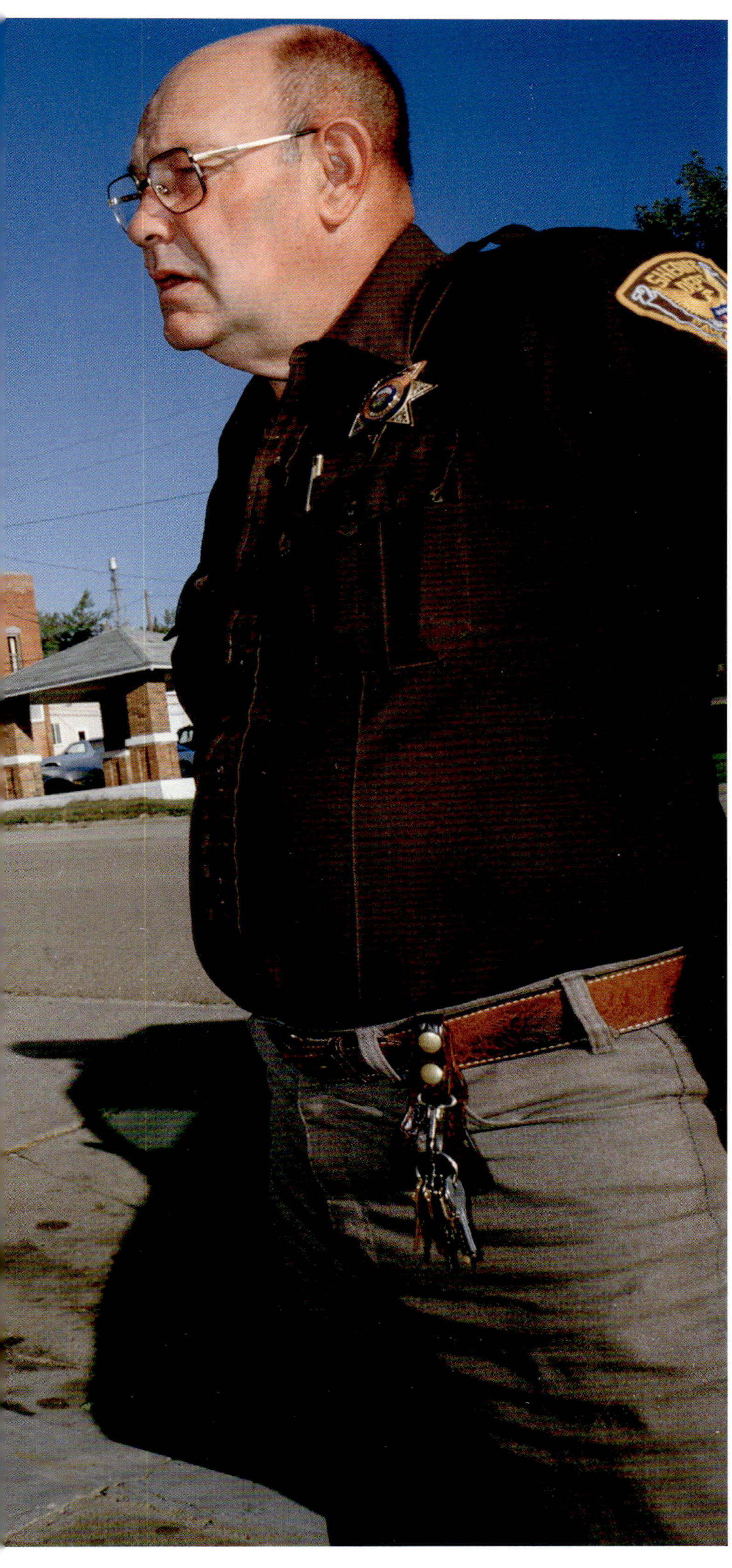

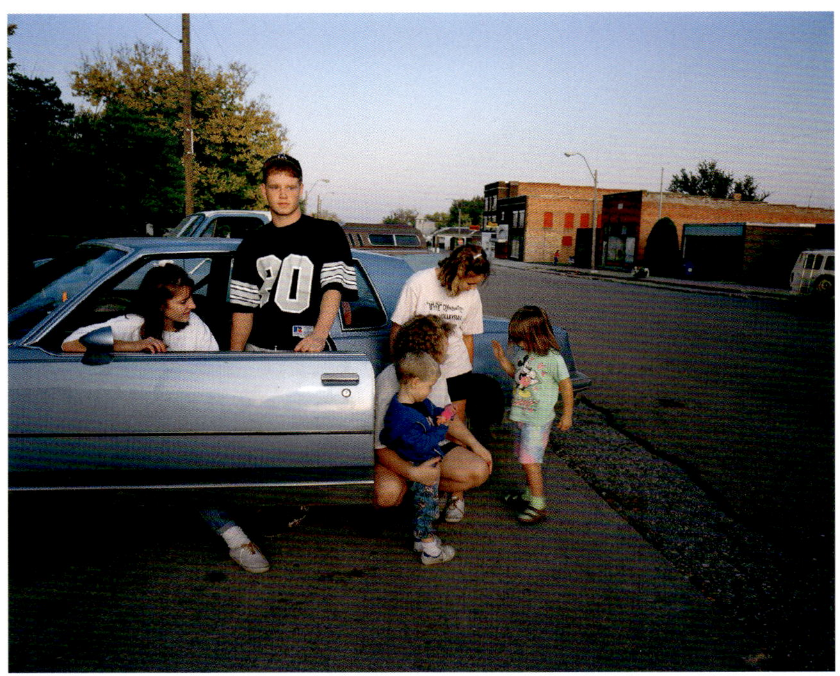

Matt Kuhlman, pictured in 1992 when he was 18, stands alongside his girlfriend Melissa Bernadt (in car).

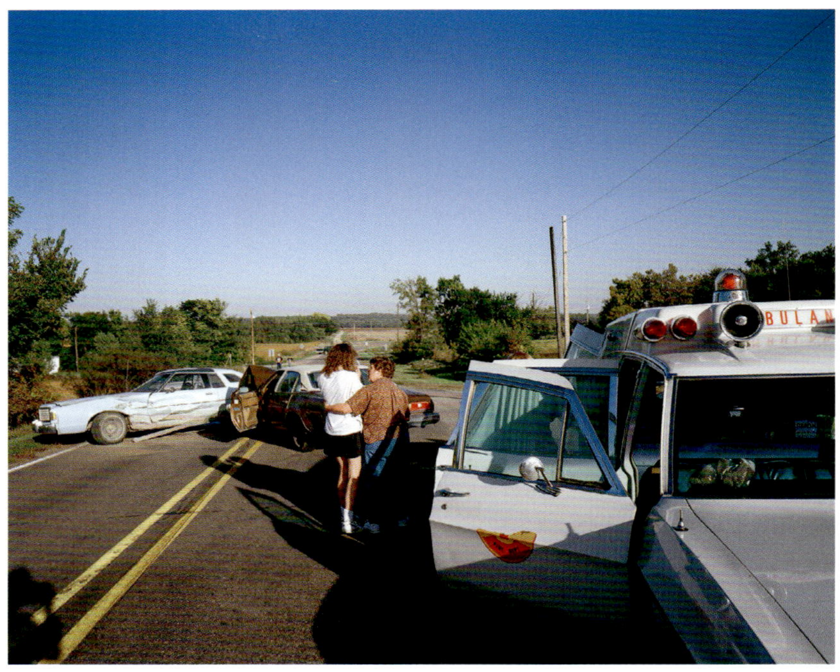

Angie Beethe is comforted after having had an accident in her father's car. She was on her way to her school's 1992 homecoming game, where she was to be a cheerleader.

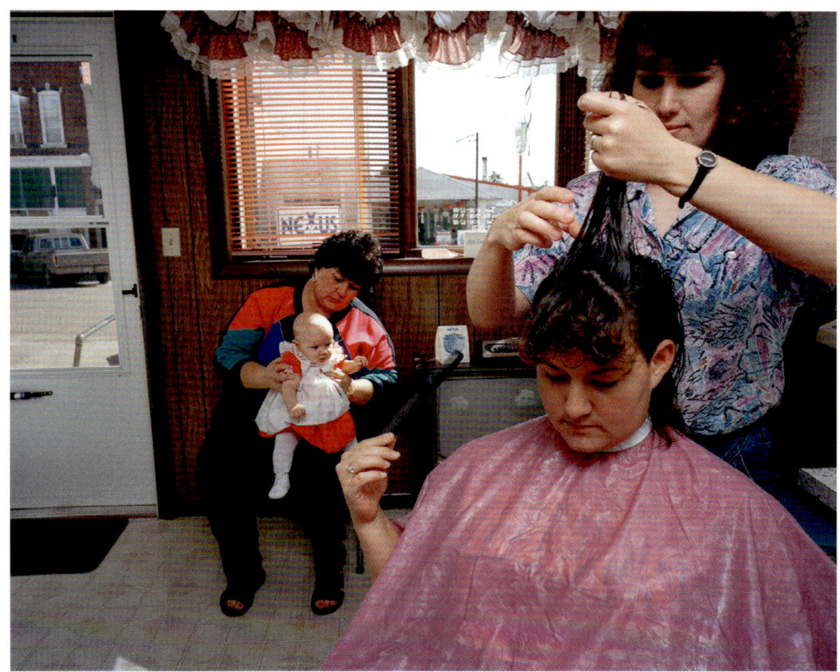

Kelly Freeman, aged three months, sits on her grandmother's knee at the hairdresser's, in 1992.

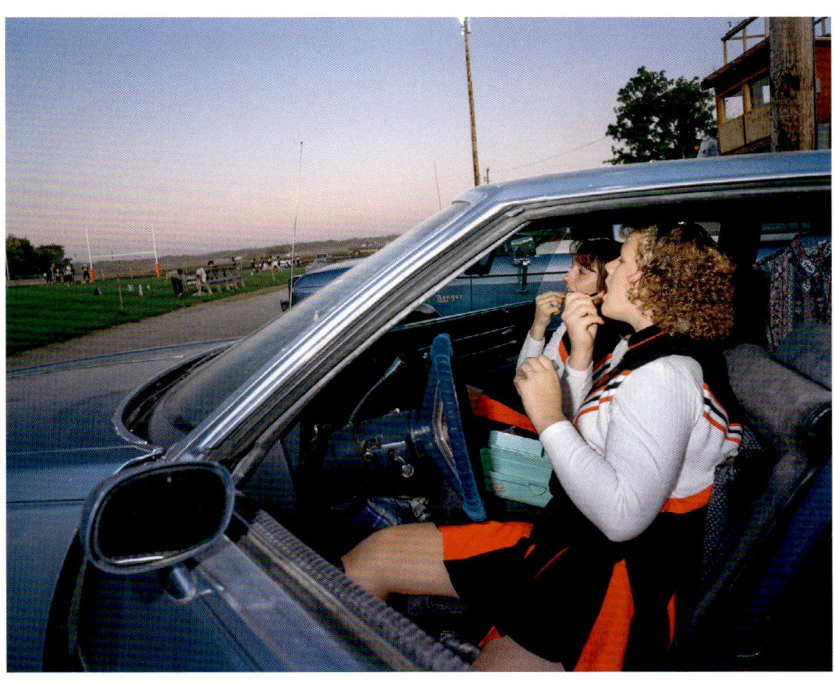

Cheerleaders Melissa Bernadt and Jennifer Burnedt prepare for the evening's homecoming game, in September 1992. *Following spread*: Garrett Rogge rests on the floor of his in-laws' home after a hard working day.

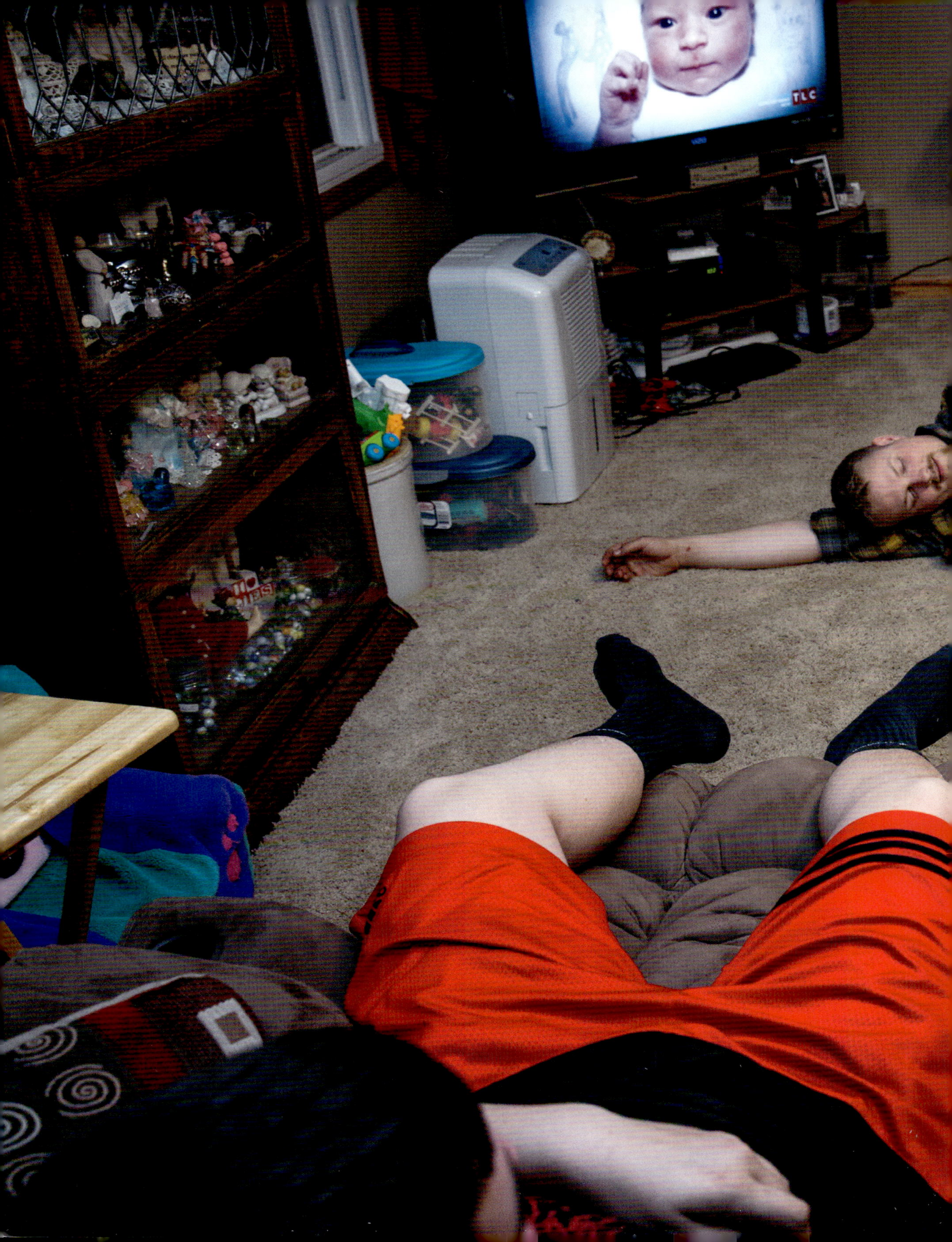
TLC

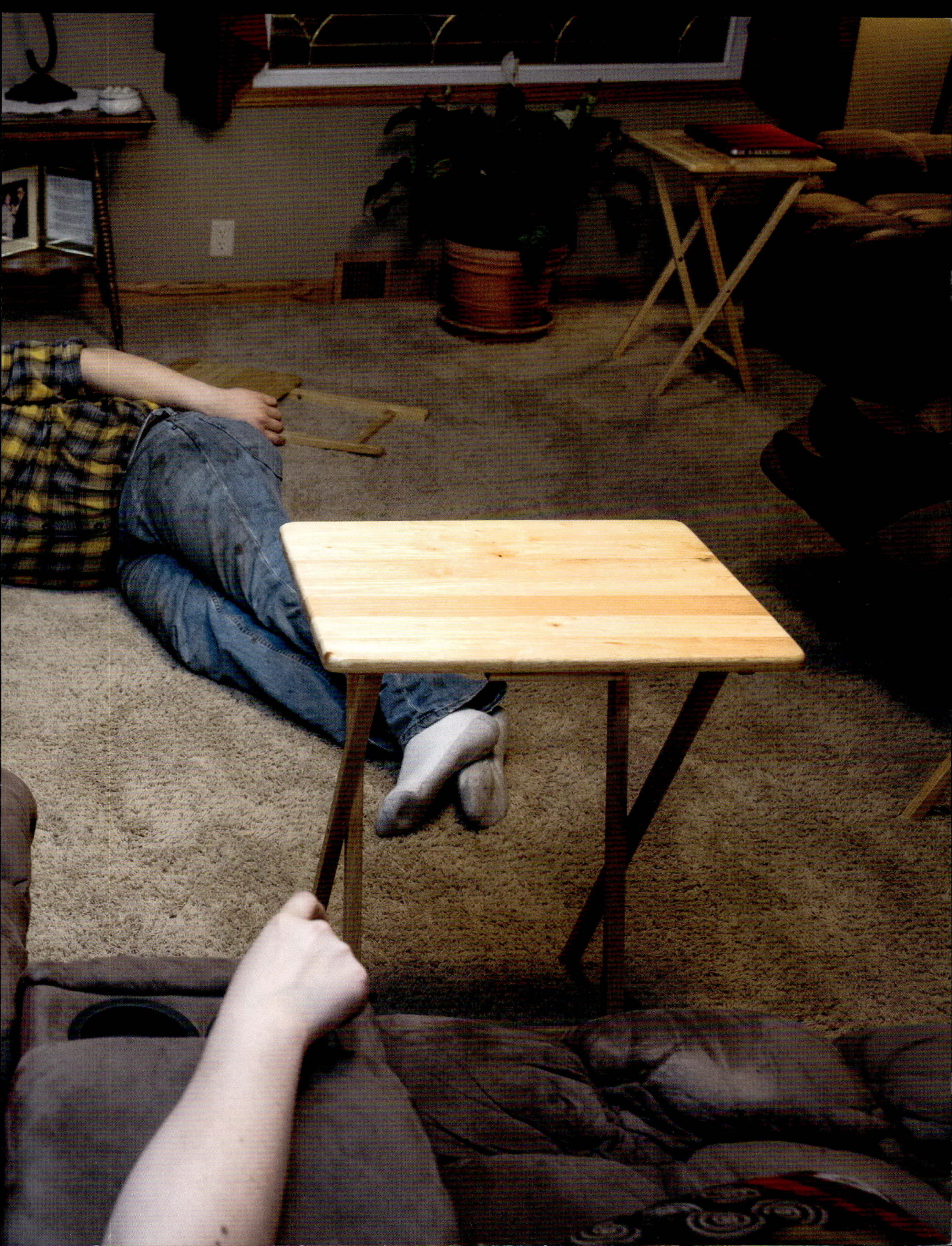

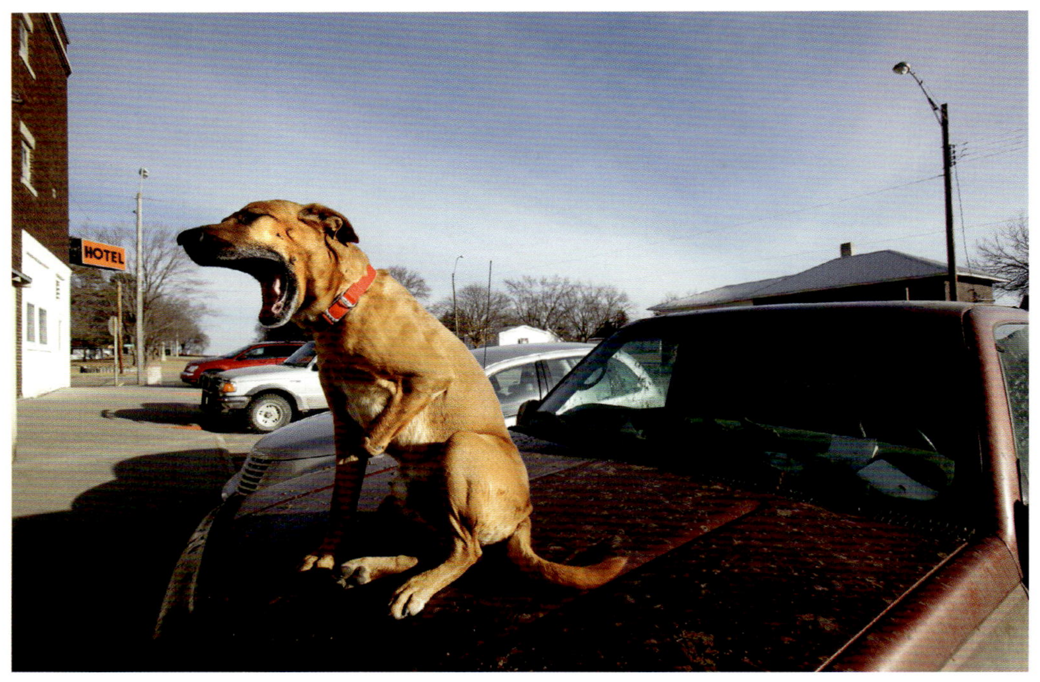

Randy Freeman's dog, Puppy, lost a paw after running into a combine harvester.

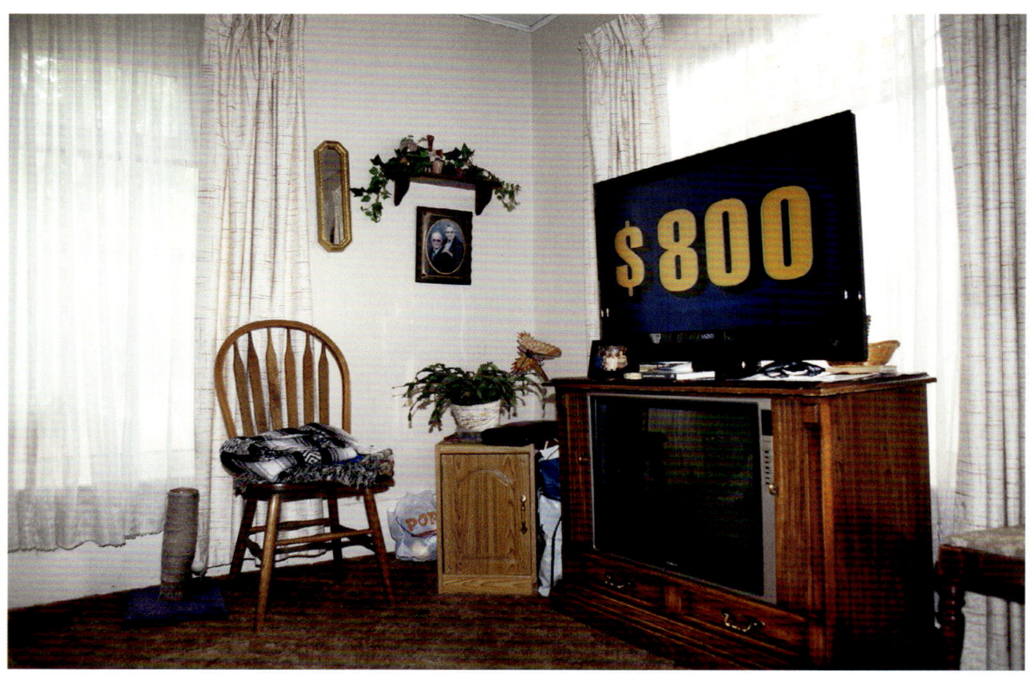

Naomi Pope's living room, in 2012.

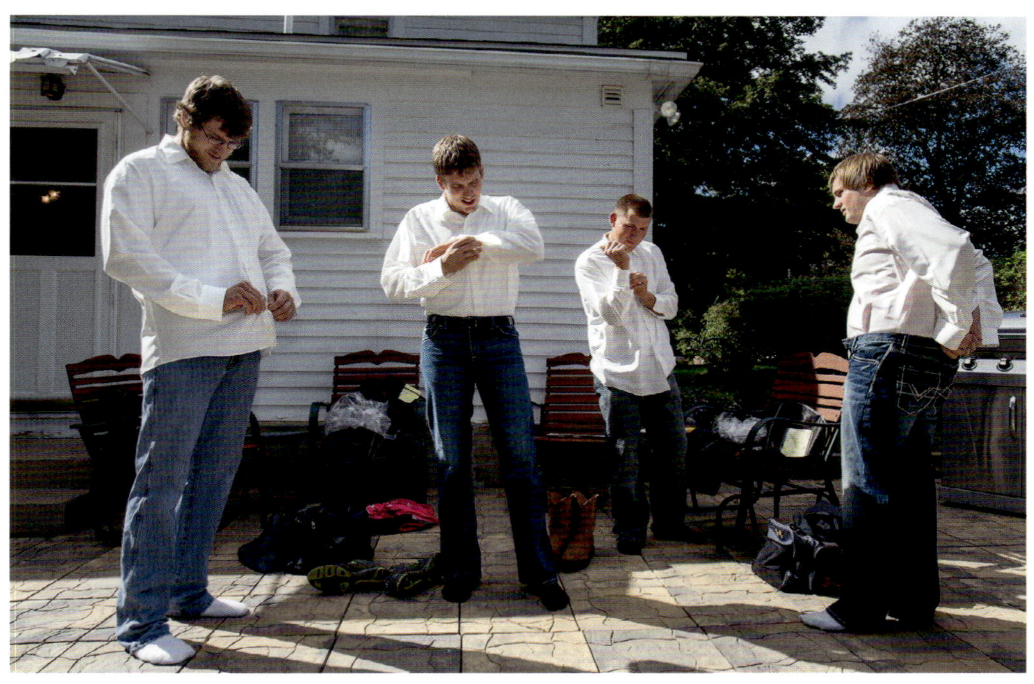

Groomsmen prepare for Kelly Freeman's wedding, on 5 October 2013.

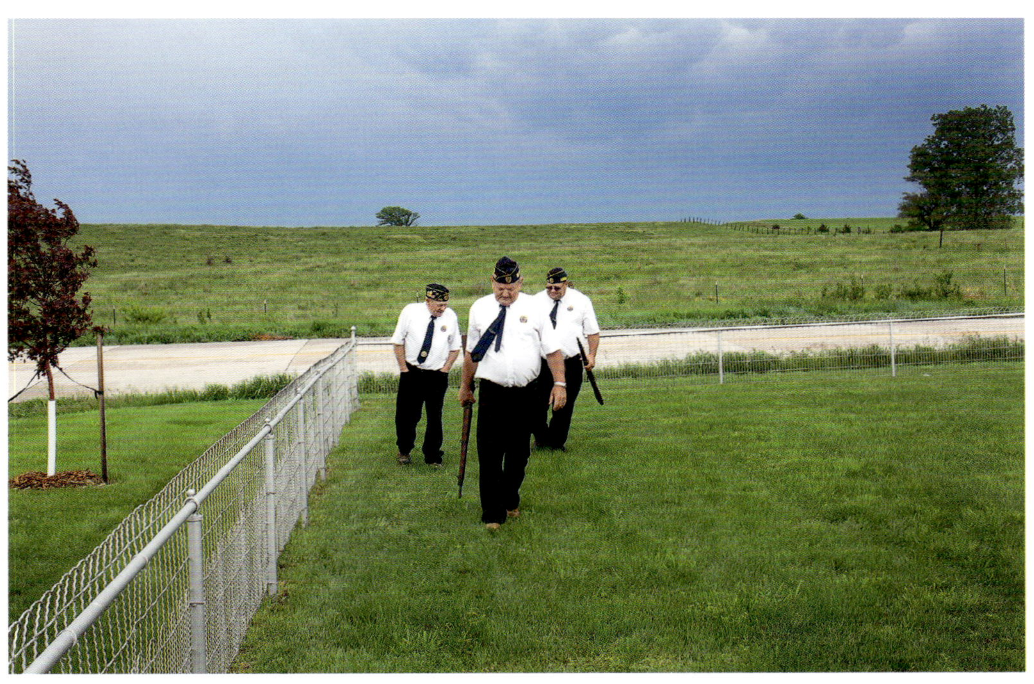

Memorial Day at the Lutheran cemetery outside Table Rock.

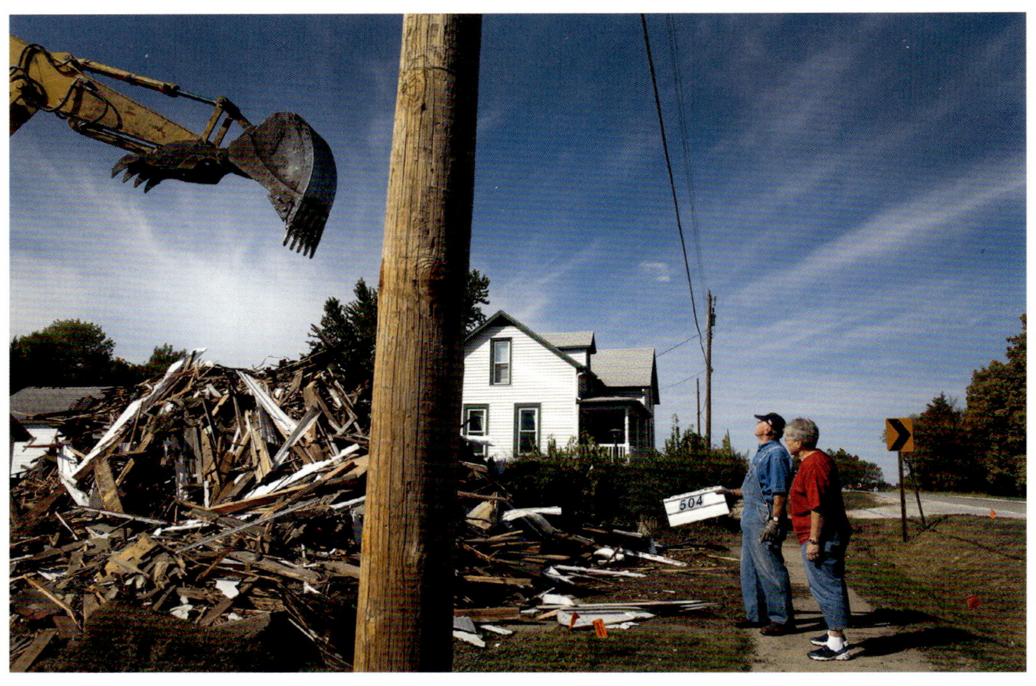

Bob and Frances Blecha watch as their house is torn down. Lightning set fire to it in the summer of 2012.

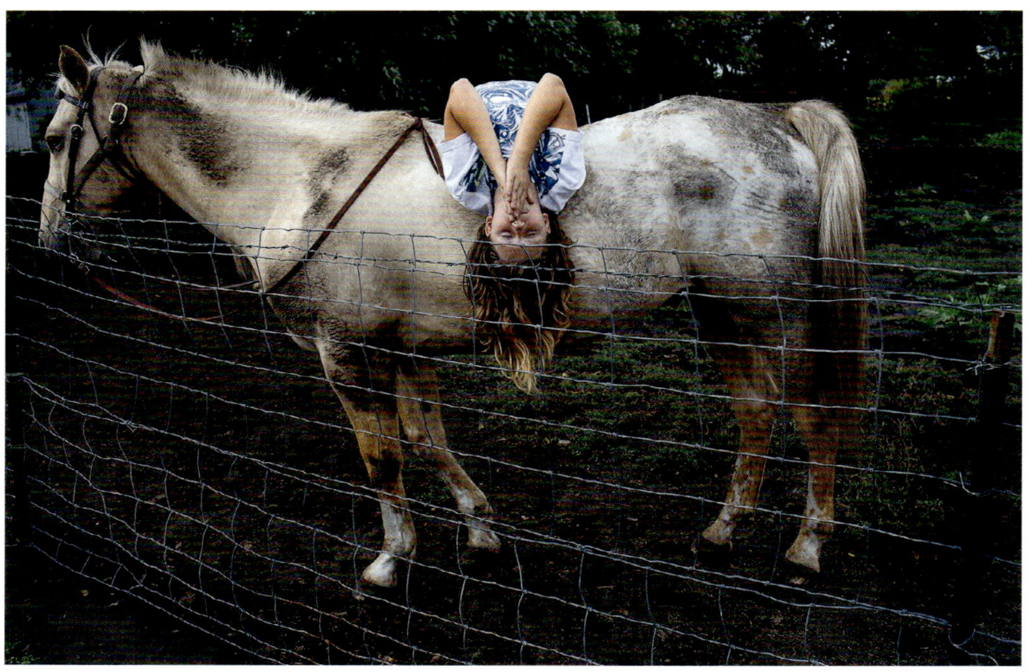

Sarah Barrs lies over her horse's back, in October 2013.

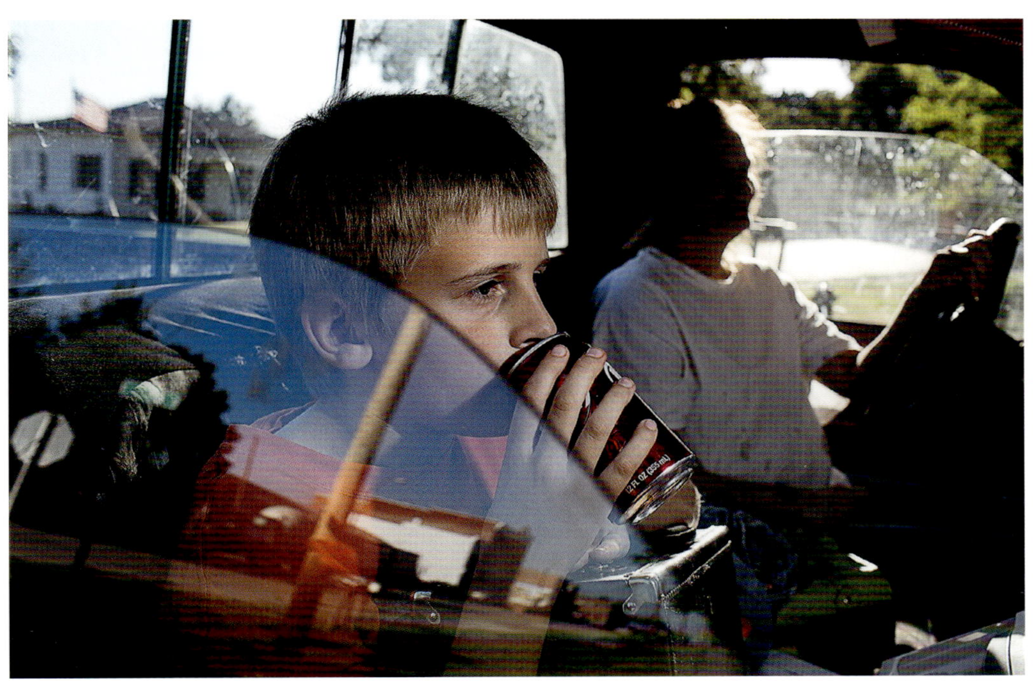

Leslie Blank takes her son Joe home from a music lesson, in the fall of 2013.

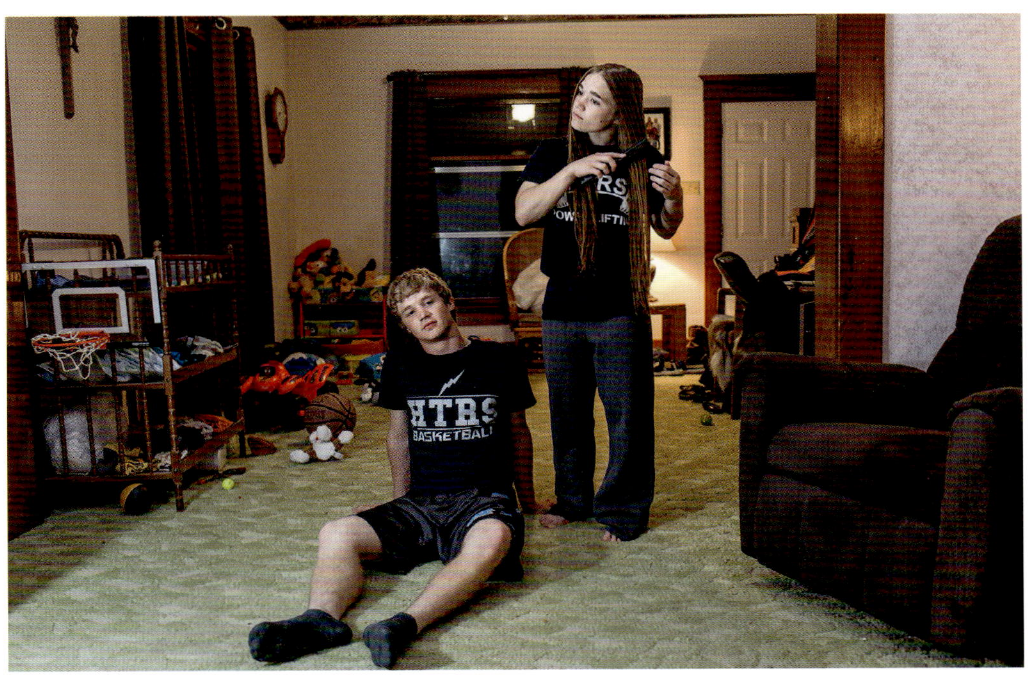

Matt Kuhlman's children, Schuyler (18) and Bailey (17), pictured at home in May 2015.
Following spread: Cheerleaders at Table Rock School's 1992 homecoming game.

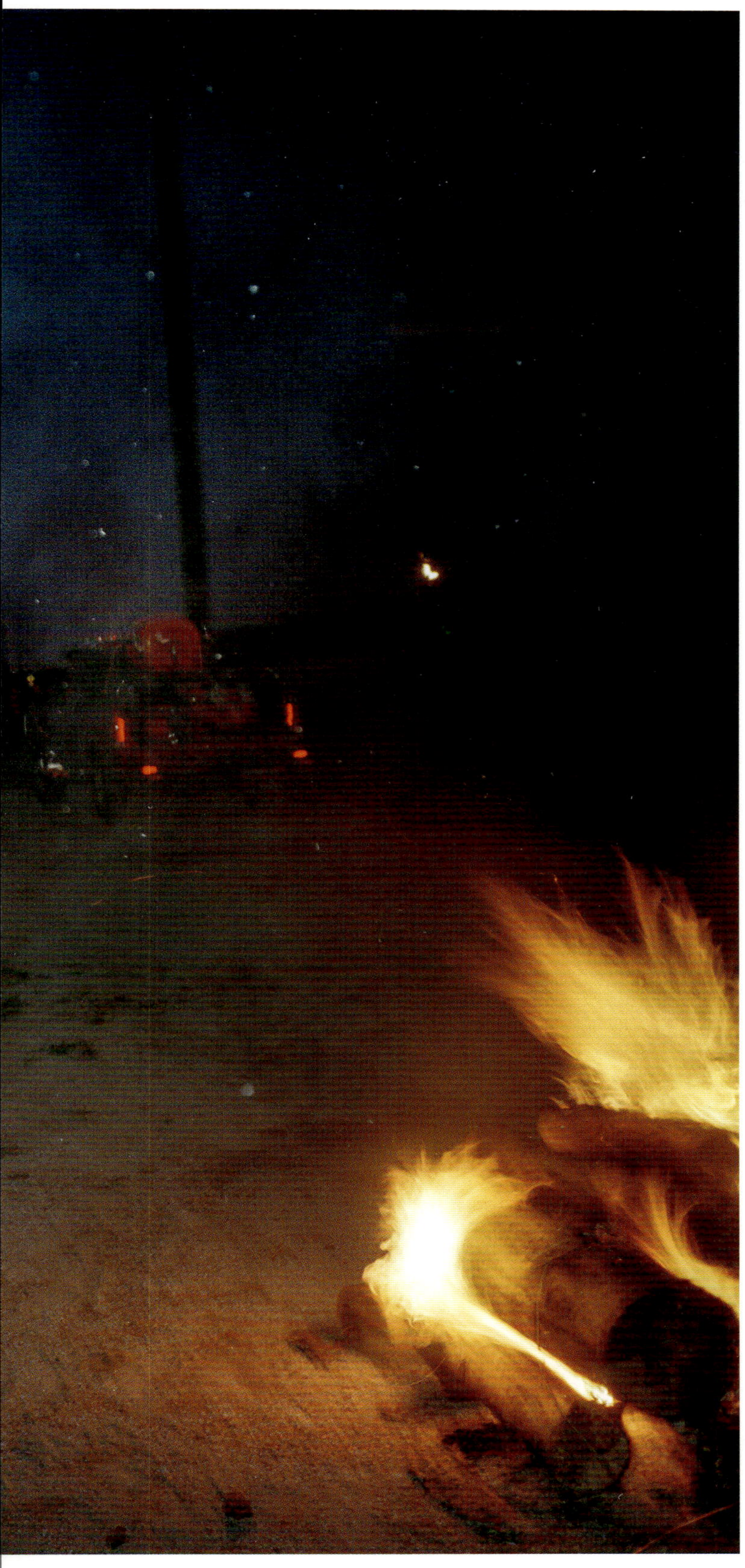

The 2017 Jury

Chair: Stuart Franklin, UK, photographer Magnum Photos
Mary F. Calvert, USA, independent photojournalist
Luciano Candisani, Brazil, nature photojournalist
Claudi Carreras Guillén, Spain, independent curator, editor and photography researcher
Helen Gilks, UK, managing director Nature Picture Library
Yumi Goto, Japan, independent photography curator
Kelli Reed Grant, USA, photography director Yahoo News
Marco Grob, Switzerland, photographer
Tanya Habjouqa, Jordan, photographer NOOR and founding member Rawiya
Eman Mohammed*, Palestine, photographer and multimedia photojournalist
Aïda Muluneh, Canada/Ethiopia, founder and director Addis Foto Fest
Andrei Polikanov, Russia, visual director Takie Dela online media
Kira Pollack, USA, director of photography and visual enterprise *Time*
Adam Pretty, Australia, photographer Getty Images
Pim Ras, the Netherlands, photographer *AD Sportwereld*
João Silva, Portugal/South Africa, staff photographer *The New York Times*
Wim van Sinderen, the Netherlands, senior curator The Hague Museum of Photography
Goran Tomasevic, Serbia, chief photographer East Africa Reuters
Susan White, USA, photography director *Vanity Fair*
Christian Ziegler, Germany, photographer

Secretaries:
David Griffin, USA, owner DGriffinStudio
Maria Mann, USA, consultant international relations EPA

* Eman Mohammed was unable to travel to Amsterdam from the United States following legal advice she received concerning the US president's executive order of 27 January 2017, restricting the rights of individuals from select countries. Eman's place on the General Jury was taken by Tanya Habjouqa.

Participants

In 2017, 5,034 photographers from 126 countries submitted 80,408 images in the photo contest. The participants are listed here according to nationality, as filled in by them in the entry registration system.

Afghanistan
Rada Akbar / Hedayatullah Amid / Mohammad Atif Aryan / Mohammad Ismail / Jalil Rezayee / Naseer Turkmani

Albania
Arben Bici / Edvin Celo / Petrit Kotepano / Valdrin Xhemaj / Gentian Shkullaku

Algeria
Zohra Bensemra / Fethi Sahraoui

Argentina
Rodrigo Abd / Paula Acunzo / Humberto Lucas Alascio / Rodrigo Alfaro / Maximiliano Amena / Martin Arias Feijoo / Facundo Arrizabalaga / Walter Astrada / Juan Manuel Baialardo / Carlos Barria / Araz Bedros / Néstor J. Beremblum / Dominique Besanson / Pablo Bobbio / Marcos Brindicci / Maximiliano Carlos Vernazza / Pedro Castillo / Mario De Fina / Fernando de la Orden / Walter Díaz / Augusto Famulari / Emmanuel Fernandez / Sebastian Gimenez / pablo ariel gomez / Claudio Herdener / Daniel Jayo / Oliver Kornblihtt / Andres Kudacki / Maximiliano Luna / Blas Martinez / Juan Medina / Patricio Murphy / Atilio Orellana / Sebastian Pani / Pablo Ernesto Piovano / Natacha Pisarenko / Angel Ricardo Ramírez / Héctor Rio / Rodrigo Ruiz Ciancia / Alejandro Sala / Juan Sandoval / Matias Sarlo / Mario Sayes / Cristian Scotellaro / Martin Sobral / Eduardo Soteras / Juano Tesone / Pablo Tosco / Franco Trovato Fuoco / Irina Werning

Armenia
Anush Babajanyan / Eric Grigorian / Hrant Khachatryan

Australia
Michael Aw / Nicolas Axelrod / Ben Baker / Darian Berehulak / Philip Brown / Steve Christo / Warren Clarke / Tim Clayton / Brett Costello / Morne De Klerk / Stephen Dupont / Jason Edwards / Mark and Jenny Evans / John Feely / Michael Franchi / Andrea Francolini / Luka Fuda / Kate Geraghty / Ashley Gilbertson / Craig Golding / Steve Gosch / David Gray / Katherine Griffiths / Phil Hillyard / Ian Alfred Hitchcock / Heath Holden / Blair Horgan / Bradley Kanaris / Rohan Kelly / Nicholas Laham / Sylvia Liber / Gordon McComiskie / Ted McDonnell / Justin McManus / Andrew Merry / Paul Miller / Palani Mohan / Nicholas Moir / Angus Mordant / Peter Morgan / Dean Mouhtaropoulos / Fabian Muir / Barry O'Brien / Jason O'Brien / David Dare Parker / Marta Pascual Juanola / Martine Perret / Edvina Pickles / Ryan Pierse / Scott Portelli / Andrew Quilty / Peter Rae / Mark Ralston / Asanka Ratnayake / Warren Richardson / Quinn Rooney / Raphaela Rosella / Jayne Russell / Sam Ruttyn / Dean Saffron / Russel Shakespeare / Marko Sommer / Cameron Spencer / Virginia Star / Adrian Steirn / David Tacon / Andrew James Tauber / Jay Town / Darrian Traynor / Lisa Maree Williams / Toby Zerna

Austria
Heimo Aga / Simon Alber / Heinz-Peter Bader / Christian Bruna / Matthias Cremer / Rudolf Klaffenböck / Stefan Kleinowitz / Herbert Kratky / Gregor Kuntscher / Miroslav Kuzmanovic / Mario Marino / Eugenia Maximova / Josef Polleross / Andreas Pranter / Gregor Sailer / Erwin Scheriau / Alexander Schmidjell / Christian Thiess / Aram Voves / Nurith Wagner-Strauss / Sebastian Wahlhuetter / Claudia Ziegler / Martin Zinggl

Azerbaijan
Rena Effendi / Ilkin Huseynov / Ilgar Jafarov / avid Mammadov / Dilavar Najafov

Bangladesh
Md. Maruf Hasan Abhi / A.M. Ahad / Parvez Ahmad / Firoz Ahmed / Shm Mushfiqul Alam / Shafiqul Alam / Monuril Alam / Samsul Alam / Apu Jaman / K.M. Asad / Mohammad Asad/ Zakir Hossain Chowdhury Auniket / Khandaker Azizur Rahman / Milton Bennett / Pulock Biswas / Turjoy Chowdhury / Rasel Chowdhury / Suvra Kanti Das / Faiham Ebna Sharif / Abul Khaer Muhammad Emdadul Islam / Md.Ibrahim Khalil / Md. Enamul Hasan Enam / Saydul Fateheen / Ismail Ferdous / Indrajit Ghosh / Khaled Hasan / Mamun Hossain / Mashruk Ahmed Iftekhar Hossain / Nazrul Islam / Shikder Jahan / Momena Jalil / Fahad Kaizer / Zahidul Karim / Riasat Alve Kazi / Md Rafayat Haque Khan / Naymuzzaman Khan / Md. Shahnewaz Khan / Md. Zakirul Mazed Konok / Alamin Leon / Sourav Loskar / Mamunur Rashid Mamun / Mohammad Reaz Uddin / Suman Paul / Abdur Rahman / Reza Shahriar Rahman / Sony Ramany / Probal Rashid / Mohammad Fahim Ahamed Riyad / MD Tanveer Hassan Rohan / Azim Khan Ronnie / Md. Abdus Salam / Jewel Samad / Naman Protick Sarker / Shadman Shahid / Salahuddin Ahamed Shamim / Md. Khalid Rayhan Shawon / Reaz Ahmed Sumon / Md. Shamsul Haque Suza / Rahiul Talukder / M Yosuf Tushar / AKM Shehab Uddin / Md. Akhlas Uddin / Md. Hadi Uddin / Jashim Uddin Salam / Qamruz Zaman

Belarus
Sergey Balay / Anton Dotsenko / Viktor Drachev / Denis Dziuba / Sergei Gapon / Katsiaryna Harayeva / Uladzimir Hrydzin / Alexander Khitrov / Dimitrij Leltschuk / Andej Liankievich / Oksana Manchuk / Yuliya Matskevich / Sergei Pahotin / Eugene Reshetov / Vitus Saloshanka / Volha Shukaila / Aliaksandr Vasiukovich / Sviatlana Yerkovich / Tatyana Zenkovich

Belgium
Claire Allard / Zaza Bertrand / Benoit Bou / Nicola Bouvy / Hendrik Braet / Frederik Buyckx / Isabel Corthier / Johannes De Bruycker / Patrick De Roo / Peter de Voecht / Marika Dee / Anthony Dehez / Bieke Depoorter / Oscar Dhooge / Tim Dirven / Laurent Dubrule / Alexander Dumarey / James Arthur Gekiere / Brigitte Grignet / Gaelle Henkens / Justin Jin / Roger Job / François Lenoir / Nicolas Maeterlinck / Olivier Matthys / Mashid Mohadjerin / Virginie Nguyen Hoang / Olivier Papegnies / Vincent Peal / Gaspare Dario Pignatelli / Vincent Rocher / Jonas Roosens / Gaël Turine / Geoffroy Van Der Hasselt / Liza Van der Stock / Katrijn van Giel / Sébastien Van Malleghem / Kristof Van Meirvenne / Wouter van Vaerenbergh / David Verberckt / John Vink / Dirk Waem / Keoma Zec

Bolivia
Verónica Avendaño / Sergio Daniel Caballero / Steve Camargo Zenteno / Gonzalo Contreras del Solar / Patricio Crooker / David José Flores Saavedra / Juan Karita / Marcelo Pérez del Carpio / Wara Maria Leandra Vargas Lara

Bosnia and Herzegovina
Haris Calkic / Armin Durgut / Sljivo Husein / Haris Memija / Midhat Poturovic / Damir Sagolj

Brazil
José Carlos Alexandre / Raphael Alves / Paulo Amorim / Keiny Andrade / Eduardo Anizelli / Alberto César de Araújo / Felipe Barcellos / Paulo Barreto Tavares Cavalcanti / José Carlos Barretta / Lunaé Basile Parracho / Guilherme Bergamini / Thiago Bernardes / Eurivaldo Bezerra / Julio Bittencourt / Marcela Bonfim / Daniel C. Kfouri / André Camara de Mello e Silva / Emiliano Capozoli / Leonardo Carrato / Gabriel Chaim / Rodrigo Coca Lopes / André Augustus Coelho Cardoso / Julio Cesar Bello Cordeiro / Leonardo Correa / Marizilda Cruppe / Ailton Rocha da Cruz / Felipe Dana / Carlos Eduardo de Almeida / João Paulo De Araujo Pinto / Diego de Campos Padgurschi / João Luiz de Franco / Eduardo Lima de Oliveira / Thiago Leon de Oliveira Quiroz / Alex Ferro de Oliveira Ramos / Mastrangelo de Paula Reino / Garbiela Di Bella / Marcio Antonio Dias Pimenta Machado / Angelo Antonio Duarte / Calil Elias Neto / Alan Kardec Epifânio Alves / Chris Faga / Marcio Rodrigo Ferreira Machado / Rogério Florentino Pereira / Flavio Forner / Fernando Frazão de Queiroz / Ramiro Furquim Filho / Luis Eduardo Galdieri / Luiz Carlos Gomes / Bruno Leonardo Gomes Morais / Bernardo Guerreiro / Antonio Pereira Lacerda Junior / Luisa Lauxen Dörr / Odair Leal / Mauricio Lima / Ulisses Lima Job / Alexandre Macedo / Jorge Macêdo / Tiago Machado Carneiro / Benito Maddalena / João Maximiano Mafra de Laet / Cezar Magalhaes / Teresa Cristina Maia Dantas de Góes / Ricardo Marcondes Nogueira / Daniel Soares Marenco / Alice Martins / Paulo Martins Pinto / Luiz Maximiano / Ana Mendes / Alexandre Meneghini / Henry Milléo / Ricardo Moraes / Luiz Ricardo Moreira da Silva / Paulo Henrique Pampolin / Diorgenes Pandini / Rahel Patrasso da Silva / Amanda Perobelli / Mauro Pimentel / Alexandre Pottes Macedo & João Correia Filho / Leonardo Ramos de Miranda Henriques / Livia Rangel da Rocha Radwanski / Claudio Reis / Marcio Resende de Mendonça e Silva / Murilo Cezar Ribas / Sergio Ricardo Oliveira / Mauricio Alexandre Rocha Lima / André Rodrigues / Jonne Roriz / Albari Rosa da Silva / Alessandro Ruaro / Albery Santini Jr. / Antonio Scorza / Alexsandro Silva/ André Sousa Borges / Wilton Sousa junior / Clayton Souza / Jean Souza Lopes / Rogério Stella Santos / Ricardo Stuckert / Roberto Sungi Pedrão / Leandro Taques / Fabio Alarico Teixeira / Thelma Vidales / André Felipe Vieira / William Volcov / Weimer de Carvalho Franco / Adriana Zehbrauskas

Bulgaria
Mehmed Aziz / Minko Chernev / Dimitar Dilkoff / Nicolay Doychinov / Assen Ignatov / Boryana Katsarova / Blagoy Kirilov / Dimitar Kyosemarliev / Juia Lazarova / Julia Paskova / Hristo Rusev / Vladimir Shokov / Anastas Tarpanov / Teodor Todorov / Vlado Trifonov / Victor Troyanov / Ladislav Tsvetkov / Hristo Vladev

Burkina Faso
Yempabou Ahmed Ouoba

Cambodia
Tang Chhin Sothy

Canada
Logan Abassi / Carlo Allegri / Kiran Ambwani / Tyler Anderson / Alexis Aubin / Tanya Bindra / Mark Blinch / Normand Blouin / Christopher Bobyn / Amber Bracken / Bernard Brault / Cole Burston / Kitra Eden Cahana / Darren Calabrese / Martin Chamberland / David Champagne / Andrew Clark / Arianne Clément / Jessie Craig / Barbara Davidson / Daniel Desmarais / Chris Donovan / Thierry du Bois /

Pascal Dumont / Darryl Dyck / Jessica Earnshaw / Stephanie Foden / Brent Foster / Kevin Frayer/ Julie Gascon / Shixu Gu / Gary Hershorn / Colin Horabin / Michel Huneault / Sara Hylton / Marta Iwanek / Olivier Jean / Emiliano Joanes / Emily Kassie / Jeremy Kohm / Nick Kozak / Jean Levac / Laura Leyshon / Peter Mather / Valérian Mazataud / Jo-Anne McArthur / Allen McInnis / Jeff McIntosh / Ryan McLeod / Lance McMillan / Jaclyn McRae-Sadik / Yoanis Menge / Muse Mohammed / Christopher Morris / Mandel Ngan / Guang Niu / Gary Nylander / Brennan O`Connor / Jen Osborne/ Ed Ou/ Louie Palu / Rosa Park / Renaud Philippe / Wendell Phillips / Andre Pichette / Eduard Plante-Fréchette / Maude Plante-Husaruk / Melissa Renwick / Vaughn Ridley / Norman Jean Roy / Frédéric Séguin / John Simpson / Brant Slomovic / Dvid Maurice Smith / Adrienne Surprenant / Larry Towell / Martin Tremblay / Michel Tremblay / Richard Tsong-Taatarii / Alexa Vachon / Ian Willms / Patrick Woodbury / Tanya Workman / Cory Wright / James Young / Iva Zímová

Chile
Orlando Barría Maichil / Tomas Pablo Fernandez / Rodrigo Eliseo Garrido Fernandez / Javier Godoy Fajardo / Raúl Goycoolea / Mariola Bernarda Guerrero Sepulveda / Tomás Munita / Carlos Newman / Cristian Andres Ochoa Espinoza / Alejandro Olivares / Cristobal Olivares Araya / Ronald Patrick / Hector Retamal / Pedro Alfonso Rojas Jorquera / Luis Sergio / Carlos Vera / Carlos Villalon / Christian Zapata / Ernesto Javier Zelada Celis

China
Weimin An / Bai Kelin / Xue Bai / Bayasule Bao / Ying sheng Bi / Deng Bo / Sheng Xiang Cai / Zhiyuan Cai / Guangwen Cao / JianXiong Cao / Jun Cao / Min Cao / Tong Cao / Xueqin Cao / Zhi Zheng Cao / Zhigang Cao / Zongwen Cao / Liang Chang / Yicen Che / Chang Rong Che / Chao Chen / Dong Chen / Fan Chen / Gang Chen / Gangfeng Chen / Guimin Chen / Ji Chen / Jian Chen / Jianping Chen / Jianqiang Chen / Jianqiang Chen / Jianyu Chen / Jianyuan Chen / Jianzhen Chen / Jie Chen / Junjie Chen / Li Chen / Liang Chen / Mao Hui Chen / Qiang Chen / Ronghui Chen / Ruilin Chen / Ruishi Chen / Ruiyuan Chen / Shujiang Chen / Wei Chen / Weibin Chen / Weixi Chen / Xiangcheng Chen / Xiaotie Chen / Xiaoyue Chen / Xiurong Chen / Xuan Chen / Yan Chen / Yangfu Chen / Yin Chen / Yingjie Chen / Yongcheng Chen / Yongheng Chen / Youchen Chen / Zhenming Chen / Zhiqiang Chen / Zhiwei Chen / Zhongqiu Chen / Zhuohui Chen / Ding Cheng / Xuliang Cheng / Yiheng Cheng / Yongzhi Chu / Ma Chun Bin / Hu Cong / Genyuan Cui / Heping Cui / Jun Cui / Li Cui / Ling Cui / Maoyuan Cui / Nan Cui / Feie Dai / Liqun Dai / Jia Dai Feng Fei / Sun De Li / Liangming Deng / Weijian Deng / Zhigang Deng / Ting Ding / Ren Dong / Shuming Dong / Yalin Dong / Shaolin Dou / Yiming Dou / Jinen Du / Jingbo Du / Jinxing Du / Yang Du / Dayong Duan / Fangbin Fan / Liwen Fan / Liyong Fan / Yulei Fan / Qianhua Fang / Sheng Fang / Yunfeng Fang / Zhenhong Fang / Cheng Fa Feng / Junkuan Feng / Qiang Feng / Shuni Feng / Ding Fu / Liang Fu / Qiang Fu / Sibo Fu / Yingdong Fu / Pan Gan Ming / Hetao Gao / Liequan Gao / Wei Gao / Wenxiu Gao / Xing Gao / Xiaoming Ge / Yaqi Ge / Bencai Gong / Gongwenbin Gong / Wei Gong / Zijie Gong / Jia Gu / Jing Gu / Shan Hong Gu / Song Gu / Xiaolin Gu / Yi Gu / Yifan Gu / Jun Guan / Chen Guo / Guanghui Guo / Guizhong Guo / Ji dong Guo / Jijiang Guo / Jing Guo / Jingyu Guo / Liliang Guo / XianZhong Guo / Xiao Guo / Xin Guo / Yijiang Guo / Yong Guo / Yongfen Guo / ZhiHua Guo / Yang Hai / Lile Han / Yan Han / Yunmin Han / zhiming Han / He Hao / Chunsheng He / Haiyang He / Jiao He / Ou He / Yanguang He / Yi He / Yong An He / Yuanquan He / Jianjun Hei / Guoliang Heng / Mingsheng Hong / Zhongmin Hong / Shuwang Hou / Yu Hou / Yu Hou / Guoqing Hu / Jianhuan Hu / Lingyun Hu / Tiexiang Hu / Tingmei Hu / Weiguo Hu / Yonghui Hu / Jian Hua / Tudeng Huadan / Baojia Huang / Changbo Huang / Dongmei Huang / Heng Ri Huang / Hongfeng Huang / Jianjun Huang / Jianming Huang / Jianyuan Huang / Jin Huang / Jingyue Huang / Lun Qian Huang / Qingdang Huang / Songhe Huang / Xirui Huang / Yan Huang / Yue Huang / Yuejia Huang / Yufei Huang / Yunping Huang / Yuyang Huang / Zhe Huang / Tian Huo / Long Sheng Ji / Guorong Jia / Lei Jia / Tianyong Jia / Yanan Jia / Jiang Hao / Lin Jiang / Wen Hua Jiang / Wenhua Jiang / Yan Jiang / Youqun Jiang / Xiaodong Jiao / Sheng Jiapeng / Liwang Jin / Siliu Jin / Xiaolan Jin / Yi Jin / Wang Jing / Fan Jinyu / Rao Jun / Wang Jun / Liu Junyang / Aijie Kang / Linyi Kang / Zhao Kang / Xu Kangping / Xiangming Kong / Huimin Kuang / kuangbinqi Kuang / Jing Lai / Qiaoquan Lai / Xinlin Lai / Hongguang Lan / Yezuo Lan / Naiyi Lei / YaPing Lei / Yuting Lei / Pang Wai Leung / Aimin Li / Bin Li / Celiang Li / Chun Yan Li / Chunling Li / En Li / Fan Li / Fang Li / Feng Li / Ga Li / Gang Li / Guanyu Li / Guibin Li / Huaifeng Li / Jiangang Li / JianLin Li / Jiangsong Li / Jiaping Li / Jing Li / Junhui Li / Junjian Li / Ke Li / Linlin Li / Ming Li / Qiang Li / Qianhao Li / Quanhai Li / Shujing Li / Shuying Li / Wei Li / Xianjun Li / Xiaoguo Li / Xiaolei Li / Xin Li / Yanan Li / Yang Li / Yong Li / Yushan Li / Yuze Li / Zhenqi Li / Zhenyu Li / Yi Lian / Meng Liang / Yilong Liang / Ying Fei Liang / Jin Liangkuai / Feng Liao / Pan Liao / WenXiong Liao / Xiong Liao / Xueming Liao / Zhengyan Liao / Shi Lifei / Chen Lin / Feng Lin / Hui-Yi Lin / Jiaxian Li / Mingbin Lin / Minming Lin / Qiao Sen Lin / Qishu Lin / Shi Fang Lin / Song Lin / Wu Dan Lin / Wu Wang Lin / Xiong Lin / Xu Lin / Yun Lin / Zuxian Lin / Baosheng Liu / Bin Liu / Bingsheng Liu / Bo Liu / Chang Liu / Changming Liu / Changyan Liu / Chengliang Liu / Dajia Liu / Dan Liu / Debin Liu / Fengrui Liu / Guanguan Liu / Guoxing Liu / Han Feng Liu / Hang Liu / Jian Liu / Jiang Liu / Jiani Liu / Jie Zhi Liu / Junhua Liu / Lei Liu / Li Liu / Liangjin Liu / Mei Hong Liu / Qingyun Liu / Rongqin Liu / Shuailiang Liu / Shuisheng Liu / Shutong Liu / Song Liu / Tao Liu / Weiqiang Liu / Xiaolan Liu / Yan ao Liu / Yongmei Liu / Youzhi Liu / Yuyang Liu / Zhankun Liu / Zhongcan Liu / Zhou Lixin / Wei Long / Yongping Lou / Fanjing Lu / Guang Lu / Minqiang Lu / Xubo Lu / Ying Lu / Shengjie Luan / Yu Lun / Hua Luo / Luohui Luo / Shanxin Luo / Yong Luo / Jiming Lv / Ning Lv / Ting Chuan Lv / Zhongbin Lv / Hao Lyo / Jie Ma / Juan Ma / Nan Ma / Qianli Ma / Xiaobo Ma / Yuandong Ma / Huiqiao Man / Shang Wen Mao / Yanzheng Mao / Fei Maohua / Ao Miao / Yong Miao / Qingzhu Min / Jiwu Mu / Saikeli Muhushi / Zhiping Nan / Li Xiang Ni / Feng Ning / Zhouhao Ning / Deng Pan / Haisong Pan / Jingcao Pan / Jinming Pan / Songgang Pan / Yu Pan / Zhiwang Pan / Changtong Peng / Dan Peng / Nian Peng / Ziyang Peng / Feng Pu / Xiaoxu Pu / Heng Qi / Hui Qi / Shihui Qi / Li Qi Zheng / Haifeng Qian / Jin Qian / LuBin Qian / Jianguo Qiao / Bin Qin / Wanshou Qin / Zhao Qing / Taijian Qiu / Weirong Qiu / Yan Qiu / MengJun Ran / Wen Ran / Yongxia Rao / Chunpu Ren / Shi Chen Ren / Xi Ren / Xihai Ren / Xiuting Ren / Fen Ruan / Zhonghua Sha / Xiaohui Shan / Gen Shun Shang / Huage Shang / Ying Shao / Bohan Shen / Yanjun Shen / Youguo Shen / Yu Shen / Yunfeng Shen / Zhijun Shen / Bai Shi / Tao Shi / Weimeng Shi / Yi Shi / Weiping Shu / Yuxi Si / Aly Song / Gangming Song / Jinyu Song / Kai Song / Li Song / Linji Song / Weihua Song / Xinhua Song / Ziyu Song / Bo Su / Jixiang Su / JunJie Su / Qiaojiang Su / Shaolong Su / Yu Su / Guoshu Sun / Jiandong Sun / Jianhui Sun / Jie Sun / Li Sun / Lin Sun / Shubao Sun / Wen Sun / Zhimao Sun / Jianwei Tan / Wendong Tan / Huiji Tang / Jie Tang / Jun Tang / Junlin Tang / Mingzhen Tang / ShouXin Tang / Yijun Tang / Yinfeng Tang / Huan Tao / Tao Tao / Zheng Tao / Haiguang Tian / He Tian / Jian Tian / Jieyan Tian / Yuan Tian / Lei Wan / Aimin Wang / Changshu Wang / Chen Wang / Cheng Wang / Fanqi Wang / Fengzhan Wang / Guorong Wang / He Wang / Hongsong Wang / Hui Wang / Jian Wang / Jianguo Wang / Jianing Wang / Jicheng Wang / Jin Wang / Lei Wang / Lili Wang / Liqiang Wang / Mianli Wang / Ming Wang / Pan Wang / Peng Wang / Pingsheng Wang / Qin Wang / Qing Wang / Ruobang Wang / Shanyuan Wang / Shen Wang / Shouzhi Wang / Suping Wang / Taiheng Wang / Tiejun Wang / Wei Wang / Weiwei Wang / Xiangyang Wang / Xiao Wang / Xiaobing Wang / Xiaohong Wang / Xiaoke Wang / Xiaoming Wang / Xueya Wang / Yan -Chuan Wang / Yanggang Wang / Yi Wang / Ying Ying Wang / Yixuan Wang / Yong Wang / Yuheng Wang / Yunliang Wang / Zhanqi Wang / Zhendong Wang / Zhenyu Wang / Zicheng Wang / Gesheng Wei / Liang Wei / Ming Wei / Tao Wei / Xiaodong Wei / Xingqi Wei / Zheng Wei / Cao Weisong / Wsir Wsir / Changqing Wu / Di Wu / Duanhong Wu / Hailang Wu / Hong Wu / Hongjun Wu / Huaming Wu / Jianmin Wu / Jiaxiang Wu / Jin Wu / Jingli Wu / Junjie Wu / Junsong Wu / Kai Wu / Linhong Wu / Weize Wu / Wenbing Wu / Wengang Wu / Wowei Wu / Xiao Rong Wu / Yong Gang Wu / Youliang Wu / Zhengjian Wu / Wu Wu Jie Di / Haibo Xi / Donghai Xia / Shiyan Xia / Weicong Xia / Xuejun Xia / Zhaxi Xia Wu / Shulian Xiao / Wensong Xiao / Xiong Xiao / Yijiu Xiao / Dan Xie / Gangjun Xie / Hongmei Xie / Hua Xie / Jiujiang Xie / Kuangshi Xie / Longxiang Xie / Minggang Xie / Yi Xin / Shengwen Xiong / Zhaohua Xiong / Bin Xu / Chen xu / Dezhi Xu / Haifeng Xu / Huoju Xu / Jingxing Xu / Jiye Xu / Junkui Xu / Kaikai Xu / Li Xu / Minhao Xu / Ping Xu / Shiwei Xu / Weihua Xu / Yi Xu / Gangqiang Xuan / Yubin Xue / Bailiang Yan / Han Yan / Jing Yan / Silin Yan / Yin Yan / Bo Yang / Cai Yang / Chenglong Yang / Da Yang / Donghui Yang / Guang Yang / Haodong Yang / Huafeng Yang / Hui-quan Yang / Jian Yang / Kejia Yang / PengWei Yang / Qianfu Yang / Shenlai Yang / Shutian Yang / Tongyu Yang / Xinyu Yang / Xiuqiong Yang / Yang Yang / Yaoye Yang / Yingcong Yang / Youde Yang / Yousheng Yang / Zhonghua Yang / Dong Yao / Huabei Yao / Qiang Yao / Hongbing Ye / Kai Ye / Shuyong Ye / Wei Ye / Gang Yin / Peiyu Yin / Yonghong Yin / Li Yong / Sihang You / Genling Yu / Guanghua Yu / Hong Chun Yu / Huaqiang Yu / Jijian Yu / Ming Yu / Ping Yu / Tong Yu / Yonghua Yu / Liyang Yuan / Peide Yuan / Hongjun Yue / Yuewei Yue / Hongbo Yun / Cao Yv-Qing / Demeng Zeng / Junshang Zeng / Mei Zeng / Shaoxi Zeng / Wei Zeng / Yipeng Zeng / Kai Zha / Jianfeng Zhai / Jianlan Zhai / Yan Zhan / You Bing Zhan / Yu Zhan / Bin Zhang / Cheng Zhang / Chengbin Zhang / Chuansong Zhang / Cuncheng Zhang / Deqiang Zhang / Dian Zhang / Feng Zhang / Han Zong Zhan / Hong Zhang / Hongwei Zhang / Hui Zhang / Huoshun Zhang / Jian Zhang / Jie Zhang / Jin Zhang / Jinqi Zhang / Junmin Zhang / Kechun Zhang / Lei Zhang / Lide Zhang / Lijie Zhang / Peijian Zhang / Qiang Zhang / Ruomeng Zhang / Shibo Zhang / Tao Zhang / Tinaming Zhang / Wei Zhang / Weichun Zhang / Wengliang Zhang / Xiaohong Zhang / Xingyong Zhang / Yanlong Zhang / Yifan Zhang / Yifu Zhang / Yingnan Zhang / Yongtao Zhang / Yongyan Zhang / Youqiong Zhang / Yuan Zhang / Yujie Zhang / Zhao Zhang / Zhaozeng Zhang / Zheren Zhang / Zhiming Zhang / Zhitao Zhang / Zhou Zhang / Changming Zhang / Zhang Zhang Hongwei / Caixia Zhao / Chengyi Zhao / Chongyi Zhao / Heting Zhao / Hongzhi Zhao / Huai Zhao / Jiangning Zhao / Jingdong Zhao / Jingwei Zhao / Jinyu Zhao / Jun Zhao / Peigen Zhao / Wang Zhao / Xiangrong Zhao / Yi Zhao / Yong Zhao / Zuemin Zhao / Xuebao Zhen / Chengle Zheng / Dong Lin Zhen / Ji Zhen / Kaixia Zheng / Kanghua Zheng / Xiaomei Zheng / Xiaoqun Zheng / Xinqing Zheng / Yao De Zheng / Yong Sheng Zheng / ZW Zheng / Leiying Zhi / Sun Zhijun / Bing Wen Zhong / Guanyong Zhong / He Zhong / Huan Zhong / Liming Zhong / Zhenbin Zhong / Zhihu Zhong / Zhitang Zhong/ Wang Zhong Ju / Cunyun Zhou / En Zhou / Gukai Zhou / Guoqiang Zhou / Jincheng Zhou / Lichun Zhou / Na Zhou / Pinglang Zhou / Qing Zhou / Saiqiong Zhou / Shengli Zhou / Xiao Zhou / Xiaogang Zhou / Xiaoping Zhou / Xin Zhou / Xinghua Zhou / Xuejun Zhou / Changle Zhu / Haiwei Zhu / Hongbo Zhu / Jialei Zhu / Jianxing Zhu / Jun Zhu / Lijian Zhu / Qi Zhu / Qingfu Zhu / Xingxin Zhu /

Xiyong Zhu / Yibin Zhu / ZhiHui Zhu / Zibohong / Biyu Zou / Dongxiong Zou

Colombia
Luis Acosta / Ruven Afanador / Cristhian Agudelo / Luis Henry Agudelo Cano / Eliana Aponte Tobar / Juan d Arredondo / Luis Benavides / Felipe Caicedo Chacón / Ramon Campos Iriarte / Juan Fernando Cano Munoz / Nelson Oswaldo Cárdenas Ferreira / Abel Enrique Cardenas Ortegon / Camilo Diaz / Milton Diaz Guillermo / Salym Fayad / Daniel Garzón Herazo / Lina Maria Hidalgo Acevedo / Luis Eugenio Lizarazo García / William Fernando Martínez Beltrán / Carlos Julio Martinez Tamara / Ricardo Mazalan / Claudia Alexandra McNichols / Alberto Mira Mora / Juan David Paez Sanchez / Leon Dario Pelaez Sanchez / Bernardo Peña / Jaime Pérez Munevar / Federico Rappa / Federico Rios / Henry Romero / Camilo Rozo / Manuel Salvador Saldarriaga Quintero / Nelson Alexander Sierra Gutierrez / Victor Hugo Soto Galeano / Joana marcela Toro Mora / Javier Vanegas / Esteban Vanegas Londoño / Carlos Velasquez / Mauricio Alberto Villamizar/ Donaldo Zuluaga Velilla / Diego Andres Zuluaga Zuluaga

Costa Rica
Daniel Garzón Herazo / Priscilla Mora Flores / Rafael Pacheco Granados

Croatia
Boris Koziak / Dragan Matic / Marijan Murat / Hrvoje Polan / Damir Senčar / Sanjin Strukic

Cuba
Milton Diaz Guillermo / Salym Fayad / Ismael Francisco / Eduardo Javier Garcia / Ismael Francisco Gonzalez Arceo / Adalberto Roque / Yander Alberto Zamora de los Reyes

Cyprus
Belal Doufesh / Yiorgos Doukanaris / Andreas Iacovou / Aleksandar Ljubojevic

Czech Republic
Hana Connor & Filip Jandourek / Eloy Costa Arias / Camilo Diaz / Martin Divisek / Hynek Glos / Michael Hanke / Jaromír Hanzlík / Jana Hunterova / Šimon Jiráček / Tomas Junek / Radek Kalhous / Stanislav Krupar / Lukáš Mach / Michal Novotny / Jiri Nykodym / Pavel Radosta / Vladimir Rys / Jarmila Stukova / David Tesinsky / Petr Toman / Daniel Vojtech / Roman Vondrouš / cJan Zatorsky

Denmark
Steven Achiam / Joachim Adrian / Morten Albek / Cicilie Sigrid Andersen / Abbid Anwar / Nicolas Asfouri / Jens Astrup / Lasse Bak Mejlvang / Søren Bidstrup / Stine Bidstrup / Anders Birch / Marcus Trappaud Bjørn / Jeppe Bøje Nielsen / Thomas Borberg / Andreas Hagemann Bro / Jeppe Carlsen / Casper Holmenlund Christensen / Mads Christensen / Casper Dalhoff / Miriam Dalsgaard / Charlotte de la Fuente Nørregaard / Michael Drost-Hansen / Jacob Ehrbahn / Simon Bruun Fals / Finn Frandsen / Betina Garcia / Kasper Glendorf Palsnov / Jan Grarup / Marie Hald / Bjorn Stig Hansen / Ulrik Hasemann / Helle Arensbak / Mikkel Hørlyck / Lars Horn / Jan Høst-Aaris / Kristian Hvidtfeldt Buus / Peter Klint Busk Jørgensen / Lars Just / Jens Juul / Lasse Kofod / Lars Krabbe / Nanna Kreutzmann / Asger Ladefoged / Joachim Ladefoged / Martin Lehmann / Thomas Lekfeldt / Nikolai Linares Larsen / Bax Lindhardt / Mathias Løvgreen Bojesen / Mohammed Massoud Morsi / Nils Meilvang / Lars Moeller Jensen / Thomas Nielsen / Mads Nissen / Sigrid Ryge Nygaard / Daniel Rye Ottosen / Jeannette Pardorf / Rasmus Degnbol Pedersen / Janus Engel Rasmussen / Søren Rønholt / Simon Skipper Christiansen / Anders Rye Skjoldjensen / Cécile Smetana Baudier / Carsten Snejbjerg / Morten Stricker / Sisse Graabech Stroyer Andersen / Michael Svenningsen / Gregers Tycho / Jens Welding Øllgaard / Kaspar Wenstrup

Dominican Republic
Jorge Manuel Cruz Diaz / Miguel Gomez / Adriano Rosario Hernandez

Ecuador
Santiago Borja / Rodrigo Buendia / Anamaria Chediak / César Morejón Castillo / Galo Armando Paguay Becerra / Diego Pallero Torres / Rodolfo Párraga Quiroz / Marcos Pin / Sergio Augusto Poveda Chavez / Isadora María Romero / Mijail Leonardo Vallejo Prut

Egypt
Ahmed Mostafa Abd El-gwad / Motaz Ahmed / Amr Alfiky / Mohamed Anwar / Omnia Arfin / Ahmed Ashraf / Kim Badawi / Nour El Refai / Mohammed Elshamy / Waled Gebril / Ahmed Hamed / Mohamed Hossam El-Din / Heba Khalifa / Heba Khamis / Ashraf Mohamed Talaat / Ayman Aref Saad EL-Din / Nader Saadallah

El Salvador
Mauricio Alexander Cáceres García / Omar Carbonero / Yuri Cortez / Josué Abisaí Guevara Flores / Lissette Esperanza Lemus Sánchez / Víctor Osvaldo Martínez Peña / Frederick Meza Díaz Md

Estonia
Dmitri Kotjuh / Tairo Lutter / Joosep Martinson / Brigit Püve

Finland
Marina Ekroos / Rio Gandara / Jukka Gröndahl / Esko Jämsä / Markus Jokela / Sami Kero / Heidi Kirjavainen / Petteri Kokkonen / Arttu Laitala / Saara Mansikkamäki / Juhani Niiranen / Jussi Nukari / Jari Peltomäki / Miikka Pirinen / Hannu Rainamo / Kaisa Rautaheimo / Janne Riikonen / Heikki Saukkomaa / Mikko Vähäniitty / Akseli Valmunen / Markus Varesvuo

France
Cyril Abad / Olivier Adam / Pierre Adenis / Pascal Aimar / Denis Allard / Bruno Arbesú / Christophe Archambault / Lilian Auffret / Patrick Aventurier / Hugo Aymar / Laurent Bagnis / Joan Bardeletti / Martín Barzilai / Pascal Bastien / Eric Baudet / Patrick Baz / Jean-Jacques Bernard / Cyrille Bernon / Martin Bertrand / Franck Bessiere / France Billon / Guillaume Binet / Didier Bizet / Julien Blanc / Raphaël Blasselle / Vincent Boisot / Régis Bonnerot / Jérôme Bonnet / Sébastien Boué / Pierre Boutier / Franck Boutonnet / Eric Bouvet / Gabriel Bouys / Thomas Bregardis / Edouard Bride / Arnaud Brunet / Axelle Budan de Russé / Martin Bureau / Anne-Laure Camilleri / Francesco Carella / Sarah Caron / Sophie Carrère / Fabrice Catérini / Bruno Chapiron / Nathanael Charbonnier / Denis Charlet / Antoine Chauvel / Patrick Chauvel / Sandra Chenu Godefroy / Olivier Chouchana / Thomas Coex / Olivier Corsan / Stéphane Coutteel / Pierre Crom / Julien Daniel / William Daniels / Guillaume Darribau / Georges Dayan / Béatrice de Géa / Philippe de Poulpiquet / Veronique de Viguerie / Benjamin Decoin / Pascal Della Zuana / Mathias Depardon / Bénédicte Desrus / Eric Dessons / Jean Jérôme Destouches / Stephen Dock / François Dufor / Fred Dufour / Sophie Ebrard / Alain Ernoult / Eric Facon / Julien Faure / Bruno Fert / Franck Fife / Anna Filipova / Corentin Fohlen / Emeric Fohlen / Julie Franchet / Eric Gaillard / Michel Garcia / Sebastian Gil Miranda / Thomas Girondel / Baptiste Giroudon / Julien Goldstein / Daniel Jeremias Gonzalez / Olivier Grunewald / Marie Guilland / Jeoffrey Guillemard / Simon Guillemin / Valery Hache / Christian Hartmann / Laurent Hazgui / Guillaume Herbaut / Philippe Huguen / Patrick James / Gérard Julien / Jérémie Jung / Laurent Kalfala / François Xavier Klein / Stephane Klein / Pascal Kobeh / Jean-Philippe Ksiazek / Benedicte Kurzen / Alain Laboile / Fréderic Lafargue / Stephane Lagoutte / Francis Latreille / Etienne Laurent / Sébastien Leban / Vianney Le Caer / Michel Le Moine / Rose Lecat / Vincent Lecomte / Christophe Lepetit / Herve Lequeux / Christian Lombardi / Amélie Losier / John MacDougall / Jean Christophe Magnenet / Stephane Mahe / Stephane Mantey / Pierre-Philippe Marcou / David Mareuil / Francois Xavier Marit / Pierre Marsaut / Catalina Martin-Chico / Adrien Matton / Nadège Mazars / Georges Merillon / Isabelle Merminod / Nicolas Messyasz / Denis Meyer / Jean-Christian Meyer / Gilles Mingasson / Michaël Monnier / Tuul & Bruno Morandi / Thomas Morel-Fort / Olivier Morin / Jean-Claude Moschetti / Mao Moumene / Alain Mounic / Jean François Mutzig / Sebastien Nogier / Frederic Noy / Olivier Robin / Jeff Pachoud / Matthieu Paley / Franck Paubel / Guillaume Payen / Alexis Pazoumian / Romain Perrocheau / Benjamin Petit / Frédéric Mery Poplimont / Brice Portolano / Anne-laure Pouchard Serra / Mathieu Pujol / Noël Quidu / Yann Rabanier / Zacharie Rabehi / Theo Renaut / Tristan Reynaud / Franck Robichon / Alexis Rosenfeld / Véronique Roux Voloir / Séverine Sajous / Thomas Samson / Lise Sarfati / Norbert Scanella / Jan Schmidt-Whitley / Christophe Simon / Michel Slomka / Jeremie Souteyrat / Marion Staderoli / Benoit Stichelbaut / Frederic Stucin / Jeremy Suyker / Thierry Suzan / Mehdi Taamallah / Myriam Tangi / Antoine Tempé / Pierre Terdjman / Pierre Teyssot / Antonin Thuillier / Gia-Dinh To / Vincent Tremeau / Théophile Trossat / Emilien Urbano / Marion Vacca / Yoan Valat / Laurent Van der Stockt / Thibault Vandermersch / Marylise Vigneau / Antoine Vincens de Tapol / Valerio Vincenzo / Maurice Virivau / Christophe Viseux / Franck Vogel / Delphine Warin / Vincent Wartner / Mélanie Wenger / Philippe Wojazer / Raphael Yaghobzadeh Patrick Zachmann / Adlan Ziadi-Mansri

French Guiana
Karl Joseph

Gambia
Dawda Bayo

Georgia
Irakli Dzneladze / Ketevan Kardava / Ketevan Mghebrishvili / Dina Oganova / Olga Tsiskarishvili-Soselia

Germany
Anne Ackermann / Emine Akbaba / Michael Bahr / Lajos Eric Balogh / David Baltzer / Lars Baron / Marcus Barthel / Gil Bartz / Leonora Baumann / Michael Bause / Peter Bauza / Siegfried Becker / Xiomara Bender / Fabrizio Bensch / Lars Berg / Toby Binder / Dominik Bindl / Dominic Blewett / Joerg Boethling / Stefan Boness / Hubert Brand / Verena Brandt / Hermann Bredehorst / Frank Bredel / Philipp Breu / Hansjürgen Britsch / Anika Büssemeier / Dominik Thomas Butzmann / Reinaldo Coddou / Antonino Condorelli / Christina Czybik / Stefan Dauth / Reinhard Dirscherl / Sven Döring / Anna Domnick / Emile Alain Ducke / Thomas Duffé / Willi Effenberger / Johannes Eisele / Thomas Eisenhuth / Andreas Endermann / Andreas Engelhard / Daniel Etter / Enrico Fabian / Ralf Falbe / Christina Feldt / Fabian Fiechter / Kilian Foerster / Walter Fogel / Sascha Fromm / Jürgen Fromme / Maurizio Gambarini / Walter Geiring / Mario Gerth / José Giribás Marambio / Christoph Gödan / Oliver Goernandt-Schade / Stefan Gregor / Marvin Ibo Güngör / Julia Gunther / Patrick Haar / Kerstin Hacker / Miguel Hahn & Jan-Christoph Hartung / Johannes Hartig / Benjamin Haselberger / Alexander Hassenstein / Gerhard Heidorn / Marc Heiligenstein / Juliane Herrmann / Katharina Hesse / Karl-Josef Hildenbrand / Harald Hohenthal / China Hopson / Sandra Hoyn / Angelika Jakob / Claudia Janke / Britta Jaschinski / Hannes Jung / Christian Jungeblodt / Kati Jurischka / Rainer

Jysch / Mohammad K.Zoyari / Sebastian Kahnert / Jonas Kakó / Enno Kapitza / Birte Kaufmann / Corinna Kern / Claus Kiefer / Dagmar Kielhorn / Björn Kietzmann / Anselm Kissel / Karolin Klüppel / Alexander Koerner / Bjorn Eric Kohnen / Marcus Koppen / Maren Krings / Stephan Krudewig / Patricia Kühfuss / Simone Kuhlmey / Ksenia Kuleshova / Moritz Küstner / Matthias Lange / Bartek Langer / Martin Leissl / Timo Lieber / Christoph Lienert / Ralf Lienert / Alexandra Lier / Kai Löffelbein / Gerhard E. Ludwig / Marcel Maffei / Ute Mans / Werner Mansholt / Erik Marquardt / Uwe H. Martin / Noel Matoff / Fabian Matzerath / Jens Meyer / Thorsten Milse / Sascha Montag / Johannes Moths / Lena Mucha / Mark Mühlhaus / Johannes Müller / Jörg Müller / Hans-Maximo Musielik / Merlin Nadj-Torma / Frank Neßlage / Wolfgang Noack / Ali Noureldin / Ricardo Nunes / Jonas Opperskalski / Reimar Ott / Ingo Otto / Jens Palme / Melina Papageorgiou / Ladislav Perenyi / Thomas P. Peschak / Kai Oliver Pfaffenbach / Michael Probst / Stephan Rabold / Markus Georg Reintgen / Sascha Rheker / Stefan Richter / Astrid Riecken / Martin Rose / Norbert Rosing / Kaveh Rostamkhani / Helena Maria Schaetzle / Peter Schatz / Dietmar Scherf / Analisa Schindler / Laurin Schmid / Roberto Schmidt / Harald Schmitt / Kirstin Schmitt / Jakob Schnetz / Julius Schrank / Markus Schreiber / Annette Schreyer / Thomas Schreyer / Olaf Schuelke / Frank Schultze / Lukas Schulze / Hartmut Schwarzbach / Kai Schwörer / Patrick Seeger / Bertram Solcher / Martin Specht / Andy Spyra / Bente Marei Stachowske / Wolfgang Stahr / Johannes Stein / Heike Steinweg / Björn Steinz / Stephanie Wolff / Nikita Tereshin / Karsten Thormaehlen / Christian Thum / Ryu Voelkel / Stefan Volk / Philipp von Ditfurth / Anke Waelischmiller / Franz Waelischmiller / Richard Walch / Oliver Weiken / Fabian Weiss / Sebastian Wells / Ludwig Welnicki / Sebastian Widmann / Kai Wiedenhoefer / Arnd Wiegmann / Claudia Yvonne Wiens / Ann-Christine Woehrl / Rainer Wohlfahrt / Oliver Wolff / Solvin Zankl / Anna Katharina Zeitler / Sven Zellner

Ghana
Eric Gyamfi

Greece
Alexandros Avramidis / Socrates Baltagiannis / Yannis Behrakis / Evangelos Bougiotis / Thomas Daskalakis / Christina Georgiadou / Petros Giannakouris / Louisa Maria Gouliamaki / Lakovos Hatzistavrou / Alexandros Katsis / Konstantina Klossi / Gerasimos Koilakos / Yannis Kolesidis / Alkis Konstantinidis / Yannis Kontos / Stefanos Kouratzis / Georgios Makkas / Kostas Mantziaris / Alexandros Maragkos / Vasilis Maroukas / Dimitri Mellos / Aris Messinis / Sakis Mitrolidis / Giorgos Moutafis / Christos Ntountomis / Anna Pantelia / Myrto Papadopoulos / Giannis Papanikos / Antonis Pasvantis / Michalis Patsouras / Kostas Pikoulas / Nikos Pilos / Fotios Plegas Gavrilakis / Konstantinos Tsironis / Orhan Tsolak / Angelos Tzortzinis / Aristidis Vafeiadakis

Guam
Ed Crisostomo

Guatemala
Santiago Billy / Guillermo Esteban Estrada Biba / Sergio Joel Muñoz Rodriguez / Luis Soto Maldonado

Haiti
Florian Alvarez / Homère Cardichon / Dieu Nalio Chery

Hong Kong
Cheuk Fai Chan / Kam-Tong Chung / Chun Wai Fu / Katat Ho / Chung Ming Ko / Billy H.C. Kwok / Chun Tung Lam / Yik Fei Lam / On Man Kevin Lee / Chak Tung Li / Kwan Ho Lo / Siu Wai Lui / Alastair Pike / Wing Kai Tsang / Wai Kin Kenji Wong / Wing Chun Wong / Chun Leung Yu

Hungary
Zoltán Balogh / Balázs Béli / Krisztián Bócsi / Maximiliano Gabriel Braun Ibanez / Gyula Czimbal / Gabor F.Toth / Bertalan Feher / Gabor Garamvari / Balazs Gardi / Eszter Horvath / Marton Kallai / Bea Kallos / Tamas Kaszas / Marton Magocsi / Szilvia Magyar / Bence Mate / Balazs Mohai / Zoltan Molnar / Simon Móricz-Sabján / András Polgár / Milan Radisics / Zsolt Reviczky / Levente Safrany / István Csaba Sánta / Tamas Schild / Balázs Somorjai / Daniel Soós / Akos Stiller / Peter Szalmas / Robert Szaniszlo / Laszlo Szirtesi

Iceland
Ólafur Steinar Gestsson / Vilhelm Gunnarsson / Christina Simons / Pall Stefansson / Gisli Svendsen

India
Abhijit Alka Anil / Bindu Arora / Mahesh Kumar Asodha / Bijuraj Ayilliath Kuttiyeri / Pratik Dutta Babu / Pritam Bandyopadhyay / Shome Basu / Salil Bera / Ritesh shukla Betu / Adil Hussain Bhat / Narendra Bisht / Biju Boro / Arunchandra Bose / Soumya Sankar Bose / Balarka Brahma / Ranjan Basu Bulbul / Mohammed Thanseer Ck Chakkalakkunnan / Rana Chakraborty / V.S. Vijaya Bhaskara Rao Chalasani / Suresh Kumar Chinnasamy / Kamakhya Kumar Choudhary / Ravi Choudhary / Rupak Chowdhuri / Mohd Yasin Dar / Sanjit Das / Shantanu Das / Sucheta Das / Sudipto Das / Supranav Dash / Arko Datto / Amit Dave Rameshchandra / Mandar Deodhar / Uday Deolekar / Vinod Divakaran / Devendra Dube / Gajanan Dudhalkar / Akhil E.S. Enchikkalayil / Tara Chand Gawariya / Mijannur Rahaman Gazi / Akash Ghosh / Sayantan Ghosh / Dev Gogoi / Ashish Shankar Gupta / Rajat Gupta / Sanjeev Gupta / Sanjay Arjun Hadkar / Arvind Kumar Jain / Jainish Vig / Manoj Kumar / Kailash Mittal / Aditya Kapoor / Sankha Kar / Emmanual Karbhari / Harikrishna Katragadda / Ahmer Khan / Faisal Khan / Saumya Khandelwal / Praveen Khanna / Nayan Khanolkar / Vibi Job Kottekavil / Nidhish Krishnan / Rajesh Kumar / Subir Kumar Dutta / Raj Kumar / Prabhat Kumar Verma / Zishaan Akbar Latif / Shankar Lattur Rathinam / Atul Loke / Arun M. / Periasamy M. / Shivang Mehta / Riyasannamanada Mohamedreyas / Samir Mohite / Arindam Mukherjee / Muzamil Shafi Mattoo / Showkat Nanda / Anupam Nath / Yawar Nazir / Sudharmadas Nr Neelamkulangara / Hemant Padalkar Ravindra / Swastik Pal / Venkata Sunder Rao Pampana / Josekutty Panackal / Swapan Parekh / Partha Pratim Hazarika / Anand Patel / Peethambaran Payyeri / Ravi Posavanike / Anshuman Poyrekar / Kunal Pradeep Patil / Sathish Kumar Purushothaman / Altaf Qadri / Qamar Sibtain / Ashish Raje Subhash / Ravindran Ramalingam / Pattabi Raman / Kannekanti Ramesh Babu / Riya Sharma / Vicky Roy / SL Shanth Kumar Sambasivam Leela / Sajeesh Sankar / Ruby Sarkar / Neeta Satam / Arijit Sen / Ajeet Kumar Shaah / Anil Shakya Kumar / Divyakant Divyakant / Mahesh Shantaram / Anand Sharma / Arun Sharma / Smita Sharma / Subhash Sharma / Anand Shinde / Raju Mahadev Shinde / Danish Siddiqui / Sharath Babu Siddoju / Anand Singh / Satpal Singh / Akash Singh Chauhan / Chetan Soni / Mehta Sonu / Uday Kumar Sripathi / Anantha Subramanyam K. / Manish Swarup / T Mohandas Thattankandy / Vishnu V. Nair Thundathil / Harish Tyagi / Nitin Umare / Sriharsha Vladamani / Karan Vaid / Palla Sreenivasu Vasu / Himanshu Vyas / Aditya Waikul / Chirag Wakaskar / Danish Ismail Wani / Atish Wankhede

Indonesia
Andri Mardiansyah Aan / Sutanta Aditya / Yuan Adriles / Yuniadhi Agung / Dita Alangkara / Binsar Bakkara / Arie Basuki / I Gusti Bayu Ismoyo / Mushaful Imam Bin M Djen Umar / Ronny Adolof Buol / Riski Cahyadi / Suwandi Chandra / Johannes Christo / Albert Damanik / Ivan Damanik / M Awaluddin Fajri / Fahmi Fajri Utama / Iggoy Fitra Yogi / Emily May Gunawan / Arif Gunawan AM / Hariandi Hafid / Jongki Handianto / Fully Handoko / Boy Harjanto / Akrom Hazami / Afriadi Hikmal / Donal Husni / Herry Ibrahim / Ulet Ifansasti / Fauzan Ijazah / Ferganata Indra Riatmoko / Resha Juhari / Subekti Kasdan / Juni Kriswanto / Lasti Kurnia / Feri Latief Pujianto Johan Leo / Abriansyah Liberto / Ali Lutfi / Chaideer Mahyuddin / Maman Sukirman / Irsan Mulyadi / Hway Sheng Pang / Agung Parameswara / Anton Raharjo / Ramdani / Ardiles Rante / Aman Rochman / Veri Sanovri / Yuli Seperi / Arnold Simanjuntak / Slamet / Agus Susanto / Muhammad Adimaja Syariffudin Hamid / Muhammad Syofri Kurniawan / Tatan Syuflana / Jefri Andi Putra Tarigan / Mokhamad Zubaidillah Ube / Nova Wahyudi / B.D. Kentjono Seto Wardhana / I Putu Sayoga Wicaksana / Taufan Wijaya / Rony Zakaria / Zulkifli

Iran
Mehdi Abbasi / Fateme Abedi / Gholamreza Ahmadi / Mohammad Akhlaghi / Babak Aliasgharian / Mostafa Alizadegan / Azad Amin Rashti / Azin Anvar Haghighi / Amir Aslan Arfa Kaboudvand / Seyed Ehsan Bagheri / Amin Bahrani / Hamed Barchian / Amir Behroozi / Amin Berenjkar / Azadeh Besharati / Solmaz Ghadimlou Daryani / Adis Easagholian / Sajjad Ebrahimi / Javad Erfanian Aalimanesh / Mohsen Esmaeilzadeh / Hossein Fatemi / Mohammad Mehdi Fazlollahi / Marjan Foroughi / Arez Ghaderi / Hassan Ghaedi / Mojgan Ghanbari / Masou Gharaei / Saeed Gholamhoseini / Reza Golchin Kouhi / Alireza Goudarzi / Seyed Hossein Hadaeghi / Ahmad Reza Halabisaz / Ali Hamed Haghdoust / Abdollah Heidari / Marziyeh Heydarzadeh Aghdam / Hadi Hirbodvash / Majid Hojati / Seyed Mahmood Hosseini / Seyed Mohammad Mehdi Hosseini / Amin Mohammad Jamali / Shayan Javan Khoshdel / Khashayar Javanmardi / Ehsan Jazini / Younes Jolfaie Azar / Morteza Kanani / Younes Khani / Saeed Mahbadi / Abolfazl Mahrokh / Mohamad Javad Maktabi / Maryam Mazrooei / Behrouz Mehri / Ahmad Moeinijam / Hamzeh Mohammad Hosseini / Abedin Mohammadi / Masoud Mohammadi / Mahin Mohammadzadeh / Karim Mohseni Arjmand / Mehdi Monem / Shaghayegh Moradian Nejad / Mohammad Ali Najib / Amir Narimani / Shahab Naseri / Hamed Nazari / Hassan Nezamian / Morteza Nikoubazl / Javid Nikpour / Hossein Sadri Nobarzad / Ebrahim Noroozi / Roshan Norouzi / Mehdi Nosrati / Adel Pazyar / Moslem Poorshamsi / Morteza Pournejat / Soran Qurbani / Ata Ranjbar Zeydanlou / Mohammad Mahdi Razavi / Zohreh Saberi / Zahra Saboniha / Hossein Sadri / Majid Saeedi / Abdollah Safa / Milad Safabakhsh / Farhad Safari / Sajad Safari / Seyed Ali Saleh / Mojtaba Salek / Ako Salemi / Soheila Sanamno / Mohsen Sanei Yarandi / Sohrab Sardashti / Babak Sedighi / Mehdi Shahnazari / Hashem Shakeri / Aitai Shakibafar / Jalal Shamsazaran / Seyed Madyar Shojaeifar / Aydin Siami / Sadegh Souri / Seyed Mehdi Taghavi / Farshid Tighehsaz / Omid Vahabzadeh / Mohamad Hossin Velayati / Bahram Yazdanpanah / Faramarz Zareian / Reza Zirakpuordehkordi / Hossein Zohrevand

Iraq
Ahmad al-Rubaye / Rwa Faisal / Abdul Hameed Hussein Karam / Feriq Ferec Mahmood / Hadi Mizban / Younes Mohammad / Ali Haider Ujam

Ireland
Jonathan Beamish / Desmond Boylan / Deirdre Brennan / Matt Browne / Cyril Byrne / Aidan Crawley / James Crombie / Lauren Crothers / Kieran Doherty / Andrew Downes / Denis Doyle / Arthur Ellis / David Farrell / Brian Gavin / David Hayes / Keith Heneghan / John Kelly / Clodagh Kilcoyne / Ernie Leslie / Eric Luke / Dara Mac Dónaill / Michael Mac Sweeney / David Maher /

Andrew McConnell / Cathal McNaughton / Charles McQuillan / Denis Minihane / Paul Mohan / Brendan Moran / Seamus Murphy / Piaras Ó Mídheach / Michael O' Neill / Douglas O'Connor / Kenneth O'Halloran / Pedraig O'Reilly / Joe O'Shaughnessy / Fergal Phillips / Ivor Prickett / Ray Ryan / Billy Stickland / Dermot Tatlow / Morgan Treacy / Eamon Ward / Robert Whelan

Israel
Nir Alon / Eli Atias / Oded Balilty / Roni Ben Ari / Rafael Ben Ari / Michel Braunstein / Elinor Carucci / Rina Castelnuovo / Gil Cohen Magen / Natan Dvir / Dror Garti / Dan Haimovich / Ziv Koren / Felix Lupa / Tali Mayer / Shay Mehalel / Omer Messinger / Lior Mizrahi / Jorge Novominsky / Daniel Reiter / Emil Salman / Ahikam Seri / Avishag Shaar-Yashuv / Danielle Shitrit / Uriel Sinai / Abir Sultan / Gali Tibbon / Miriam Tsachi / David Vaaknin / Oded Wagenstein / Kobi Wolf / Gili Yaari / Ilia Yefimovich / Orna Zietman / Oren Ziv / Ronen Zvulun / Ohad Zwigenberg

Italy
Anna Adamo / Daria Addabbo / Edoardo Agresti / Andrea Alai / Livia Alcalde Patane / Salvatore Alibrio / Marco Alpozzi / Francesco Anselmi / Angelo Antolino / Simone Aprile / Michele Ardu / Giampiero Assumma / Giovanni Attalmi / Tommaso Ausili / Carlo Gianferro / Luigi Avantaggiato / Mario Badagliacca / Diana Bagnoli / Antonio Baiano / Luigi Baldelli / Danilo Balducci / Jacob Balzani Lööv / Federico Barattini / Massimo Barberio / Alessandro Barcella / Filippo Bardazzi & Laura Chiaroni / Emilio Barillaro / Matteo Bastianelli / Azzurra Becherini / Francesco Bellina / Valentino Bellini / Daniele Belosio / Marina Berardi / Valerio Berdini / Simone Bergamaschi / Massimo Berruti / Leonello Bertolucci / Marco Bertorello / Giorgio Bianchi / Matteo Biatta / Sulejman Bijedic / Valerio Bispuri / Paolo Bona / Simona Bonanno / Marcello Bonfanti / Federico Borella / Gregorio Borgia / Michele Borzoni / Alfredo Bosco / Maëlle Grand Bossi / Marco Bottelli / Luca Bracali / Majlend Bramo / Roberto Brancolini / Luisa Briganti / Francesco Broli / Annamaria Bruni / Luca Bruno / Grazia Bucca / Fabio Bucciarelli / Mario Bucolo / Fulvio Bugani / Patrizia Burra / Antonio Busiello / Teo Butturini / Stefano Butturini / Vittore Buzzi / Jean-Marc Caimi & Valentina Piccinni / Turi Calafato / Danilo Campailla / Giulia Candussi / Erica Canepa / Cinzia Canneri / Marco Cantile / Stefano Cantù / Emanuele Capoferri / Federico Caponi / Giovanni Capriotti / Alessandro Carboni / Andrea Carboni / Eleonora Carlesi / Giuseppe Carotenuto / Daniele Casciari / Davide Casella / Remo Casilli / Marco Casini / Marco Casino / Luca Catalano Gonzaga / Bruno Cattani / Gianluca Cecere / Pierfrancesco Celada / Loredana Celano / Giancarlo Ceraudo / Gianluca Checchi / János Chialá / Alfredo Chiarappa / Matteo Chinellato / Giuseppe Chiucchiu / Alberto Cicchini / Giuseppe Ciccia / Francesco Cinque / Martina Cirese / Paola Ciriello / Pier Paolo Cito / Tomaso Clavarino / Giovanni Cocco / Alex Coghe / Arianna Colliard / Betty Colombo / Emanuela Colombo / Massimo Colombo / Francesco Comello / Daniele Coppa / Luigi Corda / Antonio Corocher / Alfredo Covino / Emiliano Cribari / Massimo Cristaldi / Thomas Cristofoletti / Gianluca Crivellin / Diego Cupolo / Fabio Cuttica / Alessandro D'Angelo / Alfredo D'Amato / Cinzia D'Ambrosi / Albertina d'Urso / Enrico Dagnino / Stefano Dal Pozzolo / Daniel Dal Zennaro / Barbara Dall'Angelo / Chiara Dazi / Edgard De Bono / Dario De Dominicis / Stefano De Luigi / Serena De Sanctis / Lino De Vallier / Linda de'Nobili / Luciano del Castillo / Giovanna Del Sarto / Edoardo Delille / Giulia Piermartiri / Andrea Depaoli / Alvaro Deprit / Andrea Di Biagio / Ilaria Di Biagio / Giovanni Di Cecca / Gianluca Di Fazio / Pietro Di Giambattista / Adamo Di Loreto / Armando Di Loreto / Andrea di Martino / Alessandro Di Meo / Danilo Garcia Di Meo / Giulio Di Sturco / Giovanni Diffidenti / Alessandro Digaetano / Simone Donati / Linda Dorigo / Patrizia Dottori / Gabriele Duchi / Angelo Emma / Salvatore Esposito / Antonio Faccilongo / Gabriele Facciotti / Alessandro Falco / Andrea Falcon / Giuseppe Fama / Andrea Fantini / Maurizio Faraboni / Massimo Ferrero / Gerardo Filocamo / Vito Finocchiaro / Gaetano Fisicaro / Vincenzo Floramo / Giovanni Fontana / Mario Fornasari / Nicola Fossella / Renato Franceschin / Andrea Frazzetta / Aldo Frezza / Roberto Fumagalli / Vito Fusco / Gabriele Galimberti / Gianfranco Gallucci / Alessandro Gandolfi / Angelo Gandolfi / Alessandra Garagnani / Marco Garofalo / Stephanie Gengotti / Riccardo Ghilardi / Filippo Maria Gianfelice / Raffaella Gianolla / Antonio Gibotta / Pierluigi Giorgi / Claudio Giovannini / Alberto Giuliani / Alessandro Grassani / Annibale Greco / Emiliano Grillotti / Eugenio Grosso / Marco Gualazzini / Gianluigi Guercia / Stefano Guidi / Francesco Guidicini / Giulia Iacolutti / Marina Imperi / Evandro Inetti / Fabrizio Intonti / Alessandro Iovino / Roberto Isotti / Jacopo Landi / Oskar Landi / Silvia Landi / Francesco Lastrucci / Emanuela Laurenti / Mirco Lazzari / Francesca Leonardi / Laura Lezza / Giacomo Liverani / Vincenzo Livieri / Nicola Lo Calzo / Luca Locatelli / Marco Longari / Silvia Longhi / Nicola Longobardi / Davide Lopresti / Guillermo Luna / Luca Lupi / Elvio Maccheroni / Francesca Maceroni / Giacomo Maestri / Alessandro Magagna / Diego Maggioni / Francesca Magnani / Nicola Maiani / Alessio Mamo / Karl Mancini / Livio Mancini / Francesca Manolino / Gianmarco Maraviglia / Paolo Marchetti / Giulia Marchi / Alberto Maretti / Nicola Marfisi / Cesare Martucci / Adriano Valerio Marzi /Enrico Mascheroni / Alex Masi / Antonio Masiello / Roberto Masiero / Cristina Mastrandrea / Antonio Mazzarella / Antonello Mazzei / Laura Melesi / Ugo Mellone / Lorenzo Meloni / Myriam Meloni / Claudio Menna / Giovanni Mereghetti / Hermes Mereghetti / Marco Merlini / Erik Messori / Gabriele Micalizzi / Simone Migliaro / Stefano Miliffi / Dario Mitidieri / Pierpaolo Mittica / Diego Mola / Mimi Mollica / Vincenzo Montefinese / Davide Monteleone / Luciano Monti / Stefano Morelli / Agnese Carlotta Morganti / Filippo Mutani / Giulio Napolitano / Luigi Narici / Annalisa Natali Murri / Roberto Nistri / Giovanni Norrito / Antonello Nusca / Oli Olivieri / Gianluca Oppo / Roberto Orrù / Alessio Paduano / Giulio Paletta / Giorgio Palmera / Lorenzo Palmieri / Simona Pampallona / Manfredi Pantanella / Marco Panzetti / Savino Paolella / Paolo Woods / Alessia Paradisi / Francesca Valentina Partesi / Mattia Passarini / Paolo Patrizi / Paolo Pellegrin / Carlo Pellegrini / Matteo Pellegrinuzzi / Paolo Pellizzari / Alessandro Penso / Luciano Perbellini / Massimo Percossi / Viviana Peretti / Simone Perolari / Leonardo Perri / Lucia Perrotta / Raffaele Petralla / Paolo Petrignani / Emiliano Pinnizzotto / Manfredo Pinzauti / Piergiorgio Pirrone / Giulio Piscitelli / Michele Piscitelli / Francesco Pistilli / Alberto Pizzoli / Fausto Podavini / Massimo Podio / Francesca Pompei / Patrizia Posillipo / Antonio Presta / Tommaso Protti / Alessandro Puccinelli / Maike Pullo / Cesare Quinto Di Cameli / Marco Racchichini / Tommaso Rada / Cristiano Ragab / Sergio Ramazzotti / Giuseppe Rampolla / Simone Raso / Ezio Ratti / Massimiliano Rella / Stefano Rellandini / Andreja Restek / Paolo Robaudi / Renata Romagnoli / Alessio Romenzi / GIanluca Rona / Rocco Rorandelli / Gabriele Rossi / Max Rossi / Nicoló Filippo Rosso / Alessandro Rota / Mario Rota / Marcello Russo / Patrick Russo / Mario Sabatini / Andrea Sabbadini / Marco Sales / Laura Salvinelli / Andrea Giuseppe Sanfilippo / Antonio Sansica / Rossella Santosuosso / Simone Sapienza / Emanuele Satolli / Giorgio Scala / Stefano Schirato / Federico Scoppa / Emanuele Scorcelletti / Francesca Semerano / Andi Shtylla / Michele Sibiloni / Christian Sinibaldi / Luca Sola / Andreas Solaro / Paolo Sollazzo / Attilio Solzi / Davide Spada / Mario Spada / Alita Spano / Mauro Spanu / Massimo Spinolo / Marina Spironetti / Andrea Staccioli / Angela Stagnitta / Herbert Steele / Nicolas Tarantino / Christian Tasso / Sebastiano Tomada / Dario Tommaseo / Gianfranco Tripodo / Filippo Trojano / Alessandro Trovati / Lorenzo Tugnoli / Serena Tulli / Mirko Turatti / Nicola Ughi / Mauro Ujetto / Stefano Unterthiner / Mattia Vacca / Clara Vannucci / Angela Varricchio / Antonello Veneri / Filippo Venezia / Filippo Venturi / Luca Veronesi / Paolo Verzone / Federico Vespignani / Mirko Viglino / Fabrizio Villa / Daniele Vita / Daniele Volpe / Francesca Volpi / Filippo Zambon / Stefania Zamparelli / Erberto Zani / Barbara Zanon / Bruno Zanzottera / Sandra Zarneshan / Elisabetta Zavoli / Francesco Zizola / Nicola Zolin / Mattia Zoppellaro / Lorenzo Zoppolato / Paola Zorzi / Vittorio Zunino Celotto

Jamaica
Andrew Smith / Jermaine Barnaby

Japan
Koji Aoki / Takashi Aoyama / Yasuyochi Chiba / Kenji Chiga / James Whitlow Delano / Toru Hanai / Takumi Harada / Yusuke Harada / Naohiko Hatta / Noriko Hayashi / Kazushi Hirose / Kazuo Horiike / Eugene Hoshiko / Madoka Ikegami / Tomonori Iwanami / Taichi Kaizuka / Taro Karibe / Yosuke Kashiwakura / Issei Kato / Keisuke Kato / Naoko Kawamura / Kyung-Hoon Kim / Rei Kishitsu / Toshifumi Kitamura / Koide Yohei / Hirotsugu Komiya / Rei Kubo / Dai Kurokawa / Shingo Kuzutani / Naoki Maeda / Hiroyasu Masaki / Hiroko Masuike / Kimimasa Mayama / Iwasaki Minoru / Takashi Nakagawa / Takuma Nakamura / Shiro Nishihata / Takao Ochi / Nozomu Ogawa / Kosuke Okahara / Hiroshi Okamoto / Takashi Ozaki / Kyujiro Sakamaki / Hiroto Sekiguchi / Kazushige Shirahata / Akira Suemori / Ryuzo Suzuki / Satoshi Takahashi / Atsushi Taketazu / Mika Tanimoto / Masayuki Terazawa / Takeshi Tokitsu / Sachie Torikai / Yoshio Tsunoda / Naotsune Umemura / Kenichi Unaki / Daisuke Wada / Jun Yasukawa / Yuta Yasumoto

Jordan
Jaber abdulkhaleq / Ahmad Gharabli / Muhammed Muheisen / Raed Qutena

Kazakhstan
Grigoriy Bedenko / Ivan Bessedin / Zhanar Karimova / Anna Shakurskaya / Ksenia Show

Kenya
Georgina Goodwin / Kevin Midigo / Lameck Nyagudi / Brian Ochieng / Humphrey Odero

Korea
Jinsub Cho / Seong Joon Cho / Woohae Cho / Dong Jun Choi / Hyungrak Choi / Yoo Jin Choi / Jao Hong/ Kim In Chul / Heon-Kyun Jeon / Hanjo Jung / Sanghwan Jung / Ha Dong Kim / Hong-Ji Kim / SeongGwang Kim / Un Ho Ko / Sung Chan Koo / JoonHeon Lee / Byeongsik Lim / Jun Michael Park / Jungkeun Park / Kim Seong-Ryong

Kosovo
Fisnik Dobreci / Admir N Idrizi / Jetmir Idrizi / Armend Nimani

Kyrgyzstan
Danil Usmanov

Latvia
Valdis Brauns

Lebanon
Mustapha Elakhal / Wael Hamzeh / Saër Karam / Hussein Malla / Hasan Shaaban / Marwan Tahtah / Charbel Torbey / Rodrigue Zahr

Libya
Assan Albarghathi

Lithuania
Vidmantas Balkūnas / Ramunas Danisevicius / Tadas Kazakevicius / Sofija Korf / Kazimieras Linkevičius / Almantas Mickus / Domantas Pipas / Rita Stankeviciute / Berta Tilmantaitė

Luxembourg
Alain Schroeder

Macedonia
Goran Anastasovski / Nake Batev / Tomislav Georgiev / Georgi Licovski / Toshe Ognjanov

Madagascar
Rija Emadisson / Mamiarisoa Georges Raelisaona

Malaysia
Tan Chee Hon / Wei Seng Chen / Stefen Chow / Chai Hin Goh / Glenn Guan / Fazry Ismail / Firdaus Latif / Shang Leo / Jeffry Lim Chee Yong / Azhar Mahfof / Ahmad Yusni Mohammad Said / Mohd Rasfan Mohd Nor / Mohamed Sairien Nafis / Kah Vee Pan / Aizuddin Saad / Mohd Samsul Said / Lo Sook Mun / Chen Soon Ling / Ee Long Tan / Sang Tan / Fok Loy Wong / Lay Peng Yeap / Zulfadhli Zulkifli

Malta
Darrin Zammit Lupi

Mauritius
George Michel / Kadrewvel Pillay Vythilingum

Mexico
Octavio Aburto / Theda Acha / Guillermo Arias / Gerardo Avila / Francisco Javier Belmont Bautista / Juan Cárdenas / Carlos Cazalis / Narciso Contreras / Alejandro Cossio Borboa / Juan Carlos Cruz / José Rafael Cruz Vázquez / Gustavo Duran De Huerta Patiño / Mario Ernesto Dominguez Bravo / Eduardo Feldman / Carlos Angel Ferrer / Gerardo Enrique Flores López / Héctor Javier García Ibarra / Eliud Gil Samaniego / Fernando Gomez / Oscar René González de la Torre / Quetzalli Nicte Ha González Pérez / Claudia Guadarrama Guzmán / Hector Guerrero / Emmanuel Guillén Lozano / David Guzmán González / Guillermo Hernandez Martinez / Rodrigo Jardon / Jose Francisco Jimenez Castro / Jaime Kastro / Hector David Lopez Ramirez / Eduardo Loza Vázquez / Prometeo Jorge Rodríguez Lucero / José Pedro Martínez / Yael Martínez / Victor Medina / Alberto Alejandro Millares Méndez / Jordi Montiel Ramos / María Elena Muñoz Bonilla / Mauricio Palos / François Pesant / Alejandro Prieto / Rodrigo Reyes / Juan Carlos Sánchez Díaz / Enrique Serrato / Ramon Sienra Cravioto / Diego Ricardo Sierra Moreno / Jordi Sifuentes / Luis Octavio Silva Hoyos / Jonathan Telles Corvera / Ricardo Vargas Sánchez / Eduardo Verdugo

Moldova
Denis Buchel / Ramin Mazur / Vasile Platon

Mongolia
Rentsendorj Bazarsukh / Davaanyam Delgergargal / Badamkhand Sodnom / Battulga Vandandorj

Mozambique
Victor Marrao

Myanmar
Kaung Htet / Thet Htoo / Min Myo Nyan Win Ko Myo / Hkun Lat / Minzayar Oo / Soe Zeya Tun

Namibia
Karel Prinsloo

Nepal
Nabin Baral / Bijaya Rai / Navesh Chitrakar / Angad Dhakal / Skanda Gautam / Narendra Shresta / Niranjan Shrestha / Prashit Sthapit / Susheel Kumar Shrestha

The Netherlands
Catrien Ariëns / Saskia Aukema / Marcel Bakker / Michael Ballak / Jan Banning / Amit J. Bar / Shirley Barenholz / Rob Becker / Hugo Bes / Maarten Boersema / Theo Bosboom / Yvonne Brandwijk / Jurriaan Brobbel / Maartje Brockbernd / Arjan Bronkhorst / Jet Budelman / Cleo Campert / René Clement / Eelkje Colmjon / Rachel Corner / Roger Cremers / Merlin Daleman / Chris de Bode / Henk de Boer / Sacha de Boer / Ingrid de Groot / Anjo de Haan / Raymond de Haan / Gerrit de Heus / Angeliek de Jonge / Bas de Meijer / Ralph de Pagter / Sonja de Sterke / Helen de Vries / Sander de Wilde / Peter Dejong / Hester den Boer / Jacqueline Dersjant / Henk Jan Dijks / Jasper Doest / Ellis Doeven / Chantal A.F.M. Douwes / Marc Driessen / Willeke Duijvekam / Mathilde Dusol / Jan Everhard / Michael Floor / Flip Franssen / Hans Gerritsen / Reinier Gerritsen / Guillaume Groen / John Gundlach / Robbert Frank Hagens / Ruben Hamelink / Eddo Hartmann / Isabelle Hattink / Roderik Henderson / Piet Hermans / Inge Hondebrink / Laura Hospes / Jasper Juinen / Erwin Kessing / Paul E. Ketelaar / Chris Keulen / Arie Elbert Kievit / Joris Knapen / Ton Koene / Bart Koetsier / Carla Kogelman / Kees Krick / Suzanne Liem / Bas Losekoot / Marinka Masséus / Olivier Middendorp / Ilvy Njiokiktjien / Paco Nunez / Jeroen Oerlemans / Anneloes Pabbruwee / Mardoe Painter / Liesbeth Parlevliet / Frans Poptie / Michel Porro / Pim Ras / Roman Ronny Rozenberg / Chantal Ruisseau / Maikel Samuels / Bram Schilling / Geert Snoeijer / Corné Sparidaens / Friso Spoelstra / Jan-Joseph Stok / Eric Stolk / Pieter ten Hoopen / Cris Toala Olivares / Ton Toemen / Frank Trimbos / Sander Troelstra / Robin Utrecht / Richard van Bennekom / Peter van Breukelen / David van Dam / Patrick van Dam / Anne van de Pals / Kees van de Veen / Mona van den Berg / Freek van den Bergh / Marcel van den Bergh / Joris van Gennip /Gé-Jan van Leeuwen / Dennis van Lingen / Kadir van Lohuizen / Inge van Mill / Paul van Riel / Marielle van Uitert / Koen van Weel / Eddy van Wessel / Frank Viergever / Mickey Vissers / Teun Voeten / Pascal Vossen / Roger Waleson / Bert Wieringa / Fleur Wiersma / Emily Wiessner / Henk Wildschut / Sinaya Wolfert / Daimon Xanthopoulos

New Zealand
Martyn Aim / Mark Aitken / Greg Baker / Scott Barbour / Martin de Ruyter / Robin Hammond / Andy Jackson / Iain McGregor / Michael Scott / Mark Taylor / Cornell Tukiri

Nicaragua
Carlos Herrera

Nigeria
Abayomi Ademola Akinlabi / Adekunle Joshua Ajayi / Olubunmi Muftau Azeez Azeez / Pius Utomi Ekpei / Suleiman Husaini Jibril / Emmanuel Osodi / Oluwafemi Wahabi

Norway
Jarle Aasland / Odd Andersen / Stein Jarle Bjorge / Tom Henning Bratlie / Terje Bringedal / Bjorn Steinar Delebekk / Tommy Ellingsen / Furunes Eskil Wie / Andrea Gjestvang / Eirik Grønningsæter / Johnny Haglund / Pål Hermansen / Katinka Hustad / Adrian Øhrn Johansen / Anne-Stine Johnsbråten / Dorthe Karlsen / Anne Marit Larsen / Klaudia Lech / Kyrre Lien / Robert James McPherson / Aleksander Nordahl / Kristine Nyborg / Kim Nygård / Ken Opprann / Line Ørnes Søndergaard / Audun Rikardsen / Haavard Saeboe / Therese Alice Sanne / Vegard Wivestad Grøtt

Pakistan
Fayyaz Ahmed / Abdul Baqi / Ahmed Ramzan Mohammed Ramzan / Mahammad Sajjad / Akhtar Soomro / Tauseef Zafar

Palestine
Ibraheem Abu Mustafa / Ahmad Al-Bazz / Issam Alasmar / Mohammad Alhaj / Musa Alshaer / Laura Boushnak / Ahmed Deeb / Mustafa Hassona / Mahmoud Issa / Ahmed Jadallah Salem / Majdi Mohammed / Mohammed Asad Muhaisen / Mussa Qawasma / Sameh Rahmi / Mohammed Saber / Mohammed Salem

Panama
Scarlett Fontecha

Peru
Eitan Abramovich Samesas / Omar Lucas Arapa Castro / Mariana Bazo / Ernesto Benavides del Solar / Juan Sebastian Castaneda / Sharon Castellanos Tuesta / Gladys E. Alvarado Jourde / Hector Emanuel / Wilfredo Nolazco Fernández Ojeda / Carlos Garcia Granthon / Marco Garro / Guillermo Gutierrez Carrascal / David Martín Huamaní Bedoya / Franz Renzo Krajnik Baquerizo / Carlos Americo Lezama Villantoy / Miguel Ángel Mejía Castro / Uriel Montúfar / Erick Winder Nazaro Gil / Musuk Nolte Maldonado / Manunel Roca / Leslie Searles / José Alberto Sotomayor Jiménez / Milko Torres Ramirez / Gihan Tubbeh / Christian Yonathan Ugarte Bravo / Santiago Paul Vallejos Coral / Javier Zapata

The Philippines
Ezra Acayan / Louis Aslarona / Jes Aznar / Xyza Bacani / Keith Kristoffer Bacongco / Mark Louis Balmores / Noel Celis / Alexis Carlo Corpuz / Claro Fausto Cortes / Mark Cristino / Czeasar Dancel / Gregorio, Jr. Dantes / Linus Escandor II / Aaron Favila / Carlo Gabuco / Victor Kintanar / Rafael Resty Lerma / Francis Malasig / Bernardo Tawatao / Hannah Maria Carmina Reyes / Emlyn Hope Rillon / Fernando Sepe / Bernardino Testa / Jake Verzosa / Vicente Jaime Villafranca / Jophel Ybiosa

Poland
Iwona Abessolo / Michal Adamowski / Michal Adamski / Piotr Apolinarski / Mateusz Baj / Andrzej Banas / Anna Bedyńska / Marek Berezowski / Marcin Bielecki / Piotr Bieniek / Piotr Bławicki / Filip Błażejowski / Bartosz Bobkowski / Andrzej Bochenski / Oliver Britton / Jadwiga Brontē / Kamil Broszko / Jan Brykczynski / Mateusz Budzisz / Monika Bulaj / Grzegorz Celejewski / Justyna Cieślikowska / Filip Cwik / Łukasz Cynalewski / Wiktor Dabkowski / Darek Delmanowicz / Krystian Dobuszynski / Jacek Fota / Anna Freindorf / Daniel Frymark / Jakub Gadek / Dominik Gajda / Robert Gajda / Maciej Gillert / Kornelia Glowacka-Wolf / Łukasz Głowala / Arkadiusz Gola / Krzysztof Gołuch / Jan Graczyński / Andrzej Grygiel / Wojciech Grzedzinski / Marek Grzesiak / Maciej Grzybowski / Bartosz Hołoszkiewicz / Andrzej Hulimka / Iwona & Maciej Jabłoński / Krzysztof Jakubczyk / Marcin Jamkowski / Mariusz Janiszewski / Piotr Jaruga / Monika Jaśkowska-Bablok / Pawel Jędrusik / Adam Jędrysik / Maciej Jeziorek / Tomasz Jodlowski / Karolina Jonderko / Bartlomiej Jurecki / Łukasz Kaczanowski / Maciej Kaczanowski / Marcin Kadziolka / Krzysztof Kalinowski / Slawomir Kaminski / Tomasz Kawka / Grzegorz Klatka / Adam Klimek / Tytus Kondracki / Tadeusz Koniarz / Luc Kordas / Michał Kosc / Slawomir Kowalewski / Andrej Koziar / Damian Kramski / Arkadiusz Kubisiak / Jacek Labedzki / Adam Lach / Pawel Łączny / Marek Lapis / Arkadiusz Lawrywianiec / Tomasz Lazar / Damian Lemański / Maria Litwa / Marcin Lobaczewski / Michał Luczak / Maciej Luczniewski / Krystian Maj / Aleksander Majdanski / Grażyna Makara / Marek Maliszewski / Maciej Margas / Tymon Markowski / Katarzyna Markusz / Omar Marques / Boguslaw Maslak / Wojciech Matusik / Gregory Michenaud / Justyna Mielnikiewicz / Andrzej Mikulski / Rafal Milach / Joanna Mrowka / Michał Mrozek / Maciek Nabrdalik / Borys Niespielak / Mikolaj Nowacki / Konstancja Nowina Konopka / Jakub Ochnio /

Patryk Ogorzałek / Zbigniew Osiowy / Tomasz Padlo / Adam Panczuk / Mieczyslaw Pawlowicz / Kacper Pempel / Grzegorz Piaskowski / Magdalena Pierwocha / Mirosław Pieślak / Leszek Pilichowski / Paweł Piotrowski / Robert Pipała / Agnieszka Rayss / Jakub Robowski / Justyna Rojek / Bartosz Rozalski / Artur Rusek / Wojciech Ryzinski / Alicja Rzepa / Sławek Rzewuski / Karolina Sekuła / Darek Sepiolo / Rafał Siderski / Michał Sita / Mateusz Skwarczek / Łukasz Skwiot / Mariusz Smiejek / Tomasz Sobczak / Michal Solarski / Waldek Sosnowski / Waldemar Sowiński / Wojciech Strozyk / Dawid Stube / Waldek Stube / Lukasz Swiderek / Jakub Szafrański / Michal Szalast / Elwira Magdalena Szczecian / Lukasz Szelag / Aleksandra Szmigiel-Wiśniewska / Kamil Szumotalski / Tomasz Szustek / Jacek Taran / Dawid Tatarkiewicz / Piotr Tracz / Jacekt Turczyk / Aleksander Wasyluk / Artur Widak / Jerzy Wierzbicki / Przemysław Wierzchowski / Wiktoria Wojciechowska / Grzegorz Wójcik / Witold Woszczyna / Marcin Zaborowski / Julia Zabrodzka / Marek Zakrzewski / Dominika Zarzycka / Arleta Monika / Dawid Zielinski

Portugal
Bruno Aleixo / Miguel Angelo Ribeiro Lopes / Rodrigo Antunes Cabrita / Fábio Augusto / Victor Manuel Barros / Carlos Barroso / José Júlio Barulho da Silva / Ana Brígida Moreira Mendes / Rui Caria / José Carlos Carvalho / Nuno José Carvalho de Moura / Henrique Casinhas / Sérgio Cipriano / Bruno Colaço / Leonel de Castro / Rodrigo Miguel De Freitas Antunes / Manuel de Moura / Gonçalo Delgado / Carlos Gustavo Dias Lopes Pereira / Rui Duarte Silva / Jose Fernandes / Nuno Fernandes / Paulo Figueiredo / Lara Jacinto / Hugo Joel Ramos / Eduardo Leal / Sérgio Lemos / Francisco Leong / Raphael Lima de Oliveira Santos / Artur Machado / Ruben Mália / Sara Matos / Pedro Miranda / Pedro Noel da Luz / Paulo Nunes dos Santos / Antonio José Pedrosa Silva Costa / Luis Pereira Barbosa / Jorge Manuel Pereira Monteiro / João Paulo Pimenta / João Pina / Rui Pires / Miguel Proença / Ricardo Ramos / Miguel Ribeiro / Daniel Rodrigues / Pedro Miguel Rosa Teodosio Ferreira / Francisco Salgueiro / Paulo Manuel Sargo Escoto / José Sarmento Matos / Tiago Miguel Semiao Carvalho de Miranda / Bruno Simões Castanheira / Pedro Simões Ferreira / Marcos Sobral / Nuno Veiga

Puerto Rico
Andre Kang

Romania
Jozsef Balint / Petrut Calinescu / Corneliu Cazacu / Dorin Chiotea / Ioana Cîrlig / Ionel Sorin Furcoi / Vadim Ghirda / Cornel Gingarasu / Amnon Gutman / Ioana Moldovan / Cristian Munteanu / Andrei Pungovschi / Mircea Restea / Calin Strajescu / Tudor Stefan Vintiloiu

Russia
Alexey Abanin / Alexei Akseshin / Evgeny Alekseev / Malgavko Alexey Sergey / Elena Anosova / Petr Antonov / Alexander Anufriev / Andrey Arkhipov / Vladimir Astapkovich / Maxim Babenko / Vyacheslav Bakin / Veronika Beletskaya / Dimitri Beliakov / Victor Berezkin / Dmitry Berkut / Julia Borovikova / Kristina Brazhnikova / Viacheslav Buharev / Denis Butin / Konstantin Chalabov / Dmitriy Chelyapin / Andrey Chepakin / Artem G. Chernov / Elena Chernyshova / Roman Demianenko / Boris Dolmatovsky / Pavel Dubensev / Ilias Farkhutdinov / Alexander Fedorenko / Vadim Fedotov / Evgeny Feldman / Filippov Alexey / Vladimir Finogenov / Anton Gainanov / Mary Gelman / Andrey Golovanov / Pavel Golovkin / Mikhail Grebenshchikov / Yuri Gripas / Galina Halilova / Sergei Ilnitsky / Daria Isaeva / Ksenia Ivanova / Olya Ivanova / Victoria Ivleva / Mikado Kadachnikov / Oleg Kargapolov / Anton Karliner / Yury Khodzitskiy / Sergei Kivrin / Anton Klimov / Vasiliy Kolotilov / Oleg Konstantinov / Nickolay Koreshkov / Kristina Kormilitsyna / Eduard Korniyenko / Vladimir Korobitsyn / Maxim Korotchenko / Dmitry Kostyukov / Ludmila Kovaleva / Denis Kozhevnikov / Yuri Kozyrev / Olga Kravets / Alexandr Kryazhev / Kirill Kudryavtsev / Sergey Kuksin / Alexey Kunilov / Vladimir Lamzin / Viktor Leushin / Dmitrii Linnikov / Natalia Lvova / Maxim Marmur / Aleksandr Martynov / Vadim Massalimov / Ekaterina Maximova / Vladimir Melnik / Valery Melnikov / Raisa Mikhaylova / Viatcheslav Mitrokhin / Mikhail Mordasov / Maria Morina / Anton Mukhametchin / Ovik Mushegyan / Juri Nesterenko / Stanislava Novgorodtseva / Sergey Novikov / Vitaliy Novikov / Maria Novoselova / Natalya Onishchenko / Valentinas Pecininas / Vladimir Pesnya / Sergey Pesterev / Sergey Petrov / Ilya Pitalev / Maria Plotnikova / Natalya Podunova / Alexandr Polyakov / Vladimir Pomortsev / Oleg Ponomarev / Sergey Ponomarev / Pronin Andrey / Sergey Pyatakov / Eva Rapoport / Julia Raskova / Andrey Rassanov / Ekaterina Rezvaya / Maria Romakina / Andrey Rudakov / Anastasia Rudenko / Maria Rudnaya / Salavat Safiullin Uralovich / Fyodor Savintsev / Alexander Scherbak / Andrey Shapran / Tatiana Sharapova / Valeriy Sharifulin / Oleg Shashkov / Sergey Shchekotov / Anastasia Shpilko / Anna Shulyateva / Ksenia Sidorova / Mikhail Sinitsyn / Ramil Sitdikov / Yulia Skorobogatova / Anna Skorokhodova / Olga Smirnova / Alexander Stepanenko / Aleksandra Striapunina / Sergei Stroitelev / Julia Sundukova / Grigory Sysoev / Fyodor Telkov / Dmitry Tkachuk / Anastasia Tsayder / Maria Turchenkova / Yuri Tutov / Kirill Umrikhin / Anton Unitsyn / Alexander Usanov / Grigoriy V. Yaroshenko / Sergey Vasiliev / Sergey Vdovin / Alexander Vedernikov / Vladimir Velengurin / Sergei Vinogradov / Tatiana Vinogradova / Pavel Volkov / Vladimir Vyatkin / Anastasya Yerofeyeva / Victor Yuliev / Oksana Yushko / Konstantin Zavrazhin / Dima Zharov & Liza Zhakova / Anatoly Zhdanov / Artem Zhitenev

Rwanda
Jean Ndayisenga

Saint Kitts and Nevis
Wayne Lawrence

Saudi Arabia
Tasneem Alsultan

Serbia
Igor Čoko / Predrag Dedijer / Marko Djurica / Marko Drobnjakovic / Andrej Isakovic / Dejan Jankovic / Marija Jankovic / Milovan Milenković / Nemanja Pancic / Igor Pavicevic / Sava Radovanovic / Marko Rišović / Marko Rupena / Tamás Tóth / Dragomir Vukovic

Singapore
Suhaimi Abdullah / Ooi Boon Keong / Young How Whee / Zann Huizhen Huang / Jacqueline Mei Hwee Koh / Kevin Chin Ping Lim / Yaohui Lim / Yong Teck Lim / Lionel Ng / Chi Yin Sim / Terence Chiang Seng Tan / Chih Wey Then / Desmond Teck Yew Wee / David Wirawan / Maye-E Wong

Slovakia
Martin Balaz / Andrej Balco / Martin Cervenansky / Rene Fabini / Dorota Holubová / Jan Husar / Adriana Katona / Peter Korcek / Karol Stollmann / Gabriel Szabo

Slovenia
Luka Dakskobler / Jošt Franko / Jaka Gasar / Maja Hitij / Ciril Jazbec / Mitja Kobal / Matjaz Krivic / Miro Majcen / Matej Pušnik / Matjaz Tancic / Tadej Znidarcic / Matija Zorman

Somalia
Mohamed Abdiwahab / Feisal Omar

South Africa
Pieter Bauermeister / Angus Begg / Nic Bothma / Gare John Bright / Jay Caboz / Paul Joseph Daylin / Antoine de Ras / Jillian Edelstein / Nardus Engelbrecht / Brenton Geach / Ihsaan Haffejee / Stefan Heunis / Phandulwazi Jikelo / Christiaan Kotze / Francisco J. Little / Kim Ludbrook / Moeletsi Mabe / Gideon Mendel / Joy Meyer / Eric Miller / James Oatway / Samantha Reinders / Shaun Roy / Marc Shoul / Siphiwe Sibeko / Alon Skuy / Brent Stirton / Caroline Suzman / Alexia Webster / John Wessels / Mark Wessels / Graeme Williams

Spain
Victoria Adame Lopez / Pedro Luis Ajuriaguerra Saiz / Ruben Albarran Beltran / Martí Albesa Castañer / Asier Alcorta Hernández / Cristina Aldehuela / Benito Alonso Pajares / Joan Alvado Cárcel / Delmi Alvarez / Adrian Alvarez Cueto / José María Álvez / Samuel Aranda / Celestino Arce Lavin / Javier Arcenillas / Pablo Argente Ferrer / Juan Arias Soler / Bernat Armangue / Toni Arnau / Gonzalo Arroyo Moreno / Lluís Artús / José Aymá Gonzalez / Javier Aznar / Joan Manuel Baliellas / Manuel Ballesteros Roque / Raúl Barbero Carmena / Alvaro Barrientos Gòmez / Ignacio Barrios / Consuelo Bautista Riveros / Edu Bayer / Iván Benítez Forniés / Victor J Blanco / Pablo Blazquez Dominguez / Jordi Boixareu / Albert Bonsfills / Manu Brabo / Jordi Busquets Nuell / Albert Busquets Plaja / Tomas Calle / Enrique Calvo / Olmo Calvo Rodríguez / Sergi Camara Loscos / Salvador Campillo Alba / Miguel Candela / Felipe Carnotto Díaz / Daniel Casares Román / Ricardo Cases Marin / Cristobal Castro / Javier Cebollada / José Manuel Cendón / Pablo Cobos Terán / Ignacio Maria Coccia / Jordi Cohen Colldeforns / Jose Colon Toscano / Mireia Comas Franch / Maria Contreras Coll / Fabrizio Cortesi / Joan Costa García / Ramon Costa Lôpez / Carlos de Andrés / Jose Luis De la Cuesta Solera / Joan de la Malla / Elena del Estal Martínez / Marcelo del Pozo / Oscar del Pozo / Emilio José Delgado Fraile / Cesar Dezfuli / Nacho Doce / Adrián Domínguez / Santiago Donaire / Daniel Duart / Sergio Enríquez-Nistal / Vidal Escalante / Ramon Espinosa / Oscar Espinosa / Joaquín Farrero MartÍnez / Erasmo Fenoy / Javier Fernandez / Claudio Fernandez de la Cal / Jorge Fernandez Garces / Alexandra Fernandez Rico / Luis Fernandez Rodriguez / Jesus Fernandez Salvadores / Jorge Fuembuena / Quico García / Rodrigo García / Vicente García / Jesús García / Jose Manuel Garcia de Porras / Rodrigo Garcia Rodriguez / Pablo Garcia Sacristan / Ricardo Garcia Vilanova / Maria Dolores García-Ajofrín Romero-Salazar / Juan Francisco Garrido Sanchez Toledo / Juli Garzon Comas / Rafael Gassó / Eugenio Gay Marín / Carlos Gil / José Pascual Gil Rubio / Sonia Giménez Bellaescusa / Susana Girón / Júlia Girós / Rafael Gómez Arjones / Joaquin Gomez Sastre / David González / Mdolors Gonzalez - Luumkab / Albert Gonzalez Farran / Pedro Pablo González Rodriguez-Armestre / Marisol González Veiga / Amador Guallar / Francisco Javier Guiñales Gutiérrez / Rafael Gutiérrez / Tarek Halabi Alonso / Jose Haro Sanchez / Antonio Heredia Sánchez / Nacho Hernandez / Diego Ibarra Sánchez / Luis Ignacio Tejido Garcia / Maria Jou Sol / David Juliá Etxabe / Emilio Lavandeira Villar / Jaime León / Sebastian Liste / Antonio López Diaz / Jorge López Muñoz / Jose Manuel Lopez Perez / José A. López Soto / Nuria López Torres / Juan Carlos Lucas / Javier Luengo / Cesar Julio Manso Arroyo / Rafael Marchante / Clara Margais Abeya / Aníbal Martel Peña / Guillermo Martínez / Roberto Martínez Astorgano / Andrés Martinez Casares / Ángel Martinez Colina / Héctor Mediavilla / Angel Medina García / Jacobo Medrano / Patrick Meinhardt / Francesc Melcion / Yeray Menéndez / Jose María Mercado Montero / Pablo Miranzo Macià / David Molina / Ruth Montiel Arias / Alfonso Moral / Emilio Morenatti / Raúl Moreno / Marcos Moreno Castillo /

Jesus Moron Martin / Albert Naya / Cristina Núñez Baquedano / Daniel Ochoa de Olza / David Oliete Casanova / Ana Palacios / Santiago Palacios / Alberto Garcia Palomo / Ana Isabel Pascual Guerra / Jordi Perdigó / Francis Pérez / Jose Luis Pérez / Juan José Pérez Monclús / Francisco Javier Pérez Moure / Juan Antonio Pérez Vela / Jose Pesquero Gomez / Encarnación Pindado González / Jordi Pizarro / Dani Planas Labad / Inigo Plaza Cano / Anna Pons Semelis / Judith Prat / Pedro Puente / Paco puentes Gracìa / David Ramos / Elias Regueira Garcia / Pau Rigol / José Miguel Riopa Alende / Ángel Rivas Hernández / Sergio Rodriguez / Jose Luis Rodriguez Sanchez / Alberto Hugo Roja Luque / Jaime Rojo / Jordi Ruiz Cirera / Abel Ruiz de Leon / Marìa del Mar Sáez Martínez / Eduardo Saiz Rodrigo / Daniel Salvà / Lluìs Salvadó Icart / Txema Salvans / Moises Saman / Baldesca Semper Dìaz / Borja Sanchez / Miguel Angel Sánchez / Eduardo Sánchez de León Herencia / Ivan Sanchez Pinto / Javier Sanchez-Monge Escardo / Marc Sañé / Miguel Sebastian Sebastian / Francisco Seco Martin / Enrique Shore Kohan / Jose Ramon Silveira Rodriguez / Faustino Soriano Marco / Carlos Spottorno / Juan Teixeira Vázquez / Javier Teniente Lago / Gabriel Tizon Vazquez / Almudena Toral / Xvier Torres Bachetta / Felipe Trueba / Raùl Urbina Alvarez / Jose Uris Domingos / Francisco Uriz Domezáin / Quintina Valero / Joan Valls / Rubén Vázquez / Juan Carlos Vázquez Osuna / Jesús Vecino Domìnguez / Domingo Venero Barberán / Susana Vera / Jaime Villanueva / Alvaro Ybarra Zavala / Jordi Zaragoza Alòs

Sri Lanka
M.A. Pushpa Kumara / Sanka Vidanagama / Buddhika Weerasingh Nishantha

Sudan
Mohamed Abdallah

Surinam
Roy Ritfeld

Sweden
Joakim Ahlström / Anders Andersson / Christian Andersson / Urban Andersson / Vedran Arnautovic / Andreas Bardell / Elin Berge / Niclas Berglund / Anette Brolenius / Henrik Brunnsgård / Lars Dareberg / Åke Ericson / Malin Fezehai / Jan Fleischmann / Anders Forngren / Niklas Hallen / Niclas Hammarström / Paul Hansen / Anders Hansson / Lotta Härdelin / Casper Hedberg / Robert Henriksson / Peter Holgersson / Torbjörn Jakobsson / Olof Jarlbro / Jesper Klemedsson / Pavel Koubek / David Lagerlöf / Roger Larsson / Fred Lerneryd / Jonas Lindkvist / Nora Lorek / Beatrice Lundborg / Daniel Malmberg / Joel Marklund / Jack Mikruit / Henrik Montgomery / Anette Nantell / Michael Nasberg / Daniel Nilsson / Nils Petter Nilsson / Thomas Nilsson / Cletus nelson Nwadike / Louise Margareta Nylén / Axel Oberg / Malin Palm / Tommy Pedersen / Emilia Petersson Ellafi / Katarina Premfors / Carl Sandin / Åsa Mikaela Sjöström / Vilhelm Stokstad / Linus Sundahl-Djerf / Don Titelman / Ola Torkelsson / Ann Tornkvist / Roger Turesson / Elisabeth Ubbe / Joachim Wall / Tom Wall / Magnus Wennman / Peter Wixtröm

Switzerland
Niels Ackermann / Zalmaï Ahad / Sébastien Anex / Daniel Auf der Mauer / Denis Balibouse / Franco Banfi / Fabian Biasio / Christian Bobst / Pit Buehler / Stéphanie Buret / Mischa Christen / Fabrice Coffrini / Michele Crameri / Ladislav Drezdowicz / Sebastien Feval / Yvain Genevay / Pablo Nadir Yanick Gianinazzi / Laurent Gilliéron / Markus Harald Bühler-Rasom / Christian Herbert Hildebrand / Patrick Bruno Kraemer / Alexander Kühni / Pascal Mora / Christophe Moratal / Edouard Musy / Massimo Pacciorini-Job / Anna Pizzolante / Jean Revillard / Roland Schmid / Rolf Simeon / Lazar Simeonov / Dominic Steinmann / Simon Tanner / Xavier Voirol / Michael von Graffenried / Andreas Walker / Stefan Wermuth / Luca Zanetti / Matthieu Zellweger / Michael Zumstein

Syria
Sameer al-Doumy / Karam al-Masri / Carole Alfarah / Ameer Alhalbi / Mohammed Badra / Abd Doumany / Beha El Halebi / Ibrahim Haj Ibrahim / Mostafa Mohamad Haj Omar / Thaer Mohammed / Mahmoud Muhammed Deeb / Hüseyin Nasır / George Ourfalian / Yahya Racco / Mahmoud Rawas / Mohammed Sheikh / Aref Tamawe

Taiwan
Boheng Chen / Cho Pang Chen / Ying-Ying Chiang/ Yuankai Chou / Chia-Chang Hsieh / Hsieh Ming Hsiu / Tzu Chiang Huang / Tzu Cheng Liu / Li Chun Ma / Wu Po-Yuan / Yu Hsuan Sheu / Yingting Shih / Man Chiu Siu / Jilson Seckler Tiu / Chih-Wei Yu / Chun-Te Yuan

Tanzania
Othman Michuzi

Thailand
Piti Anchaleesahakorn / Sirachai Arunrugstichai / Tanat Chayaphattharitthee / Ekkarat Punyatara / Natis Sirivatanacharoen / Rungroj Yongrit

Trinidad and Tobago
Andrea De Silva

Tunisia
Mohamed Amine Ben Aziza / Zied Ben Romdhane / Amine Landoulsi

Turkey
Yasin Akgul / Metin Aktas / Hakan Burak Altunoz / Sener Yilmaz Aslan / Mahmut Bunyami Aygun / Kürsat Bayhan / Özkan Bilgin / Tolga Bozoglu / Ünal Çam / Aydin Çetinbostanoglu / Ismail Coskun / Cagdas Erdogan / Salih Zeki Fazlıoğlu / Cem Genco / Ilker Gurer / Ozan Guzelce / Mehmet Karaca / Barbaros Kayan / Yunus Keleş/ Bulent Kilicv / Ertugrul Kilic / Haşim Sezgin Kılıç / Celil Kırnapcı / Ozan Kose / Daghan Kozanoglu / Levent Kulu / Chris McGrath / Mehmet Emin Menguarslan / Burak Milli / Sahan Nuhoglu / Burhan Ozbilici / Atılgan Özdil / Riza Ozel / Okan Ozer / Emin Özmen / Gurcan Ozturk / Ali Ihsan Öztürk / Ziya Ramoglu / Italo Rondinella / Selcuk Samiloglu / Emin Sansar / Bulent Selcuk / Murat Sengul / Sedat Suna / Huseyin Emre Tazegul / Furkan Temir / Arif Hudaverdi Yaman / Uğur Yıldırım / Oguz Yoruk

Uganda
Edgar Batte

Ukraine
Mykola Bochek / Mishka Bochkarev / Arthur Bondar / Oleh Dubyna / Oleskii Furman / Gleb Garanich / Sergei Grits / Igor Lefimov / Osman Karimov / Denys Kopylov / Oleksandr Kromplias / Dmytro Kromplias / Andrey Lomakin / Efrem Lukatsky / Tetyana Lyuta / Oleg Makovskyi / Pavlo Maydikov / Olya Morvan / Oleg Nikitenko / Serhii Nuzhnenko / Mykhaylo Palinchak / Stepan Rudik / Oleksandr Rupeta / Anatolii Stepanov / Ruslan Stepanov / Ivan Tykhy / Roman Vilenskiy / Yuriy Voroshylov

United Arab Emirates
Kamran Jebreili

United Kingdom
Rachel Adams / Andrew Aitchison / Ed Alcock / Livesey Alex / Sachelle Babbar / Emily Bates / Richard Beaven / John Beck / Guy Bell / Vince Bevan / Charlie Bibby / Jon Bond / Harry Borden / Russell Boyce / Andrew Boyers / Joshua Bright / Clive Brunskill / Simon Bruty / Jason Bryant / Will Burrard-Lucas / Jason C Larkin / Gary Calton / James Cannon / Michael Carroll / Brian Cassey / Benjamin Cawthra / Matt Cetti-Roberts / David Chancellor / Wattie Cheung / Matthew Childs / Mark Chilvers / D J Clark / Paul Clarke / Phil Clarke Hill / Garry Clarkson / Nick Cobbing / Guy Corbishley / Vicki Couchman / Damon Alexander Coulter / Carl Court / Alan Crowhurst / Ben Curtis / Simon Dack / Prodeepta Das / Jon Davey / Jack Davison / Daniel Day / Carl de Souza / Adam Dean / Peter Dench / Adrian Dennis / Nigel Gordon Dickinson / Kieran Dodds / Luke Dray / Luke Duggleby / Giles Duley / Thomas Richard Dunwoody / Mike Egerton / Rick Findler / Julian Finney / Jason Florio / Joel Ford / Stuart Forster / Ian Forsyth / Peter James Fox / Stuart Freedman / Christopher Furlong / Sean Gallagher / Kieran Galvin / Dan Giannopoulos / Joel Goodman / Sophie Green / Laurence Griffiths / Neil Hall / Charlie Hamilton James / Geoffrey Hammond / Rod Harbinson / Brian Harris / Olivia Harris / Graham James Harrison / Rahman Hassani/ Matthew James Rowland Hill / Paul Hilton / Adam Hinton / Sam Hobson / Katherine Holt / Daniel Homewood / Rip Hopkins / James Howard / Mike Hutchings / Grey Hutton / Susannah Ireland / Paul Jacobs / Thabo Jaiyesimi / Thomas Jamieson / Thomas Jenkins / Ed Jones / Richard Jones / Nadav Kander / Michael Kemp / Edward Keogh / Chin Kiu Lee / Louis Leeson-Smith / Bryn Lennon / Robert Leslie / David Levene / David Levenson / Tom Lovelock / Mikal Ludlow / Amy Lyne / Alasdair MacLeod / Murdoch MacLeod / Ian MacNicol / Dylan Martinez / Clive Mason / David Mbiyu / Patrick McCann / Vikki McCraw / Mark McEvoy / Tim McGuinness / Hannah McKay / Toby Melville / Kois Miah / Yui Mok / Eddie Mulholland / Vincent Mundy / Mark Naftalin / Zed Nelson / Lucy Nicholson / Tom Nicholson / Cian Oba-Smith / Fleur Olby / Fiorenza Panke / Elizabeth Pennington / Gerry Penny / John Perkins / Charles Pertwee / Christopher Pillitz / Tom Pilston / Olivier Pin-Fat / Mike Pinches / Lucy Piper / Peter Powell / Gilles Price / Howard Pugh / Louis Quail / Andy Rain / Darran Rees / Michael Regan / Kiran Ridley / Ben Roberts / James Robertson / Nigel Roddis / David Rose / William Rose / Jacob Russell / Honey Salvadori / Oliver Scarff / Michael Schofield / Bradley Secker / Justin Setterfield / Simon Sharp / David Shaw / Robbie Shone / John Sibley / Anthony Smith / Ben Smith / Lee Smith / Craig Stennet / Dominic Storer / Rob Stothard / Sean Sutton / Shi Tang / Sam Tarling / Paul Taylor / Edmond Terakopian / Andrew Testa / Claire Thomas / Ed Thompson / Abbie Trayler-Smith / Tommy Trenchard / Michael Tubi / Mary Turner / Nick Turpin / James Veysey / Jackson Wade / Christopher Warde-Jones / Filip Warwick / Sophie Wedgwood / Edward Whitaker / Alex Whitehead / Mathieu Willcocks / Jonathon Williams / James Williamson / Jamie Wiseman / Andrew Sun Tun Wong / Matt Writtle / Chris Young / Tariq Zaidi / Betty Zapata

United States
Nadin Abbott / Myriam Abdelaziz / Mustafah Abdulaziz / Lynsey Addario / Sumaya Agha / Heather Ainsworth / Micah Albert / Jonathan Alcorn / Cassi Alexandra / Diana Zeyneb Alhindawi / Carol Allen-Storey / Mary Altaffer / Daniel A. Anderson / Scott Anderson / Maggie Andresen / Jason Andrew / John Angelillo / Drew Angerer / Bryan Anselm / Karen Anthony / Ben Arnon / Marc Asnin / Rose Baca / Jonathan Bachman / Stephanie Bassos / David Bathgate / Taylor Baucom & Todd Rosenberg / William Allen Baxter / Max Becherer / Robert Beck / Keith Bedford / Michael Belleme / Al Bello / Bruce Bennett / Noah Berger / Josh Bergeron / Emily Berl / Alan Berner / William Keith Birmingham / Rebecca Blackwell / Michael Blake / Tali Blankfeld / Sarah Blesener / Sarah Blesener / Victor Blue / Jabin Botsford / Anna Boyiazis / Desmond Boylan / Matthew Scott Brauer / William

Bretzger / Paula Bronstein / Jeffrey Brown / Milbert Brown / Andrea Jean Bruce / Vernon Bryant / Joe Buglewiczv / Matthew Busch / Alexandra Buxbaum / Renée Byer / Andrew Caballero-Reynolds / Zackary Canepari / Ricky Carioti / Rachael Cerrotti / Dominic Chavez / Ray Chavez / Barry Chin / Jimmy Chin / Paul Chinn / Ringo Chiu / André Chung / Jamie Chung / Giles Clarke / Jay L. Clendenin / Douglas R. Clifford / Nadia Shira Cohen / Robert Cohen / Oliver Contreras / Thomas Cordova / Gary Coronado / Chad Cowan / Peter Crabtree / Andrew Craft / Manuel Crisostomo / Logan Russell Cyrus / Jonathan Daniel / Lauren DeCicca / Lloyd DeGrane / Gabriella Demczuk / Bryan Denton / Daniel DeSlover / Chris Detrick / Robert Deutsch / Andrea DiCenzo / Kevin Dietsch / Bobby Doherty / Gordon Donovan / Olivier Douliery / Michael Downey / Al Drago / Carolyn Drake / Rebecca Droke / Sam Dykes / Aristide Economopoulos / Dorothy Edwards / Matt Eich / Sean Elliot / Loren Elliot / Ronald Erdrich / Josh Estey / Alissa Everett / Timothy Fadek / Steven M. Falk / Katie Falkenberg / Megan Farmer / Candace Feit / Gina Ferazzi / Adam Ferguson / Jon Ferrey / Stephen Ferry / Deanne Fitzmaurice / Lauren Fleishman / Charles Fox / Tom Fox / Bill Frakes / Ric Francis / Ross Franklin / Dustin Franz / Misha Friedman / Noah Friedman-Rudovsky / Trevor Frost / John Fulgencio / Phyllis Galembov / Armando Gallo / Samip Gandhi / Preston Gannaway / Mark Garfinkel / Mark Garten / Ryan Garza / Robert Gauthier / Derek Gee / Salwan Georges / Danny Ghitis / Jonathan Gibby / David Gilkey / Joseph Giordano / Cassandra Giraldo / David Goldman / Andrew Gombert / Glenna Gordon / Michael Gouldingv / Pat Greenhouse / Michael Greenlar / Osie Greenway / Mike Groll / Adrienne Grunwald / Justin Brice Guariglia / Anna Gueorguieva / Robert Gumpert / Caroline Gutman / David Guttenfelder / Carol Guzy / Jane Hahn / Bob Hallinen / Matthew Hamon / Josh Haner / Michael Hanson / Mark Edward Harris / Lori Hawkins / Jared Haworth / Todd Heisler / Michael Henninger / Ryan Henriksen / Seth Herald / Gerald Herbert / Max Herman / Gary Hershorn / Edward Hersom / Tyler Hicks / Erik Hill / Edward J. Hille / Matthew Hinton / Brendan Hoffman / Sarah Hoffman / Jeremy Hogan / Jim Hollander / Loren Holmes / Mark Holtzman / Alexandra Hootnick / Christopher Horner / Sarah Hoskins / Lucas Jackson / Warzer Jaff / Terrence Antonio James / Jay Janner / Monique Jaques / Shannon Jensen Wedgwood / Lynn Johnson / Allison Joyce / Joel Angel Juarez / Greg Kahn / Hyungwon Kang / Ed Kashi / Ivan Kashinsky / Karen Kasmauski / Carolyn Kaster / Reseph Keiderling / Stephanie Keith / David Kennerly / Laurence Kesterson / Natalie Keyssar / Pete Kiehart / John Kim / Michael Kim / John Kimmich / Kohjiro Kinno / Paul Kitagaki Jr / Martin Klimek / David Kluthо / Mackenzie Knowles-Coursin / Meridith Kohut / Niko Koppel / Isadora Kosofsky / Lisa Krantz / Suzanne Kreiter/ Elizabeth Kreutz / Teresa Kruszewski / Jack Kurtz / Gioia Kuss / Rod Lamkey / Wendy Sue Lamm / John Lamparski / Ashley Landis / Justin Lane / Nancy Lane / Jerry Lara / Erika Larsen / Adrees Latif / Gillian Laub / Lewis Lecka / Brian Lehmann / Erik Lesser / Marc Lester / Heidi Levine / Andrew Scott Lewis / Sara Lewkowicz / David Liittschwager / Dina Litovsky / Jim Lo Scalzo / John Locher / Saul Loeb / Alfred Lopez / Katharine Lotze / Benjamin Lowy / Kirsten Luce / M. Patricia Lynch / Chris Machian / Erik Madigan Heck / Jose Luis Magana / Michael Magers / Brandon Magnus / M. Scott Mahaskey / Mark Makela / Andre Malerba / Melina Mara / Diana Markosian / Pete Marovich / Dan Marschka / Joel Martinez / Pablo Martinez Monsivais / Noah Mascarin / AJ Mast / Tim Matsui / Joanne Matuschka / David Maung / Dania Maxwell / Jake May / Scott Mc Kiernan / Peter McBride / Matthew McClain / John McDermott / Michael McElroy / Ken McGagh / Maddie McGarvey / David Gordon McIntyre / Kirk McKoy / Joseph McNally / Bruce McNamee / Eric Mencher / Susan Merrell / Justin Mark Merriman / Rory Merry / Nhat Meyer / Sebastian Meyer / Vladislav Meytin / Johnny Miller / Douglas Mills / Lianne Milton / Donald Miralle / Logan Mock-Bunting / Pablo Monsivais / Philip Montgomery / Andrew Moore / John Moore / Christopher Morrisv / Laura Morton / vJulius Motal / Bonnie Jo Mount / Pete Muller / Jordan Murph / Edward Murray / Amanda Mustard / Jacob Naughton / Sol Neelman / Andrew Nelles / Greg Nelson / Robin Rayne Nelson / Steve Nesius / Gregg Newton / Jonathan Newton / Landon Nordeman / Lisbeth Norton / Michael Patrick O'Neill / Christopher Occhicone / Adriane Sage Ohanesian / Katie Orlinsky / Francine Orr / Darcy Padilla / Michele Palazzo / Stuart Palley / Ilana Panich-Linsman / Karen Pearson / Peggy Peattie / Caitlin Penna / Joseph Penney / Jessica Pepper-Peterson / Lucian Perkins / Brian Peterson / Mark Peterson / Scott Peterson / David Phillip / Steve Phipps / Matthew Pillsbury / Spencer Robert Platt / William B. Plowman / Robert Pluma / Lane Thomas Plummer / Suzanne Plunkett / Smiley Pool / Lisette Poole / Mamta Popat / Joshua Prezant / David Lee Proeber / Staton Rabin / Connor Radnovich / Joseph Raedle / Erick Rasco / Mark Reinstein / Mark Reis / Andrew Renneisen / Tim Revell / Drew Reynolds / Emilie Richardson / Andy Richter / Jessica Rinaldi / Annie Risemberg / Joshua Ritchie / Amanda Rivkin / Kevin Rivoli / Lawrence Roberts / Michael Robinson Chavez / Ricardo Rocamora / James Rodriguez / Paul Rodriguez / Gabriel Romero / Aaron Rosenblatt / Angela Rowlings / Radcliffe Roye / Jeffrey Russell / Robert Sabo / Griselda San Martin / Paul Sancya / David Sanders / RJ Sangosti / Alyssa Schukar / Susan Schulman / Erika Schultz / Robin Schwartz / Stacie Scott/ Danielle Scruggs / Gallup Sean / Andrew Seng / Andrew Seng / William Serne / Ezra Shaw / Callie Shell / Ting Shen / Charles Shoemaker / Charlie Shoemaker / Ricci Shryock / Tsedenya Simmie / Denny Simmons / Jimmy Simmons / Steve Simon / Mike Simons / Luis Sinco / Jeff Siner / Wally Skalij / Brian Skerry / Laurie Skrivan / Brendan Smialowski / Bryan Smith / Byron Smith / Patrick Smith / Steven G. Smith / Brian Snyder / Nichole Sobecki / Kenneth Somodevilla / Brianna Soukup / Andrew Spear / Jeremiah Stanley / John Stanmeyer / Shannon Stapleton / Susan Stava / George Steinmetz / Chase Stevens / Stephanie Strasburg / Jordan Strauss / Scott Strazzante / Andrew Sullivan / Justin Sullivan / Lawrence Sumulong / Chitose Suzuki / Joseph Swide / Hilary Swift / Joseph Sywenkyj / John Taggart / Mario Tama / Wei Tan / Nima Taradji / Mark J. Terrill / Shmuel Thaler / Eric Thayer / Shawn Thew / Bryan Thomas / Lonnie Timmons III / Tara Todras-Whitehill / Jonathan Torgovnik / Alex Tracy / Erin Trieb / Robert Tringali / Richard Tsong-Taatarii / Nicole Tung / Thomas Turney / Christopher Tyree / Jane Tyska / Dana Ullman / Don James Urquhart / Gregory Urquiaga / Peter van Agtmael / Joseph Van Eeckhout / Carolyn Van Houten / William van Overbeek / Alba Vigaray / Danielle Villasana / José Luis Villegas / Ami Vitale / Sarah Voisin / Stephen Voss / Evan Vucci / Fred Vuich / Mark W. Kelley / Chang W. Lee / Craig Walker / Eric Wambsgans / Jeffrey Warner / Elizabeth Waterman / Lannis Waters / Susan Watts / William Weeks / John Wendle / Jim West / Andrew White / Jared Wickerham / Christian Wilbur / Danny Wilcox Frazier / Andrew Wilhelm / Rick T. Wilking / Samuel Wilson / Damon Winter / Dan Winters / Alex Wroblewski / Devin Yalkin / Marcus Yam / Caroline Yang / Lei Yang / Anna Yanishevsky / Cengiz Yar / Nico Young / Daniella Zalcman / Mark J. Zaleski / Ariel Zambelich / Jingtao Zhao

Uruguay
Roberto Calvino / Gabriel Alejandro Cusmir Cúneo / Julio Etchart

Uzbekistan
Vladimir Jirnov

Venezuela
Gustavo Bandres / Donaldo Barros / Juan Pablo Bellandi / Juan Carlos Barreto / Oscar B. Castillo / Alejandro Cegarra / Luis Cobelo / Jaime De Sousa / Carlos Garcia Rawlins / Roberto Jesus Gil Padrino / León Giménez / Hugo Andrés Gutiérrez Taberne / Carlos Hernandez / Alejandro J Paredes Perez / Vladimir Marcano / Humberto Matheus / Rodolfo Antonio Mejías Molina / Jacinto Oliveros / Javier Eduardo Plaza Camacho / Carlos Sanchez / Ronaldo Schemidt / Malva Suárez / Jimmy Villalta

Vietnam
Nam Hai Bach / Binh Duong / Lai Khanh / Anh Dũng Lê / Than Hai Nguyen / Viet Thanh Nguyen / Khanh Nguyen Thanh / Thai Khuong Tran / Thao Vu Xuan

Yemen
Sumaia Al-hamaly / Maad al-Zikry / Yahya Arhab / Mohammed Omer Barassm / Mansour Mohen

Zimbabwe
Philimon Bulawayo / Columbus Mavhunga / Tsvangirayi Mukwazhi / Zinyange Auntony Ruzvidzo / Aaron Ufumeli / Tafadzwa Ufumeli

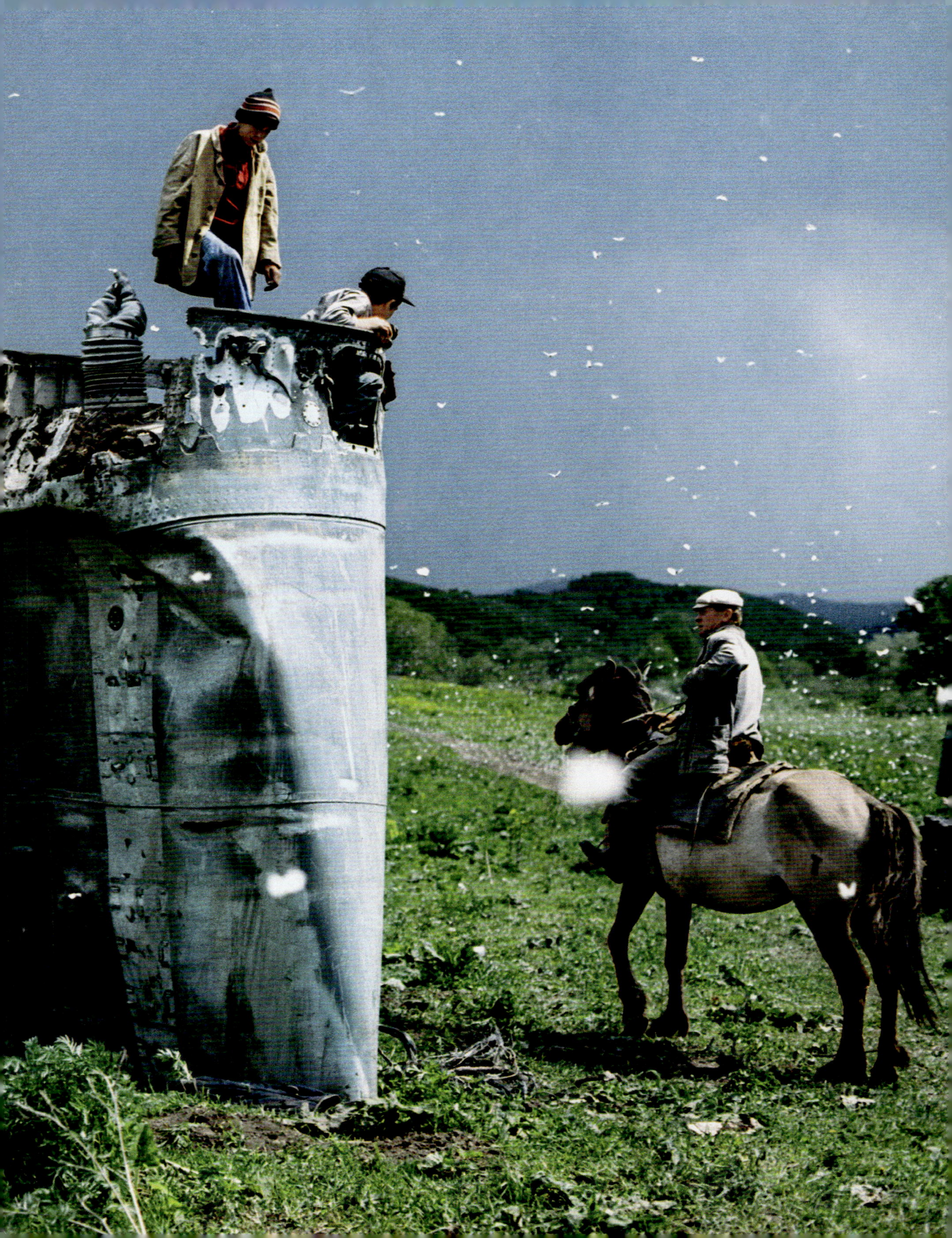

Schilt Publishing
Peter Martensstraat 121
1087 NA Amsterdam, the Netherlands
Tel. +31 (0)20 528 69 12
www.schiltpublishing.com

Distributed in North America by Ingram Publisher Services
One Ingram Blvd.
LaVergne, TN 37086, United States of America
Tel. +1 866 400 5351
ips@ingramcontent.com

Managing Editor
David Campbell
Editor
Rodney Bolt
Production Coordinator
Anne Colenbrander
Picture Coordinator
Thera Vermeij
Research Coordinator
Rosalyn Saab
Research
Jerzy Brinkhof
Yi Wen Hsia
Babette Warendorf
Zoe Zizola

Art Director
Teun van der Heijden
Design
Heijdens Karwei, Amsterdam, the Netherlands
www.heijdenskarwei.com

Print & Logistics Management
KOMESO GmbH, Stuttgart, Germany
www.komeso.de
Lithography, printing and binding
F&W Druck- und Mediencenter GmbH, Kienberg, Germany
www.fw-medien.de
Paper
Maximat Prime, 300 / 150 g
Produced by UPM, distributed by IGEPAgroup

Production Supervisors
Maarten Schilt
Yasmin Keel

ISBN 978 90 5330 887 5

World Press Photo Foundation
World Press Photo, founded in 1955, is an independent, non-profit organization based in Amsterdam, the Netherlands.

#WPPh2017

World Press Photo receives support from the Dutch Postcode Lottery and is sponsored worldwide by Canon.

Supporters
Delta Lloyd • ING • Unique • VCK logistics

World Press Photo holds the official accreditation for good practices from the Central Bureau on Fundraising (CBF).

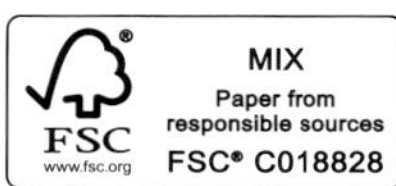